Bc

D1563503

JOURNAL FOR THE STUDY OF THE PSEUDEPIGRAPHA
SUPPLEMENT SERIES
26

Editors
James H. Charlesworth
Lester L. Grabbe

Roehampton Institute London Papers
3

Sheffield Academic Press

The Scrolls and the Scriptures

Qumran Fifty Years After

Edited by
Stanley E. Porter and Craig A. Evans

Journal for the Study of the Pseudepigrapha
Supplement Series 26

Roehampton Institute London Papers, 3

Copyright © 1997 Sheffield Academic Press

Published by
Sheffield Academic Press Ltd
Mansion House
19 Kingfield Road
Sheffield S11 9AS
England

Typeset by Sheffield Academic Press
and
Printed on acid-free paper in Great Britain
by Bookcraft Ltd
Midsomer Norton, Bath

British Library Cataloguing in Publication Data

A catalogue record for this book is available
from the British Library

ISBN 1-85075-844-1
ISBN 1-85075-845-X pbk

CONTENTS

Part II
THE SCROLLS AND THE SCRIPTURES OF ISRAEL

Part III
THE SCROLLS AND EARLY CHRISTIANITY

Part IV
THE SCROLLS AND EXTRA-BIBLICAL TEXTS

FOREWORD

Like its two predecessors in the series of Roehampton Institute London
Papers, this book arises out of a conference organized within the Institute by the Faculty of Arts and Humanities, the Digby Stuart Chaplaincy and the Centre for Advanced Theological Research. Once again
the conference was run by a small team, headed up by Professor Stanley
Porter (Head of Theology and Religious Studies at Roehampton Institute
London), Father Michael Hayes (Chaplain at Digby Stuart College, one
of the four constituent colleges of the Institute) and myself (Dean of
the Faculty of Arts and Humanities). This time, however, we were working with the Dead Sea Scrolls Institute of Trinity Western University,
and I need to thank Professor Craig Evans for his assistance in making
many of the contacts and early arrangements that resulted in the parti-
cipation of many of the world's foremost Dead Sea Scrolls scholars.

The conference, which was entitled 'The Dead Sea Scrolls and the
Bible', was held at Digby Stuart College in February 1997. Of course,
1997 was the fiftieth anniversary of the discovery of the Scrolls, and we
knew that by getting in early in the year we could steal a march on other
scholarly attempts to mark this anniversary. Whether or not this was the
reason, we certainly attracted papers of the highest quality and readers
of this volume will be the long-term beneficiaries of this proud achieve-
ment. The sharp focus of the topic and the fact that most of the dele-
gates were familiar with, if not experts in, the field, meant that speakers
and workshop leaders easily stimulated informed and instructive responses from their audiences and fellow participants. The result was an
instant sense of community, and those of us who were new to the topic
not only learnt a great deal very quickly but, thanks to the fellowship
and goodwill generated by our educators, were soon confident enough
to feel we were genuine participants in the event.

That event is over, but this book is a new event, with a life of its
own. My thanks to the editors—Stanley Porter and Craig Evans—for
giving it life and urging it into the world.

Neil Taylor

ABBREVIATIONS

AAW	Approaching the Ancient World
AB	Anchor Bible
ABRL	Anchor Bible Reference Library
AGJU	Arbeiten zur Geschichte des antiken Judentums und des Urchristentums
AOAT	Alter Orient und Altes Testament
BA	*Biblical Archaeologist*
BARev	*Biblical Archaeology Review*
BASOR	*Bulletin of the American Schools of Oriental Research*
BASP	*Bulletin of the American Society of Papyrologists*
BDB	F. Brown, S.R. Driver and C.A. Briggs, *Hebrew and English Lexicon of the Old Testament*
BDF	F. Blass, A. Debrunner and R.W. Funk, *A Greek Grammar of the New Testament*
BHS	*Biblia hebraica stuttgartensia*
Bib	*Biblica*
BICS	*Bulletin of the Institute for Classical Studies*
BJRL	*Bulletin of the John Rylands University Library of Manchester*
BJS	Brown Judaic Studies
BKAT	Biblischer Kommentar: Altes Testament
BSJS	Brill's Series in Jewish Studies
BSO(A)S	*Bulletin of the School of Oriental (and African) Studies*
BZAW	Beihefte zur *ZAW*
CBQ	*Catholic Biblical Quarterly*
CBQMS	*Catholic Biblical Quarterly*, Monograph Series
ConBOT	Coniectanea biblica, Old Testament
CRINT	Compendia rerum iudaicarum ad Novum Testamentum
CSCT	Columbia Studies in the Classical Tradition
DBSup	*Dictionnaire de la Bible, Supplément*
DJD	Discoveries in the Judaean Desert
DSD	*Dead Sea Discoveries*
ETL	*Ephemerides theologicae lovanienses*
GRBS	*Greek, Roman, and Byzantine Studies*
HALAT	W. Baumgartner *et al.*, *Hebräisches und aramäisches Lexikon zum Alten Testament*
HeyJ	*Heythrop Journal*
HSM	Harvard Semitic Monographs
HSS	Harvard Semitic Studies
HTR	*Harvard Theological Review*

HUCA	*Hebrew Union College Annual*
ICC	International Critical Commentary
IDBSup	*IDB*, Supplementary Volume
IEJ	*Israel Exploration Journal*
Int	*Interpretation*
JBL	*Journal of Biblical Literature*
JewEnc	*The Jewish Encyclopedia*
JJS	*Journal of Jewish Studies*
JNES	*Journal of Near Eastern Studies*
JQR	*Jewish Quarterly Review*
JRS	*Journal of Roman Studies*
JSNT	*Journal for the Study of the New Testament*
JSNTSup	*Journal for the Study of the New Testament*, Supplement Series
JSOT	*Journal for the Study of the Old Testament*
JSOTSup	*Journal for the Study of the Old Testament*, Supplement Series
JSPSup	*Journal for the Study of the Pseudepigrapha*, Supplement Series
JSS	*Journal of Semitic Studies*
JTS	*Journal of Theological Studies*
LCL	Loeb Classical Library
LD	Lectio divina
NovT	*Novum Testamentum*
NovTSup	*Novum Testamentum* Supplements
NTS	*New Testament Studies*
NTTS	New Testament Tools and Studies
OTP	J.H. Charlesworth (ed.), *The Old Testament Pseudepigrapha*
PEQ	*Palestine Exploration Quarterly*
RB	*Revue biblique*
REJ	*Revue des études juives*
RevQ	*Revue de Qumran*
RSB	*Religious Studies Bulletin*
SBLEJL	SBL Early Judaism and its Literature
SBLMS	SBL Monograph Series
SBLRBS	SBL Resources for Biblical Study
SBLSBS	SBL Sources for Biblical Study
SBLSCS	SBL Septuagint and Cognate Studies
SBT	Studies in Biblical Theology
SEÅ	*Svensk exegetisk årsbok*
SJ	Studia judaica
SJLA	Studies in Judaism in Late Antiquity
SPB	Studia postbiblica
STDJ	Studies on the Texts of the Desert of Judah
TDOT	G.J. Botterweck and H. Ringgren (eds.), *Theological Dictionary of the Old Testament*
TOTC	Tyndale Old Testament Commentaries
TRu	*Theologische Rundschau*
TS	*Theological Studies*

TSAJ	Texte und Studien zum antiken Judentum
TU	Texte und Untersuchungen
UTB	Uni-Taschenbücher
VT	*Vetus Testamentum*
VTSup	*Vetus Testamentum*, Supplements
WBC	Word Biblical Commentary
WUNT	Wissenschaftliche Untersuchungen zum Neuen Testament
ZNW	*Zeitschrift für die neutestamentliche Wissenschaft*
ZPE	*Zeitschrift für Papyrologie und Epigraphik*
ZTK	*Zeitschrift für Theologie und Kirche*

LIST OF CONTRIBUTORS

Philip S. Alexander, University of Manchester
Andrea E. Alvarez, Trinity Western University, Langley, BC, Canada
Richard Bauckham, University of St Andrews, Scotland
George J. Brooke, University of Manchester
Philip R. Davies, University of Sheffield
James D.G. Dunn, University of Durham
John Elwolde, University of Sheffield
Craig A. Evans, Trinity Western University, Langley, BC, Canada
Peter W. Flint, Trinity Western University, Langley, BC, Canada
Arthur Gibson, Roehampton Institute London
Lester L. Grabbe, University of Hull
Charlotte Hempel, University of Birmingham
Richard S. Hess, Roehampton Institute London
John Jarick, Roehampton Institute London
Timothy H. Lim, University of Edinburgh, Scotland
Kevin McCarron, Roehampton Institute London
Brook W.R. Pearson, Roehampton Institute London
Stanley E. Porter, Roehampton Institute London
Jacqueline C.R. de Roo, Roehampton Institute London
James M. Scott, Trinity Western University, Langley, BC, Canada
Loren T. Stuckenbruck, University of Durham
Al Wolters, Redeemer College, Ancaster, ON, Canada

FROM QUMRAN TO ROEHAMPTON:
FIFTY YEARS OF RESEARCH AND REFLECTION ON THE SCROLLS

Stanley E. Porter and Craig A. Evans

In the last century, there have been many important archaeological discoveries that have helped us to understand more fully the world and text of the Bible. For example, one thinks of the many significant sites that have been excavated, such as Ur and Ebla to name only two, as well as the caches of papyri discovered in the sands of Egypt. Arguably the most important archaeological discovery for biblical scholarship, however, has been the Dead Sea Scrolls. They have captured the public imagination and have generated a great deal of controversy—learned and popular alike. The controversial aspects have run the gamut. The first debate centred on their authenticity and their age. Did they really date from the turn of the era, during the period of Herodian rule of Judaea? A few did not think so, contending that they dated to the medieval period. However, a whole panoply of dating criteria has since apparently settled the matter in favour of Hasmonaean and Herodian dating (i.e. 200 BCE to 50 CE). The next question concerned who wrote the Scrolls. Early on it was suggested that the Essenes had much to do with the Scrolls, writing some and collecting others. Although still the majority view, this theory has been vigorously challenged, especially in recent years. Linked to this debate is the question of how the Scrolls relate to early Christianity. Some have claimed that the Scrolls are anti-Christian; others that the Scrolls are Christian. These untenable views have rightly been rejected by most scholars, but to what extent and in what ways the Scrolls shed light on the world of Jesus and the early Church remain very important questions. Finally, a great deal of controversy still surrounds the release in 1991 of the unpublished Scrolls (mostly from Cave 4). After years, even decades, of scholarly clamouring for access to the unpublished Scrolls, Ben Wacholder and Martin Abegg reassembled the texts from an unpublished concordance that had been prepared in Jerusalem by some of the early Scrolls scholars and had circulated among those who had had access to the Scrolls.[1] Shortly after the appearance of Wacholder and Abegg's first fascicle, Robert Eisenman and James Robinson published the Palestine Archaeological Museum photographs of these Scrolls,[2] and the director of the Huntington Library of San Marino, California, announced that he would make the library's microfilm of these photographed texts available to qualified scholars.[3] Some threatened lawsuits, and in one notable instance an Israeli scholar successfully sued the owner and publisher of a popular biblical archaeology magazine. But the dust has settled for the most part, and scholars in numbers larger than ever are engaged in the painstaking task of reassembling the fragments and making sense of them.[4] The major series that publishes these texts is 'Discoveries in the Judaean Desert', which published its first volume in 1955, and, with a recently revised and expanded editorial board, is continuing the editorial process of making these documents available.[5]

One of the most intriguing features of the Scrolls is the diversity of the collection itself. Of the approximately 867 documents, some 220 are Bible scrolls. All of the books that make up the Hebrew Bible, with the exception of Esther, are represented,[6] though many in small

1. B.Z. Wacholder and M.G. Abegg, Jr, *A Preliminary Edition of the Unpublished Dead Sea Scrolls* (4 fascicles; Washington: Biblical Archaeology Society, 1991–96).

2. R.H. Eisenman and J.M. Robinson, *A Facsimile Edition of the Dead Sea Scrolls* (2 vols.; Washington: Biblical Archaeology Society, 1991).

3. For photographs of the Scrolls, see E. Tov (ed.), *The Dead Sea Scrolls on Microfiche* (Leiden: Brill, 1993); G.J. Brooke (ed.), *The Allegro Qumran Collection on Microfiche* (Leiden: Brill, 1996).

4. For a succinct and well informed discussion of the unfolding of these events, see J.C. VanderKam, *The Dead Sea Scrolls Today* (London: SPCK; Grand Rapids: Eerdmans, 1994), pp. 1-27.

5. (Oxford: Clarendon Press, 1955–), now under the editorship of Emanuel Tov, with approximately fifteen or so volumes having appeared. A second series that is publishing the Scrolls in a systematic way is J.H. Charlesworth (ed.), *The Dead Sea Scrolls: Hebrew, Aramaic, and Greek Texts with English Translations* (Princeton Theological Seminary Dead Sea Scrolls Project; Tübingen: Mohr [Paul Siebeck]; Louisville: Westminster/John Knox, 1994–), in which three volumes have appeared to date.

6. This assumes that the survival of fragments of Ezra indicates that Nehemiah was known at Qumran. There are no fragments of Nehemiah itself, but in the

fragments. Of the remaining non-Bible scrolls we have sectarian documents, such as the Damascus Document (CD + 4QD), the Rule of the Community (1QS + 4QS + 5QS), the War Scroll (1QM + 4QM), the Thanksgiving Hymns (1QH), and most of the *pesharim* or commentaries (for example 1QpHab, 4Q161–174).[7] Many of the Scrolls cannot be said to be the products of the community of the 'new covenant'.[8] Apocryphal and pseudepigraphal documents have been found. Imaginative retellings of biblical narratives, collections of biblical passages, calendars, hymns, and apocalyptic materials in ample numbers are among these documents. 4QMMT, the letter that discusses 'some of the precepts of Torah', has proven to be one of the most interesting writings in this collection.[9]

The first cave containing Scrolls was discovered fifty years ago.[10] Therefore it is not surprising that several international conferences have been scheduled for this year, 1997,[11] and a number of 'jubilee' volumes, such as the present one, are in production.[12] *The Scrolls and*

Hebrew Bible this book is combined with Ezra.

7. For a convenient listing of the Scrolls, along with selected bibliography, see S.A. Reed (ed.), *The Dead Sea Scrolls Catalogue: Documents, Photographs and Museum Inventory Numbers* (rev. and ed. by M.J. Lundberg and M.B. Phelps; SBLRBS, 32; Atlanta: Scholars Press, 1994).

8. The Qumran sectarians are increasingly referred to as the 'community of the new covenant'. See VanderKam, *The Dead Sea Scrolls Today*, pp. 111-12; S. Talmon, 'The Community of the Renewed Covenant: Between Judaism and Christianity', in E. Ulrich and J.C. VanderKam (eds.), *The Community of the Renewed Covenant: The Notre Dame Symposium on the Dead Sea Scrolls* (Christianity and Judaism in Antiquity Series, 10; Notre Dame: University of Notre Dame Press, 1994), pp. 3-24 (12-17).

9. See J. Kampen and M.J. Bernstein (eds.), *Reading 4QMMT: New Perspectives on Qumran Law and History* (SBL Symposium, 2; Atlanta: Scholars Press, 1996).

10. 1947 is the usual date. It is given as '1946 or 1947' in M.O. Wise, M.G. Abegg, Jr, and E.M. Cook, *The Dead Sea Scrolls: A New Translation* (London: HarperCollins, 1996), p. 4. There have even been reports that one or two of the caves were discovered as early as the 1930s.

11. Major conferences include those at Jerusalem (July) and Princeton (November). Regional meetings of the Society of Biblical Literature, as well as the national meeting in San Francisco (November), and the symposium at Trinity Western University sponsored by the Dead Sea Scrolls Institute (March), have devoted sections to the Scrolls and to the golden anniversary of the discovery of the first cave.

12. E.J. Brill has announced a two-volume jubilee collection, edited by P. Flint

the Scriptures: Qumran Fifty Years After results from one of the first international jubilee conferences (22–23 February) and is the only one to appear in print in the very year in which the conference was held.[13]

The Roehampton Institute London conference, sponsored by the Faculty of Arts and Humanities, the Centre for Advanced Theological Research, and the Digby Stuart College Chaplaincy, in conjunction with the Dead Sea Scrolls Institute of Trinity Western University, was favoured by an unusually rich and interesting collection of papers. Further refined in the light of discussion and further reflection, they have been arranged in the present volume under four major headings. The papers that make up Part I speak to the larger problems concerned with the historical and literary context of the Dead Sea Scrolls. Philip Davies's paper outlines the uncertainties of our knowledge of who wrote the Scrolls and of the true meaning of this diverse collection of writings. Tracing the history of Scrolls scholarship Davies offers a salutary warning against reading the Scrolls in the light of older, rigid notions of 'Judaism' of late antiquity. Charlotte Hempel rightly calls into question the once widely held idea that the Scrolls bear witness to the beliefs of a small, fringe movement outside of mainstream Judaism. She finds that the Scrolls reflect a cross-section of Jewish life and thought in the Palestine of late antiquity. Lester Grabbe seconds the important caveats raised by Davies and Hempel, calling for 'daring proposals' and 'new hypotheses to explain the data'. Part I is brought to a conclusion by two challenging and innovative essays. The philosopher and theologian Arthur Gibson applies literary-critical and philosophical concepts of metaphor to the language about God in the Scrolls, Hebrew Bible, Septuagint and New Testament. Kevin McCarron, whose expertise is English literature—not the Dead Sea Scrolls—offers readers a lively 'outsider's perspective' on the Scrolls and their scholarship. His reading of 'The Seductress' text (4Q184) will sensitize experts and nonexperts alike to literary and pyschological dimensions of these ancient documents that specialists sometimes overlook.

The papers found in Part II speak to the ways in which the Scrolls

and J. VanderKam. J.C.B. Mohr (Paul Siebeck) has also announced a jubilee volume, edited by J. Charlesworth.

13. We wish to thank Sheffield Academic Press for its efficient and timely efforts to ensure this publication's appearance, especially Mrs Jean Allen, Managing Director, and Steve Barganski, Managing Editor.

may help us understand better the text and early interpretation of the Scriptures of Israel. Richard Hess examines the text of Judges as preserved in 4QJudg[a]. He calls into question the claim some have made that this document preserves a primitive, pre-deuteronomistic text type of Judges. John Elwolde examines the use that the Temple Scroll (11QTemple) made of Numbers. He finds that the adaptation of the biblical text often reflected linguistic aspects as much as exegetical tendencies. Peter Flint and Andrea Alvarez briefly introduce the Dead Sea Psalms Scrolls, examine the main features of 4QPs[a], and present a facing Hebrew–English text of this, the most ancient of all Psalms manuscripts. John Jarick directs his attention to the 'Festival Scrolls' (Song of Songs, Ruth, Lamentations, Ecclesiastes and Esther) and what the writings of Qumran tell us about them. He finds evidence of liturgical usage of Lamentations and the Song of Songs, and speculates that Esther was not found among the Scrolls because of its urging Jews to observe Purim on the Sabbath, something the covenanters of Qumran strictly opposed.

The remaining essays of this section treat figures that in various ways contribute to eschatological and messianic ideas. Craig Evans reviews the function of the figure of David in the Scrolls. He observes that many of David's virtues, achievements, and promises contribute significantly to the messianism of the Scrolls and to the background against which early Christian beliefs about Jesus should be understood. James Dunn takes a fresh look at the much discussed 'Son of God' text (4Q246). He contends that the 'son of God' figure is not the 'son of man' figure of Daniel 7 but the promised descendant of David described in 2 Sam. 7.14. Loren Stuckenbruck argues that Qumran's 'Book of Giants' (especially as preserved in 4Q530) clarifies the traditional material on which the vision of the 'son of man' described in Dan. 7.9-10 draws. He concludes that the Book of Giants preserves a theophanic tradition in a form that has been expanded in Daniel. Recognition of this, Stuckenbruck avers, should enable interpreters to understand better the nature of the son of man vision in Daniel 7. Brook Pearson's essay rounds out Part II with a discussion of the relationship of Rabbi Aqiba and Simon ben Kosiba (or 'bar Kokhba') and the question of what light, if any, the finds of Nahal Hever might shed on these figures. Pearson proposes that the Minor Prophets contributed to the messianic identification of Simon.

The papers that make up Part III discuss the ways that the Dead Sea

Scrolls relate to early Christianity and the writings of the New Testament. In a masterful study George Brooke considers the writings that were especially important at Qumran and in the New Testament. He finds important similarities with respect to preferred books (Genesis, Deuteronomy, Isaiah and the Psalms), perspectives, and interpretative traditions. He concludes that the authors of the Dead Sea Scrolls and the New Testament were especially concerned with the restoration of humanity. Richard Bauckham reconsiders the old issue of the relationship between the Scrolls and the Gospel of John. He questions the frequently made assertion that Johannine light/darkness dualism parallels closely that found in the Scrolls. Johannine dualism derives from a Jewish milieu, to be sure, but it is a dualism quite different from what we find at Qumran. Timothy Lim reviews the problematical category 'midrash pesher', coined forty years ago by Earle Ellis, and what relevance it may have for understanding Paul's use of the Old Testament. Lim believes that it is better to understand *midrash* in 4Q174 as 'a study of' or 'an instruction deriving from' a verse of Scripture. Stanley Porter concludes this section with an analysis of the Greek papyri found in the area of the Dead Sea and their importance for understanding dimensions of the Roman east. He contends that these finds offer important insights into the linguistic milieu in Palestine and environs in the first two centuries CE, and hence regarding the environment in which early Christianity developed.

The papers in Part IV discuss some of the 'extra-biblical' texts found among the Dead Sea Scrolls. Philip Alexander treats magic texts in the Scrolls. He is particularly concerned with texts devoted to warding off evil spirits and texts that speak of divination and prediction of the future. Jacqueline de Roo explores whether or not 4Q525, a wisdom text, is sectarian. She develops important methods for ascertaining how we may distinguish this text, famous for its 'beatitudes', from traditional Jewish wisdom literature. James Scott studies the Noachic materials in the Dead Sea Scrolls. He finds a variety of traditions, cautioning that scholars should not assume that all of these traditions originally sprang from a common source. Our collection of studies concludes with Al Wolters's fascinating investigation of the Copper Scroll (3Q15). Of special interest is 12.10, which Wolters believes speaks of 'the cavern of the Presence'. If this reading is correct, then we have the 'earliest attested occurrence of the central Jewish theologoumenon שכינה'.

The papers that make up the present volume look back at the last half century of Scrolls research and review problems and progress. But these papers are also forward-looking, providing in some instances critical assessments of texts that have only become available to scholars in the last few years. As such, these papers are on the forefront of Scrolls research today. The questions with which they grapple, some of them very difficult and perhaps ultimately insoluble, are the questions that scholars will be discussing and attempting to answer in the years ahead. The present volume therefore hopes to make a worthwhile contribution to the assessment of past scholarly labours and to the work that still remains.

Part I

THE SCROLLS IN HISTORICAL AND LITERARY CONTEXT

QUMRAN AND THE QUEST FOR THE HISTORICAL JUDAISM

Philip R. Davies

Introduction

Practically everyone currently involved with the Dead Sea Scrolls agrees that far from maintaining the relatively straightforward consensus once enjoyed, Qumran studies are now beset not only by conflicting interpretations but even by a lack of consensus over some very basic descriptions.[1] Scholars concentrating in related fields such as Old Testament, New Testament, Jewish history and Christian origins used to enjoy the luxury of accommodating widely-agreed conclusions about these scrolls into their own agendas; they now have to choose between a rather extensive spread of interpretations. And, of course, it remains obvious that our understanding of the Scrolls carries implications, sometimes radical, for these related fields. The current debate, then, cannot be ignored; and to await the outcome of discussion is both impractical and imprudent. No early consensus is in prospect.

One of the fundamentally important perceptions to be affected by the Qumran scrolls is the relationship between Christianity and Judaism. Or perhaps I should say more precisely, the relationship between Judaisms and Christianities. This is the theme of the present paper, but before addressing it directly, it may be helpful to mention some of the basic issues in Qumran research on which disagreement rules, starting with the most elementary: the connection between the caves and the Qumran ruins. Although the proximity of the scroll caves and the ruins of Qumran appears to make a direct link very probable, there is nothing in the ruins that explicitly indicates the existence of so many literary texts nearby nor do the texts point to a

---

1. For a convenient review, see P.R. Davies, 'The Qumran Affair 1947–1993', *The Qumran Chronicle* 5.2 (1995), pp. 133-42; 'Was There Really a Qumran Community?', *Currents in Research: Biblical Studies* 3 (1995), pp. 9-35.

nearby site. And even given that there is at least a circumstantial connection, several explanations are possible, ranging from the possibility
that the texts were all written or copied in a Qumran *scriptorium*, to
the other extreme, that the Scrolls were hidden there after the site was
abandoned. We can force connections by identifying a *scriptorium*,
refectory and meeting room among the ruins, or even making much
of the passage in the Community Rule (1QS) 8.14 about going into the
wilderness 'to prepare the way of **** [the divine name is not writ-
ten]', or legislation in the Damascus Document (CD) for residence in
'camps'. But these links are slender. The similarities in pottery can
likewise be accounted for in several ways. Even the famous report of
Pliny the Elder, mentioning an Essene settlement 'below' Engedi,
which triggered off the investigation of Khirbet Qumran as an Essene
site, does not have to point to Qumran, now that we know of other
sites both north and south of Engedi. The water cisterns tell us that the
inhabitants of the site were Jews who observed the practice of ritual
washing, but this is not startling, while the texts themselves do not
(despite the impression often given in the secondary literature) make a
great issue of this practice in itself. There are rules about how and
when (such as in the Temple Scroll [11QTemple[a]] col. L), but no textual evidence of significantly *increased* ritual bathing.

The impasse may just have been overcome with the discovery of an
inscribed ostracon at the edge of the site.[2] It may contain the word
yahad, which is a name used in the Community Rule for its community. If the reading is correct, it will be a great relief, though not
everyone will think the problem is solved. But unfortunately the
reading is not certain, leaving ample room for dissent. If it is true that
scholarship is about creating problems rather than solving them, then
Qumran scholars are currently among the most successful of all.
Individually we are proposing all manner of solutions; collectively the
variety of these solutions is itself a major problem.

Thus, for instance, the student of the Qumran ruins can be informed
that they represent the relics of a trading post, a villa, a factory, a

---

2. Now published (since the preparation of this paper): F.M. Cross and E.
Eshel, 'Ostraca from Khirbet Qumran', *IEJ* 47 (1997), pp. 17-28.

monastery, a fort and a spiritual health farm.[3] Indeed, some combinations of these are possible, since we cannot demonstrate that the place was used by the same people or for the same purpose throughout its 150 or so years of occupation in the Graeco-Roman period.

The other basic problem on which Qumran scholars cannot agree is the nature of this collection, or perhaps even collections, of texts. Once these manuscripts could easily be referred to as a sectarian library, in which everything that was not biblical (i.e. about 75% of the texts) could be taken to represent the views of the owners of the library. But that idea is long gone. We do not in any case know what 'biblical' means in the context of the Qumran texts, and, even allowing that the producers and owners of the texts had the notion of a category of Scripture, there remains the problem of distinguishing among the remaining manuscripts so-called 'sectarian' from so-called 'non-sectarian' writings, which means, in effect, writings already known from outside this collection as against those only known within it.[4] A further problem is that of the eight hundred or so distinct manuscripts that can be reconstructed, very few indeed can be positively identified as having been written by the same scribe. Furthermore, the Scrolls attest different kinds of Hebrew, different ways of writing it, and different conventions of preparing the manuscripts for writing. There are differing editions of 'scriptural' texts but even important variations in so-called 'sectarian' texts (such as between 1QS and 4QS, 1QM and 4QM). The idea that the Qumran archive was a collection of texts even largely written at Qumran has therefore been largely abandoned, and it now seems widely agreed that many or most were brought there from elsewhere.

The student of Qumran, then, confronts a large number of variable factors. Do these represent an archive? A library? Several libraries?

3. The most recent discussion of the state of play is P.R. Davies, 'Khirbet Qumran Revisited', in M. Coogan, L. Stager and J.C. Exum (eds.), *Scripture and Other Artifacts: Essays on the Bible and Archaeology in Honor of Philip J. King* (Louisville: Westminster/John Knox, 1994), pp. 126-42.

4. Some slightly better distinctions have recently been suggested, such as isolating texts whose ideology or vocabulary coheres with 1QS; so D. Dimant, 'The Qumran Manuscripts: Contents and Significance', in D. Dimant and L.H. Schiffman (eds.), *Time to Prepare the Way in the Wilderness: Papers on the Qumran Scrolls* (STDJ, 16; Leiden: Brill, 1995), pp. 23-58. But whether 1QS should be definitive in this regard is questionable; why should there not be more than one kind of 'sectarianism' in this collection?

And where were these libraries or archives originally? At Qumran? At Essene centres throughout Judah? In public and private libraries in Jerusalem and/or Jericho? Mutual denunciations and scornful dismissal among the proponents of various positions do not (or should not) obscure the fact that the evidence really does permit a range of conclusions. It hardly needs adding that, if the Scrolls are a product, or were a library, of one distinct Judaism or form of Judaism, we have not exhausted the possibilities of disagreement. Among the identifications enjoying contemporary support are Essenes, Sadducees, Zealots, early Christians, and otherwise unknown Covenanters!

Serious doubt in any one of the fundamental areas just mentioned would be exhilarating for our field. Doubt in so many simultaneously is frustrating, or even, as Oscar Wilde might have put it, careless. Wherever one scholar takes a view on one of these issues, as we all have to at some point, she or he immediately parts company with a number of colleagues. Discussion is, of course, possible, and at conferences it proves to be largely productive and congenial. But there are also some whose views (or personalities) are such that they cannot or will not participate in meaningful talks with others. Yet even within the circle of those who wish to argue and discuss, there currently exists a range of intellectually respectable differences wider than most cognate disciplines experience. Sometimes I have imagined that I can hear the senior common room at Harvard buzzing with the comment 'we told you this would happen: this is what comes of publishing too many texts too quickly'!

Is it too dramatic to assert that we have reached a point where whether we like it or not we really have to start all over again from square one and ask, before we do anything else, 'Why are there manuscripts in these caves? Who put them there? Who wrote them, who owned them? Who did what at ancient Qumran?' Such an agenda would, of course, prohibit a great deal of current research, which proceeds on the basis that answers to these questions can be either taken for granted or delivered with some conviction. My own feeling, however, is that a period spent concentrating on the *contents* of the Scrolls, making sure of responsible reconstruction of readings and structures, elucidating their ideologies, assembling their agreements and differences, and attending to their textual histories might not be a bad thing. Perhaps we can manage for a while without committing ourselves to a 'big picture'?

Well, that may sound commendable, but it needs some qualification. In the humanities (just as in the sciences), research is driven by hypotheses. One cannot easily generate important research without some wider notion of the significance of what one is doing. And this is the theme of my paper, more or less. The question I have been asked most often by journalists, radio interviewers and documentary makers is 'why are the Dead Sea Scrolls important?' It is, I think, a question that all of us ought to try to answer, even if we answer differently. We owe it to the general public, but we also need to keep the question at the forefront of our own research, and in discussion among ourselves.

Judaism and Christianity in the History of Scrolls Research

The variety of scholarly views on the Qumran scrolls has as much to do with modern ideologies as with the ancient ones we are attempting to reconstruct. It has been a commonplace that every reconstruction of the historical Jesus creates a figure congenial to the researcher, be that Schweitzer's existentialist Jesus, Crossan's Irish Jesus or Wright's evangelical Anglican Jesus. The same is true about ancient Judaism and ancient Christianity, which scholars are likewise tempted to conceive after their own ideals. Theories about the significance of the Scrolls represent in some respects (I emphasize this qualification) a struggle over contemporary definitions.

A moment's reflection on the discovery and publication of these texts shows that ever since the moment of their discovery, they have been the object of ecumenical transaction. They were discovered in what was then Palestine by *Ta'amireh* Bedouin and passed, some into the possession of Eliezer Sukenik, a Hebrew University professor, and some, via a Christian cleric, to the Christian West, before they were physically reunited in the Shrine of the Book in Jerusalem. The recovery of the remainder took place after the partition of Palestine, which left the Qumran area outside the state of Israel, in territory annexed by Jordan, which appointed a French school to take charge of excavating the site of Qumran. No Jews, let alone Israelis, were (regrettably, but understandably) allowed to work on these scrolls. Most of the interest in their significance came from Christian scholars, though one or two were atheists, such as Wilson, Allegro and Dupont-Sommer. These stimulated a good deal of popular debate about whether or not the Scrolls undermined the originality of the Christian religion, and the controversy attracted much public interest (as it still does), but little professional support. On the Jewish side, not a tremendous amount of interest was taken even of the Scrolls from Cave 1. Despite some attempts to make them Pharisaic (Louis Ginzberg, Chaim Rabin) they were regarded, as they were on the Christian side, as belonging on the fringes of Judaism, as the product of a secluded sect. It is broadly true that the Scrolls were studied largely by Christians and thus, inevitably, in terms of Christian agendas. For this no apology is needed, since more Christians than Jews are actually interested in the academic study of ancient Judaism, and, were it not for the prolixity of Jacob Neusner, most books on the subject probably still would be written by Christian scholars. The exclusion of a major Jewish interest was certainly due in large measure to political circumstances. But, ironically, it had been the Jews who pressed for partition of Palestine, and so the blame for the state of affairs that excluded them from the initial research cannot be directed elsewhere (this is usually overlooked in discussion of such matters).

Yet for the first thirty years of Scrolls research, Jewish scholarship displayed at least as much vitality as Christian scholarship; I need only mention the names of Sukenik, Licht, Roth, Rabin and Talmon, a few of many whose work remains important. But of course the picture changed dramatically in 1967, when the capture of East Jerusalem led to Israeli custody of most of the remaining manuscripts. However, this development did not make their contents any more accessible than they had been previously. For the Israeli Department of Antiquities (now the Israel Antiquities Authority) did not interfere in the composition of the group of editors working on the still unpublished scrolls, but left it to its own devices and in the hands of the École Biblique, until in 1987, the IAA responded to growing concern about the rate of publication and appointed, as successor to Père Benoit, John Strugnell, with a commission to complete publication by a specified deadline. Strugnell was dismissed in 1990 for reasons unconnected with the editorship of the Scrolls, and replaced by Emanuel Tov. The current team of editors has been vastly expanded and includes a large number of Jewish scholars. Inevitably, these changes of personnel have affected the context of interpretation.

However, an equally significant watershed in the understanding of the Scrolls was, I think, Yigael Yadin's seizure in 1967 of the Temple Scroll, a full edition of which was published ten years later. This text

looked rather different from the previously published Qumran materials, for instead of rejection of the Temple, it clearly celebrates a
Temple cult. Its writers clearly had not rejected the Temple as the
centre of their Judaism nor had they replaced it permanently with
some 'spiritual temple'. Even if Yadin was wrong to attribute this
text, as he did, to the *yahad*, the text itself signified a reassertion of the
themes of Law and Temple that, on the conventional dichotomies of
biblical scholarship, separated Judaism from Christianity. It underlined
fundamental *connections* between the Judaism of the Scrolls and other
Judaisms, while elucidating differences of cultic practice (among other
things).

The Jewish agenda of Scrolls interpretation thus encouraged by the
Temple Scroll was extended even further, of course, by the so-called
'Halakhic Letter', for which the notoriously anti-Jewish John Strugnell
nevertheless brought in the Jewish scholars Elisha Qimron and Joseph
Sussmann.[5] Here was a text that a Christian scholar felt could be prop-
erly analyzed only with the aid of Talmudic and linguistic expertise.
From this point onwards, it can be said that a distinctly rabbinic-
Jewish agenda has been introduced into the mainstream of Scrolls
research.

'Christianizing' the Scrolls?

We can, then, certainly speak of a period of Scrolls research in which
Christian scholarship predominated and which has been succeeded by
a period in which Jewish scholarship has played a full part. In his
Reclaiming the Dead Sea Scrolls, Lawrence Schiffman makes quite a
thesis of this change of agenda, as the title itself conveys. Schiffman
asserts that the first generation of scholars, who were

> ...primarily Christians interested in either the Hebrew Bible or the New
> Testament, did not understand the scrolls for what they really were: doc-
> uments illustrating the history of Second Temple Judaism. The few Jews
> who did enter the field and make contributions failed to get a fair hearing
> for that approach... Accordingly, research during the first period of
> scrolls studies focussed primarily on what the scrolls said, or could be
> claimed to say, about the background of Christianity. What resulted,

---

5.   E. Qimron and J. Strugnell (eds.), in consultation with Y. Sussmann and with
contributions by Y. Sussman and A. Yardeni, *Qumran Cave 4. V. Miqṣat Maʿaśe
ha-Torah* (DJD, 10; Oxford: Clarendon Press, 1994).

therefore, was a Christianized interpretation of the scrolls... More recently, both Jewish and Christian scholars... have finally turned to the Jewish character of the scrolls.[6]

Schiffman has gone further than I think he should have done, and in doing so blurred the issue that is central to my argument here: the Scrolls, he says, are Jewish, not Christian, and thus Christians have misunderstood them. How far is this claim true? It may seem self-evident enough (except to a few); but does it require closer inspection? What, after all, do the alternatives actually mean? If, for instance, Palestinian Christianity was, in the first century CE, one of many Judaisms, as a number of scholars are prepared to accept (including me), what distinction is Schiffman actually making?

Faced with the question: has study of the Scrolls moved decisively away from a Christian agenda and towards a Jewish one? The answer has to be: yes and no. It is true, as the foregoing sketch has shown, that Jewish scholarship has come to occupy a major place in Scrolls research, and has contributed its own perspective to the task previously dominated by Christian scholarship. But Schiffman is implying more than this. He claims that Scrolls scholarship in the past has been Christianized; furthermore, that the Scrolls are Jewish; and finally that modern Jews can understand the Scrolls better than modern Christians. I am not concerned here to make points for or against either Jews and Christians or Judaism and Christianity. My thesis is that the Scrolls make these kinds of distinctions problematic.

Certainly there has been a strong current of interpretation linking the Scrolls with early Christianity. Some years ago a best-selling book claimed that the Vatican had been plotting to suppress some of the Scrolls because they contained information damaging to Christianity.[7] One of the more detailed formulations of this claim was inspired by the work of not a Christian scholar, but a Jewish one, Robert Eisenman. But it had been anticipated (as the authors acknowledged) by the claims of John Allegro more than twenty years earlier that publication of the Scrolls was being frustrated, and their true interpretation hindered, by a realization on the part of the editors that these texts showed Christianity to be derivative. These opinions drew

6. L.H. Schiffman, *Reclaiming the Dead Sea Scrolls* (Philadelphia: Jewish Publication Society, 1994), p. xxiii.

7. M. Baigent and R. Leigh, *The Dead Sea Scrolls Deception* (London: Jonathan Cape, 1991).

attention to a figure who appears in some biblical commentaries and in the Damascus Document, bearing a title 'teacher of righteousness' or 'righteous teacher' or perhaps 'genuine teacher', who, as these texts imply, was persecuted by a wicked priest, fled into the wilderness, and founded a community. This community, according to the texts, rejected sacrifices and after his death awaited the return of this 'teacher'. This profile of the 'teacher' was indeed quite widely accepted, and, quite frankly, even if one stops short of Allegro's thesis[8] that the 'teacher' was crucified, there are some striking similarities between the two messianic figures and their respective communities. There are, of course, also striking differences. But both the 'teacher' and Jesus might be said to be charismatic leaders who founded Jewish messianic sects proclaiming the end of days, both inimical to the Temple establishment, and the career of each interpreted in terms of scriptural texts.

If we add to this the possible notions of sacrifice via suffering and holiness replacing the cult, of an obsession with messiahs and the calculation of the end of the world calendar, and indeed with a commendation of celibacy, we are certainly confronted with matters that the Scrolls share with early Christianity. There are further parallels between the New Testament and the Scrolls: the attitude towards divorce (not allowed at all), the figure of Melchizedek, the so-called 'son of God' text. A consistent pattern in such similarities is hard to see. These correspondences invite legitimate comparison, though they obviously do not show the Scrolls to be Christian rather than Jewish. Where Schiffman is right, however, is that little interest has been paid in Christian scholarship to features of the Scrolls that were shared with *rabbinic* Judaism: concern with the practice of holiness through obedience to the law and observation of degrees of ritual purity, a concern with the priestly service rota and the proper dates of festivals as well as the development of what we can call *halakhah*, and the use of certain midrashic techniques. On both the Jewish and Christian side the view has predominated that these scrolls were Jewish but sectarian; and thus parallels with Christianity, which could also be seen as Jewish but sectarian, were not unexpected, while parallels with rabbinic Judaism were. On both sides, however, this assumption betrayed the notion that rabbinic Judaism was somehow normative or orthodox, the

---

8. J.M. Allegro, *The Dead Sea Scrolls: A Reappraisal* (Harmondsworth: Penguin Books, 1956 [rev. edn, 1959]).

real 'Judaism', to which that Judaism called Christianity could be contrasted.

Yet I actually find it hard to judge how far the *general* reading of the Scrolls (that is, apart from certain sensational theses) was Christianized in the early days, perhaps because I was taught the standard interpretation by one of its eminent proponents, the Jewish scholar Geza Vermes. Of course, most people were interested in what the Scrolls could tell them about Christianity, because that is what Christians wanted to know. Even so, as I browsed again through the pages of the early textbooks by de Vaux, Milik and Cross and Burrows (disregarding much of what went on in German, where the topic has always tended to be monopolized by New Testament scholars), I find little of what I would define as Christianizing interpretation. I did find this quotation in Burrows's *The Dead Sea Scrolls*:

> In the Qumran texts... we now have a considerable quantity of literature cherished and produced by a dissident group of Jews during the time when the temple was standing, just after the composition of the latest books of the Old Testament, and just before and during the time when the New Testament was coming into being... The religious vocabulary of Judaism in these periods is richly illustrated by the texts. One of the most significant aspects of pre-Christian Judaism which finds expression in them is its devotional spirit. Everything that is important for Judaism in the last two or three centuries before Christ is also important for Christianity.[9]

Burrows then goes on to talk about Jesus and about Christianity. I think he represents the general Christian attitude fairly well: these texts reveal to him a Judaism that he had not expected. It was devotional! The important factor, I think, is that until these texts were recovered, Christians had cherished a rather narrow view of Judaism as a legalistic religion, and also a monolithic one. Judaism was represented by the Pharisees of the Gospels. I think many Jewish scholars felt the same, however; the religion of the rabbis perpetuated what had always been the mainstream of Judaism in the Second Temple period. But in the last thirty years or so scholars have stopped regarding Judaism in this period as either monolithic or as predominantly legalistic, and do not think that Ezra invented Pharisaism. It has been an important discovery, with far-reaching, but different implications for Christians and Jews. Christian scholars have had to revise a theologically low opinion of Judaism, abandon a set of stereotypes. Jews, who surely knew

9. M. Burrows, *The Dead Sea Scrolls* (New York: Viking, 1955), pp. 326-27.

better that Judaism never was without its 'devotional spirit', nevertheless exhibited some loyalty to the notion that Judaism had not changed
in its essentials from well before the time of Jesus or Hillel, and thus
held the Scrolls to be non-representative. That they were not 'Jewish'
in this orthodox sense was not troubling.

The majority of scholars, nevertheless, have neglected any systematic
connections between the Scrolls and Christianity, although the Scrolls
and the life of Jesus are contemporary. The presence of messianic
themes and a concern with eschatology generally have nevertheless led
some scholars to posit a species of Judaism called 'apocalyptic' and
thereby to suggest or imply a trajectory into Christianity. However,
apart from some flirtation with the possibility of John the Baptist as a
renegade Essene, the generally prevailing view remained, and in many
quarters still remains, that the Scrolls belonged to a curious dualistic
sect belonging to the mainstream of neither Christianity nor Judaism
and mentioned explicitly by neither the rabbinic corpus nor the New
Testament.

To sum up, then: Christian scholarship regarded these scrolls as
sectarian because the contents did not conform to a stereotype of
Judaism and because the Scrolls themselves expressed a hatred of the
Temple establishment and the rest of 'Israel' generally. Those features
of the Scrolls that conformed to the stereotype were quite clearly
acknowledged but not explored. Interest focused on the correspondence
of unusual traits shared by the Scrolls and Christianity, but also by the
evidence of a messianic, apocalyptic strand in Judaism that helped to
explain the ministry of Jesus. But my clear impression is that while
the approach was hardly disinterested, its results were taken to show
that Christianity was originally Jewish rather than that the Scrolls
were Christian. But even this conclusion could be seen, from the
Jewish perspective, as an attempt to drive a wedge between Second
Temple Judaism and rabbinic Judaism. Yet that wedge has been more
firmly driven in by the Jewish scholar Jacob Neusner than by any
Christian Scrolls scholar. The issue is not, as Schiffman suggests,
simply a matter of bad Christian scholarship being driven out by good
Jewish scholarship. Rather, it is about the convergence of Christian
and Jewish scholarship in a shared understanding. Indeed, in recent
Scrolls scholarship, Jewish contributions have been primary in setting
the agenda. Let me now expand on this statement.

'Judaizing' the Scrolls?

Recent scholarship on the Dead Sea Scrolls has been rejuvenated, it has to be said, by three Jewish scholars. Yet their ideas could hardly be different. Schiffman's effort to reclaim the Scrolls for Judaism falls foul of the simple observation that modern, no less than ancient, Judaism is quite varied. What kind of Judaism do modern Jewish scholars want to reclaim the Scrolls *for*?

Norman Golb, Robert Eisenman and Lawrence Schiffman are indeed all Jewish and also all American, and they are locked in mutual disagreement and some hostility. Partly the dispute is about who gets the greater publicity, but intellectually they have widely differing views about the Scrolls and different perceptions of both modern and ancient Judaism. Let me begin with Schiffman. He states that 'The DSS are our main source of information about the history of Judaism between the Bible and the Mishnah'[10]—that is, not 'between the Old Testament and the New Testament', as Burrows had put it. However, he recognizes, rather like Burrows, that through them

> we gain a glimpse of an era characterized by several competing approaches to Judaism, each claiming a monopoly on the true interpretation of the Torah. All these approaches, with the exception of the extreme Hellenizers, demanded observance of the Torah's commandments. They differed only on certain theological issues and in the particular rulings of the Law and its interpretation.[11]

So while recognizing divergence, Schiffman wants to stress that the Scrolls belong firmly within a definition of Judaism that focuses on the centrality of law. By 'Judaism' he clearly means *rabbinic* Judaism, even though he regards the authors of these texts as opposed to the Pharisees. For he is convinced that not just Pharisees, but most Jews were interested most of all in purity, the commandments, the Mosaic Law. The extent of Jewish diversity, then, is severely restricted and the Qumran texts do not fall outside the common agenda.

Robert Eisenman[12] attributes the Scrolls to a nationalistic Jewish

10. Schiffman, *Reclaiming the Dead Sea Scrolls*, p. xxi.

11. Schiffman, *Reclaiming the Dead Sea Scrolls*, p. xxv.

12. R.H. Eisenman, *Maccabees, Zadokites, Christians and Qumran* (Leiden: Brill, 1983); *James the Just in the Habakkuk Pesher* (Leiden: Brill, 1986); *James the Brother of Jesus, Recovering the True History of Early Christianity* (London: Faber & Faber, 1997).

party, variously called Maccabees, Zadokites and, later, Christians. These began as freedom fighters in the second century BCE and finished up as those of the Jerusalem Christian church led by James brother of Jesus. For Eisenman Palestinian Christianity is a form of Jewish nationalism, James its hero and Paul its enemy, the one referred to in one scroll as the 'Liar'. Eisenman's historical reconstruction, which few scholars accept, but which has impressed a number of other educated and intelligent authors,[13] is not undeserving of attention. For Eisenman reconfigures both Judaism and Christianity in a way which, whatever the problems with his precise portrait, is not at all implausible. In his Judaism of the late Second Temple period he finds piety allied to fierce nationalism and opposed to the corrupt institutions of Judaism under Herod the Great. His Christianity is of course more like his ideal Judaism, which is far from Talmudic and rather more Zionist. The Greek New Testament, representing the theology of the Greek-educated Paul, is, on Eisenman's reading, a total betrayal of the followers of Jesus. Schiffman has accused Eisenman of 'taking the Scrolls away from the heritage of the Jewish people', presumably by making them Christian. But with as much, if not more plausibility, Eisenman could be described as reclaiming early Palestinian Christianity for Judaism, placing it firmly in the context of a militant nationalistic messianism. At the same time he distances from Judaism, from the Scrolls and even from its own origins that which most Christians take as Christianity. Like Schiffman, he regards the Scrolls as embodying the essence of Judaism, perhaps even the mainstream of Judaism, a Judaism concerned with Torah but also with a strong anti-Greek and anti-Roman agenda, a 'zeal for the law' that was fired by a passionate interest in eschatology, a belief in divine intervention and a strong messianic doctrine. Eisenman and Schiffman would therefore both see themselves as reclaiming the Scrolls for Judaism, though they differ very dramatically on what they think Judaism essentially *was* and what early Christianity was in relation to it. While I find Schiffman's scholarship methodologically more scrupulous, I find Eisenman's view of late Second Temple Judaism rather more congenial, though I do not accept his interpretation of the Scrolls. That the New Testament does not offer a reliable

13. For example, Baigent and Leigh, *Dead Sea Scrolls Deception*, and N.A. Silberman, *The Hidden Scrolls: Christianity, Judaism and the War for the Dead Sea Scrolls* (New York: Grosset Putnam, 1994).

picture of the followers of Jesus in Palestine between the death of their messiah and their flight from Jerusalem when the revolt against Rome broke out strikes me as almost self-evident, though it is hardly the consensus of New Testament scholars.

The last of the three Jewish writers on Qumran to be considered is Norman Golb.[14] He does not think there is any sect behind the Scrolls, nor any connection between their authorship and Qumran. For him, the Scrolls came from Jerusalem when Romans besieged it and they represent the contents of several libraries. The contents of the Scrolls, in his view, are indicative of the entire spectrum (or almost the entire spectrum) of Judaism at the turn of the era, and thus show it to exhibit a highly variegated pattern. This view, the most radical of all for Scrolls research, has proved a very useful catalyst in breaking open the last vestiges of consensus about the Scrolls and their relationship to Qumran and a Qumran sect. It is thanks to Golb as much as anyone that we are effectively starting again from scratch. Golb is not much interested in what 'Judaism' might mean in ancient Judaea, but as a historian of Judaism he is aware of its highly diverse character. He is primarily a historian of mediaeval Judaism, and his study has taught him that Judaism is prone to great diversity.

There are some problems with Golb's position, of course, as with the others just mentioned; it is hard to deny that certain themes characterize the Scrolls, and that some sects and sectarian views seem to be very well represented. Some kind of connection between the site of Qumran and the Scrolls also seems probable, though to be fair Golb does not rule that out completely; he only denies that there was a community at Qumran that either wrote or owned the manuscripts. But if he himself maintains a fairly inflexible position, his view is amenable to modification: these various libraries brought to Qumran for safe keeping may have comprised or included collections of particular groups opposed to the established authorities in belief and practice; one such group may have lived at Qumran (though whether this last point is of much importance is debatable). There is, though, more uniformity among the Scrolls than Golb allows for, even as there is less uniformity than many other scholars allow for.

One of the points that my review of these scholars has endeavoured to establish is that each of them adopts a different view both of the

14. N. Golb, *Who Wrote the Dead Sea Scrolls? The Search for the Secret of Qumran* (New York: Charles Scribner's Sons, 1994).

Scrolls and of Judaism. Each could be said to be 'Judaizing' the Scrolls, but in conformity with a different definition of Judaism. Schiffman is an orthodox Jew, educated in Talmud, for whom Torah-centred rabbinic Judaism represents what was always to him the essence of Judaism. There is, nevertheless, a view, adopted by some Jewish and Christian scholars, that rabbinic Judaism represents as radical a turn in Judaism as did Pauline Christianity, abandoning Temple and cult, abandoning sacrifice, abandoning priesthood and transforming the themes of land and messiah. But for Schiffman, reclaiming the Scrolls for Judaism means showing that they are compatible with *his* Judaism, which is indeed the normative religious Judaism of later times and of today.

Eisenman is not a religious, but a secular Jew. His Judaism is much more tied up with national pride, with the political agenda that modern Zionism and the creation of the state of Israel have made possible. He does not, I think, approve of the religious character of the state of Israel, but he admires those Jews of ancient times who fought against imperial forces in the name of Judaism, believing that only political independence could guarantee the kind of 'righteousness' with which his Sadducee-Qumran-Zealot-early Christians were obsessed. Eisenman sees these texts as revealing the true nature of *popular* Judaism, as opposed to that of a corrupt pro-Roman establishment, and certainly as opposed to that denial of true Judaism that he would see in Paul, who, together with Herod the Great, receives Eisenman's most extreme hatred.

Finally, Norman Golb, is I would hazard, a cultural Jew. He is not interested in the question of a historically-defined religious essence of Judaism, but rather in Jewish cultural identity. His reading of the Scrolls, then, indicates to him a pluriformity. Judaism was a rich and diverse culture in late Second Temple Judaism, with legal observance only one of a number of possible manifestations. This represents a different kind of challenge to Schiffman than does Eisenman. But between them these three have made the running; no-one can claim that the Scrolls are lacking a Jewish agenda, or indeed, Jewish agendas. That is to my mind very welcoming, and the fact that modern Judaism (not to mention modern Jewish historical scholarship) can be so diverse encourages me in my suspicion that it was just as diverse two thousand years ago, if not more so.

Judaism before Judaism

Even before the end of the first century CE, Christianity constituted a diverse array of systems, and over the next 300 years or so it continued to develop, though thanks to the imperial infrastructure a degree of doctrinal and institutional cohesion was achieved, so that a number of 'Christian' beliefs and practices were excluded as heresy and, of course, political, social and linguistic differences ensured that 'Catholic' western Christianity became only one of several Christianities to survive and to become the orthodox Christianity of the Roman Empire and then of the medieaval and modern periods.

Rabbinic Judaism began after the destruction of the Second Temple[15] in 70 CE and, like western Christianity (the version with which it has had mostly to deal), did not develop fully until centuries later. Both religions were highly influenced by each other, consolidating themselves in mutual opposition. Both, of course, have also continued to develop up to modern times; both have various 'reformed' versions. Despite a common historical origin, each is a quite different religion. But there was, of course, a time when neither existed as a religious system, and that is the time when the Qumran scrolls were written. We are caught in a linguistic trap in speaking about the religion of their time and place: we use the term 'Judaism' for the religion(s) of Judah and of those communities outside Judah that belonged to the *ethnos* of the Judaeans, and we also use it of the religion of the rabbis. But while Christianity is certainly excluded from *rabbinic* Judaism it has an equal birthright, at least in principle, in the Jewish religion that precedes both later systems. To say that the Scrolls are 'Jewish', then, does not mean that they are rabbinic rather than Christian. In theory it might be possible to decide that the Judaism or Judaisms of the Qumran Scrolls are generally closer to one or other of the systems that later emerged from Second Temple Judaism. But my own assessment of the evidence suggests that in actual fact no such proclivity can be definitively established.

And so it is necessary to confront the phenomenon of 'Judaism before Judaism'. The Qumran scrolls are part of the *prehistory* of both Christianity and rabbinic Judaism. They come from the land and

---

15. Herod's Temple was in fact at least the third Judaean/Jewish Temple on the site, and was still short of completion at the time of its destruction.

the culture that constituted the womb of both these religions, for even
though both were shaped substantially outside Judah (Rome, Galilee,
Babylonia), both were born there.[16] If this is a correct perception, the
Scrolls throw fresh light not just on Christianity and rabbinic Judaism
individually, *but on the processes that generated their divergence*. A
few examples can be offered. The War Scroll allows us to appreciate
the strong mix of religion and nationalism that explains, perhaps
better than Josephus's account (which is informed by a somewhat
dubious thesis), the kinds of feelings that prompted Jews of different
kinds to go to war with Rome; we can perceive very clearly from this
and from many other Qumran scrolls the calculations of a world calendar, including an end of history that was believed to be imminent.
The Scrolls convey quite extensively (though not exclusively) the
sense of time coming to a climax, the sense of partial abandonment by
its god of the nation as a whole, and the need to preserve a pure element within it ready for the final cleansing. There is evidence, too, of
the search for communion with heaven apart from a Temple which
was tainted by impure priests, though not the abandonment of the *idea*
of a perfect Temple. This attachment to a Temple, even if understood
as a heavenly one, is of course found in different ways in both rabbinic Judaism and in the New Testament also, although both grew up
without a Temple on earth. It is Christianity, nevertheless, that has
preserved (or recreated) the priestly caste and the altars and the
sacrificial terminology, and rabbinic Judaism that preserves better the
notion of physical holiness. The Scrolls, of course, exhibit both
aspects.

The Scrolls also evidence uses of Scripture that both rabbinic
Judaism and Christianity inherited and exploited. That the Scriptures
contain secrets of the end is, however, a belief more characteristic of
Christianity than rabbinic Judaism, while the reverse is true of the
commitment to the Law of Moses as binding on Israel. The search for
truth in the stars is a continuing Jewish theme, as the texts from the
Cairo Genizah show, though not officially condoned. But according to
Matthew Jesus' birth was indicated by a star too. And so one could go

16. It is hardly necessary to point out that, culturally speaking, Judaea cannot be
sharply separated from the rest of the Graeco-Roman world; but physical proximity
to the Temple did make an important difference, and rabbinic religion is *theoretically*
predicated on life in the Land, if the Mishnah be taken as the first systematic statement of that Judaism.

on to illustrate by further examples (discipline, attitudes to sexuality, charisma, discipleship, anthropology [1QH]) how aspects of the Scrolls are developed now in Christianity and now in rabbinic Judaism, and occasionally in both, more or less equally.

Perhaps we can go a step further and scrutinize the tensions between some of the ideas that these texts contain, such as between the goals of personal holiness and national redemption; between human and heavenly redeemers; between faith and knowledge as the means of salvation (a salvation definable in different ways); between free will and predestination; between an anthropology of human holiness and an anthropology of human depravity. We can also see in the Scrolls typical features of sectarian mentality: traces of a persecution complex, a corporate identity fortified by official opposition, something which both early Christianity and rabbinic Judaism experienced and have the marks to show (the language of 'election', the cult of martyrdom and the threat/promise of final judgment persist in both religions). These tensions, which sometimes approach the status of contradiction, may lead us to conclude that the Qumran texts do not represent any single Judaism, any coherent system.

But that would not necessarily follow. Religious systems are not entirely coherent, despite the best effort of theologians, because they answer to emotional as well as intellectual aspirations. What I suggest is that even if the Scrolls represent a fairly narrow segment of the religious life of ancient Judaea (of which I am not yet convinced), that segment may well constitute a reasonably representative sample of that religious life in all its diversity. If, as can plausibly be argued, the Temple remained (until its destruction) one cohesive element, the major common denominator in the definition of any kind of Judaism, there was not a corresponding common denominator of belief or practice. The fall of the Temple may therefore have been a major factor in the rise of rabbinic Judaism and the development of Christianity precisely because the tensions within Judaean religion could not sustain a single religious system without it. Indeed, even the two 'orthodox' systems could not contain them, for they manifested themselves at times in other forms of Christianity and Judaism that the rabbis and the Church managed to squeeze out of the system, though never entirely to dispose of: various kinds of what we call Gnosticism (and that certainly has strong roots in the Qumran literature), Manichaeism, astrology, magic, and so on.

The Importance of the Qumran Scrolls

I suppose that whether or not we are religious ourselves, the worlds of the Old Testament, the New Testament and the classical period have exerted a powerful influence on our culture: they have constituted, and still do, an alternative universe, depicted in thousands of stories and works of art. That ancient world was indeed *historically* the begetter of our Western civilization. Europe adopted a Christian culture that mixed Semitic and Graeco-Roman values. In the United States, the presence of a large, visible and active Jewish population has given this culture a vitality that Europe's vibrant Jewish population contributed in the nineteenth century. But the fate of that population reminds us that the opposition between Judaism and Christianity has defaced our civilization for centuries. Now, from two thousand years ago, the world that gave birth to both rabbinic Judaism and Christianity is illuminated by these scrolls from the Dead Sea caves. Whatever the popular conceptions or misconceptions surrounding them, such writings have much to tell us about the religious, political and social forces that combined to shape our Judaeo-Christian mentality through two major religious systems. Neither of these two religions is eternal; there was a time when neither existed, and they were indeed begotten and not created, out of specific historical circumstances, but also out of an already very rich Judaean religious heritage. That heritage lies documented before us. The last thing we should do is fight over who 'owns' them, or whose heritage they are; because to do so is to blind ourselves to one of the most important insights they have to offer.

QUMRAN COMMUNITIES: BEYOND THE FRINGES
OF SECOND TEMPLE SOCIETY

Charlotte Hempel

Introduction

It is the purpose of this paper to outline a number of recent developments in Qumran studies and to draw out their implications for assessing the significance of the Scrolls for biblical studies. I will divide
what follows into two main parts. In the first section I will review a
number of factors that have contributed to the widely-held view that
the chief value of the non-biblical scrolls is their witness to the beliefs
and practices of a small group on the fringes of late Second Temple
society.[1] In the second section I will endeavour to show that such a
view has been radically called into question by more recent developments in Qumran studies.

The Push to the Fringes

On the traditional view espoused in many textbooks the Qumran settlement and library are seen as the centre of a single community
whose views are expressed in the so-called sectarian literature. This
basic conception has a number of important corollaries.

1. A Qumran-Centric Vantage Point
A considerable problem for the proponents of this view is the presence among the so-called sectarian writings of documents that are
clearly at variance with one another, compare most notably the

---

1.   J.T. Milik sums up his outline of the history of the Essenes in his influential
monograph *Ten Years of Discovery in the Wilderness of Judaea* (trans. by
J. Strugnell; London: SCM Press, 1959), p. 98, as follows: 'To sum up, the
Essenes remained on the outskirts both of the life of the Jewish people [. . .] and of
that of the early Christians in their formative days'.

Damascus Document (CD) and the Community Rule (1QS). These differences are often accounted for by arguing that whereas the Community Rule legislated for a community resident in the vicinity of Qumran, the Damascus Document was composed by that same group for members living outside of Qumran. Thus, it is frequently argued that even documents that presuppose a different lifestyle, such as the Damascus Document, have been commissioned, sanctioned, and probably written by the Qumran centre.[2]

In short, the significance of divergences between texts were downplayed, and it was assumed that the 'nerve-centre', Qumran, promulgated a unified rationale that runs through the 'sectarian' literature.

This programme of harmonization was expanded to include the descriptions of the Essenes in the classical sources as well as the archaeological evidence recovered at Qumran. Note J.T. Milik's introductory words to a chapter on the history of the Essenes:

> We will first cite a passage found in Pliny [...] and summarize the results of the excavations of the Qumrân region, adding a discussion of such Qumrân texts as are relevant to the sect's history. [...] we shall attempt to *synthesize* [emphasis mine] this material, together with the data to be found in classical writers, in a picture of the history of the Essene movement and of the Qumrân settlement.[3]

Milik's monograph set a very influential trend early on in the history of Qumran research—a trend that is now being re-thought. What is advocated here is an overarching synthesis of archaeology, texts found in caves, and the statements of the classical authors. This procedure does not do justice to any of the three bodies of evidence, a point forcefully made with reference to the archaeological evidence by Davies.[4]

---

2. A number of pertinent points on the detrimental effect of what they call the 'mother-house hypothesis' have recently been made by M.O. Wise, M.G. Abegg, Jr, and E.M. Cook in the introduction to their volume of translations, *The Dead Sea Scrolls: A New Translation* (London: HarperCollins, 1996), pp. 16 and 20. The term 'mother house' is used with reference to the Qumran settlement by Milik, *Ten Years of Discovery*, p. 90.

3. Milik, *Ten Years of Discovery*, p. 44.

4. See P.R. Davies, 'How Not to Do Archaeology: The Story of Qumran', *BA* 51 (1988), pp. 203-207; reprinted in P.R. Davies, *Sects and Scrolls: Essays on Qumran and Related Topics* (South Florida Studies in the History of Judaism, 134; Atlanta: Scholars Press, 1996), pp. 79-87.

F.M. Cross, another pioneer of Qumran Studies, introduces his chapter on the Essenes with a comparable programme for harmonization:

> In the discussion to follow we wish to trace the process of historical *synthesis*, the *combination* [emphasis mine] of data dug up by the spade, culled from classical writers, and sifted out of the scrolls themselves...[5]

Note the use of the term 'synthesis' or 'synthesize' by both Milik and Cross, as well as Cross's phrase 'the combination of data'.

The traditional view outlined above did view the Qumran library as partially extending beyond the fringes of society in as far as it supposes a second order of Essenes reflected in the Damascus Document, for example. Qumran was nevertheless regarded as the centre or the purest form of Essenism, if you like. As Milik put it, the Essenes 'bequeathed to us the books of their chief monastery'.[6]

Such an overall view of the non-biblical Qumran corpus is not found exclusively in books from the early decades of Qumran research. The Edinburgh doctoral dissertation by Mark Boyce may be cited as a recent example.[7] Boyce's work provides a close study of the Admonition of the Damascus Document. He deals with the Laws of the same document in an Appendix where he argues that CD 10.10–12.18 reflects:

> a more advanced stage of the sect with some 'members', or branches within the sect, now allowed to hold property, marry, and mix with the Jewish population rather than living a segregated ascetic existence.[8]

Elsewhere, Boyce describes the probable purpose of the Damascus Document:

> so that those who lived away from Qumran should have a document to keep them on the straight and narrow.[9]

Boyce's analysis here is saturated with presuppositions, and his interpretation of the evidence is, though not impossible, not the natural

---

5.   F.M. Cross, *The Ancient Library of Qumran* (Philadelphia: Fortress Press, 3rd edn, 1995), pp. 54-55.

6.   *Ten Years of Discovery*, p. 43. For a critique of the use of monastic terminology with reference to Qumran, cf. Davies, *Sects and Scrolls*, pp. 83-84.

7.   For a summary of Boyce's conclusions, cf. A.S. van der Woude, 'Fünfzehn Jahre Qumranforschung (1974–1988)', *TRu* 57 (1992), pp. 1-57 (55-56).

8.   M. Boyce, 'The Poetry of the Damascus Document' (PhD diss., University of Edinburgh, 1988), p. 390.

9.   'Poetry of the Damascus Document', p. 309.

reading of the evidence. It seems more likely to me that those parts of
the Laws of the Damascus Document that reflect a life-style integrated
into wider Jewish society originated with a group that had never segregated in the first place. The existence of an earlier, 'purer', segregated phase is no more than a supposition which I would not want to
adopt.[10]

In sum, the Qumran-centric vantage point from which the evidence
of the Scrolls was being interpreted from the earliest phase of
Qumran studies has been a major factor in establishing the view that
we are dealing with a 'fringe phenomenon'.

2. *The Location of the Qumran Site*
A related issue is the influence of the location of the Qumran site on
the interpretation of the contents of the nearby caves. The remoteness
and isolation of the Qumran site has contributed to viewing the contents of the non-biblical scrolls as largely expressing the views of an
isolated community. This is a point well made recently in the introduction to the new translation of the Dead Sea Scrolls by Michael
Wise, Martin Abegg, and Edward Cook, who note,

> One of the effects of the Standard Model has been to distance the scroll
> writers geographically and ideologically from the Judean mainstream: they
> were insular, monastic dropouts.[11]

Curiously by 'Standard Model' they seem to mean virtually everybody
except themselves, since they repeatedly mention Lawrence Schiffman
as an exemplary exponent. Schiffman has, of course, recently proposed a new 'model' himself by forcefully promoting Sadducean origins of the Qumran scrolls.[12]

---

10. In this context note the remarks by George Brooke, 'The Temple Scroll: A
Law Unto Itself?', in B. Lindars (ed.), *Law and Religion: Essays on the Place of the
Law in Israel and Early Christianity by Members of the Ehrhardt Seminar of
Manchester University* (Cambridge: James Clarke, 1988), pp. 34-43 (39). See also
M.A. Knibb, 'The Place of the Damascus Document', in M.O. Wise (ed.), *Methods
of Investigation of the Dead Sea Scrolls and the Khirbet Qumran Site: Present
Realities and Future Prospects* (New York: The New York Academy of Sciences,
1994), pp. 149-62.
    11. *The Dead Sea Scrolls: A New Translation*, p. 28.
    12. Cf. *The Dead Sea Scrolls: A New Translation*, pp. 26-27 and again p. 30.
For Schiffman's position, cf. L.H. Schiffman, 'The Sadducean Origins of the Dead
Sea Scroll Sect', in H. Shanks (ed.), *Understanding the Dead Sea Scrolls: A Reader*

The Pull away from the Fringes

Before discussing a number of recent developments in Qumran studies some general remarks are required. My reference to 'the pull away from the fringes' inevitably provokes the question: where to? From the fringes to the centre would perhaps be the expected and most natural answer. I am deliberately avoiding any references to a centre or a mainstream of contemporary Judaism, however, since this concept has become increasingly challenged in recent years.[13] A further difficulty in assessing accurately the wider background of the Scrolls is the limited nature of our evidence, a point well made recently by Martin Goodman.[14] Put very briefly, our evidence of late Second Temple society is limited, and we are forced to rely on the few pieces of the jigsaw puzzle that have survived. Recent developments in Qumran studies might add—or more precisely relocate—some pieces of the jigsaw puzzle that makes up late Second Temple Judaism. And to stay with the image of the jigsaw puzzle, these pieces are not necessarily confined to the edge of our puzzle.

1. *Recent Developments in the Study of the Non-Biblical Literature from Qumran*
Recent years have seen a number of important developments in Qumran studies. One of these is the realization that key documents such as the Damascus Document and the Community Rule are composite works. Pioneering work in this area was done by Jerome

from the Biblical Archaeology Review (London: SPCK, 1992), pp. 35-49; *idem*, *Reclaiming the Dead Sea Scrolls: The History of Judaism, the Background of Christianity, the Lost Library of Qumran* (Philadelphia: Jewish Publication Society, 1994). For a critical response to Schiffman's proposals, cf. J.C. VanderKam, 'The People of the Dead Sea Scrolls: Essenes or Sadducees?', in Shanks (ed.), *Understanding the Dead Sea Scrolls*, pp. 50-62; also J.A. Fitzmyer, 'The Qumran Community: Essenes or Sadducean?', *HeyJ* 36 (1995), pp. 467-76.

13. Cf. Davies, *Sects and Scrolls*, p. 2; see also K. Berger, *Jesus and the Dead Sea Scrolls: The Truth under Lock and Key?* (trans. J.S. Currie; Louisville: Westminster/John Knox, 1995), p. 28.

14. M. Goodman, 'A Note on the Qumran Sectarians, the Essenes and Josephus', *JJS* 46 (1995), pp. 161-66; cf. also G. Stemberger, *Jewish Contemporaries of Jesus: Pharisees, Sadducees, Essenes* (trans. A.W. Mahnke; Philadelphia: Fortress Press, 1995), p. 2.

Murphy-O'Connor, who studied the literary growth of both the
Community Rule[15] and the Admonition of the Damascus Document.[16]
Whether or not one agrees with all the conclusions arrived at by
Murphy-O'Connor, which are in any case in need of some revision in
the light of new evidence from Cave 4, he was able to demonstrate the
complex literary developments that shaped these documents.
Moreover, the work of Murphy-O'Connor and subsequent studies by
others, such as Philip Davies's work on the Damascus Document[17] or
Michael Wise's work on the Temple Scroll,[18] have highlighted the
need to study the Qumran texts with much the same methodological
tools as are common place in biblical studies, such as source criticism
or redaction criticism, to name but two.[19] Some would say that these
approaches are outmoded in modern biblical studies, but that is a
debate I will not enter into here. Thus, whereas early Qumran scholarship tended to promote a programme of harmonization, recent
scholarship is acknowledging diversity and complexity, not only from
one document to the next, but even within individual documents.

Furthermore, a number of scholars have recently proposed
hypotheses on the nature and interrelationship of the Qumran library

15. J. Murphy-O'Connor, 'La genèse littéraire de la Règle de la communauté', *RB*
76 (1969), pp. 528-49. See also J. Pouilly, *La règle de la communauté de Qumrân:
son évolution littéraire* (Cahiers de la Revue Biblique, 17; Paris: Gabalda, 1976).

16. J. Murphy-O'Connor, 'An Essene Missionary Document? CD II,14–VI,1',
RB 77 (1970), pp. 201-29; 'A Literary Analysis of Damascus Document VI,2–
VIII,3', *RB* 78 (1971), pp. 210-32; 'The Critique of the Princes of Judah (CD
VIII,3-19)', *RB* 79 (1972), pp. 200-16; 'A Literary Analysis of Damascus
Document XIX,33–XX,34', *RB* 79 (1972), pp. 544-64; 'The Damascus Document
Revisited', *RB* 92 (1985), pp. 223-46.

17. P.R. Davies, *The Damascus Covenant: An Interpretation of the 'Damascus
Document'* (JSOTSup, 25; Sheffield: JSOT Press, 1982).

18. M. Wise, *A Critical Study of the Temple Scroll from Qumran Cave 11*
(Studies in Ancient Oriental Civilization, 49; Chicago: Oriental Institute, 1990). See
also the earlier studies by A.M. Wilson and L. Wills, 'Literary Sources of the
Temple Scroll', *HTR* 75 (1982), pp. 275-88; P. Callaway, 'Source Criticism of the
Temple Scroll: The Purity Laws', *RevQ* 12 (1986), pp. 213-22; and L.H.
Schiffman, 'The Laws of War in the Temple Scroll', *RevQ* 13 (1988), pp. 299-311.

19. In this context see the pertinent methodological observations made recently by
Charlesworth and Strawn in J.H. Charlesworth and B.A. Strawn, 'Reflections on
the Text of *Serek ha-Yahad* Found in Cave IV', *RevQ* 17 (1996), pp. 403-35 (408-
10).

and the settlement that in different ways move away from viewing Qumran as the centre of a radical fringe group. Thus, Hartmut Stegemann in his most recent publications no longer speaks of the 'Qumran community' but instead coined the expression 'the main Jewish Union of Second Temple times' or 'die Essenische Union'.[20] Shemaryahu Talmon proposes that the Qumran site, rather than being seen as the permanent place of residence for the Qumran community, was used as a place of retreat where male community members spent limited periods in celibacy preparing for the eschatological battle.[21] Moreover, Norman Golb has argued that the Scrolls and the site are not related, a position radically challenged, however, by the recent discovery of an ostracon in the wall extending south from the main buildings which is thought to contain the term *yahad*, the technical self-designation of the community as found in the sectarian scrolls.[22]

An important methodological development has been the recognition that the non-biblical scrolls reflect more than one community—this is reflected in the title of my paper. This was argued, for example, by Philip Davies with reference to the Admonition of the Damascus Document.[23] What is more, Florentino García Martínez has made an important contribution to this debate.[24] In essence García Martínez argues that, among the non-biblical scrolls, we need to distinguish between works or parts of works that go back to the Essene parent movement of the Qumran community, and those that go back to the

20. H. Stegemann, 'The Qumran Essenes—Local Members of the Main Jewish Union in Late Second Temple Times', in J. Trebolle Barrera and L. Vegas Montaner (eds.), *The Madrid Qumran Congress* (Leiden: Brill, 1992), I, pp. 83-166; and *idem, Die Essener, Qumran, Johannes der Täufer und Jesus* (Freiburg: Herder, 1994).

21. S. Talmon, 'Qumran Studies: Past, Present, and Future', *JQR* 85 (1994), pp. 1-31. See also *idem*, 'The Community of the Renewed Covenant: Between Judaism and Christianity', in E. Ulrich and J.C. VanderKam (eds.), *The Community of the Renewed Covenant* (Notre Dame: University of Notre Dame Press, 1994), pp. 3-24.

22. The ostracon has now been published by F.M. Cross and E. Eshel as 'Ostraca from Khirbet Qumran', *IEJ* 47 (1997), pp. 17-28.

23. *Damascus Covenant*, esp. pp. 173-97.

24. F. García Martínez, 'Qumran Origins and Early History: A Groningen Hypothesis', *Folia Orientalia* 25 (1988), pp. 113-36. See also F. García Martínez and J. Trebolle Barrera, *The People of the Dead Sea Scrolls: Their Writings, Beliefs and Practices* (trans. W.G.E. Watson; Leiden: Brill, 1995), esp. pp. 77-96.

Qumran community. He sees the latter as a group that emerged after a split within the Essene movement. In addition to these two types of evidence García Martínez further suggests the presence of material that goes back to a 'formative period' when the differences between the parent movement and the Qumran community crystallized. One may well want to take issue with some of the details of García Martínez's proposals or Davies's analysis. However, perhaps the most significant contribution of both scholars is their emphasis on more than one community being represented by the non-biblical scrolls. On García Martínez's basic model, that is, the Qumran community and its parent movement, it becomes less obvious which texts should be associated with the community resident in the vicinity of Qumran, and how much influence the Qumran group had on the wider movement. If we think of the Qumran group as a splinter group that had segregated from its parent movement, then it is unlikely that this group had any influence on the organization and leadership of the parent group.

In other words, if we are able to distinguish those texts or parts of texts that originated with the parent movement of the Qumran group, we are in possession of firsthand evidence from a Jewish group in Late Second Temple times that never withdrew to Qumran nor was it dominated by those who had done so. Finally, only after close study of the literary evidence should we proceed to attempt to relate the results of this work to other bodies of evidence such as the archaeological evidence and the reports on the Essenes in the classical sources.

Having outlined a number of developments of the ways in which we read long known texts from Qumran I will now turn to the significance of new evidence that has recently become widely accessible to students of the Scrolls.

2. *New Evidence*
A considerable amount of unpublished material coming mainly from the wealth of fragments discovered in Cave 4 has now been made available to the world of scholarship at large since the early nineties. I would like to discuss two types of new evidence.

a. *Manuscripts that throw new light on long known texts.* A number of manuscripts from Cave 4 provide additional copies of key Qumran texts. Probably the most important of these are the numerous Cave 4 manuscripts of the Community Rule[25] and the Damascus Document.[26]

The Cave 4 versions of the Community Rule attest a number of significant variants from the Community Rule from Cave 1.[27] Let me draw out just one feature of 4QS vis-à-vis 1QS, and comment on its potential significance for the present argument. The famous teaching on the two spirits in 1QS 3.13–4.26, which is frequently described as 'Qumran theology' at its most developed and in its purest form, is missing from a number of Cave 4 manuscripts of the Community Rule. Geza Vermes has pointed out that 4QS^d (4Q258), for instance, lacks the equivalent to 1QS 1–4.[28] The teaching on the two spirits is thus not intrinsically linked to the communal legislation, and by implication the community legislated for, in 1QS 5–9, and may well have originated independently of that material and/or outside of that community. It can, therefore, no longer be taken for granted that the two-spirits passage should be regarded as Qumran doctrine *par excellence.*[29]

25. Cave 4 revealed ten copies of the Community Rule: 4Q255–264 (4QS^{a-j}).

26. Eight ancient manuscripts of the Damascus Document were recovered from Cave 4: 4Q266–273 (4QD^{a-h}).

27. An edition and translation of the Cave 4 manuscripts of the Community Rule prepared by E. Qimron and J.H. Charlesworth is available in J.H. Charlesworth (ed.), *The Dead Sea Scrolls: Hebrew, Aramaic, and Greek Texts with English Translations* (Princeton Theological Seminary Dead Sea Scrolls Project, 1; Tübingen: Mohr [Paul Siebeck]/Louisville: Westminster/John Knox, 1994), pp. 53-103. Cf. also G. Vermes, 'Preliminary Remarks on Unpublished Fragments of the Community Rule from Qumran Cave 4', *JJS* 42 (1991), pp. 250-55; *idem*, 'Qumran Forum Miscellanea', *JJS* 43 (1992), pp. 300-301; C. Hempel, 'Comments on the Translation of 4QS^d I,1', *JJS* 44 (1993), pp. 127-28; S. Metso, 'The Primary Results of the Reconstruction of 4QS^e', *JJS* 44 (1993), pp. 303-308. Further, most recently, Charlesworth and Strawn, 'Reflections', and P.S. Alexander, 'The Redaction-History of *Serek ha-Yahad*: A Proposal', *RevQ* 17 (1996), pp. 437-53.

28. *The Dead Sea Scrolls in English* (Harmondsworth: Penguin Books, 4th edn, 1995), p. 90.

29. Even the otherwise very cautious treatment of the subject of 'Qumran theologies' in J.H. Charlesworth's introduction to the recent reissue of Helmer Ringgren's classic study *The Faith of Qumran* still puts the two-spirits passage on a theological pedestal. Whereas Charlesworth rightly speaks of 'theologies at Qumran' in the plural, he describes the teaching on the two spirits as follows: 'A profound cosmic dualism tends to shape the documents composed at Qumran, and this was expressed in a definitive form in the Rule of the Community (1QS 3-4)...' H. Ringgren, *The Faith of Qumran: Theology of the Dead Sea Scrolls* (new introduction by

The Cave 4 manuscripts of the Damascus Document, moreover, provide a great deal of additional legal material that is lacking from the mediaeval copies of the work.[30] Of particular interest is the additional penal-code material that is found in three manuscripts.[31] The relationship between the Community Rule and the Damascus Document emerges as a much more complex one in the light of extensive overlap in the penal code in both documents.[32] The view, hitherto taken for granted, that this penal code expresses the nitty-gritty of life at Qumran now needs to be argued for rather than assumed.

b. *New texts that lack clear sectarian features.* Apart from shedding important new light on long-known texts the contents of Cave 4 also include a large amount of new material that lacks clear sectarian features.[33] Milik attempted to account for this material in the 1950s as follows:

> In some manuscripts of Cave IV there are collections of halakic prescriptions with no specific allusion to a community of either the Damascus or Qumrân types. It is possible that these manuscripts contain the rules for groups of 'tertiaries', copied by the expert scribes of Qumrân.[34]

Much depends on what Milik means by the expression 'copied by the expert scribes of Qumrân' here. I suspect he implies composition as well as copying since he seems to argue that these documents, though addressed to groups outside of Qumran, were nevertheless authorized at Qumran. Those new texts that lack references to a community context can equally be taken to testify to halakhic, liturgical, sapiental,

---

J.H. Charlesworth; New York: Crossroad, expanded edn, 1995), p. xix.

30. See J.M. Baumgarten, *Qumran Cave 4. XIII. The Damascus Document (4Q266–273)* (DJD, 18; Oxford: Clarendon Press, 1997).

31. These are 4QD^a [4Q266], 4QD^b [4Q267], and 4QD^e [4Q270].

32. Cf. J.M. Baumgarten, 'The Cave 4 Versions of the Qumran Penal Code', *JJS* 43 (1992), pp. 268-76, and C. Hempel, 'The Penal Code Reconsidered', in M. Bernstein and J. Kampen (eds.), *Legal Texts and Legal Issues* (Leiden: Brill, forthcoming).

33. Cf. the observations by Devorah Dimant in 'The Qumran Manuscripts: Contents and Significance', in D. Dimant and L.H. Schiffman (eds.), *Time to Prepare the Way in the Wilderness* (STDJ, 16; Leiden: Brill, 1995), pp. 23-58.

34. *Ten Years of Discovery*, p. 90.

and exegetical[35] traditions that originated outside of the confines of the Qumran community. This latter possibility seems the more likely to me.

Conclusion

To conclude, in the light of recent developments in Qumran studies, assessments of the significance of the Qumran finds for biblical studies like the following by Günter Stemberger are in need of considerable revision:

> The Qumran texts [...] are an essential source for Jewish history since the Maccabean period. Nevertheless, the increased interest in the Essenes stimulated by discoveries made during the last few decades should not obscure the fact that they were a rather marginal, radical group.[36]

By contrast, I hope to have shown that the non-biblical literature discovered in the Qumran caves sheds light far beyond the confines of a small and isolated fringe group.[37] A great deal of detailed work is still being done, however, by students of the Scrolls in order to attempt to determine which texts reflect the Qumran community in the narrow sense and which shed light on a wider movement.

35. Note the comments by George Brooke with reference to 4Q252 in '*4Q252* as Early Jewish Commentary', *RevQ* 17 (1996), pp. 385-401 (399-401).

36. Stemberger, *Jewish Contemporaries of Jesus*, p. 1.

37. See the apposite comments by Davies, *Sects and Scrolls*, p. 2 and Berger, *Jesus and the Dead Sea Scrolls*, pp. 38-39, 66. Also most recently G.J. Brooke's review of J.H. Charlesworth (ed.), *Jesus and the Dead Sea Scrolls: The Controversy Resolved* (New York: Doubleday, 1995), in *DSD* 3/3 (1996), pp. 332-34.

THE CURRENT STATE OF THE DEAD SEA SCROLLS:
ARE THERE MORE ANSWERS THAN QUESTIONS?

Lester L. Grabbe

With the large number of Qumran scrolls recently published or made available in preliminary form by partial publication, description, or individual studies, only a few people with the time and energy can truly be said to be on top of this new knowledge. I do not claim to be one of those; indeed, I have never claimed to be a Scrolls specialist even though my PhD mentor was William Brownlee. Nevertheless, I dabble in the Scrolls now and then, as I must if I want to be a historian of the Second Temple period, as I try to be.

Much of the work on the Scrolls has been of a literary nature, and many valuable studies have advanced our knowledge considerably. As someone who attempts to be a historian, however, I see some dangers, not only in the present, but also in earlier studies, which can impede progress. I draw attention to three of these here: (1) an uncritical attachment to a past consensus, (2) a failure to make properly critical historical judgments, and (3) the continued politicization of Qumran scholarship.

An Uncritical Attachment to a Past Consensus

One of the most salutary events in recent scholarship is the injection of new theories about the origin of the Scrolls and/or the Qumran community. In the first decade or so after the unveiling of the initial find in 1947, a number of different identifications were proposed (e.g., the Pharisees,[1] the Ebionites,[2] and the Zealots[3]). An early

1. C. Rabin, *Qumran Studies* (Oxford: Clarendon Press, 1957).
2. J. Teicher in a series of articles in *JJS* 2–5 (1950–54).
3. C. Roth, *The Historical Background of the Dead Sea Scrolls* (Oxford: Basil

identification of the Cairo Damascus Document was that it was a Sadducean-related product.[4]

The majority of scholars soon settled on the Essene identification of the community, and this has continued to dominate scholarship up to the present.[5] The result is that one sees even recent articles that refer to the 'Essenes at Qumran' or the like without discussion or qualification.[6] Such complaisance is totally unwarranted. The Essene thesis is far from proved; at the very least, there are still major questions about the classical sources describing the Essenes and about their relationship to the Qumran scrolls. It is not yet time to talk about 'Qumran' and 'Essene' as interchangeable terms.[7]

I like a consensus as much as the next scholar, but when we think we have answers, that is often when the real work stops. Progress comes with questions. We must ask questions and we must question— both are vital if the field is to advance. There is nothing more dangerous than using a consensus as the basis of an argument. The late Samuel Sandmel was known mainly for his writings on the two first-century figures Philo and Paul, but he wrote several classic articles about methodology which deserve to be known and read by every

Blackwell, 1958); G.R. Driver, *The Judaean Scrolls: The Problem and a Solution* (Oxford: Basil Blackwell, 1965).

4. R.H. Charles, 'Fragments of a Zadokite Work', in R.H. Charles (ed.), *Apocrypha and Pseudepigrapha of the Old Testament in English* (2 vols.; Oxford: Clarendon Press, 1913), II, pp. 785-834.

5. It is usually credited to E. Sukenik, *Megillot Genuzot* (Jerusalem, 1948), p. 16 (as cited by N. Golb, *The American Scholar* 58 [1989], pp. 179-80, 628-29; I have not seen this work of Sukenik), though John Trevor has claimed that the identification was suggested to Sukenik by others (*The American Scholar* 58 [1989], p. 626).

6. A random example is Torleif Elgvin, 'The Reconstruction of Sapiential Work A', *RevQ* 16 (1993–95), pp. 559-80: 'it [Sapiential Work A] was highly regarded within the Essene Community... this early Essene writing...' (p. 559). Many more examples could be cited since one comes across them constantly.

7. My criticisms do not apply to those who attempt to defend the Essene hypothesis with critical arguments. For example, the 'Groningen hypothesis' is in many ways a revitilization of the Essene hypothesis. See F. García Martínez, 'Qumran Origins and Early History: A Groningen Hypothesis', *Folio Orientalia* 25 (1988), pp. 113-36; F. García Martínez and A.S. van der Woude, 'A "Groningen" Hypothesis of Qumran Origins and Early History', *RevQ* 14 (1989–90), pp. 521-41. A recent criticism of an aspect of it is given by T.H. Lim, 'The Wicked Priests of the Groningen Hypothesis', *JBL* 112 (1993), pp. 415-25.

scholar. One of his last articles was on 'The Comfortable Theory'.[8] As he showed, we all have an affinity for the comfortable theory, and he did not exempt himself from that stricture. It gives us a sense of stability. No one likes to be in a state of perpetual uncertainty, which means that we always like to appeal to a thesis which is already accepted as proved. The trouble is, very little can be considered 'proved beyond doubt' in scholarship, and Qumran is certainly no exception.

For this reason, I welcome new theories, such as the recent ones arguing that the Scrolls are Sadducean[9] or that they have nothing to do with Qumran but originated in Jerusalem.[10] I even welcome those views which many scholars consider unlikely or even eccentric.[11] Even if these theories are wrong, they may provide insights into aspects of the Scrolls not noticed by anyone before. If nothing else, they make us realize that very basic matters are far from settled and that we should take nothing for granted. The only theories I do not welcome are those of amateurs who play on the conspiracy anxieties

8.   'Palestinian and Hellenistic Judaism and Christianity: The Question of the Comfortable Theory', *HUCA* 50 (1979), pp. 137-48. Another article, more often cited, is his 'Parallelomania', *JBL* 31 (1962), pp. 1-13.

9.   Y. Sussman, 'The History of *Halakha* and the Dead Sea Scrolls: A Preliminary to the Publication of 4QMMT', *Tarbiz* 59 (1989–90), pp. 11-76; Appendix 1 of E. Qimron and J. Strugnell (trans.), *Qumran Cave 4. V. Miqṣat Ma'aśe ha-Torah* (DJD, 10; Oxford: Clarendon Press, 1994), pp. 179-200, gives an English translation of the text but not all the notes of the preceding article; L.H. Schiffman, 'The New Halakhic Letter (4QMMT) and the Origins of the Dead Sea Sect', in Z. Kapera (ed.), *Papers on the Dead Sea Scrolls Offered in Memory of Jean Carmignac*. I. *General Research on the Dead Sea Scrolls, Mogilany 1989* (Qumranica Mogilanensia, 2; Cracow: Enigma Press, 1993), pp. 59-70 (slightly different version in *BA* 53 [1990], pp. 64-73); *idem*, 'Miqsat Ma'aśeh Ha-Torah and the *Temple Scroll*', *RevQ* 14 (1990), pp. 435-57. Similar conclusions with regard to 11QT have been arrived at by J.M. Baumgarten, 'The Pharisaic–Sadducean Controversies about Purity and the Qumran Texts', *JJS* 31 (1980), pp. 157-70. On my critique of this thesis, see below and the study in note 24.

10.   N. Golb, *Who Wrote the Dead Sea Scrolls?* (New York: Charles Scribner's Sons, 1995).

11.   E.g., R. Eisenman, *Maccabees, Zadokites, Christians and Qumran: A New Hypothesis of Qumran Origins* (SPB, 34; Leiden: Brill, 1983); B.E. Thiering, *Jesus and the Riddle of the Dead Sea Scrolls: Unlocking the Secrets of his Life Story* (Garden City, NY: Doubleday, 1992).

of the general public and peddle ignorance and innuendo to those without the knowledge to evaluate the claims.

A Failure to Make Critical Historical Judgments

Although many specialists in the Dead Sea Scrolls dabble in history, most of them—not surprisingly—focus on the literary or related aspects of the writings. The specialities brought have been formidable as, for example, in *halakhah*. Each of these is important, and together they have brought great insights to the study of the Scrolls. But the context in which this interpretation goes on is a historical one, and yet the historical deductions made are often quite shallow or myopic, as if done by formula: quote your Qumran passage, make a quick foray to your book shelf for a hasty (and by preference somewhat inaccurate) read of Whiston,[12] draw a couple of facile connections and, presto, a piece of pre-packaged, ready-to-serve historical reconstruction. It's quick, it's cheap, and it's readily available; it's like going to your neighbourhood DIY store.

You may think I exaggerate, but not by very much. Josephus has the honour of being one of the most quoted and least read figures of antiquity. An enormous amount of work has gone into assessing the strengths and weaknesses of Josephus as a historian, yet so many of those who quote his works seem to be in total ignorance of very basic historiographic studies.[13] The last word has not been said about

12. William Whiston translated the works of Josephus into English in 1736. This translation became a staple version for English speakers, only being superseded by the appearance of the Loeb edition (H.St.J. Thackeray *et al.*, *Josephus* [LCL; London: Heinemann; Cambridge, MA: Harvard University Press, 1926–65]). Nevertheless, Whiston's version continues to be reprinted and is still widely used. It has recently been re-edited, with the paragraph numbers of the Greek editions inserted into the text (*The Works of Josephus: Complete and Unabridged* [Peabody, MA: Hendrickson, new updated edn, 1987]).

13. See my critical remarks and the various important secondary studies cited in *Judaism from Cyrus to Hadrian*. I. *Persian and Greek Periods*; II. *Roman Period* (Philadelphia: Fortress Press, 1992; British edition in one-volume paperback, London: SCM, 1994), pp. 4-13. To my mind the best overall study on the critical problems with using Josephus is still S.J.D. Cohen, *Josephus in Galilee and Rome: His Vita and Development as a Historian* (CSCT, 8; Leiden: Brill, 1979). See also the recent volume of essays: F. Parente and J. Sievers (eds.), *Josephus and the History of the Greco-Roman Period: Essays in Memory of Morton Smith* (Studia Post-Biblica, 41; Leiden: Brill, 1994).

Josephus by any means, but the scholar who would not dare make a statement about a passage from the Hebrew Bible without first checking the major commentaries and handbooks will blithely quote Josephus without apparently being aware of any of the elementary critical considerations necessary to evaluate his account. The following examples all involve Josephus in one way or another.

a. *'Seekers-after-Smooth-Things'*

The identity of the 'Seekers-after-Smooth-Things' as the Pharisees has become a truism of scholarship. The argument goes something like this: Since the Qumran community is the Essenes, whom would they be opposed to? Because the Pharisees were the main religious group among the Jews, the Pharisees were probably their enemies. If so, 'Seekers-after-Smooth-Things' (*dôrsê hahălāqôt*) is a play on 'Interpreters of the Laws' (*dôrsê hahălākôt*). This interpretation is clinched when we read in 4QpNah 1.7 that the 'Lion of Wrath' hangs the Seekers-after-Smooth-Things alive. This is clearly Alexander Jannaeus who crucified 800 Pharisees. This interpretation is often assumed without significant argument.[14]

There is only one problem with this interpretation. It is based on unproved assumptions and on a misreading of Josephus. The assumption that the Pharisees were the only candidates for the title is blinkered; in addition to the variety of groups we know of at the time, there were likely many groups whose existence we can only guess at. The word play has no power of proof since it becomes significant only when the Seekers-after-Smooth-Things have been identified with the Pharisees. Alexander Jannaeus indeed crucified 800 men, and slaughtered their families before them as they died, according to Josephus, and this is most likely the incident referred to in 4QpNah which says that 'he will hang men alive' (1.7: אנשים חיים יתלה). But when we read in Josephus who these men were, we are nowhere told that they were Pharisees.

---

14. See, for example, M.P. Horgan, *Pesharim: Qumran Interpretations of Biblical Books* (CBQMS, 8; Washington: Catholic Biblical Association, 1979), pp. 161, 173-77. The most recent treatment is the following, though unlike some he does attempt to justify the identification: L.H. Schiffman, 'Pharisees and Sadducees in *Pesher Nahum*', in M. Brettler and M. Fishbane (eds.), *Minhah le-Nahum: Biblical and Other Studies Presented to Nahum M. Sarna in Honour of his 70th Birthday* (JSOTSup, 154; Sheffield: JSOT Press, 1993), pp. 272-90.

Josephus has two accounts of the incident. In the *War* (1.4.1–6.4 §§85–131), he simply refers to a general opposition to Jannaeus; the Pharisees are not even mentioned. The same applies to the *Antiquities* (13.13.5-14.2 §§372–83).[15] In each case, what Josephus says is that 'the nation' (*to ethnos*) revolted. On one occasion Jannaeus killed 6000 Jews; at another time he killed 50,000 over a period of six years. Finally, 'the Jews' called for the Seleucid ruler Demetrius III Acaerus to come against the Hasmonaean king. Although Jannaeus lost the battle, Demetrius withdrew, and Jannaeus continued his fight with his own people; this ended in 800 opponents being crucified and their families slaughtered. It may well be that Pharisees were among the opposition to Jannaeus, but the context makes it clear that it was far wider than any one group.[16]

15. Contrary to many, Schiffman recognizes and acknowledges this ('Pharisees and Sadducees', p. 277), though he goes on to argue that, nevertheless, the Pharisees are in the mind of the writer. His main arguments are an appeal to *m. Suk.* 4.9 which refers to a high priest who spilled the water libation on his feet and the *baraita* in *b. Qid.* 66a (correct Schiffman's 61a) which mentions the Pharisaic opposition to Alexander Jannaeus. Both these arguments depend on assumptions which Schiffman does not discuss or justify.

In the first case, *if* the Mishnah passage refers to Jannaeus and *if* this is the same incident as in *Ant.* 13.13.5 §172, what evidence is there that the ones who pelted him and revolted were Pharisees? Neither the Mishnah nor Josephus suggests as much. The Tosephta (*t. Suk.* 3.16) makes the actor a Boethusian; one text of the Babylonian Talmud (*b. Suk.* 48b), a Sadducee; another, an anonymous priest (*b. Yom.* 26b). The Pharisees are not mentioned in any of our sources, yet Schiffman seems to assume that we must have to do with a Pharisee–Sadducee dispute. Josephus, the earliest source, gives no hint of a Pharisee–Sadducee dispute being involved here.

As for the other argument, *b. Qid.* 66a may well be parallel to *Ant.* 13.10.5-6 §§288–98, but Josephus makes the Hasmonaean John Hyrcanus. Why should we give precedence to the story from the Bavli that it was Jannaeus? But leaving aside the question of whether the much later anecdotes of rabbinic literature are trustworthy remembrances of an event centuries earlier for the moment, I find a more fundamental flaw in the reasoning: the argument in each case assumes that for Pharisees to oppose Jannaeus means that all his opposition must necessarily be Pharisaic and only Pharisaic. Such does not follow either logically or from the information provided by Josephus, who never makes the Pharisees the sole opponents of Jannaeus. Neither of the two main points in Schiffman's argument provides substantial support for the view that the 'Seekers-after-Smooth-Things' must be Pharisees in 4QpNah.

16. It is true that at a later point, the *Antiquities* (13.15.5 §§398–404) tells the story of how Jannaeus, on his death bed, tells his wife to make allies of the Pharisees, a story not found in the *War*. This is the only indication of a Pharisaic

Thus, while the Pharisees might be included in the epithet 'Seekers-after-Smooth-Things', our primary source Josephus gives us no reason to think that Pharisees in particular were the opponents of Jannaeus or that they were the only ones crucified by him. It seems most likely that the epithet 'Seekers-after-Smooth-Things' was a useful one for the sect to use for any of its Jewish enemies, and did not have a consistent usage.[17] However, my point is the superficial way in which an identification has been made without a proper critical historical enquiry in most cases.

b. *The Thesis of Norman Golb*[18]

My second example concerns Norman Golb's thesis about the origin of the Scrolls. I alluded to this above as an example of a welcome new theory, though welcoming it does not mean I therefore embrace it. Golb's hypothesis attempts to explain the characteristics of the Scrolls'

opposition to Jannaeus and represents part of a Pharisaization of the later narrative. The narrative in the *Antiquities* is suddenly swarming with Pharisees where the *War* had none. There are various explanations for this. For example, if the *War* represents a shortening of Nicolaus of Damascus's account, it may be that the *Antiquities* more closely represents what Nicolaus wrote. The question then would be. Why would Josephus want to 'de-Pharisaize' his narrative? He shows no sign anywhere of finding references to Pharisees a problem. On the other hand, the opposite could be the case. That is, when he wrote the *Antiquities*, his particular *Tendenz* required that he make the Pharisees the prime movers at this point in his history, in which case the Pharisees have been artificially introduced. In any case, it is difficult to be certain of the correct reason why the *Antiquities* has Pharisees when the *War* does not. But in the relevant part of our story, both the *War* and the *Antiquities* make the opposition to Jannaeus a widespread phenomenon and not one limited to a specific group such as the Pharisees.

17. Cf. D. Pardee, 'A Restudy of the Commentary on Psalm 37 from Qumran Cave 4', *RevQ* 8 (1972–73), pp. 163-94; also P.R. Davies, *Behind the Essenes: History and Ideology in the Dead Sea Scrolls* (BJS, 94; Atlanta: Scholars Press, 1987), pp. 87-105, who notes that stereotyped expressions might have different meanings in different contexts.

18. His most recent work is given in n. 10 above. The thesis was presented and defended in several articles, including 'The Problem of Origin and Identification of the Dead Sea Scrolls', *Proceedings of the American Philosophical Society* 124 (1980), pp. 1-24; 'Who Hid the Dead Sea Scrolls', *BA* 48 (1985), pp. 68-82; 'The Dead Sea Scrolls: A New Perspective', *The American Scholar* (1989), pp. 177-207, 628-32; 'Khirbet Qumran and the Manuscripts of the Judaean Wilderness: Observations on the Logic of their Investigation', *JNES* 49 (1990), pp. 103-14. For a detailed assessment of his book, see my review in *DSD* 4 (1997), pp. 124-28.

contents by arguing that they originated in Jerusalem libraries which were taken to various caves for physical protection during the siege of Jerusalem. It has the advantage of taking into account the archaeology of Qumran, giving a historical context to the Scrolls, and not once evoking Jesus, the Vatican, or unidentified flying objects.

My main criticism of Golb is that he presents a theory which investigates the historical situation only superficially. He draws on historical sources to defend his theory, primarily Josephus, but he has not pursued the historical investigation far enough. What appears initially to be the strength of the theory is actually its weakest point. The question is whether it is likely or even possible that large collections of scrolls were spirited out of Jerusalem during the siege. Thanks to Josephus, we have a detailed account of the situation in Jerusalem before and during the Roman siege. There are several points to take note of in this context.[19]

Civil war broke out in Jerusalem already at the beginning of the revolt in the summer of 66 CE (*War* 2.17.2-9 §§408–48). The archives were captured and destroyed because it was thought that records of debts were preserved there (2.17.6 §427). But we have to keep in mind Josephus's particular *Tendenz* in the *War*. He wants to make a separation between a few hot-headed rebels, on the one hand, and the bulk of the 'people' (*dēmos*) or the 'moderates' (*metrioi*) who opposed the war and were only very reluctantly brought into it, on the other. Golb quotes a later episode in which John of Gischala fled to Jerusalem and reported on the Roman capture of Galilee.[20] At that time, 'the people' perceived the impending disaster to come upon Jerusalem. Golb sees this as evidence that it finally dawned on them what was coming, and they began to make plans to take the manuscripts out of the city. What Golb does not seem to realize is that Josephus often makes such comments. He says the same thing in several earlier passages: in *War* 2.17.10 §§455–56 the 'moderates' are already anticipating their fate at the hands of the Romans. Similarly,

19. The most detailed source of information on the situation before and during the final siege is Josephus's *War*, mainly books 4–6. A general summary of the siege is found in Chapter 7 of my *Judaism from Cyrus to Hadrian*. The best study of the Jerusalem siege is J.J. Price, *Jerusalem under Siege: The Collapse of the Jewish State 66–70 CE* (BSJS, 3; Leiden: Brill, 1992).

20. *Who Wrote the Dead Sea Scrolls?*, pp. 143-45, quoting *War* 4.3.1-2 §§121–28.

as the leaders prepare for war, the 'moderates' foresee the disasters to come and lament their fate (2.22.1 §§647–49). What Josephus is doing in these instances (in addition to his theme about who was responsible for the war) is exploiting the general literary techniques of raising feelings of *pathos* in the readers of his account, one of these techniques being anticipation of the catastrophe to come.[21] Therefore, the theme periodically occurs in which the 'people' (as opposed to the rebels) realize the great suffering about to come on Jerusalem.

What Josephus has hidden is the extent to which the very groups of society that he exonerates as opposed to the war were in fact the main leaders of it, the aristocracy and the priests.[22] Therefore, when Josephus has this very group fearing the destruction of Jerusalem, he is simply employing a literary device, and we would be foolish to take his statements at face value. What he does tell us is that various opposing Jewish groups were once again at each other's throats, apparently by late 67 (*War* 4.3.2–9.12 §§128–584). They also watched the gates fairly well, even if messengers sometimes got through (cf. 4.4.3 §236). This party strife continued until the Romans set siege to the city (5.1.1–6 §§1–38), at which point the various Jewish factions united against the common enemy (5.2.4 §71), though skirmishes with one another were renewed periodically (5.3.1 §§98–105).

Although Josephus does state that people feared for their lives and some even prepared to leave Jerusalem during the first siege of Cestius, this danger passed (*War* 2.19.6 §538); he does not suggest at any point that people thought of taking books to hide away from Jerusalem. On the contrary, he shows how difficult a massive removal of books would be and thus the unlikelihood of it. Even if a few individuals fled for their lives, the indication is that the Jews of Jerusalem as a whole expected to resist the Romans to the last, and strong efforts

---

21. There was a long tradition among Hellenistic historians of using 'pathetic' and tragic elements in their accounts. Even those such as Thucydides (1.21-22) and Polybius (2.56.10-12), who spoke against such elements themselves, actually made use of them. This is a well-known phenomenon in Josephus, though it is usually mentioned only in passing, and full studies are difficult to find. On the phenomenon in general, see A.J. Woodman, *Rhetoric in Classical Historiography: Four Studies* (London: Croom Helm, 1988); F.W. Walbank, 'Tragic History: A Reconsideration', *BICS* 2 (1955), pp. 4-14; *idem*, 'History and Tragedy', *Historia* 9 (1960), pp. 216-34; C. Gill and T.P. Wiseman (eds.), *Lies and Fiction in the Ancient World* (Exeter: University of Exeter Press, 1993).

22. See Price, *Jerusalem under Siege*.

were made to keep anyone from leaving (cf. *War* 4.6.3 §§377–88). When it became clear that the city was doomed, it was far too late to think about moving libraries out of the city; the individuals who tried to escape were turned back or murdered for the most part. Golb points out that some individuals managed to elude the Roman sentries to bring in supplies.[23] This example provides no support for his theory, however—it is one thing to bring in vital supplies to fighters defending the city; it is quite another to try to transport out books, which had a good chance of being detected and could just as easily have been hidden in the city itself.

During the siege, a few people managed to slip by the rebel guards and escape (cf. *War* 5.10.1 §§420–23), but it was to save their own skins, not those of sheep or goats. Golb does not explain why people would leave the city to hide books if they were expecting to return to be besieged. Nor does he explain why the books would have been taken to the Qumran region when the site of Khirbet Qumran was now garrisoned by Roman troops who just might have been alert enough to notice groups of Jews carrying wagon- or donkey-loads of scrolls to the surrounding caves—some right under their noses—for hiding. Masada might serve for this purpose, but Qumran? Hardly.

There are lots of points one could discuss about Golb's theory, and some points will be more convincing than others, but it seems to me to founder on the historical context which initially seems to be one of its strengths.

c. *4QMMT*

In the 1980s when a couple of articles revealed some tantalizing information about *Miqṣat Ma'aśe ha-Torah* or 4QMMT, and became available to a limited number of scholars, and a *samizdat* version was accessible to some of the rest of us, the word went around that it would revolutionize our understanding of Second Temple Judaism. Now, 4QMMT is finally available, almost forty years later than it should have been. It is an extremely valuable document, but has it revolutionized what we know of Judaism of the time?

Several have seen evidence in 4QMMT (and the Temple Scroll) that the Qumran community was Sadducean and that their opponents were Pharisees. This is based on the halakhic rulings in 4QMMT which

---

23. Golb, *Who Wrote the Dead Sea Scrolls?*, p. 146, quoting *War* 5.12.1 §§496–98.

either agree with Sadducean teachings or which seem to be polemic
against Pharisaic rulings. The argument is not simple, and a full
appreciation of it would require one to work through the various texts
and examples offered in defence of the thesis. I have argued against
this thesis for two main reasons.[24] The first of these is that the supposed parallels between Sadducean and Pharisaic teachings do not on
the whole stand up to investigation, but this will not be discussed further here.

My other reason for opposing the Sadducean hypothesis is based on
historical considerations and has two aspects to it. The first is that this
thesis simply bypasses some of the recent work on the Pharisees and
Sadducees. For example, the *editio princeps* ignores recent studies on
the Sadducees using the Greek and other sources.[25] A huge debate on
the Pharisees has been going on in the past quarter century or so, but
much of this is disregarded by the editors and others who support the
Sadducean hypothesis. I agree that 4QMMT can potentially feed into
this debate, but to develop a theory based almost exclusively on the
internal contents of 4QMMT and some Tannaitic passages without reference to other sources is very one-sided.

The second historical problem is that the hypothesis as generally
stated creates a second Sadducean group *ex hypothesi* alongside the
Sadducees we thought we knew from Josephus and other sources. I am
always suspicious of the 'duplex' method of writing history. This
approach assumes, whenever two sources do not agree, that each
source is talking about a similar but separate group or event. Instead
of evaluating the sources and examining them critically, it naively

24. '4QMMT and Second Temple Judaism', in F. García Martínez (ed.), *Legal
Texts and Legal Issues: Second Meeting of the IOQS, Cambridge, 1995* (Leiden:
Brill, forthcoming).

25. For example, Qimron and Strugnell (*Qumran Cave 4. V*) hardly mention
J. LeMoyne (*Les Sadducéens* [EB; Paris: Lecoffre, 1972], one reference on p. 117),
while more recent studies are omitted entirely, such as A.J. Saldarini, *Pharisees,
Scribes and Sadducees in Palestinian Society: A Sociological Approach* (Wilmington,
DE: Glazier, 1988); G. Baumbach, 'The Sadducees in Josephus', in L.H. Feldman
and G. Hata (eds.), *Josephus, the Bible and History* (Leiden: Brill, 1988), pp. 173-
95; E. Main, 'Les Sadducéens vus par Flavius Josèphe', *RB* 97 (1990), pp. 161-
206; W. Poehlmann, 'The Sadducees as Josephus Presents Them, or the Curious
Case of Ananus', in A.J. Hultgren, D.H. Juel, J.D. Kingsbury (eds.), *All Things
New: Essays in Honor of Roy A. Harrisville* (Word and World Supplement Series,
1; St Paul, MN: Luther Northwestern Theological Seminary, 1992), pp. 87-100.

takes each source at face value. For example, when Josephus mentions a Sanballat, he must be different from the Sanballat in Ezra–Nehemiah. Thus, we end up with three Sanballats,[26] four Ben-Hadads,[27] and two sanhedrins.[28] Now we have another group of Sadducees, but this is a group which apparently had little to do with the group known from Josephus and related sources. Contrary to the popular saying, 'The more, the merrier', it is a case of 'the more, the less convincing'.

The Continued Politicization of Scholarship

Politics have always played a part in scholarship and will continue to do so. This is unavoidable because it is a part of being human. Nevertheless, I strongly disagree with those who think that it is all politics.[29] Most of us feel that there is still room for reasoned argument. If not, why do we waste our time presenting arguments?

It is not necessary here to rehearse the rather disreputable way in which many of the unpublished Scrolls were kept out of the public domain, even when they could have been published in preliminary form already forty years ago,[30] not to mention that those who had

26. This is the solution of Frank Cross, perhaps best expressed in his well-known article, 'A Reconstruction of the Judean Restoration', *JBL* 94 (1975), pp. 4-18 (reprinted in *Int* 29 [1975], pp. 187-203). See my critique, 'Josephus and the Reconstruction of the Judean Restoration', *JBL* 106 (1987), pp. 231-46. It seems clear to me that Josephus's story is based on Nehemiah but, because of his ignorance of the Persian period, he misdates it to the time of Alexander. There is a second Sanballat apparently attested among the Samaritan finds, though the document which dates the seal has not been published.

27. A Bar Hadad is mentioned in both the Melqart and the Zakkur inscriptions; it may well be that the same person is attested in the ancient Near Eastern sources. In any case, the creation of up to four Ben Hadads comes from a naive reading of the biblical text. See J.M. Miller in J.A. Dearman and J.M. Miller, 'The Melqart Stele and the Ben Hadads of Damascus: Two Studies', *PEQ* 115 (1983), pp. 95-101.

28. E.g., H. Mantel, 'Sanhedrin', *IDBSup* (1976), pp. 784-86.

29. This is certainly the impression given by the address of L.A. Hitchcock, presented at the Society of Biblical Literature meeting in New Orleans, November 1996, at least in the oral presentation and the discussion section (I have not seen the written form of her paper). I actually do not believe that this is what she really thinks, but a more nuanced presentation would have been preferable.

30. I am sure I am not the only one who feels some anger to find that 4QMMT had been in large part reconstructed by 1959 and yet it was not even published in

access to them published articles based on them which others could not check. I can remember only a few years ago when someone complained on the IOUDAIOS e-mail discussion group about the fact that 4QMMT was unavailable, another participant replied, with what seemed to me a rather supercilious sniff—assuming you can give a supercilious sniff by e-mail—that Sussman's article[31] was available. For some reason, several of us did not feel that Sussman's article was a sufficient substitute for the real thing.

There were clearly lessons to be learned, but I am not sure they have been. I still see the same attitudes that want to decide matters not on the basis of freely available texts and a forum which allows various views and interpretations to be expressed but on the basis of personality, whom you studied with, who your friends are, and partisan politics.

None of us is able to practice completely disinterested scholarship, I readily admit. There is not enough time to examine every theory in the depth required, so we all give more weight to the interpretations and views of those we trust and those we judge to be good scholars. All of this we take for granted.

What does disturb me is the way that someone should attempt to prevent a fair hearing to others. Without being able to confirm the facts, I do believe—to some extent—Norman Golb's complaints that there have been some endeavours to exclude him from meetings and other opportunities to defend his views because they were not the accepted ones.[32] But I also take his interpretation with a grain of salt. After all, he is not unknown, he has published a number of articles in well-known journals, his book featured in the Ancient and Medieval History Book Club, and above all he has tenure. He is big enough to take care of himself. What really causes concern is when one hears stories that there have been threats to the careers of young scholars

preliminary form because 'certain major questions of introduction had to be solved' (Qimron and Strugnell [eds.], *Qumran Cave 4. V*, p. vii). This is especially galling when Strugnell still found the time to publish a very critical review ('Notes en marge du volume V des "Discoveries in the Judaean Desert of Jordan"', *RevQ* 7 [1969–71], pp. 163-276) of John Allegro (*Qumran Cave 4. I [4Q158–4Q186]* [DJD, 5; Oxford: Clarendon Press, 1968]) who had at least published his share of the Scrolls, whatever the deficiencies of his publication.

31. Sussman, 'The History of *Halakha*'.

32. Claims to this effect are made in *Who Wrote the Dead Sea Scrolls?*, especially Chapters 10–11.

who do not toe certain lines; of course, this is only an ugly rumour since no scholar would ever contemplate doing such a thing.

Such things as lawsuits, boycotts, cartels, all seem designed only to impede the free exercise of scholarship. Some use popular media, such as *The Biblical Archaeology Review*, as a way of attacking or intimidating others. It seems to me that if someone is not willing to say and defend something in a scholarly publication, they should not be saying it in a popular one. No doubt I am old-fashioned, but I continue to believe that the merits of an argument are more important than personalities or external factors.

Conclusions

I return now to my original theme, as expressed in the paper's title. What Qumran scholarship needs now is a recognition of how uncertain it all is. The Qumran material recently published only confirms how much we really do *not* know, and we need to admit our ignorance. I have no objection to new theories and new explanations of the data as we know them. What I do object to are theories which simply repeat old assumptions and shibboleths without examining them and which show a cavalier approach to the sources as a whole. Wide-ranging theories, daring proposals, new hypotheses to explain the data—these are what we need. Any theory will have its weak points and its imaginative reconstructions. The presence of these is not fatal in itself. The question is how well it makes sense of all the data currently known, even if not every *i* has been dotted or *t* crossed. But scholars must be willing to criticize their own theories as rigourously as those of others, and that is frequently lacking. Too often the answers are given before the questions are asked. The questions must come first; only then will the answers follow.

GOD'S SEMANTIC LOGIC:
SOME FUNCTIONS IN THE DEAD SEA SCROLLS AND THE BIBLE

Arthur Gibson

I

I will begin by stating the exploratory presuppositions of this study. This paper is concerned with the functions of *'l[w]hym* in the Dead Sea Scrolls and the Hebrew Bible, together with their relations to *theos, theoi, angelos* and *angeloi* in the LXX and New Testament quotations. The obvious significance of such investigation for concepts of God will not be pursued below, though presentation reflects the relevance of analysis for such presuppositions. This paper resumes earlier work for a philosophy of language with applied linguistics (commenced in Gibson 1981, 1998d). In Part II of this study I will propose analysing applied semantics by deploying logic theory of meaning, implementing my view that logic and semantics are species of live metaphor. Part III is concerned to implement Part II as a function to develop literary theory.

Prior to semantic excavation, a site-survey of intellectual policies employing sampling techniques, one which attempts to make explicit the subsumed links between ideology and semantics, is apt. This study of the semantic logic of terms for 'God' is here situated to introduce and connect a multi-disciplinery scenario. Its applicability hopefully will be generalized by future research as a contribution to the questions of what it is to be language, and to be logic. Although the linguistic exploration of the Dead Sea Scrolls is proceeding apace, literary theory, as well as current narrative theory conjoined with linguistic research in other languages (for example the type of work produced by Kermode 1991, Bowie 1993 and Prendergast 1986 in French, and Chinca 1977 in German), has yet to be added to Dead Sea Scrolls maps, even allowing for their less than fulsome literary worlds. The issue of the reference of divine terms, and what is to be reference, have no full account in such literary research, however. To address this topic one has to pass beyond the treatment of theistic terms in philosophy of religion, to the more significant and technical analyses produced by analytical philosophers (for example, variously: Dummett 1991, 1993; Lewis 1986; Sluga 1980; Stern 1995; Summerfield 1996).

There are obviously vexed problems that disrupt attempts to connect the (often imperialist) territories of literary theories and logics (in addition to the difficulties of generalizing over competing options within each domain). The topic of intentionality is merely one cross-mapping possibility between the two disciplines, which could facilitate continental drift to complementary overlap, but without tectonic collision, in the examination of divine referring expressions. Roughly, intentionality is the presupposition implemented as a semantic value of a referring term, such as *'lwhym*, in its relation to its purported referent. From the standpoints of literary research, the quite different researches of Bowie (1993) and of Bouveresse (1995), as well as Descombes (1992, 1995), construct routes linking psychoanalysis with literary criticism to address issues of intentionality. Bouveresse's 1995 study explicitly considers relations of Wittgenstein's (1997) ouvre to Freudian and literary interpretation—a sort of French Eurostar expression of ecumenical links with, yet usually spurned by, Anglo-Saxon philosophy.

Unfortunately, within the land of analytical philosophy, as Geach (1980) has trenchantly argued, many underground references lead along incomplete protest tunnels, or, contrary to the advertised named destinations and departure times, do not refer at all. In this respect not only have we much to learn from profoundly logical excavations currently under way, though they are as yet themselves incomplete and fraught with disagreement, but unfortunately typical analytical philosophy has no account of, or no allowance for, a connection between philosophical logic and literary criticism. Clearly, the assessment of dead languages amounts to an extreme and problematic instance of such a conjunction, not least because intentionality is a presupposition used in live native use of 'God', whereas live intuition is displaced by the modern linguist's own learnt instinct as a presupposition in frequency of, say, *'lwhym* in a Dead Sea Scrolls text.

Logic in early stages of development and self-assessment had long, often unhelpful, though now largely ignored, applications to the Bible (see Evans 1985). Institutional imperialisms hold sway over areas of logic. Yet, as Dummett (1991) remarks and demonstrates, the problems of logic are deeper and more unexpected than philosophers typically expect. Perhaps consequently, analytical philosophy's use of logic is typically taken to be alien or in opposition to literary analysis, ecumenical though the latter is. It is a criterion of analytical philosophy that its fundamental axiom is: any analysis of thought must go through an examination of language, and in principle offer a plausible philosophy of language (cf. Dummett 1993: 129-30). But a peculiar feature of almost all analytical philosophy is that generally there is no interest in analysis of a particular language, especially its literary uses, to contribute to the foregoing criterion. If it were the case that we had already reached a position to render such an analysis redundant, all well and good; but analytical philosophy is astronomically far from such a destination, together with disagreement as to what would count as the stipulation of what it is to be language, and its relations to natural languages.

In these respects unresolved areas of applied meaning-theory in the semantics of the Dead Sea Scrolls and the Bible impinge on partially unsolved issues in the logical theory of meaning. A selective conjunction of both can illuminate each. We are in fact unclear about what it is to be a relation between one actual language and a logical theory of meaning. As with all languages, we have no exhaustive decision-procedure for specifying the holistic structure of Hebrew. This is further complicated by the asymmetry between a live native-based analysis of language and what we cannot perform for a dead language since, for the latter, there is no corresponding function for native user-intuitions. A semantic theory for a dead language (even if it is only implicitly presupposed, or is a premise to which Semiticists have to be committed as a function of their arguments) is accordingly an over-generalization which goes beyond the hitherto explored data. The main task of applied semantics is to discover the means to infer a symmetry between semantics usage and generalization. Logic may both aid this programme and yet reflect the same type of restriction by labouring under its own limits.

Concerning a logical theory of meaning, the conjunction of 'logic' with 'theory of meaning' sets in motion a concern with inference and generalization applied to the project of defining what it is to be true— or false—interpretation. This latter feature is often misplaced.

Dummett (1993: 130) strikes the right note: 'a complete thought is to be characterized as that which it makes sense to qualify as true or false'. True *or* false. Application of logic theory to the Dead Sea Scrolls and the Bible is not a programme whose minimal condition for success is for it to identify what is true (though once such a programme is realized, the criteria for such an interpretation will already have been supplied). In so far as logic has any success in isolating what it is to be language, it can be employed to interpret aspects of groups of linguistic features whose representation is a matter of significance or dispute, though it is not a decision-procedure by which the logician can impose imperialism. As with any epistemological conception, including literary appreciation, we only expose those properties of language which our presuppositions attract, together with accidental discoveries or inventions of sense. We usually have too confident an assumption that our theories determine exactly what it is to be the subject they target. We too easily fail to notice excess space ignored by our perception since the latter is not a recognitional concept of what it is to be the object-language of our analysis. (For example, the European anarchistic anti-logic avant-garde in the 1918–30 period was anything but new, and used logic, while Whitehead and Russell's *Principia* confused premises with assumptions. No doubt the present study will unconsciously furnish its own instances.)

In addition to the above scope which can be circumscribed by true/false logics, deviant logics can sometimes be applied to interpret linguistic phenomena. Many typical deviant logics can be derived indirectly from bivalent (true/false) logical calculuses (see Haack 1971), and thus be networked into a generalized framework. It would be an anachronistic misrepresentation of this type of project, however, to envisage that the application of logic to language, ancient or modern, is the mere formalization of a narrative. The deeper and more significant logical issues for applied linguistics reside within the purvue of philosophical logic or theory of meaning; namely, the attempts to dig out what it is to be a language, and how creative narrative challenges and disputes its own roles. In particular, for the present paper's purposes, logic is not a methodological manifesto—it will be brought in (largely informally) only where the main priority, of investigating issues in the Dead Sea Scrolls, warrants it.

A way forward for both the construction of the linguistics of a given language, say Hebrew or Greek, and the scope of logic, for example concerning what is reference and function, is to align such concerns in study of a problematic core-term in a body of literature. To give full-throttle to such an investigation would be to choose two such sets of uses in two languages in which contentions of mirroring and collision of semantic values occurs. The employment of terms translated 'God' in the Dead Sea Scrolls and the Bible facilitates such an investigation.[1] The discussion of what is representation is already controversial prior to the introduction of conceptions of God to the debate. Prendergast (1986) revolutionized the arena by reviving mimesis as a counter-intuitive normatively unstable feature whose point is lost when it is not at the frontier of creative risk but institutionalized, as it often has been in theological tradition. The structure of personification poetics, at least in English literary studies, is much better understood now, thanks to Paxson (1994). It remains for us to explore the possible creative and logical conjunction of destabilized mimesis with personification. Presumably 'God' is the most exotic instance of this conjunction. Although I demur from Priest's (1995) paraconsistent logic (in which a proposition can be true and false), his investigation, of how to transcend the limits of thought in language to infinity, breaks with a tradition of restrictions which notions of the transcendental God in ancient literature contravened. The use of *'l[w]hym* in the Dead Sea Scrolls and Hebrew Bible is a case of counter-intuitive mimesis which personifies God by suturing transcendence to a finite expression, I shall argue.

II

a. *When Angels Go Proxy for God*
When Newsom (1985: 24) discussed Qumran angelology in the liturgical text 4QShirShabb, she observed that:

> Many occurrences of *'lwhym* in the Shirot are ambiguous and might refer either to God or to angels, though such expressions as *kwl 'lwhym* (4Q40; 1 i 32, 32-33) and *mlk 'lwhym* (4Q400 2 5) unequivocally attest

---

1.   Michael Dummett (1991: 17) writes of a similarity between problems of the meaning of 'God' and logic: 'Perhaps a polytheist cannot mean the same by "God" as a monotheist; but there is a disagreement between them, all the same. Each denies that the other has hold of a coherent meaning; and that is just the charge made by the intuitionist against the classical mathematician.' We could replace the term 'polytheist' by opposing belief in an angel's role using the term *'lwhym*, so as to adjust this contrast for our purpose.

the use of *'lwhym* for the angels. A biblical basis for *'lwhym* = angels is
provided by Pss. 8.6; 82.1, 6; 97.8; 138.1; etc.

Before proceeding to the task of semantic analysis, a note is appropriate on the orthography of the MT *'lhym* in relation to the Dead Sea
Scrolls *'lwhym*. The form of the Dead Sea Scrolls probably only
reflects a tendency to write fuller forms in later Hebrew. But we
should allow the possibility that it could mark some unknown semantic
tonal or lexical contribution. In any case, as Ulrich (1995: 109) points
out, the orthography of a number of biblical books from Qumran is
inconsistent. Just how or if these reflect any semantic function is
unclear. In view of the role of *'lhym*, for example, to code judges in
Exod. 21.6, together with the import of earlier traditions of orthography at Qumran and their irregular yet (possibly uneven) mirroring
of practices generally in Palestine, it is worth reproducing Ulrich's
(1995: 116) observation on the relevant orthography of 4Qpaleo-
Exod^m: although it tends towards a fuller orthography, it remains in
the moderate range, with *'lhym* spelled without *waw*. Newsom (1992:
41) points out that, for example, in 4Q374 *'lhym* occurs 41 times,
with *'lwhym* once. If we take the view that at least some of the paleo-
Hebrew manuscripts predate Qumran (while agreeing to the possibility that paleo-Hebrew copying was practiced there), as well as
allowing for manuscripts with the Jewish script being copied in and
away from Qumran, we need further analysis to reach a conclusion as
to the identity of the presence or absence of *waw* in *'lhym*. Schuller
(1992: 97) observes that the non-canonical psalm 4Q381 15 employs
'lhy, even where the MT and others have YHWH. Qimron (1992: 366)
judges that here the Dead Sea Scrolls morphology of Hebrew was
probably not influenced by the MT. But there is the question of the
influence of Daniel, if it is as early as Stefanovic (1992) suggests.
More generally, if Stefanovic's conclusion exposing further links
between Old Aramaic and Daniel is correct, we will have radically to
re-assess such relations. The following remarks leave a space for the
solution to these larger problems, and avoid tying the difference of
form to its conclusions. Nevertheless it is clear from the use of
'lwhym in 4QShirShabb that Newsom's claim is true for a possible
equation between the term and 'angels'; but what this notion of
identity ('=') is, is up for interrogation.

As it is expressed by her, Newsom's foregoing equation ''*lwhym* =
angels' is an absolute identity relation 'x = y'. But as it stands this

allows no difference between the two terms, and unless Newsom was supposing that *'lwhym* is here only a term for 'angel', and not 'God', then we would be committed to an angel who irreducibly is God and nothing less than God, which seems not to be her point. Obviously, since she, rightly, asserts that *'lwhym* 'might refer to God or to angels', we should extirpate her infelicity in logic to accord with the spirit of her observation, to become: 'x = y respecting a function (or set of functions) F'. (This approach to identity is well developed by Geach 1980.) That is to say, since in her view (I think correctly) "*'lwhym*...might refer to God', it is more accurate to define the identity sign '='—the equation—to be one of relative identity, that is, any referent or subject going proxy for God who, or which, does so by satisfying or manifesting features ascribed to God. (As with predicate logic and natural languages, such an equation is applicable whether or not the resulting narrative ascriptions are true or false; and so this schema is applicable to polemical contexts in the Dead Sea Scrolls and the MT, etc., where the term *'lwhym* is used of subjects who are denounced, or many intentional contexts.)

In the aforementioned quoted judgments Newsom supposes that the Hebrew 'refers' to either God or angels. Leaving aside, for the present, what is intended in her remarks by 'reference' (a study of Smiley 1982 would be helpful to clarify reference here), we should query this disjunctive contrast between reference to 'God' or to 'angels' for *'lwhym*.[2] This referential alternation does not have to follow from the linguistic data, though sometimes it is applicable. The present paper is concerned with those more problematic contexts where the disjunction does not apply. In these uses I shall argue that there is reference inclusive of God and angel in the semantic function of *'lwhym*. Such a proposal is separable from and not necessarily in conflict with the employment of *'lwhym* in, for example, 11QMelch, interpreted as used of Melchizedek. It is not here an occasion to enter into, but to note as important, the complex interplay in the Qumran *Sabbath Shiroth* of the ideal transcendental angelic priestly typology, where Newsom (1990) has introduced us to important background for this

2. So I do not exclude the possibility of a semantic difference matching the difference in orthography between *'lwhym* in some Dead Sea Scrolls MSS and *'lhym* in the Hebrew Bible, though my present study attempts to allow either eventuality. For further discussion on the Exodus orthographic issue, see Sanderson 1986, and Ulrich and Sanderson 1992.

issue. Possibly Melchizedek is identified as the priest in the assembly of God at the consecration of the angelic priests (cf. Horton 1976). Such contexts, implementing thematic interplay between transcendent and human references, appear to circumscribe, not dispute, the interaction of *'lhym* as a designator of transcendent and human agents.

No doubt, there is vagueness in some uses of *'lwhym*; but such a judgment may too easily obscure a measurable, albeit dense, sense of *'lwhym* in groups of narratives. *'lwhym* is not a term with an entirely singular sense; but I shall argue that the word is neither homonymic nor indeterminate. A plausible scenario for such an *'lwhym* function would be (very roughly) that of an agent whose function is to go proxy for another bearer while also manifesting its own individuality: for example, an angel standing for the intended (contextually relevant elements of) God's identity. Although this is not entirely parallel with regard to the semantics of *ml'kym* (messengers), yet there is some overlap with *'lhym* with the role of communicating something (from God, or whoever) and its related action. This contiguity of sense reflects similarity in some of their contexts. Schiffman (1989: 49-51) describes the presence of the *ml'kym* in 1QSa, the Rule of the Congregation, which emphasizes the bearers of *ml'kym* as present in the assembly. These are messengers from heaven who, according to Schiffman, are to stand alongside humans; and he notes Bokser's (1985) suggestion that they represent the divine presence. The uses of *'lwhym* pick out the aspects of the bearers that go proxy for God as qualitatively apt realizations of (pertinent features of) deity. Often narratives (such as 11QMelch) employ the term to remonstrate with those agents who have failed to manifest the *'lwhym* identity (or features of it), but who, by dint of position or purported function, are bearers of this divine term.

Before discussing texts, it might assist to spell out some basic aspects of this agency proposal. The thesis I am advancing binds together the quite separable roles of depicting angel and God. In this perspective the function of *'lhym* is to mediate properties of the referent of a subject (usually God) through a mediating function (frequently, a transcendental angel, though sometimes a human). This is a counter-intuitive use of personification, and we could draw in Paxson's (1994) literary analysis of the latter term to fill out how the notion applies to this in narrative form. The view presupposes that what has often been thought to be ambiguity (and let us not confuse this term with 'vagueness', for which see Williamson 1996) is a double-tier function within the expression *'lhym*. On this analysis, *'lwhym*'s sense is that of an agent(s) mediating another subject's intentions and/or likeness. (We should of course distinguish this use of 'intention' from 'intentional'.) I am not entering into having to postulate an author's intention with which the author writes. The point of the foregoing is that within the semantic field there is a functional use which maps *'lwhym* with an agency sense. This use of 'intention' is therefore an intertextual function;[3] it is not here an equation between authorial voice and author, though this connection is not thus disbanded by this more modest applied linguistic priority. To be sure, one might propose that the unconscious (such as refined by Bouveresse 1995 assessing Wittgenstein and Freud, or with Bowie 1993 deconstructing Lacan 1966, or an amalgum of both) itself has an extended and metaphoric relation to intertextual relations within a semantic field, and retrieve some such notion of an intention of an author(s) mapped into a text, tantalizingly unstable though such a counter-intuitive conception would be (for which see Gibson 1998a). The complex conception of the expression of a communal intention in tradition, as a function of this type of theory, is clearly an important requirement for future research.

b. *Referring to God*
Given the formal arguments concerning 'reference'/'refers', here briefly summarized,[4] we should employ the categories of reference for *'lwhym* indirectly and with caution. It seems clear that *'lwhym* is not a proper name: it is quantifiable by the article, and scope operators such as *kwl*; it does not appear as a proper name for a group, but as a description. And there is within *'lwhym* the ossified plural form, still largely unexplained functionally, and possibly susceptible of being triggered into plural function by paronomasia. Such data require the notion of *'lwhym* ascribing its semantic properties in nominal form identity or characteristics to God. That is to say, *'lwhym* does not of itself refer. Rather, it is true (or false) of its referent, much in the same way a predicate is true of its subject. For a term such as *'lwhym* to have a reference, in Newsom's sort of use, tends to trigger or be read with the presupposition that of itself *'lwhym* rigidly designates

3. See Gibson (1998c and 1998d) for 'intertextuality'.
4. See Dummett 1991: Chapter 5; Gibson 1981: Chapter 2; and Gibson 1997.

by reference; a role only proper to, for example, YHWH. But even if these formal analyses be opposed, the thesis being advanced in this paper still stands on a variety of other interpretations of the linguistic data.[5]

When *'lwhym* is used of a transcendent Melchizedek in 11QMelch it evidently functions to pick out a single bearer. But the scroll requires *'lwhym* to be employed as a description covering a set of such subjects, not least because of its quotation of Ps. 82.1 representing the assembly of such bearers. In the scroll the heavenly Melchizedek is an agent manifesting God's identity. The fact that the plural form is employed here, and of a singular, maps into usage a stress on *'lwhym* as a function which delineates qualities of a type, and not a proper-name like value.

'lwhym neither mediates one person, nor yet allows one to deem other subjects within its scope as homonyms, and it has a very large plural set. But *'lwhym* mediates the identity of God in such a way that God is presented in the first person, or the *'lwhym*'s acts are identified as God's, when the *'lwhym* are accepted as God-sent. As with a merger of televisions with their presenters, they broadcast subjects different from themselves, though their chosen subject imposes advertising constraints. Ed Sanders[6] contributed to reformulating our relations to ancient Christian and Jewish traditions. Two of his points are relevant here. First, Sanders circumscribes the view that after the Babylonian exile Jewish texts tended to employ an intermediary to represent God, and he notes that this does not imply God's remoteness. Secondly, Sanders highlights the idea that, for Palestinian Judaism, close reading of sacred writings brings the pious reader into God's presence. I wish to re-orientate these two points, and propose a general thesis: in appropriate uses, an intermediary *is* God's presence, under a relative identity notion of identity discussed above and below. Derrida's (1978) view of metaphysics is that it circumscribes the presence of a transcendental property, while he would dispute that any meaning can yield such support. For him, the claim of a presence entails the absence of the feature it linguistically proposes. With *'lwhym*, albeit in a radically different world, they suture absence and presence, exemplifying *différance* and thus marking that the referent

5.   See Gibson (1997) regarding the thesis of indexical predication which could be applied here.

6.   E.g. Sanders (1977) and (1985).

of, say YHWH, is both present in manifestation while entirely Other.

A recent trend in Old Testament scholarship rightly emphasizes the contrast in sacred biography between a biographic subject and the 'likeness' of the subject.[7] But some uses of *'lwhym* are part of a theme in which God's identity is mediated by an earthly or heavenly agent going proxy for God. Relative identity is shared between a subject and its representative, or that agent who goes proxy for the subject, or a facet of it, as with the angel reproducing aspects of God. Its internal logic is parallel, in relevant ways, with other relations such as father and son, or any relation in which two or more subjects share common properties or one comes to personify or go proxy for another. This alleviates the problem of the plural, because part of the syntax of *'lwhym* being employed is a switch mechanism that multiply implements singular and/or plural bearers, because part of the semantics involves mediation of qualities between agent and final referent. Much of the terminology in the narrative fields of *'lwhym* includes fellowship language (*'m*, Exod. 3.12, etc.). So the relational tonal semantics are not solely those of 'relation to', but 'relationship with' referring and referent, presence and believer/witness. Thus the deep structure of this feature is that the term, in a certain narrow sense, always has a potential function of a plural subject, going proxy for one (Other) subject. The characterization here is provisional and brief, to be filled out later.

If such a sketch is accurate, we need to re-organize the contrasts and assumed conflicts between singular God versus plural agents to which the term *'lwhym* applied. Angelic uses of this term do not compete with the prime sense of the God-referent to whom this term is finally applied. Agents have the term employed of them because their likeness functions, or is intended to manifest, God's identity. Perhaps to encapsulate the semantic relations here, the notion of a portrait is helpful: it both satisfies its own criterion of identity as an artwork, and in doing it felicitously represents, with interpretation, the identity of that for which it goes proxy and accordingly to which it refers. The creative research of Macé (1993) complements this approach by composing an explanation of reproduction of personalized visual image in literary form employing abstract predicates in prose; he uses the figure of a camera to achieve this. Imaging and interpretation coincide to satisfy a

7.   See Nigosian (1993).

criterion of identity here in which semantic indeterminacies can be so unified in creativity to comply with a consistent function: the role of the narrative and its characters going proxy for another identity, that of God. The sheer density of such a possibility, rather than indeterminacy, is a fecund source for breeding new types of representation.

c. *'Theoi' in John's Gospel and* 'lhym
We should not neglect John 10's *theoi* in Christological discussion:

> (A) *Egō eipa theoi este*
> I said, you are gods.

The key logic in (A) is that of, roughly, an equation whose deep structure binds plural subjects with a relative identity function: a 'set of "x's = y" respecting F', where 'F' stands for a set of properties which can be used as a criterion of identity for the equation and/or for the subject.

This quotation from Ps. 82.6 is blended into John's argument between Christ and Jews about the question of his identity and the relationship between father and son. Jesus is presented as claimant to be the son of God (a phrase we do well to isolate from 'God the son', not only because of the plural form *bny 'lhym* in Psalm 82). Yet the narrative in which (A) is set presents the Jews as interpreters who take this to be a different claim, that of equality with God. The passage in John 10 ascribes to Jesus an argument which not only opposes but is deployed to dispute this claim. The narrative takes Christ to cite (A) as a counterpoise to the allegation of his equality to God. Strangely, he applies an expression—*theoi*—that enacts an overkill for the task by applying some sense of divinity not to him, but to figures lowlier than he—human judges. By inference, these are the very people whom he is castigating for sarcastically elevating him to equality with God. This reads, if anything, like an explicit rebuttal of attempts to attach a substance or absolute identity sense in the reference to God. The narrative pluralizes—quantifies—semantics and existence to range over mortals. To be sure, there are a number of changes of sense and divergence between Psalm 82 and John 10; yet it should be noted that we cannot dismiss the foregoing by using the information that the Psalm is Hebrew while John is Greek, since the agency sense is not only constituted by the plural form: the case for agency resides in the narrative frame and rhetoricized functions of the virtual reality matching semantic fields of Psalm 82 and John 10.

The singular term for 'God' is central to Christology. The rarity of singular uses of *ho theos* applied to Christ in the New Testament comprises a position in such semantic fields which are fractured by many post-New Testament uses. However, as Barnes (1995a and 1995b) discovers, and Milbank (1997) develops it, Augustine's almost totally neglected later, more mature writings on the Trinity, not least in their uses of the Old Testament, raise fundamental questions which provoke directions for a 'social model' in relational issues regarding 'God'. Nevertheless, in *de Trinitate* (1.13), whilst quoting Ps. 82.6, Augustine entirely ducks the use of it in Jn 10.30, even though later citing the adjacent verse when he comes to examine Jn 10.30, 'I and my father are one', noting that it is plural not singular (instantiating, so it seems, Tertullian's puzzling over why this 'one' is neuter). Controversially consequent on these critical perspectives, one can measure the employment of *ho theos* when applied to the son of God in Heb. 1.8, quoting Ps. 45.7: 'Your throne, O God'. If we take the approach supported by this type of translation, this quotation cannot of itself be taken to dislocate the agency sense of the *'lhym* origins of *ho theos*: it confirms it. The bearer of *'lhym* envisaged by the composer of Psalm 45 was hardly implementing a substance ontology, particularly since the plural form there and an earthly king in a narrative reflect a contract with and further differentiation of the juridical use of *'lhym* (appropriate for a stylized Solomon) in Exod. 21.6 of a singular subject. In Heb. 1.8, however, the second use of *ho theos* qualifies and functionally subordinates (by anointing) the bearer of the first term to this second. 'God, your God', is a phrase consistent with the Dead Sea Scrolls and Hebrew Bible presupposition of non-singular use *'lhym*, which is also in harmony with monotheistic representation of a singular referent (or set of relevant features of its identity). In this priority, uses of *'lhym* mediate a depiction of the referent of YHWH (or the final referent of *'lhym*) while also coding a representational function and discrete identity (or relevant set of properties) of the agent of the final referent of *'lhym*. The double use of *'lhym* or an agent manifesting the final deity referent is so sharp in Psalm 45 as to approach Socratic irony for those unaccustomed to the role of the discerning reader of agency: just before the agency use of *'lhym* in Ps. 45.7, we are told in v. 3 that God has blessed the king forever. In 4QBerakhot (4Q286–290), *[hw]d whdr*, 'glory and majesty', blesses the earthly king, integrating an allusion to Ps. 45.4 (see Nitzan 1994: 60) in such a way as to mirror Heb. 1.8's use of the agency theme in divine reference. The transfer of *hdr* to the king here generalizes the scope of the *'lhym* agency use to the themes which implement it. In the Qumran Psalms Scroll 11QPs[a], after the last psalm, 150, *hdr* is employed in the 'Hymn to the Creator' in a manner reminiscent of Ezek. 43.2, ascribing such divine qualities to the angels (cf. Weinfeld 1995).

The utilization of the Old Testament semantic field and theme in Heb. 1.8 stands in unexpected but consistent relation to the other plural translation of *'lhym* as *angelous* in Heb. 2.7, which cites Ps. 8.5. It seems naive to ascribe ignorance of this semantic state of affairs to the author on the grounds of a traditional polemical, citation-text mentality that handles programmatic material which, for him, is ossified with respect to agency functions. This is particularly so in view of the rich array of targumic and multifarious Greek translational directions in which the linguistic material continued to develop both before and after the Old Testament, within the other Dead Sea Scrolls societal groupings, and not least throughout the New Testament era. There are also the complex unresolved states and relations of the Dead Sea Scrolls Psalms to the Masoretic Psalter (see Flint 1994). Although the extant parts of the Dead Sea Scrolls Psalms 1–89 are more uniform than later ones, there is still ignorance concerning their roles and polemic identities. This cluster of problems is subject to more indeterminacy since we cannot adequately generalize over the textual family identities of the Dead Sea Scrolls, even concerning nonaligned textual elements (see Tov 1995). These factors, together with the postulated pre-Qumran distinct sources for (some of) the texts deposited/discovered at Qumran (cf. Schiffman 1995), and with, for example, the differences between the later fixed Psalter and the Qumran scrolls—generally uniform though such activity was—further disrupt a smoothing out of appeal to a fixed stylized use of 'proof-texts'. Given the foregoing, and the author of Hebrews' acquaintance with the Hebrew singular and plural agency functions of *'lhym* in Psalms 45 and 8, picked out by different Greek nouns, the agency schema of the Hebrew Dead Sea Scrolls and Hebrew Bible is explicitly programmed into New Testament use. Such a distribution does not entail that a term is used with the same thesis in different semantic fields. But the situation as characterized above does place limits on theological conjecture, which exclude an absolute identity and/or substance conception within the New Testament.

d. *Philosophy of Live Genetic Metaphor*
This puzzle is enriched by the genetic metaphors of sonship in many
Dead Sea Scrolls and Hebrew Bible contexts, of which Psalm 82 and
John 10 are ironized exotic instances. Some traditional theology
assumes antecedently that the shift from plural 'sons of God' to the
singular 'son of God' is a difference of ontology, with a divine substance attached to the latter. John's Gospel offers no terminology to
specify this, though John develops the theme of the only begotten son.
Thomas's later affirmation of 'My lord and my God', in its use of
'God' does not ontologically go beyond the application of *'lwhym* in
Ps. 45.6, and does not quite concur with an LXX 'Lord God' matching
a phrase with YHWH in it. Obviously, even so, there is a special type
of quality—not only degree of unique divine sonship—being advanced
in John; but my point is that this is not crafted from uses of 'God'
which involve an ontology of substance. Instead there appears to be a
functional theme of agency with 'God', keyed by uses of translations
of *'lwhym*, which extends into a genetic metaphor of unique sonship.
Clearly this sonship domain occupies various levels, from Psalm 82's
plural 'sons of God' to Christ, the uniquely begotten one; this uniqueness is constituted by a sonship relationship for which there is no
precedent in terms of it occurring earlier than the semantics it has in
the New Testament. But the precedent of a typology for unique sonship appears to arise from the semantics of *'lhym* developed in the
Hebrew Bible and the Dead Sea Scrolls, in which a criterion of identity for reproducing God through an agent is ontologically switched
into the begetting of a son for God the father.

e. *Melchizedek and* 'lwhym
Rowland (1982) has discussed how the use of Psalm 82 in 11QMelch
has parallels with the *Testament of Abraham* and with the *Similitudes*
concerning the heavenly court figure. Whether or not we are disposed
to accept his dating of 50 CE for the Jewish texts, or wish to take an
older date, his scrutiny of the background is valuable, particularly if
the Dead Sea Scrolls or parts of them were composed away from
Qumran or were combined with other narratives which led to their
influence upon the evolution of tradition in the Dead Sea Scrolls. The
coincidence of Jewish texts and Gospel may be informative for their
disputing in some commonly shared historical arenas.
    11QMelch does not of course cite Ps. 82.6, though it employs vv. 1-
2; but this gap of thematic development within Psalm 82 is partly

overcome since v. 6 utilizes some terms and interrelations which are introduced in the opening of the psalm. The appropriate lines of the scroll read:

9. *hw'h hqṣ/q lšnt hrṣwn lmlky ṣ[dq]l... [ ]*
wqdwšy 'l lmm[š]lt mšpṭ k'šr ktwb

He decreed the acceptable year for Melchizedek...
and the holy ones of God for judgment's rule;
as it is written

10. *'lyw bšyry dwyd 'šr 'mr 'lwhym [n]ṣb b'[dt 'l]*
bqwrb 'lwhym yšpwṭ w'lyw 'm[r ']lyh

Concerning him in the songs of David, who said:
'lwhym stands in the congregation of God; in
among 'lwhym, he judges. And concerning him, he says:

11. *lmrwm šwbh 'l ydyn 'mym w'šr '[mr 'd mty t]špwṭw*
'wwl wpny rš'[y]m tš['w s]lh.

Return you on high. God shall judge the peoples;
and that he said: *How long will you judge unjustly,*
and elevate the wicked's face? Selah.

My translation here italicizes the scriptural quotations or allusions. Isaiah 61.2 fragmentarily occurs in l. 9's 'acceptable year'; l. 10b cites Ps. 82.1; ll. 10b and 11a deploy parts of Ps. 7.8-9, with Ps. 82.2 enclosing the sequence in l. 11b. The employment of some of these expressions, including 'Melchizedek', in New Testament contexts additional to John, exemplified by Fitzmyer (1971), de Jonge and van der Woude (1965–66) and van der Woude's (1965) edition of the scroll, highlights some features shared between John's use of Greek and Semitic material, and the Melchizedek scroll, even allowing for the differences of thesis and development reflected in both groups of literatures. When Heb. 1.8 states that 'the son' bears the title *ho theos*, this parallels the application of *'lwhym* in the rulership context to Melchizedek in l. 10 of 11QMelch, which matches the above ingredients and narrative frame of Heb. 1.8 citing Ps. 45.7:

(B) *ks'k 'lhym: ho thronos sou ho theos.*

Emerton (1960) maintained that (A) above is associated with the use of *theoi* to represent angels. Yet 'associated' here, if true, has to include a contrast with 'angels' respecting (B) and (A), because of their subjects, though certainly the Hebrew Bible elsewhere has *'lhym* indicating angels, if one accepts the primary semantic value of the LXX and New Testament Greek translations of the term. A generalized account needs to incorporate and explain both why 'angels' appear to be susceptible of the same word as humans and the incarnation. As mentioned in the foregoing, there is the celebrated case in Ps. 8.5:

> (C) *wthsrhw m'ᵉt m'lkym: elattosatosas auton brachu*
> *ti par angelous.*

This quotation, taken up in Heb. 2.7, reflects a narrow translation tendency; it is also similar to Ps. 137.1, *angelon*, and Ps. 97.7, *angeloi*. In these LXX passages the translation is an agency-relation function, one that overlaps with those of (A) and (B). But (C) explicitly presents the value of the angelic component, while humans in (A) replace this angelic value even though the agency function is equivalent for (A), (B), and (C).

f. *Is Quantification Divine?*

It might be assumed that the rendering of *theos* is due to a liberalizing tendency because of a partial ossification of the term in, for example, ritual or festal usage. But this sort of approach does not allow for Alexander's (1972: 64) view that, for example, Aquila's retention of the plural *theoi* in Gen. 6.2 is due to the translator's attention to a functional requirement.

This nest of issues also obliquely engages the shift from plural to singular subject at the semantic level which is syntactically undifferentiated in the *'lhym* form. It is worth proposing here for consideration the idea that there is a live metaphoric or even idiomizing contribution of *-ym* in *'lhym*. The concept of metaphoricity ascribed to syntax is itself a vast subject for investigation.[8] This topic relates to

---

8.   An analogy to introduce, as well as connect, the issue with other linguistic phenomena for future generalization could be provided by noting the work in Gibson 1981 and 1998c: Chapter 3.3. The ossified semantic 'contents' of a proper name when subject to paronomasia are triggered into having a semantic value assigned to it. Normally, of course, the proper name is solely a referring term whose value is to satisfy a given criterion of identity, for example such as that of the bearer of YHWH. When paronomasia is created by the narrative function of a proper name, the mention (and not only use) of, say, the paronomastic thematized explanation of the 'meaning' of YHWH (for example in Exod. 3.12-15) is concurrent with the use of YHWH as a referring term. I leave aside here the above proposal of an idiomizing notion, though I address it in a proper name context, in Gibson 1981, 1998c.

the differentiation between the use of an expression in a narrative and the way in which it itself can be cross-referred to or mentioned, or in some way alluded to by other words or functions within the narrative, in addition to its typical use. Quantification itself (for our purposes here, plural to singular shifts) to some degree seems to display counter-intuitive[9] properties, and this can disrupt the semantic applicability of a formal syntactic paradigm. One unexpected feature of the proposed inter-relation between logic and language for the present purpose is the identity of predication.

Whatever the eventual estimation assigned to the founder of modern logic, Frege,[10] his exposure of the predicative identity of quantification was the first such analysis. Informally expressed, it is the interpretation of quantifiers like *kwl*, *-ym*, *hkl*, and some uses of *h-*, as predicative or ascriptive functions. A function is an incomplete expression which ascribes a property to a referent, mediating that function by its attachment to a subject term. In principle, this parallel with predication leads to analysis of relations between quantifiers and predicate expressions (fragments and complex groupings). The point of this conception for *'lhym* is that it furnishes a basis for identifying the functional inter-connection between a singular reference to God and the plural use of agent media (for example, *angeloi, theoi*). It seems clear that the main focus of such functional cross-connections, even thematically, is that the media of representation (angels, people, the incarnation) are presented to depict, manifest, reveal or embody the Other (subject). This coding of the transcendent God as present in a functional relationship with an agent of manifestation is a contrast which has some parallel with Derrida's (1978) use of *différance*. That transcendence is marked in language, and is itself a violation of the limits of finite language: what is coded to be present is marked for its referent as an absence. Without wishing to suppose that Qumran and Hebrew Bible readers were aware of this formulation, their narratives' concerns with the presence versus absence of divine features in the use of language is taken to be a function of revelation and immanence. It appears to be the case that the logical semantics of God in *'lhym*, as well as its then as yet future translational histories, is

9. For a study of 'counter-intuition', see Gibson 1998c, and indirectly Lewy, 1976.

10. Works by Frege 1969; see the research by Geach 1980, Dummett 1981; for a different approach, see Lewis 1986.

tantamount to a complex unconscious mirror of *'lhym*'s intertextual relations of its narrative fields contexts. The common Hebrew Bible conundrum of a formally plural *'lhym* with a singular subject, on this approach, may be a metaphorized use of the plural ending to code its use as a term which presupposes a medium or media of manifestation whenever God is the topic of reference. This may be construed diachronically as literary and psycholinguistic presupposition of reference for *'lhym*, which is variant in different contexts yet has some residual invariance as to dual or multiple reference involving agency.

The previous paragraph has application to aspects of 11QMelch's use of Ps. 82.1. The invariance of reference is reified, and plural/singular references maintained and extended in Jn 10.33's use of Ps. 82.6. *'lwhym* occurs in the singular and plural in 11QMelch l. 10, which quotes Ps. 82.1. The plural formation corresponds to the plural *'lhym* employed in Ps. 82.6, and which is cited in Jn 10.33. So at this level the priorities of Psalm 82, 11QMelch and John's Gospel interlock and display a common element. John 10 develops a condemnation theme in which a failure by Christ's critics to manifest the agency function of *theoi* is central to the presupposition of reference in Psalm 82 and John 10. In 11QMelch (ll. 9-10), as well as Psalm 82 and John 10, the juridical role of divine agents is the theme's pivot; this appears to match the juridical semantic reference core of Exod. 21.6's ascription of *'lhym* to juridical bearers. We may see this emphasis in 11QMelch, if we accept that 'Melchizedek' unexpectedly replaces YHWH in the scroll's apparent quotation of Isa. 61.2 (cf. Fitzmyer 1971: 262). Here Melchizedek's *'lwhym* function partially reproduces parallel functions of the Isaiah YHWH, though we need sharply to restrict and bind such quantification over the two subjects, though the intertextual relations between the passages overtly overlap. It is of course too easy to convert this into an equation that the John 10 Christ shares the functions of the scroll's Melchizedek. (In addition to many other considerations, it is not obvious that we can consistently employ 'Qumran theology' to support the equation, since the scroll's composition may not have originated at Qumran.) Parallels of function contracted by *'lwhym* in this juridical role, combined with the indictment presented in 11QMelch, Psalm 82 and John 10, are by now evident, however.

A presupposition of the general trend of the foregoing paragraphs (for convenience) can be termed a phanerosis relation. Summarily, from a standpoint of outlining *'lhym*'s basic functions, for a function to be one subject, it entails that an internal property of this conception is for such a subject to satisfy a criterion of identity of another subject: (it is true or false) that *'lhym* (angels, people) manifest God's identity. Identity is itself a tricky notion. Although God may be simple and certainly singular, in the Hebrew Bible and derivatively the Dead Sea Scrolls, God's revelatory relations and mediation are complex, not to say perplexing. But we do not have to offer a final solution on these matters to establish that representation of theistic identity is various. A consequence of examining relevant features of these matters in the present paper, as well as other studies (cf. Geach 1980, Gibson 1981), I believe, is that identity is relative. Namely, '"x = y" with regard to a function F' (where 'F' is a description or predicate-fragment); in the present context, the two (or more) such conjoined terms could be *'lhym* and YHWH (with the former instantiating an agency role such as that interpreted by *theoi* or *angeloi*, etc). Wittgenstein's (1973; cf. Summerfield 1996) pluralist approach to fixing the reference of a name enables us to show that a given use of *'lhym* satisfies at least two criteria.

First, a reference to the deity is presupposed. (Obviously if this reference is to an intended yet non-existent deity, there will be reference-failure; but the intentional semantics apes the securely referenced semantics to God, and so it has relevant functional parallels with true reference.) The metaphoric extension of these type of schemata to non-monotheistic uses of *'lhym* and comparable Northwest Semitic theophanies may help to depict the conflation between proper names and descriptions of deities which is the subject of polemics in the Hebrew Bible. The mode of emphasis in 4QMysteries (Schiffman 1995) may reflect a concern with such relations at Qumran. The very similarity of competing theological ontologies is armed by the use of the same sort of 'God' terminology, which, in the nature of the polemic, does not carry with it, in certain contexts, qualifiers that advertise the differences of predicated identity between conflicting theologies or gods. In a qualified way Pagels (1991) presents the social history of the biblical Satan as a function which is parasitic on God's society and relationships. The present study provides the structure to explain this as a Satanic mirror-image of the process of divine mediation by agency.

Secondly, an entailment of this semantic value is that there is a presupposition of an agent as logical predicate[11] internal to *'lhym*. On this analysis, then, there are two referents, and two logical predicate-fragments to *'lhym*. Of referents: YHWH, and angelic medium; of functions, the semantic value assigned a divine property (crudely, *'lh*), and the plural logical predicate *-ym*. This division of labour, however, is partly a manner of speaking; there are no grounds for supposing that one should treat this as etymology or traditional plural syntax. The recent work of Chomsky (1995) would be a profound strategy for taking this topic further as a subset of a philosophy of language and transformational syntax.

In traditional Dead Sea Scrolls, Hebrew Bible and Greek syntax conceptions, quantification is somewhat isolated in comparative terms from ascription of semantic values in predication. As far as the functions of these syntaxes go, clearly, they have significance for applied grammars, though one can also propose an extension of the critical work by Barr (1961) and Gibson (1981, 1998c) in which institutionalized semantics (such as the, still recurrent, confusion of a word with a concept) is extended to the subject of syntax. The following comment could be read as a fragmentary scenario for such a project, though with a constructive aim. The issue of quantification, in particular quantification shifts from plural to singular, and vice versa, connect with whether or not *'lwhym*, in being a function of angelomorphic categories, can also, in the same narrative space-time field function, thereby refer to (or be presupposed to be true of) a singular referent. 'Mention' is that operation in which a linguistic item within the narrative is a referent of, in this case, pun. Since 'mention' is a species of 'use' (that is, a term's function in a narrative), it would be incorrect to suppose that in principle if there is paronomasia in a term's use, then we have to accept that the contributing expression's normal use is suspended, cancelled or inoperable. In other words, there is a routing within the narrative thematics and its use of semantic values to retain, as part of the use of a term which refers or is true (or false) of its referent, a semantic contract between the contents of paronomasia and

---

11. A logical predicate is not a grammatical predicate, though the categories may sometimes coincide; as to when they do is a matter of disputed interpretation. J. Barnes (1996) offers a confrontational view of the matter using his interpretation of Aristotle. In respect of the use above, a logical predicate might characterize a function within any grammatical category if its use is a property ascribed to a subject; this is the case with certain internal properties of the class of nouns such as *'lhym*.

the usual referring function. This impinges on the above suggestion that, without falling into a diachronic conflation, there is some degree of invariancy prior to the Dead Sea Scrolls in the Hebrew Bible, carried into Qumran angelology and theistic representation, concerning the metaphorised plural ending and multiple reference and agency in *'lhym*.

Such distinctions appear to match some of the semantics in Gen. 1.26-27. This passage, notoriously, displays an apparently plural use of *'lhym* ('Let us make...'), prior to, and subsequent to, which the same form *'lhym* is qualified by singular syntax, and while narrating the same theme of plural action. The philosophy of action is a continuum between God and agents, satisfying a single criterion of identity. This is not to say, since the identity is relative to a function, that there are no criteria differentiating media from the source of reference. There is evidence of similar shifts in quantification in an Ugaritic non-monotheistic semantic field (see Gibson 1976: 281). This polemicized use seems to compete with areas in which disputes about the identity of reference engage with commonly shared frames of the form of reference. In the appropriate form, this implies that, for the states of affairs in which there is ontological disagreement, there is in Semitic material the grounds for generalized dissent because there is a presupposed parallel use of reference and quantification.

The possibility of disagreement entails the precondition that there is a set of expressions which agree with a disputing culture, for dispute to have expression. Chomsky, of course, systematized the conjecture that universal syntax has a mirror universal semantics. The status of this claim can be settled by examining reference-claims in counter-cultures to discover how quantification conjoins with reference to yield a generalized semantics. Study of the Dead Sea Scrolls in conjunction with the Bible is an historically dense instance of such a collision and partial continuity. The trick is to estimate the scale of the crash and its survivors in references to God. So we are here concerned with the identity of what it is to be a criterion of the history of ideas, exemplified by the conjunction of philosophy of language and applied linguistics.

g. *The Relative Identity Reference of* 'lwhym
Relevant logic-features that the above has proposed for the applied semantics of reference in *'lhwym*, informally stated, are (where

'object language' is constituted by data from the Dead Sea Scrolls, Hebrew Bible, and New Testament):

(1) x has the same property F as has y, where the class of Fs is constructed from predicables applied to values of x and y in the object language.

So, where 'r' stands for referring in a subject, say 'x':

(2) What x^r depicts the referent of y in the object language?

(3) The referent of y is the simulated identity of x satisfying a relative identity criterion.

Therefore:

(4) There is a dependency relation of y upon x^r since y occurs with an array of which F is a replica of corresponding elements predicated of x^r.

Thus, (4) rests on the premise that:

(5) y is the linguistic counterpart or image of x's referent correctly arranged and articulated so that y goes proxy for x^r or reproduces the specified class of x's properties.

Consequently,

(6) The identity relation '$x = y$', with '=' defined by a set of Fs occurring in the object languages, can quantify over a single referent identity which is represented by plural referring functions.

(7) The use and mention of *'lwhym* has a presupposition of agency as a function of its reference, and therefore incorporates a logical syntax which can simultaneously refer to two or more referents, with a semantic value ascribed to the final referent of the term.

III

a. *Is a Philosophy of Dead Language Literature Possible?*
Philosophers of logic have not yet discovered what possibility is. This somewhat interferes with the question. It will not escape the reader's notice that the Dead Sea Scrolls do not address this or consequent issues. Is the above question a subset of the query: 'Is a philosophy of literature possible?'

Some views settled within analytical philosophy act as an imperialism which scorns literary theory and the prospect of placing it in some sort of conjunction with logic. I am not a formalist who envisages a programme to mechanize creative literature. The frontiers of philosophical logic have, or should have, long since passed the site-debris of formalist excavations where there roamed such ghostly forms as those like Russell and a mythical plurality of simplifying Razors (see Gibson 1997). The future of logic seems to be like this: it is deeper and more complex than most have thought, like great creative Art—unexpected, counter-intuitive, and inimical to formal aesthetics. This itself approaches paradox, since logic is usually thought to be consistent generalized form with inference relations. But any predicate calculus worthy of the term entails paradoxes (cf. Sainsbury 1995; Priest 1995). So back to the drawing board. Perhaps the Dead Sea Scrolls and biblical writers, unconscious of these matters, may better furnish us by their ignorance with uses of literature that more adequately lay a path to knowledge. In other words, is literature a source for solving problems outside of itself; or, does one require solutions from outside of logic and/or philosophy so as to resolve the identity (identities) of logic?

Wittgenstein was afraid of Wittgensteinians, and would not meet Virginia Woolf. Such fragility and certainty combine to join logic and literature. To do logic is to solve everything else. The semantics of God occupy this position, though we have to do with the absence of universality in literature's history. Because we have a logical system which produces any propositions that entail paradox, then (Wittgenstein began to realize in 1929–30) we do not actually understand what it is to be a proposition—including those which are in a semantic field that has 'consistent' propositions. In a sense we have only the barest glimpse of anything significant in logic or literature. A future Renaissance would be founded on more generalized admission of this ignorance than is perhaps now possible within the confines of what is taken to be the theory of understanding. My point is that the semantics of God in ancient literature inadvertently reverses into this ignorance. To handle even straightforward expression of God presupposes a proposition about what it is to be language about God, which is itself a subset of a more general question about the identity of language.

Relations within literary and cultural theory are disturbed (cf. Steiner 1989; Said 1993; Bouveresse 1995). But Exum and Clines (1993) and their co-authors exemplify ways in which applications of literary theories and criticisms are well under way in biblical research. Ingraffia (1995) elegantly displays how such sensitivity can be complemented by introducing philosophies in poststructuralist literary research. Alferi (1989) showed how one can unexpectedly combine even a mediaeval logic with poststructuralist sensibilities. Dead Sea Scrolls research has yet to apply such scenarios. Divine reference is a fundamental area in which one can begin, not least so that the conjunction and disjunction of the Bible and the Dead Sea Scrolls may be assessed.

This is not quite the place to rehearse a formal theory attempting to resolve conflicts between philosophy and literary theory, especially in the recondite sphere of dead languages, though it almost is. Briefly and crudely stated, the fundamental element for linking applied linguistics, literary theory and analytical philosophy (the latter taken to include logic and philosophy of language) is as follows (and clearly, such a theory would have to be strong enough to operate as a generalizable explanation of language, and not be a hole-in-corner hypothesis for Dead Sea Scrolls phenomena): formal logic and philosophical logic are species of live metaphor. Literary usage is constituted by live metaphor. Reference itself is a form of live metaphor. Relations between logic and literary language are ones of live metaphor. Deep in literary usage, and deep within logic, there are logics unmapped by standard institutional traditions. A reason for this is that we are as yet in a primitive circumstance in researches into logic and literature (rather like mediaeval alchemists assuming that they discovered microphysics of metals). A surface symptom of this state of affairs is the phenomenon of counter-intuition, according to which the contradictory or contrary of a statement proved by experts in the field is discovered to be true ('Gödel's Theorem' is an instance of this, and Fermat's 'Last Theorem' is a less obvious case). This is relevant to literature because counter-intuition is a function of creativity: disclosure, concealed in literary form. It is plausible to propose that in the *Poetics* Aristotle employed logical terms metaphorically extended from Aristotle's formal metalogical writings, because he judged that formal logic and creative literature are co-extendable species of metaphor. To be sure, just because Aristotle might have been correct on the proposal, does not imply that the theses he attached to them are right. For example, as Green (1995: 37) notes, Luke's theology of God and the angels hardly allows Aristotle's distinction, which privileges the action over the actor. A stronger concept dismantles

Aristotle's thesis: a criterion of God's identity can be satisfied by another identity (contra *Poetics* 6 and 9).

Applied semantics and logic marry over the reference of a term. Part II sketched how reference is a fundamental semantic value of the Dead Sea Scrolls and the Hebrew Bible. (If one disputes standard Frege reference theory, a complex theory of indexical predication might be constructed; see Gibson 1997.[12]) I shall assume that we can, in principle, paraphrase one of these programmes into the other, in relevant reference uses, cumbersome though it would be; but I shall stick to what is better developed, that of reference theory, and propose that reference is a matter of live metaphor, with the semantics of theistic terms commonly manifesting these properties. Typically, reference has three ingredients: referring, the relation of reference, and referent. Frege in fact used only one word for the three elements, as if he metaphorically extended the scope of the one German term, derived from *deuten*. These three features are thus metaphorically related. I believe it can be shown that this can be generalized to the logic-terminology which comprises much of analytical philosophy.[13] In these respects, then, metaphor, customarily the domain of literature, constitutes the heart of analytical philosophy. There are paradoxes pervading the large fields of meaning that comprise philosophy and literature. Whereas literature glories in them, analytical philosophy has swept them under the carpet—on which we frequently stand. Therefore it eventually follows that the conjunction of live metaphor in logic and the correct recognition of the qualifying implication of the presence of paradox, construct a bridge between logic and literature. The logical semantics of God in the Dead Sea Scrolls, the Hebrew Bible and the New Testament have already effectively portrayed this in Part II.

12. This subject has not been developed in philosophical logic, though Jane Heal has commenced work on it; Gibson (1997) has ventured some proposals; and Recanati (1993) has an approach which I suggest one might modify to craft a bridge to produce a thesis of indexical predication. Indexical predication concerns the task of attempting to discover if and how predicates can fix a singular connection with a referent without a singular term or proper name-like reference.

13. This suggestion is a component in a larger investigation. For example a function x^2 has its metaphorization in any value which it takes, as with 100^2. Consequently the predicate calculus is a complex set of metaphors. These are live metaphors since there is a mapping function connecting the different expressions.

b. *Metaphoric* 'lwhym

Live metaphor has not been given extensive attention, though the expression has some currency. 'Live metaphor' is the neglected sister of 'dead metaphor': '*root* of a tree' transmogrifies in death to: '*root* of a problem', a state of health distinct to live metaphor. A live metaphor goes proxy for some other subject or property by partially reproducing the other subject as a function of its semantic value. This concurs with the frequently canvassed thesis that description of God is metaphorical, though this evident point should lead to the question of what metaphor is. Since definition is partly a disjunction of what it is not, it is embarrassing to recognize no one has yet defined what 'literal' is. Yet, for example, Hanson (1992: 560) unquestioningly states that: '[Symmachus's version of Exod. 24.10] confirms our impression that the Greek translators could accept the idea of seeing God in a vision rather than seeing him literally'; and again: 'it is possible therefore that [in Exod. 33.11] the LXX's use of *enopios enopiō* may be a slight modification of the literal Hebrew meaning' (560-61). But 'seeing him literally' and 'literal Hebrew meaning' are deconstructed by the asymmetries surrounding the presence and absence of a form of the Other in relation to a reproduction of that form, as the reader, I hope, has seen above. Consequently, I shall maintain that *'lhym* is a live metaphor, and argue that it participates in the construction of a live metaphoric thematic semantic field.

Since Aristotle's *Poetics* 21, the shifting sense of a term from one to another subject as the defining feature of dead metaphor has been given much attention. Black (1962, 1993) suggested an interaction between literal and metaphoric senses, in which it is problematic to posit a straightforward regulative contrast between the two senses. There are many subspecies of metaphor. Dead metaphor has been the central target for such research. Conversely, uses of *'lwhym* appear to satisfy requirements for being live metaphor. Live metaphor has received less sustained study. Cohen (1993) develops a thesis on metaphor which can be applied to live metaphor, though he does not use the term. He contrasts an actual 'lion' with a 'stone lion'. The latter is a live metaphor, and it reifies the actual lion so as to reproduce a likeness which therefore satisfies a criterion of identity for being a lion type, though it is not a lion. Cohen explains this as the preservation of presuppositions between actual and stone lion, together with deletion of some others (no actual fur, etc., in the case of the live metaphoric lion), and addition of others to preserve the similarity (stone legs with the live metaphor, to reproduce likeness). Here we have a semantic contract which complexly juggles with the replacement of tokens to preserve the representation of the identity of a subject. This parallels the ways in which *'lwhym* is a term that can be distributed over different media or agencies to manifest the final referent—God. The nearest state of affairs in modern experience which reflects the logic of *'lhym* agency is that of a photograph (as with Macé 1993) or televised mediation of identities. Here a 'bearer', the televised medium, mediates a criterion of identity to convey a subject which it (as a construct of instrumention) is not. Dead Sea Scrolls and biblical linguistic phenomena likewise encode visualization in the semantics of *'lwhym*, not least in the use of angels to implement the epiphanies, for example in the use of Ezek. 43.2 in the Qumran Psalms Scroll. The most explicit case of this live metaphoric reproduction is when the identity of the angel is dispersed in emergence of the first person pronoun of YHWH to which *'lwhym* is thematically joined.

The metaphoric roles of *'lwhym* are variously specialized and internally differentiated. In 11QMelch l. 9's purported use of Isa. 61.2, there 'Melchizedek' and YHWH strike different semantic contracts since the former is a divine proxy for the latter subject, in which the proper name YHWH refers to the *'lwhym* (in l. 10) who is not an agent. This switch-over is similar to the metonymy metaphor as a vehicle for personification (as advanced by Lakoff and Johnson 1981: 33-34), in which Melchizedek personifies YHWH.

In this personification by *'lwhym* there is an enriching function because two subjects become tied together, as one mediates the other. Often a personifying metaphor may employ an identity relation figuratively, such as 'I wisdom dwell with prudence' in Prov. 8.12. Likewise, photographs personify subjects, rather like angelomorphic categories which personify YHWH. The research of Deleuze (1985, 1994) complements such a distinction; in his view the film image is a presence that repeats a world outside itself, and so it inscribes a broadcast identity by something other than itself. In this perspective *'lwhym* are personifying live metaphors that go proxy for an intended divine personal identity. In a sense the Dead Sea Scrolls Melchizedek unevenly embraces these oppositions.

A structural feature of ll. 10 and 11 in 11QMelch is that the *'lwhym* construed to be the singular, as a way of describing Melchizedek, refers to God's actions that his judging agent carries out (a point mentioned in 11a). This precisely is *'l* ('God's) judging as implemented by his *'lwhym*. But 11QMelch ll. 10-11 gives priority to the singular *'lwhym* of l. 10, a member of the earth based *'lwhym*; yet this singular *'lwhym* (Melchizedek) is qualitatively distinct to them. As the contrast becomes crass, Melchizedek is instructed to return to heaven so that *'l* can judge these earthly *'lwhym*. He judges employing his judge Melchizedek in heaven, untouched by the sentences and yet being the advocate of them, with a transparent nuance on Psalm 110. The use of Psalm 82 in 11QMelch thus fairly matches the thematic rhetoric of the Psalm, and the employment of it in John 10 conforms to the *'lwhym*; as Carr (1981: 89-92) argues, this type of Melchizedek figure strongly connects with 1 Corinthians 15, where the judgment theme is developed. The condemned *'lwhym*, presumably alluded to in l. 11, which quotes Ps. 82.2, are judged defective because they do not embody the predicates which satisfy the criterion that encodes a reference to God via his agents in virtue of revealing God's judgments.

Exodus 3.2-6 depicts an equation of identity between angel and God, but which commences with the term *ml'k*, and binds the first person pronoun of YHWH with *'lhym* as medium of manifestation. The Targum translation of Ps. 8.5's *mml'ky'* embodies ancient interpretative acceptance of aspects of this relational schema, other cases occurring in Gen. 21.17-9, 22.17, 31.11-13, Judg. 6.11-16. If the Gen. 1.26-27 creation use of *'lhym*, as developed in the previous section, is accurately rendered, relationally mirrors this schema with the plural pronoun complementing *'lhym* as a single term gathering both God and angels within its subject-scope, with Ps. 8.5's allusion to creation. The likeness and image of God are replicated in the likeness and image of the agent-angels who replicate these functions in Adam, because the angels manifest the God whom they mirror. This type of semantic field and thematic interrelations between angelomorphic terminology and *'lhym* perform as a cross-fertilization of agency between transcendent categories and created form.

So in the domain of the above contexts, *'lhym* is a live metaphor of a specialized sort. Rather like (if one may be forgiven the anachronism for purposes of illustration) televised or photographed reproduction of referent identities, *'lhym* offers a claim of simulation of the identity of a referent other than the medium itself, but in which the basic function of the medium is to be that identity. On this basis, *'lhym* is the literary tautology of visual reproduction, a sort of literary painterly poetics. In short *'lhym* is a live metaphor. Perhaps Caird (1980: 66) was tracking this feature when he wrote of double reference, or double derived reference. Current research in literary theory particularly in French can be utilized to enhance the presentation of this visualization in the literary (see Gibson 1998a). The basic work stems from research on Mallarmé's *Un Coup de Dés*, its relation to symbolism, and projection of literary conceptions in narrative space and action (Bowie 1978 and 1993; Scott 1988; and Reynolds 1995). I suggest that one can paraphrase this live metaphorization into a logical narrative metaphoric world by adapting some concerns in David Lewis's (1986) thesis on the plurality of other worlds. (Clearly, this is not tantamount to accepting Lewis's ontology.) In this conception indexicality of pronoun and space-time are equatable, and co-extensive. Worlds can be reproduced in variant forms, and are accessible to each other by indexicalization. Within the ancient purview of the above Dead Sea Scrolls and biblical narrative worlds of *'lhym*, such indexicalization and matching of reified identities were the custom of the revelation of divine personal identity. Certainly, the theses in the ancient and modern worlds and their levels of formulation are fundamentally different. But the logic of live metaphor and the reproduction of a world by indexicalization have substantial parallels. Although the technologization of live metaphor by modern electronic media is vastly different from ancient religious creativity, yet the functional core of such technology has externalized a similarity between it and an ancient dynamic of divine simulation of identity by *'lhym*. This is not because of any media connection between the two; it is because both implement the conditions of the concept of communication. It is the metaphoric logic of reproduction of identities, not the technical medium, that carries and comprises the match between ancient and modern live metaphor.

In the later mediaeval European world many theologian-philosophers found it almost impossible adequately to get their heads around the reproduction of absent identities into spatially present agency, and concerning intuitive cognition and imperfect intuitive cognition, for example that of Ockham. The fourteenth-century Aureoli was a disputed exception, arguing that intuitive cognition can be truly functioning only if an individual appears to be present.[14] Since we should be aware of the great gap between ancient and modern ways of perception, we may also take opportunity to recognize the various subtlety of the narrative fields of *'lhym* that long ago offered a conception of reproducing an absent identity in present function. This purview resolves a problem thrown up by a number of ways of attempting to represent the perceived tensions of *'lhym* and its counterpart *theoi* and some uses of *theos*. Fitzmyer (1971: 261) states that the word *'lhym* must refer to others than God, though he does not seem to want to exclude reference to God; yet he does not pursue the matter. In the light of the foregoing, we see that *'lhym* is a live metaphor, with a capability of multiple reference within the one use in a narrative.[15]

c. *Reproduction of Identity in Christology*
John transforms the live metaphor typology, among other things, by stating: 'he that has seen me has seen the father; and how do you say then, "Show us the father"?' (14.9). A presupposition of this identification partly derives from the polemics of John 10. The disputants misconstrue the force of the metaphoric referring function in *theos* with regard to agency: 'you, being a man, make yourself God' (10.33). Their mythologization of Christ's relational stance is fraught with a witless almost neo-Platonic ontological litany of media misrepresentation. They seem nearly to purvey the recurrent tendency to ossify the count-noun *theos* into a proper name. Having undermined the interlocutors with the neuter 'I and my father are one [what?]', the Johanine narrator reports that the correct move is to instantiate the live metaphor of Ps. 82.6, which triggers into ironic life their singular *theos*, bound by their referent God's first person pronoun, with the plural *theoi*, which effectively quantifies over the first person and deconstructs their singularity: '"I said you are gods?" If he called them "gods", unto whom the word of God came, and the Scripture cannot be broken; Say you of him, whom the Father has sanctified, and sent into the world, you blaspheme; because I said, "I am the Son of God"?' (Jn 10.34b-36). Here the metaphoric agency function of

14. See Gibson 1997.
15. See Gibson 1981: Chapters 2 and 3, for the analysis of sense and reference in Hebrew Bible and New Testament usage which serves to provide a more formal basis for the use of reference here.

theoi, which embraces the scope of *'lhym*, is thrown down as a gaunt-let to block the equality claim. Perhaps the role of Ps. 82.6 here, and the way it acts as a deconstruction to fix the assertion of Christ being the son of God, requires attention different from some traditional treatment of John 10. The live metaphoricity of *theoi* and its relation to 'father' constitute a presupposition of inference to Christ as son of God, with the singular form *theos*. (*Monogenēs theos*, the reading of the c. 200 CE Bodmer II papyrus and the original hand of the Sinaiticus Codex in Jn 1.18, is not a problem on the present live metaphor interpretation of *theos/theoi*; improbable as the reading may be, it is sensitive to this function of live metaphor turned into the ontology of the father and the son.) The radical move, then, in terms of the antecedents of the multiple agency of the plural noun for God, is that its semantic value has a new live metaphor ontology: the conjunction of God as father of his son. For the first time this transforms the interiority[16] of the communicative relational use of *'lhym* into relational familial ontology. That is to say, the presuppositional history of crucial uses of *'lhym* is deconstructed, condensed and transformed by the creation of a new live metaphor: the former live metaphor becomes the person of which it is now conceived as the inexorable source.

In contrast, back down the road at Qumran, *'lwhym* displayed a retreat in the adoration of the past *'lwhym* as live metaphor for the mimesis of present perfect fantasy, without managing to go beyond reflections on the secrets of creation's parental relationships (4QMysteries[a] frag. 6 ii). Qumran MSS show that the terminological semantics of *'lwhym* preserved the letter of much of the Hebrew Bible semantic fields, but not the spirit of creativity in the live metaphor representation of God. The shift, from simulation of divine identity by a proxy presence, to the rebirth of the live metaphor as a vehicle for divine fatherhood and sonship, is a type of creative morphogenesis in which a counter-intuitive synecdoche is condensed from the live metaphor metonymy. Bowie (1993: 45) has offered a way of unlearning Lacan, as Lacan unlearned Freud, keeping in mind the absence from Freud of a conception of the future:

---

16. Concerning 'interiority', see Chinca (1997), which although defined within the context of Germanist mediaeval Tristan literary theory, encapsulates the way in which an external mirroring of relations has its point within the inner life, here in use of *'lhym*.

> One of the peculiar virtues of the Lacanian approach to theorizing is that it
> does not require adherence to a stabilized and jealously safeguarded lexi-
> con or conceptual arsenal. Lacan invites theorists of whatever persuasion
> to rediscover the pleasures, the mad exhilarations, of the future tense...
> 'The future' as Lacan describes it is a summons not to 'free' speculative
> play, but to inventiveness within an extirpable framework of constraints,
> just as the ripple and shimmer of his word-play... is propelled by a sense
> of paternal interdiction.

One of the tasks of literary theory here, as applied to the conjunction
of Qumran and the New Testament (without assuming any exhaustive
influence from the former to the latter), is to dislodge to the necessary
degree the notion of community from theological apologetics. How do
we explain that the original logic of, for example, John's literary
creativity came to its future from a Freudian past which has the mak-
ings of community indoctrination which typically destroys the individual authorial voice? Hobson (1995) shows how central an
unexpected digression is to originality, especially when a tradition
deems dissent a digression from relevance; in a study on Diderot's
employment of digression, she enforces the relevance of poststructuralist virtual reality for understanding why Diderot digressed. The
digression, that is, logic and literary theory for ancient virtual reality,
discovers that reality finally replaces virtuality. Accordingly, an
urgent task for the Dead Sea Scrolls and biblical research is to separate ancient egoisim from the communal subversion of originality, to
examine what it is to be literary creativity, in addition to the function
of communal tradition, as a path to construct a semantics of God.

As for the relations of logic, applied linguistics, and literary theory
which may service this complex conjunction of tradition with creativity,
we are now in a position to recognize, with Wittgenstein, as Stern
(1995) and Heal (1995) begin to demonstrate, that the distance
separating what it is to be logic and literary originality is not as great
as Frege (1969) would have us think (Dummett, for example 1991 and
1993, takes us to a new frontier in excavating these issues). The ways,
for example, Wittgenstein used dialogue (Heal 1995; Carruthers
1989), and the concept of a proposition projected in space to investigate deep issues in logic, thought and language are neglected counter-
intuitive perspectives by which to comprehend some of the greatness
of ancient literary creativity and its logics. The semantics of God is a
suitably recondite challenge to expose the identity of language.

BIBLIOGRAPHY

Alexander, P.S.
   1972   'The Targumim and Early Exegesis of "Sons of God" in Genesis 6',
             JJS: 60-71.
Alferi, P.
   1989   *Guillaume d'Ockham le singulier* (Paris: Minuit).
Barnes, J.
   1996   'Grammar on Aristotle's Terms', in M. Frede and G. Striker (eds.),
             Rationality in Greek Thought (Oxford: Clarendon Press): 175-202.
Barnes, M.R.
   1995a   'Augustine in Contemporary Trinitarian Theology', *TS* 56: 237-50.
   1995b   'De Regnon Reconsidered', *Augustinian Studies* 26.2: 51-79.
Barr, J.
   1961   *The Semantics of Biblical Language* (Oxford: Oxford University
             Press).
Barrett, C.K.
   1972   *Essays on John* (London: SPCK).
Black, M.
   1962   *Models and Metaphors* (Ithaca, NY: Cornell University Press).
   1993   'More about Metaphor', in A. Ortony (ed.), *Metaphor and Thought*
             (Cambridge: Cambridge University Press, 2nd edn): 19-41.
Bokser, B.M.
   1985   'Approaching Sacred Space', *HTR* 78: 279-99.
Bouveresse, J.
   1995   *Wittgenstein Reads Freud* (trans. C. Cosman; Princeton: Princeton
             University Press; trans. of *Philosophie, Mythologie et pseudo-science:
             Wittgenstein lecteur de Freud* [Paris: Editions de l'eclat]).
Bowie, M.
   1978   *Mallarmé and the Art of Being Difficult* (Cambridge: Cambridge
             University Press).
   1993   *Psychoanalysis and the Future of Theory: The Bucknell Lectures in
             Literary Theory* (Oxford: Basil Blackwell).
Brooke, G.J.
   1994   'Isaiah 40.3 and the Wilderness Community', in Brooke and Martinez
             (1994): 117-32.
Brooke, G.J., and F.G. Martínez (eds.)
   1994   *New Qumran Texts and Studies* (STDJ, 15; Leiden: Brill).
Brown, R.E.
   1966   *The Gospel according to John (i-xiii)* (Garden City, NY: Doubleday).
   1977   *The Birth of the Messiah* (London: Geoffrey Chapman).
Caird, G.B.
   1980   *The Language and Imagery of the Bible* (London: Gerald
             Duckworth).
Carr, W.
   1981   *Angels and Principalities* (Cambridge: Cambridge University Press).

Carruthers, P.
    1989   *The Metaphysics of the Tractatus* (Cambridge: Cambridge University Press).

Chinca, M.
    1997   *Gottfried von Strassburg: Tristan* (Landmarks of World Literature; Cambridge: Cambridge University Press).

Chomsky, N.
    1995   'Language and Nature', *Mind* 104: 1-62.

Cohen, L.J.
    1993   'The Semantics of Metaphor', in A. Ortony (ed.), *Metaphor and Thought* (Cambridge: Cambridge University Press, 2nd edn): 58-70.

Danto, A.C.
    1994   *Embodied Meanings* (New York: Farrar, Straus, Giroux).

Deleuze, G.
    1985   *Cinsma*, II (Paris: Minuit).
    1994   *Difference and Repetition* (trans. P. Patton; London: Athlone Press).

Derrida, J.
    1978   *The Truth in Painting* (Chicago: University of Chicago Press).
    1993   *Aporias* (trans. T. Dutoit; Stanford, CA: Stanford University Press).

Descombes, V.
    1992   *Proust: Philosophy of the Novel* (Stanford, CA: Stanford University Press).
    1995   'Foreword to Jacques Bouveresse', in Bouveresse (1995): vii-xiii.

Dimant, D., and U. Rappaport
    1992   *The Dead Sea Scrolls* (STDJ, 10; Leiden: Brill).

Dimant, D., and L.H. Schiffman
    1995   *Time to Prepare the Way in the Wilderness* (STDJ, 16; Leiden: Brill).

Dummett, M.
    1981   *The Interpretation of Frege's Philosophy* (London: Gerald Duckworth).
    1991   *The Logical Basis of Metaphysics* (London: Gerald Duckworth).
    1993   *The Origins of Analytical Philosophy* (London: Gerald Duckworth).

Dunn, J.D.G.
    1980   *Christology in the Making* (London: SCM Press).

Emerton, J.
    1960   'Some New Testament Notes', *JTS* NS 11: 329-36.

Evans, G.R.
    1985   *The Language and Logic of the Bible: The Road to Reformation* (Cambridge: Cambridge University Press).

Exum, J.C., and D.J.A. Clines
    1993   *The New Literary Criticism and the Hebrew Bible* (JSOTSup, 143; Sheffield: JSOT Press).

Fitzmyer, J.A.
    1971   *Essays on the Semitic Background of the New Testament* (London: Geoffrey Chapman).

Flint, P.W.
    1994   'The Psalm Scrolls from the Judean Desert: Relationships and Textual Affiliations', in Brooke and Martínez (1994): 31-52.

Frege, G.
 1969   *Frege Nachgelassene Schriften* (ed. H. Hermes *et al.*; Hamburg: Meiner).
Geach, P.T.
 1980   *Reference and Generality* (Ithaca, NY: Cornell University Press, 3rd edn).
Gibson, A.
 1976   'Judges 1.14: NEB and AV Translations', *VT* 26.3: 275-83.
 1981   *Biblical Semantic Logic* (Oxford: Basil Blackwell; New York: St Martin's).
 1997   'Ockham's World and Future', in J. Marenbon (ed.), *History of Philosophy*, III (London: Routledge).
 1998a   *Counter-Intuition* (forthcoming).
 1998b   *Divining Cosmology* (forthcoming).
 1998c   *What is Literature?* (Cambridge: Cambridge University Press, forthcoming).
 1998d   'Logical Analysis and Applied Linguistics of the Bible', new prologue to *Biblical Semantic Logic* (Sheffield: Sheffield Academic Press, 2nd edn, forthcoming).
Gibson, A., and N.A. O'Mahony
 1995   'Lamentation Sumérienne (vers—2004)', *Dédale: Le paradoxe des représentations du divin* 1 & 2: 13-14.
Green, J.B.
 1995   *The Theology of the Gospel of Luke* (Cambridge: Cambridge University Press).
Haack, S.A.
 1971   *Deviant Logic* (Cambridge: Cambridge University Press).
Hanson, A.T.
 1992   'The Treatment in the LXX of the Theme of Seeing God', in G.J. Brooke and B. Lindars (eds.), *Septuagint, Scrolls and Cognate Writings* (Atlanta: Scholars Press): 557-68.
Heal, J.
 1992   'Wittgenstein and Dialogue', in T.J. Smiley (ed.), *Philosophical Dialogues* (Oxford: Oxford University Press): 63-83
 1997   'Indexical Predicates', *Mind* 106.
Hesse, M.B.
 1966   *Models and Analogies in Science* (Notre Dame: University of Notre Dame Press).
Hobson, M.
 1995   'What is Wrong with Saint Peters. Or Diderot, Analogy and Architecture', in W. Pape and F. Burwick (eds.), *Reflecting Senses* (Berlin: de Gruyter): 54-74.
Horton, F.L., Jr
 1976   *The Melchizedek Tradition* (Cambridge: Cambridge University Press).
Ingraffia, B.D.
 1995   *Postmodern Theory and Biblical Theology* (Cambridge: Cambridge University Press).

Jonge, M., de, and A.S. van der Woude
1965–66   '11QMel and the New Testament', *NTS* 12: 301-26.
Kermode, J.F.
1990   *Poetry, Narrative, History* (Oxford: Basil Blackwell).
Lakoff, G., and M. Johnson
1981   *The Metaphors We Live By* (Chicago: University of Chicago Press).
Lewis, D.
1986   *On the Plurality of Worlds* (Oxford: Oxford University Press).
Lewy, C.
1976   *Meaning and Modality* (Cambridge: Cambridge University Press).
Macé, G.
1993   *La mémoire aime chasser dans le noir* (Paris: Gallimard).
Milbank, J.
1997   *The Word Made Strange* (Oxford: Basil Blackwell).
Newsom, C.A.
1985   *Songs of the Sabbath Sacrifice: A Critical Edition* (Harvard Semitic Studies, 27; Atlanta: Scholars Press).
1990   'He Has Established Himself Priests', in L.H. Schiffman (ed.), *Archaeology and History in the Dead Sea Scrolls* (JSPSup, 8, JSOT/ASOR Monographs, 2; Sheffield: JSOT Press), 101-20.
1992   '4Q374: A Discourse on the Exodus/Conquest Tradition', in Dimant and Rappaport (1992): 40-52.
Nigosian, S.A.
1993   'Moses as They Saw Him', *VT* 43: 399-50.
Nitzan, B.
1994   '4QBerakhot (4Q286-290): A Preliminary Report', in Brooke and Martínez (1994): 53-72.
Pagels, E.
1991   'The Social History of Satan—The Intimate Enemy', *HTR* 84: 105-28.
Paxson, J.J.
1994   *The Poetics of Personification* (Cambridge: Cambridge University Press).
Prendergast, C.
1986   *On the Order of Mimesis* (Cambridge: Cambridge University Press).
Priest, G.
1995   *Beyond the Limits of Thought* (Cambridge: Cambridge University Press).
Qimron, E.
1992   'Observations on the History of Early Hebrew (1000 BCE–200 CE)', in Dimant and Rappaport (1992): 349-61.
Recanati, R.
1993   *Direct Reference* (Oxford: Basil Blackwell).
Reynolds, D.
1995   *Symbolist Aesthetics and Early Abstract Art* (Cambridge: Cambridge University Press).
Rowland, C.C.
1982   *The Open Heaven* (London: SPCK).

Said, E.
1993   *Culture and Imperialism* (London: Chatto & Windus).
Sainsbury, R.M.
1995   *Paradoxes* (Cambridge: Cambridge University Press, 2nd edn).
Sanders, E.P.
1977   *Paul and Palestinian Judaism* (London: SCM Press).
1985   *Jesus and Judaism* (London: SCM Press).
Sanderson, J.E.
1986   *An Exodus Scroll from Qumran: 4QpaleoExod^m and the Samaritan Tradition* (Harvard Semitic Studies, 30; Atlanta: Scholars Press).
Schiffman, L.H.
1989   *The Eschatological Community of the Dead Sea Scrolls: A Study of the Rule of the Congregation* (SBL Monograph Series, 38; Atlanta: Scholars Press).
1994   *Reclaiming the Dea Sea Scrolls* (Philadelphia/Jerusalem: Jewish Publication Society).
1995   '4QMysteries^a: A Preliminary Edition and Translation', in Z. Zevit, S. Giton, M. Sokoloff (eds.), *Solving Riddles and Untying Knots. Biblical, Epigraphic, and Semitic Studies in Honor of Jonas C. Greenfield* (Winona Lake, IN: Eisenbrauns): 207-60.
Schuller, E.M.
1992   '4Q380 and 4Q381: Non-Canonical Psalms from Qumran', in Dimant and Rappaport (1992).
Scott, D.
1988   *Pictorialist Poetics* (Cambridge: Cambridge University Press).
Sluga, H.
1980   *Gottlob Frege* (London: Routledge).
Smiley, T.J.
1982   'The Theory of Descriptions', *Proceedings of the British Academy* 67: 321-27.
Stefanovic, Z.
1992   *The Aramaic of Daniel in the Light of Old Aramaic* (JSOTSup, 129; Sheffield: JSOT Press).
Steiner, G.
1989   *Real Presences* (London: Faber).
Stern, D.G.
1995   *Wittgenstein's Language and Thought* (Oxford: Oxford University Press).
Summerfield, D.M.
1996   'Fitting versus Tracking: Wittgenstein on Representation', in H. Sluga and D.G. Stern (eds.), *The Cambridge Companion to Wittgenstein* (Cambridge: Cambridge University Press): 100-33.
Tov, E.
1995   'Groups of Biblical Texts found at Qumran', in Dimant and Schiffman (1995): 85-102.
Ulrich, E.
1995   'The Paleo-Hebrew Biblical Manuscripts from Cave 4', in Dimant and Schiffman (1995): 103-29.

Ward, G.
    1995   *Barth, Derrida and the Language of Theology* (Cambridge: Cambridge University Press).

Weinfield, M.
    1995   'The Angelic Song over the Luminaries in the Qumran Texts', in Dimant and Schiffman (1995): 131-57.

Williamson, T.
    1996   *Vagueness* (London: Routledge).

Wittgenstein, L.
    1973   *Philosophical Investigations* (ed. G.F.M. Anscombe and R. Rhees; trans. G.E.M. Anscombe; Oxford: Basil Blackwell, 3rd edn).
    1997   *The Collected Manuscripts of Ludwig Wittgenstein on Facsimile CD-ROM* (ed. Wittgenstein Archives at the University of Bergen; Oxford: Oxford University Press).

Woude, A.S., van der
    1965   'Melchisedech als himmlische Erlosergestalt in den neugefundenen Midraschim aus Hohle XI', *OT* 14: 354-73.

HISTORY AND HERMENEUTICS: THE DEAD SEA SCROLLS

Kevin McCarron

'Like it or not, interpretation's the only game in town'
Stanley Fish

In his later years, the novelist Henry James became very interested in a health movement called Fletcherism, which insisted, among other draconian requirements, that every mouthful of food be chewed thirty two times. This aspect of the regime prompted one wit to observe that Henry James was the only man he ever knew who chewed more than he bit off. In this paper, in the midst of Scrolls specialists, I feel like one of the other people that the wit had known. I am not a Dead Sea Scrolls scholar, nor even a member of a religious studies department. My field is English literature, and my particular interest in the Scrolls was stimulated by Frank Cross's suggestion in his book *The Ancient Library of Qumran*:

> The recovery of editions and literary levels in biblical works begins a pro-
> cess of no small importance in biblical studies; the uniting of text-criticism
> and literary criticism in scholarly approaches to biblical literature. During
> the past century there has been a divorce between higher and lower criti-
> cism, a scandal of excessive specialization, with dreary results.[1]

I am, of course, assuming that by the 'higher criticism' here he means literary criticism. Well, certainly nobody can accuse me of being 'excessively specialized' in the area of Scrolls scholarship, but, never-theless, it is my intention to discuss history, hermeneutics and the Dead Sea Scrolls, although not in that order, and not right away. First, I want to discuss the various pleasures that could be described as 'literary' and that are, essentially, 'local' pleasures—pleasures that spring directly from an engagement with the Scrolls themselves.

---

1. F.M. Cross, *The Ancient Library of Qumran* (The Biblical Seminar, 30; Sheffield: JSOT Press, 3rd edn, 1995), pp. 182-83.

Secondly, I want to look specifically at 'The Seductress' (4Q184) and from a reading of it move on to the more 'global' issue—a consideration of the relationship between the hermeneutic and the historical processes, and the way in which interpretations of the history of the Scrolls, in which I include their reception, are trapped within precisely the same hermeneutic circle as those who offer readings of specific Qumran texts. The implications of this, for me, actually imply that the interaction between literary criticism and biblical criticism may not be as fruitful as some of us might like to think.

Although Cross implies that 'literary criticism' is a homogeneous field, there are many types of literary criticism. However, Paul Ricouer suggests in his essay 'Existence and Hermeneutics' the hermeneutic field itself can be divided into two: the 'archeological methods' (including psychoanalysis, Marxism and structuralism) and 'teleological' approaches (including phenomenology and the New Criticism). Paul Armstrong economically summarizes Ricouer's argument:

> Archeological interpretation is a hermeneutics of unmasking. For approaches of this kind, meaning is never on the surface; rather the surface is a disguise, a mask that must be demystified to uncover the meaning behind it. The rule for reading is suspicion. For teleological approaches, the rule is trust. Meaning is to be found not behind but beyond—in the goals, possibilities, and values that literary works and other cultural objects testify or try to point forward.[2]

Armstrong notes of Ricouer's teleogical approach: 'The appropriate interpretive attitude is therefore not suspicion but openness to revelation'.[3] Essentially an unsuspicious person myself, I favour the teleological approach and maintain that pleasure is a legitimate, and quantifiable, response to a text and that, in the specific case of the Dead Sea Scrolls, an 'openness to revelation' is entirely appropriate.

The literary pleasures of the Dead Sea Scrolls are, I would suggest, like the hermeneutic field itself, twofold: the pleasures of recognition and the pleasures of discovery. What higher praise could be given to the Genesis Apocryphon (1QapGen), for example, than that it is an excellent story of a thoroughly recognizable, although unfortunately rare, kind: dramatic, compulsively readable and providing the added

---

2. P. Armstrong, *Conflicting Readings* (Chapel Hill: University of North Carolina Press, 1990), p. 7.

3. Armstrong, *Conflicting Readings*, p. 8.

pleasure of ending precisely as it must do. Again, the rhetorical questions which conclude the Community Rule (1QS) perform the same function as they do in any piece of rhetoric—they initiate a dialogic relationship with the reader. In this particular case the firm declarations which characterize the rest of the text yield to a series of questions which can only be answered by the reader in the negative:

> What shall hand-moulded clay reply?
> What counsel shall it understand?[4]

Negation here serves to stress the insignificance and impotence of humanity in the presence of an omnipotent God. The same device is employed early in the first of the Thanksgiving Hymns (1QH) when the narrator asks:

> What shall a man say
> concerning his sin?
> And how shall he plead
> concerning his iniquities?
> And how shall he reply
> to righteous judgement? (p. 192).

Rhetorically manipulated into offering a response, the reader again supplies a list of negations to these questions.

Simile, as recognizable a literary device as can be found, is a particularly ubiquitous technique within the Thanksgiving Hymns. In Hymn 10 the narrator likens himself to 'a sailor in a ship/amid furious seas', and moments later employs siege imagery to depict his plight:

> But I shall be as one who enters a fortified city,
> as one who seeks refuge behind a high wall
> until deliverance (comes) (p. 209).

The geographical aptness of some of the similes in the Thanksgiving Hymns is pleasurable: 'its stem shall be like nettles in a salty land' (p. 215), and the overall conventionality of the images of lamentation, in particular, also provides the specific kind of pleasure that can be generated precisely by the recognition of convention:

---

4. G. Vermes, *The Dead Sea Scrolls in English* (Harmondsworth: Penguin, 1995), p. 89. All subsequent quotations from the Dead Sea Scrolls, unless indicated otherwise, will be from this edition. The page references will be to this edition and will be placed in the text after the quotation.

My eyes are like fire in the furnace
   and my tears like rivers of water;
my eyes grow dim with waiting,
    [for my salvation] is far from me
    and my life is apart from me (p. 216).

Vermes compares the structure of Beatitudes (4Q525) unfavourably with that of Mt. 5.3-11, noting: 'The main structural difference between Matthew and 4Q525 lies in that the former lists each time the reward of the virtue for which the people are blessed, whereas the Cave 4 text provides ordinary, mostly antithetic, parallelisms instead' (p. 286). This is true, but nevertheless the repetition of line beginnings in 4Q525: 'Blessed are those', 'He does not', 'He will not', is anaphoric and the unadorned and predictable repetition works toward maintaining a consistent note of sincerity. In its very ordinariness lies its effect on the reader.

Some of the images generate pleasure through puns, as occurs in the pun on 'kneaded' which Vermes's translation of the first Thanksgiving Hymn permits:

And yet I, a shape of clay
   kneaded in water
a ground of shame
   and a source of pollution (p. 191).

'Kneaded' here clearly means 'shaped' or 'moulded' but also evokes the sense of 'wanted', as in to be 'needed'. The reader is disconcerted by successive images of, first, power and then the loss of it, as one who is 'needed' in the second sense of the word also has power. To the objection that it is only a translation, specifically into English, that permits this reading I would only say that my reading is *of* this translation.

Other images and phrases also offer the traditional pleasure of explication. I wonder if anybody has ever read these lines from Cross's translation of 1QpHab without performing what might technically be called a 'double-take': 'This means the priest whose dishonor was greater than his honor. For he did not circumcize the foreskin of his heart but walked in ways of drunkenness in order to quench (his) thirst.'[5] 'He did not circumcize the foreskin of his heart'—well, who has? Whatever the priest's punishment he would seem at first glance to

---

5. Cross, *The Ancient Library of Qumran*, p. 115.

be unlikely to experience it in solitude. At a moment such as this, one either accepts the phrase in all its glorious bizarreness and moves on, or one looks at it again, trying to understand what it might *mean*. A critical perspective such as Feminism might choose to read the phrase as the product of a resolutely patriarchal society; one so unhealthily preoccupied with the penis as a totem of power that its imagery collapses under the linguistic burden of maintaining this phallocentricity. However, a teleological approach might choose (and I would stress this word) to focus on temporality. The hypothetical feminist reading perceives the foreskin as always part of the penis, but if the foreskin in the image is perceived as actually disassociated from it, not part of it at all, but removed precisely because it is superfluous, and, worse, because it has the potential for uncleanliness, then the priest's crime can be seen as one of retention. He has not divested himself of the superfluous and the unclean: sensuality, love of pleasure, individuality. His drunkenness is simultaneously represented as both cause and effect. The writer's decision to link a cultural practice with an individual's sin, the grossly carnal with the divinely aspirational, is, to my mind, ingenious.

There are numerous other examples of pleasures that could be described as those of recognition, but there are also some that might more accurately be described as those of discovery. Specifically, I was intrigued to encounter, among the more familiar genres within the Dead Sea Scrolls, a genre entirely new to me: the brontologia. In their discussion of 'A Divination Text (Brontologian)' (4Q318), Wise, Abegg and Cook note:

> this writing belongs to the ancient genre of *brontologia* (from Greek *brontos*, 'thunder', and *logian*, 'discourse'), which relied upon thunder to foretell the future. The ancient Mesopotamians had much earlier exploited thunder for this purpose. One such early example reads, 'When Rammanu thunders in the great gate of the Moon, there will be a slaying of Elamite troops with the sword...'[6]

The brontologia is not a genre commonly encountered in English literature—or so it seems at first glance. At second glance, however, it is possible that the genre remains hidden within western literature for nearly 2000 years, its constituent parts appropriated, subsumed and

---

6. M.O. Wise, M.G. Abegg, Jr, and E.M. Cook, *The Dead Sea Scrolls: A New Translation* (London: HarperCollins, 1996), p. 303.

integrated within other genres, until the second half of this century. The genre of brontologia may well be the antecedent of post World War Two writing which depicts nuclear apocalypse—only now have we developed technology to the point where we can mimic God's awesome destructive powers and, so to speak, mimic his voice of thunder; a voice which presages destruction. Conditions propitious, the genre of brontologia, and the Dead Sea Scrolls themselves, discovered at the same time as the H-bomb, reintroduce themselves to a new age. In addition, it can be noted that nuclear apocalypse narratives, cinematic as well as literary, are more common in science fiction than in literary fiction; the ostensibly arcane genre of the brontologia is now one of the most popular genres in western culture. There is a pleasure of a somewhat sly kind in noting that a line of development can be traced from 4Q318 'A Divination Text' to the Arnold Schwarzenegger film *The Terminator*—but it is always possible, I suppose, that this is not a pleasurable line of thought to all biblical scholars. When this paper is published I will be interested myself to see if either Schwarzenegger or *The Terminator* makes it through to the index.

A reading of the Dead Sea Scrolls offers further experiences to the literary critic. Paul Armstrong rejects Norman Holland's argument that 'each of us will find in the literary work the kind of thing we characteristically wish or fear the most', and points out 'if I mold every work to fit my own desires and defenses, no experience of reading could ever teach me anything'.[7] I agree with Armstrong's unfashionable view that literature can teach us something, and what I think can be 'learned' from the Dead Sea Scrolls is the recognition of a world view predicated on severity and austerity, on proscription and denial, on suppression and repression. One of the leading figures among the American New Critics, Cleanth Brooks, writes in his book *The Hidden God*: 'we read literary works not so much for instruction in ideas as to learn—through a kind of dramatic presentation—what it feels like to hold certain beliefs, including the pressure exerted against belief'.[8] While a Marxist reading of the Dead Sea Scrolls might emphasize the power that the priesthood construct for themselves and, more sophisticatedly, enumerate instances of the fundamental principle of exchange that pervades the relationship between man and God,

7.   Armstrong, *Conflicting Readings*, p. 27.
8.   C. Brooks, *The Hidden God* (New Haven: Yale University Press, 1963), p. 128.

and while the psychoanalytic critic might view the texts in terms of repressed libidinal energy, the metaphors and images allowed, even forced, to express linguistically a sexuality culturally prohibited, the New Critic places considerable value on this other, new version of the way the world is constructed. The Dead Sea Scrolls are suffused with radical disjunctions between light and dark, joy and lamentation, life and death. The endless lists of prohibitions, so uninviting to the modern reader, carry a subtext perhaps most perfectly articulated in the modern age by T.S. Eliot when, in another context, he famously observed 'The Spirit Killeth, the Letter giveth Life'. The Dead Sea Scrolls take absolutely for granted radical differences between— between everything. One animal may be eaten, another may not. Such emphatic distinctions reveal a world view that our own more accommodating age can only retrieve through readings which seek less to unmask deceptions than they do to reveal values.

Despite my references to the prohibitions within the Dead Sea Scrolls I would also suggest that one of the other great pleasures to be gained from reading them lies in their innocent promiscuity. I do not mean, of course, that the Scrolls themselves endorse sexual promiscuity, but rather that their current composition is generically promiscuous. In Proust's *Remembrance of Things Past*, the narrator, a boy at this time, is at Balbec for the summer and has just met Albertine, the adolescent girl who will be the love, and torment, of his adult life. In one of his most extraordinary images, Proust describes Albertine and her young friends entering the dance hall where they would go when it rained:

> As a rule we had to listen to admonition from the manager, or from some of his staff, usurping dictatorial powers, because my friends...could not enter the outer hall of the rooms without starting to run, jumping over all the chairs, sliding back along the floor, their balance maintained by a graceful poise of their outstretched arms, singing the while, mingling all the arts, in that first bloom of youth, in the manner of those poets of ancient days for whom the different 'kinds' were not yet separate, so that in an epic poem they would introduce rules of agriculture with theological doctrine.[9]

The Dead Sea Scrolls, as we have them now, similarly follow no contemporary generic or taxonomic rules; all the various genres mingle

9. M. Proust, *Remembrance of Things Past* (trans. C.K. Scott Moncrieff; London: Chatto & Windus, 1972), pp. 268-69.

promiscuously, indiscriminately. Even the presence of commentaries alongside the texts they comment upon neatly anticipates current theoretical beliefs that writing should not be hierarchized into primary and secondary texts, but that rather all forms of writing merge in a discourse we refer to as 'literary'.

However, possibly most attractive of all to a certain kind of critic is the promise, however illusory, of 'pure text'. There is certainly considerable appeal for the hermeneutically inclined reader in the absence of a named author, and there is also the extremely unusual bonus of there being little known even about the culture from within which the texts have been written. Vermes's description of the geography of Qumran: 'lifeless, silent and empty' (p. xiii), applies, for me, equally to the texts themselves—'lifeless, silent and empty', until brought to life by the act of reading. I want now to look briefly at 'The Seductress' (4Q184).

Vermes introduces this text by writing: 'A long and relatively-well preserved poem from Cave 4 depicts, by means of the metaphor of the harlot, the dangers and attractions of false doctrine' (p. 273). The novice in Scroll studies might ask at the poem's conclusion where Vermes gets the license to read the poem allegorically. In his notes to 'Commentaries on Hosea' (4Q166–67) Vermes similarly writes: 'In the first [of the fragments] the unfaithful wife is the Jewish people led astray by her lovers, the Gentiles' (p. 333). The bold 'is' here claims a similar allegorical status as 'The Seductress' for this text. But is 'The Seductress' classified, tautologously, as a wisdom poem because it is read allegorically? Taxonomy, as occurs so often, is an interpretative issue. Typology, of course, hands out many licenses but it is interesting to try and read this text without Vermes's allegorical gloss. It seems to me quite possible to read the poem and argue that not only is it not concerned with 'false doctrine', but its central character is not even a harlot. Consider the opening lines:

> ... speaks vanity
>   and... errors.
> She is ever prompt to oil her words,
>   and she flatters with irony,
>   deriding with iniquitous l[ips] (p. 273).

Clearly, these could be the words of any misogynist, describing all women. There are, of course, numerous references throughout the

Scrolls alluding to the iniquity and sinful nature of humanity. The 'Prayer for Festival' (4Q507), for example, reads: 'We are (encompassed) by iniquity since the womb, and since the breast by guilt. While we live we walk in iniquity...' (p. 265). 'The Seductress' moves very quickly into powerful images centred on perdition and damnation. The crucial lines for me occur in the last third of the poem: 'In the city's squares she veils herself/And she stands at the gates of towns'. This could indeed legitimate an allegorical reading, although not necessarily Vermes's, in that a prostitute is unlikely to be veiled in the town square, and therefore 'she' refers here to something other than woman. Equally, however, it could endorse a 'misogynistic' reading. This is not one woman, sequentially depicted as moving from one place to another, but two women, upper and lower class, and therefore, contextually, all women, waiting to sexually ensnare righteous men. There are at least three possible readings here, in addition to Vermes's. 'The Seductress' is one specific harlot; she is one harlot, but faithful enough to her type to represent all harlots; she is all women, iniquitous by nature; she is an allegorical figure representing 'false doctrine'. I would further suggest that additionally, self-referentially, 'The Seductress' can be read as an allegory of the hermeneutic process itself. Emmanuel Levinas's writings on religion persistently use a word which has considerable relevance here. Colin Davis writes of Levinas's hermeneutics:

> The reader realizes meanings which may not have been consciously placed there. Levinas frequently describes the two-way process between text and reader as *solicitation*: the reader solicits the text with his or her current interests in mind, and is in turn solicited by the text to an exploration of meaning to which those current interests make an indispensable contribution.[10]

I take 'current interests' here to include dominant theoretical assumptions.

'Solicitation', of course, is a word closely associated with prostitution; it is, essentially, a speech act which precedes a sexual act. Reading is also a linguistic act, and it precedes an interpretative act. The poem is entitled 'The Seductress' and we talk of a seductive reading; seduction is commonly envisaged as an act of persuasion and we talk of a persuasive reading. Geoffrey Harpham writes: 'Ethics is grounded in

10. C. Davis, *Levinas* (Oxford: Polity, 1996), p. 110.

the notion of resistance to temptation, but the concept can and should be generalized...'[11] I would like to take up that challenge and suggest that a sequence of interpretative possibilities, such as the one just discussed, presents what amounts to a series of temptations. Harpham writes:

> In temptation desire is illuminated, but always and only as a double desire balanced between obedience to the law and transgression, between the dictates of conscience and the impulses or drives of the mere self. In the experience of temptation we are situated at a moment of character-revealing choice...[12]

The reader who immediately reads 'The Seductress' as an allegory, or as a sexist critique of women, and presses against the text no further is in a position analogous to those who have not been tempted by the harlot at all. Only in the face of temptation can we be said to have made a decision. Where a reader does not see the possibility of other interpretations there is no act of choice, no decision. In the absence of internalized, successive interpretations there is no interpretation to speak of at all. All interpretations are self-serving, but those untested by temptation are the most self-serving of all.

In his introduction to 'The Religious Ideas of the Community' Vermes writes: 'Sexual abstinence was imposed on those participating in the Temple services, both priests and laymen; no person who had sexual intercourse (or an involuntary emission, or even any contact with a menstruating woman) could lawfully take part' (p. 57). I suspect that for many, if not all, intelligent modern people, the then-believed uncleanliness of menstruation would be used to explain the exclusion of men who had even been in contact with menstruating women. However, it seems more likely that it is life that is being excluded here: menstruation and ejaculation, blood and sperm; there are no more potent or comprehensive signifiers of life itself than these. Blood and sperm in this construction have the same symbolic weight, and what looked initially like an act of exclusion can now be seen as an act of recognition, of incorporation. Inferentially, from this reading the Temple service itself can then be seen as a ceremony very intensely focused on death. An interpretation which immediately assumes menstruating women were seen as unclean flatters us today,

11. G.G. Harpham, *The Ascetic Imperative in Culture and Criticism* (Chicago: University of Chicago Press, 1987), pp. xv-xvi.
12. Harpham, *The Ascetic Imperative*, p. 47.

who no longer organize our religious practices around such irrelevant matters, and supports the myth most desperately promulgated by modern liberal perspectives: the myth of progress. However, there is no escaping the hermeneutic circle. I notice that my own interpretation is an act of exoneration; it seeks to favourably interpret the exclusion, and my own 'objectivity' here can be seen as nothing other than deferential, patriarchical conservatism.

Accounts of the discovery and reception of the Dead Sea Scrolls, that is to say interpretations of their discovery and reception, are similarly self-serving and I would like to conclude by briefly considering some of these. All accounts of the Dead Sea Scrolls phenomenon accentuate the locale and the accidental discovery of the initial texts by a group of shepherds. Popular accounts, in particular, stress the Bedouin's immediate loss of control over the Scrolls and covert parallels are drawn between the Bedouin and ordinary people in the west, denied the right to read the Scrolls by a powerful and elite group. The geography of Qumran is also heavily stressed, and for good reasons. The power of the Scrolls' natural context here is surely inseparable from their subsequent reception. The mountains are phallic, the caves are vaginal—the Scrolls emerge from the confluence, and indeed to witness ourselves as we were so long ago is to participate more in an act of birth than in one of retrieval. But Qumran is not a place to exhaust its symbolic possibilities too quickly. The mountains which contain the caves which contained the Scrolls point to heaven, they represent the aspirational, the highest and most attractive energy; while the caves speak of mystery and of concealed depths which only the heuristic act can illuminate.

Some of the geography of the area, however, seems to be purely imaginary, rather than just extravagantly interpreted. In his best-selling *The Hidden Scrolls: Christianity, Judaism and the War for the Dead Sea Scrolls*, Neil Asher Silberman, one of the most critical of conventional, religious readings of the Scrolls, describes the cave where the first scrolls were found in this way: 'This particular cave was deep and narrow...'[13] In his account of the discovery, Jonathan Campbell makes no reference to the narrowness of the cave: 'In the morning, Muhammed edh-Dhib was the first to enter the cave...'[14]

13. N.A. Silberman, *The Hidden Scrolls* (London: Mandarin, 1995), p. 2.
14. J. Campbell, *Deciphering the Dead Sea Scrolls* (London: Fontana, 1996), p. 2.

Nor do Wise, Abegg and Cook. Nor does Vermes. I would suggest that Silberman's idiosyncratic spatialization is a projection of his interpretation of the reception of the Scrolls onto the site from which they were recovered. It precisely reflects his view of the academics who 'control' the Scrolls: deep (learned) and narrow (insufficiently interested in politics). Ideology and geography do not so much coincide here as demonstrate that the former creates the latter. Silberman is insistent throughout his book that the 'real message of the Scrolls', his favourite phrase, is 'rage against empire'. This 'radical' reading, he insists, is derided by academics. He writes: 'The scholars' discourse was civil, unemotional, analytical, and filled with the jargon of tweedy academics who were themselves voluntary exiles from the rough-and-tumble beyond the ivy walls'.[15] Here speaks a man who has never sat in a room full of academics arguing with each other over office space, car parking, or, most bloody of all, sabbaticals. He asks, in full flow: 'What did these respectable and respectful academics know of the rage of the apocalyptic outsider…?'.[16] He'd find out soon enough if he ran into one who hadn't been given a parking space. However, Silberman is surely correct when he declares: 'Studying the Scrolls can be an intensely subjective experience, in which a scholar's hopes, fears, beliefs, and preconceptions might determine what he or she sees'.[17] Many authors, of books far more scholarly than Silberman's, do not consider this possibility.

Silberman's book seems to me to answer the question posed by Wise, Abegg and Cook in their introduction: 'What do [the Scrolls] mean for us?'.[18] I would suggest that the Scrolls themselves probably do not mean much at all to the very large majority of people. But what do matter a great deal are the various interpretations of the Scrolls' contemporary reception—and suppression. Wise, Abegg, and Cook note: 'Many people today are agitated about the dawning of a new millennium'.[19] Many of these agitated people are precisely those who take pleasure from conspiracy theories and sundry myths of suppression. The interpretative act focuses, not on the text, but on the history of the text.

15. Silberman, *The Hidden Scrolls*, p .11.
16. Silberman, *The Hidden Scrolls*, p. 23.
17. Silberman, *The Hidden Scrolls*, p. 105.
18. Wise, Abegg, and Cook, *The Dead Sea Scrolls*, p. 3.
19. Wise, Abegg, and Cook, *The Dead Sea Scrolls*, p. 225.

I used to think that academics in English literature departments were aggressive to one another in print, but that was before I began reading the work of Scrolls scholars. Some may be familiar with Vladimir Nabokov's novel *Pale Fire*, in which an editor so completely takes over the text he is editing that, eventually, there is nothing left of the text, and only the incessant voice of the commentator remains. The novel is usually interpreted as a satire on academic pedantry and obsession, but such readings overlook the fact that the footnotes are, actually, where the 'real' story is to be found. The footnotes in Scrolls scholarship, particularly in the work of Robert Eisenman, also tell a fascinating story, one which is centred around a struggle for power. Eisenman's books bristle with footnotes, themselves packed with combative images and aggressive criticisms of other scholars' work. He is often brutally dismissive, but can also be deftly damning. Although one example will have to suffice, he is the master, to my mind, of the parenthetical put-down, a form so prevalent in his work it almost amounts to a new annotational sub-genre. He writes, for example, of Cross's excitement over the coin from the Tenth Roman Legion found at Qumran, which, it turns out, wasn't: 'See (however futile) Cross' complete discussion of this matter...'[20] His concluding comments in the introduction to *The Dead Sea Scrolls and the First Christians* are so suffused with metaphors of war they verge on the comical: 'This, of course, has always been a very safe vantage-point from which to attack the position of one's adversaries'.[21] And yet I raise the issue because Eisenman is surely correct in his over-arching belief, continuously implied throughout his footnotes: that interpretation does matter. Interpretation is an intrinsically political activity because power is present in the act of understanding in many forms. The issue of who is in charge in the relation between interpreter and text is, among other things, a question about the distribution of power. History does not free us from the hermeneutic circle. Armstrong writes: 'Historical understanding and literary interpretation have the same epistemological structure'.[22] Readings of individual texts, and the readings of the receptions offered to those texts will be the same interpretations.

20. R. Eisenman, *The Dead Sea Scrolls and the First Christians* (Dorset: Element Books, 1996), p. 192.

21. Eisenman, *The Dead Sea Scrolls and the First Christians*, p. xxviii.

22. Armstrong, *Conflicting Readings*, p. 103.

I began by quoting Cross's comment on the potentially fruitful interaction between literary criticism and biblical studies but, with particular reference to interpretation, possibly the most appropriate methodology for reading the Scrolls would be deconstruction. The enthusiasm with which deconstructionists signal an awareness that they write under the constant threat of erasure, is perfectly matched by the narrators of the Scrolls, who, also aware of the threat of erasure, either by Rome or God, articulate their own gloomy prospects with an equivalent anticipatory relish.

Part II

THE SCROLLS AND THE SCRIPTURES OF ISRAEL

THE DEAD SEA SCROLLS AND HIGHER CRITICISM OF THE HEBREW BIBLE: THE CASE OF 4QJUDGᵃ*

Richard S. Hess

1. *Introduction*

The fragment, 4QJudgᵃ, comprises two joined pieces some 7.6 cm high and 4.8 cm wide. Together these contain parts of nine lines of Hebrew text from Judges 6. Trebolle Barrera's (1989; 1995b) careful study of this text has led him to conclude that it comprises vv. 2-6 followed immediately by vv. 11-13. Noting that many literary critics of Judges have argued that vv. 8-10 are a literary insertion, perhaps an example of late deuteronomistic redaction, Trebolle Barrera concludes that 4QJudgᵃ is an example of an earlier literary form of Judges than that preserved in either the MT or the LXX. It is the purpose of this study to examine this contention in the light of the evidence from the Dead Sea Scrolls and that found in the MT.

Trebolle Barrera's studies of 4QJudgᵃ are important, for they represent one of many attempts by Qumran scholars to apply their readings of the Scrolls to issues of textual criticism and to move from there to relate the results to issues of literary criticism. Indeed, Trebolle Barrera's work has been singled out for special mention as a parade example of the 'marriage' of higher and lower criticism (Cross 1995: 183). He maintains that the textual evidence of 4QJudgᵃ demonstrates that it is 'an earlier literary form of the book than our traditional texts' (Trebolle Barrera 1995b: 162). In this understanding vv. 7-10 were not omitted from the Dead Sea Scroll fragment; they were not present in the first place.

It is a popular and enjoyable task to find in ancient biblical manuscripts empirical evidence for modern literary critical theories.

* I am grateful for the opportunity to discuss some ideas in this study with E. Herbert.

However, any attempt to use textual data in a theoretical model must meet the challenge that it cannot be better explained by another model. In the case of an omission in a biblical text there are examples of both unintentional and intentional scribal activity that can result in this phenomenon without resort to positing an original *Vorlage* that omitted the text.

2. *Textual Criticism*

For example, there may have been some form of haplography in the scribal copying of this manuscript. Perhaps the scribe's eyes skipped from one word or phrase beginning a verse, to a later word or phrase that was similar in appearance. Verse 11 begins as ויבא מלאך יהוה in the Hebrew text. The first words of v. 11 that are preserved in the Dead Sea Scroll fragment are אשר ליואש האביעזרי. Neither of these phrases from v. 11 are similar to the end of v. 6 or the beginning of v. 7. Therefore, haplography seems an unlikely explanation for the omission of vv. 7-10.

3. *Theology*

Another possible explanation is an intentional omission on the part of the scribe for theological reasons. In order to understand whether or not this is likely it is necessary to review the text as found in the MT. 4QJudg[a] preserves, with minor variations, Judg. 6.2-6 as in the MT translated here by the NRSV:

> The hand of Midian prevailed over Israel; and because of Midian the Israelites provided for themselves hiding places in the mountains, caves and strongholds. For whenever the Israelites put in seed, the Midianites and the Amalekites and the people of the east would come up against them. They would encamp against them and destroy the produce of the land, as far as the neighborhood of Gaza, and leave no sustenance in Israel, and no sheep or ox or donkey. For they and their livestock would come up, and they would even bring their tents, as thick as locusts; neither they nor their camels could be counted; so they wasted the land as they came in. Thus Israel was greatly impoverished because of Midian; and the Israelites cried out to the LORD for help.

Verses 7-10, although preserved in all major versions, are omitted in 4QJudg[a]. The NRSV translates:

> When the Israelites cried to the LORD on account of the Midianites, the
> LORD sent a prophet to the Israelites; and he said to them, 'Thus says the
> LORD, the God of Israel: I led you up from Egypt, and brought you out of
> the house of slavery; and I delivered you from the hand of the Egyptians
> and from the hand of all who oppressed you, and drove them out before
> you, and gave you their land; and I said to you, "I am the LORD your
> God; you shall not pay reverence to the gods of the Amorites, in whose
> land you live". But you have not given heed to my voice.'

The fragment does appear to continue with vv. 11-13, which the NRSV
renders:

> Now the angel of the LORD came and sat under the oak at Ophrah, which
> belonged to Joash the Abiezrite, as his son Gideon was beating out wheat
> in the wine press, to hide it from the Midianites. The angel of the LORD
> appeared to him and said to him, 'The LORD is with you, mighty war-
> rior'. Gideon answered him, 'But sir, if the LORD is with us, why then
> has all this happened to us? And where are all his wonderful deeds that
> our ancestors recounted to us, saying, "Did not the LORD bring us up
> from Egypt?" But now the LORD has cast us off and given us into the
> hand of Midian.'

The themes of deliverance from Egypt and guidance by God are
found both in the omitted vv. 7-10 and in the included vv. 11-13.
There is the presence of a prophet and emphases on the gift of the
land and the presence of idolatry, which are found in vv. 7-10 but not
in vv. 11-13. However, none of these themes would be omitted by any
Jewish group of the turn of the era, for whom the importance of the
prophetic word, God's blessing of the land and the judgments of idolatry were foundational parts of their faith. Nor is it likely that the
roughly contemporary account of Gideon from the pen of Josephus
will provide much help. According to Feldman (1993), miracles and
angelic appearances are downplayed by Josephus to heighten Gideon's
appeal to a Gentile audience. If this is true, then Josephus and his
environment had no influence on the edition of 4QJudg[a], which
emphasizes the angelic and miraculous and ignores human prophecy.

The absence of valid text-critical and theological reasons for the
omission of vv. 7-10 leaves the literary-critical explanation as a possibility. Could it be that 4QJudg[a] does preserve the original text while
all other versions were redacted by a scholar in the deuteronomistic
tradition? The strongest argument in favour of reserving judgment on
this is the size of the fragment. It is difficult to say whether or not
such a phenomenon can explain this omission because it is not possible

to see the larger context from which 4QJudg[a] is derived. It is difficult categorically to deny the possibility of an original omission of vv. 7-10, but it is not easy to convince on the basis of a fragment of nine lines from which over half of each line of 59 to 65 letters is missing.

4. *Masoretic Divisions*

It is, however, appropriate to consider another factor in the evaluation of this textual omission. That is the division of the Hebrew text into *parashoth*, a phenomenon well established and recorded in the Masoretic manuscripts. There the divisions are marked either by a Hebrew פ for *petucha* or by a ס for *setuma*. They are thought to define specific sections of content in the biblical text and to mark changes in ideas and thought. Thus they have been compared to the use of paragraphs in English and other modern languages. They may have served liturgical purposes, as well. Divisions similar to *parashoth* are also attested in the Qumran biblical manuscripts (Würthwein 1979: 21). Although not identical to the Masoretic texts in all cases, studies in the Qumran Pentateuchal texts, such as those recording the text of Deuteronomy (White 1993: 24, 35), reveal the presence of empty spaces in the text exactly where the *parashoth* appear in the Hebrew manuscripts of the Masoretic tradition a thousand years later.

Does this oddity have any bearing on the study of Qumran fragment 4QJudg[a]? In the MT[1] of Judg. 6.2-13 there are two *parashoth*. They occur after v. 6 and v. 10. This is exactly where a portion of the biblical text is missing in 4QJudg[a]. Is this mere coincidence, or do the *parashoth* play a role in the division and break up of the biblical text?

In order to test the possibility that the *parashoth* divisions have a role in the construction of the Qumran text of 4QJudg[a], it is of value to compare some of the other texts of the Former Prophets and to see whether the divisions match the *parashoth* in these fragments. 4QJudg[b] is reconstructed as Judg. 21.12-25. After v. 12 there is an empty space according to the reconstruction. Even though only part of the text is preserved, this single space matches the occurrence of a *parashah* after Judg. 21.12 in the MT.

4QKgs contains fragments of 1 Kgs 7.19–8.19. The reconstruction of the text allows for empty spaces after 7.26, 37, 39, 50, 51, and

---

1. For the purposes of this study, this text will be the one represented in the *Biblia Hebraica Stuttgartensia*, that is, Codex Leningrad.

8.11. These points coincide wth the *parashoth* in the MT.

In the fragments of 4QJosh[b] an empty space is located at the same location as the *parashah*, after Josh. 17.13. 4QJosh[a] may have empty spaces at the end of the fragment of Josh. 8.18 and before and after the one of Josh. 10.8-11. These are in agreement with the *parashoth* in the MT. If there is indeed an empty space between Josh. 7.15 and 16, as reconstructed by Ulrich (1995: 149), this is the only example of such a gap where there is no corresponding Masoretic *parashah*.

Especially interesting for 4QJosh[a] is the fragment containing Josh. 8.34-35, followed by a text of unknown origin, and concluding with Josh. 5.2-7. *Parashoth* in the MT appear after 8.35 and 5.1. Thus the extra-biblical insertion in this fragment occurs between the two *parashoth*.

To complete the picture of the Former Prophets from Cave 4, the text of 4QSam[a] should be mentioned. Herbert (1995: 69) found this Qumran text in agreement with 32 occurrences of *parashoth* and in disagreement in 31 cases. In addition, eighteen divisions occur in the Qumran text that do not appear in the MT. Although the Samuel text seems at variance with the others in terms of its *parashoth* and those of the MT, this may reflect its unique and special manuscript tradition. In any case, the other textual examples of the Former Prophets consistently place divisions where the *parashoth* appear in the MT.

4QJosh[a] and 4QJudg[a] have both evoked discussion because these fragments preserve texts that do not follow the sequence of the MT and LXX. Instead, they reverse the order and insert nonbiblical texts, in the case of 4QJosh[a], or they omit several verses, in the case of 4QJudg[a]. However, it may be of significance to observe that in all cases where these anomalies appear, they occur at points divided by Masoretic *parashoth*. Since the other Cave 4 Qumran texts of Joshua and Judges seem to preserve *parashoth* divisions in agreement with the MT, it may be appropriate to ask whether the scribes did not find and exercise a liberty in moving these paragraphs of their Former Prophets around, inserting and omitting sections for their own purposes, be they liturgical or otherwise. This suggestion would not compromise the integrity of any possible 'canon' from which scriptural texts might have been copied. Instead, it would recognize the flexibility in the selection, arrangement and commentary that could accompany biblical texts; a flexibility that consistently follows the *parashoth* as found in the MT.

5. *Conclusion*

In conclusion, the following reasons may be suggested for exercizing caution regarding the assertion that 4QJudg[a] exhibits an authentic piece of pre-deuteronomistic text:

First, the fragment itself is too small to warrant such a far-reaching conclusion. Additional and consistent evidence from this manuscript of Judges, if that indeed is what it is, is required before it can be assumed that the text or its *Vorlage* predates the insertion of deuteronomistic redaction. This same caution can also be applied to 4QJos[a] (Hess 1996: 19-20).

Secondly, the comparable evidence from the other fragments of Joshua and Judges suggests that the omission of 4QJudg[a] follows a tendency to insert, omit and change sections or paragraphs of biblical text at what would become the Masoretic *parashoth* divisions of text. Although these divisions are regularly according to sense, a fuller understanding of their purpose and application is appropriate before conclusions should be drawn about the relation of editorial work along these divisions and the assumptions of higher criticism.

Thirdly, when no other evidence of a pre-deuteronomistic text is at hand, it seems less likely that this lone fragment should preserve a pre-deuteronomistic text than that the fragment is part of a larger manuscript that never was intended to present the whole book of Judges but rather may have been a collection of biblical texts serving a particular liturgical purpose for the community who read it.

These conclusions do not take away from the importance of these texts for the textual criticism of the Hebrew Bible. However, they do ask questions about particular constructs of a hypothesis attached to the study of 4QJudg[a].

BIBLIOGRAPHY

Cross, F.M.
    1995   *The Ancient Library of Qumran* (The Biblical Seminar, 30; Sheffield: JSOT Press, 3rd edn).
Feldman, L.
    1993   'Josephus' Portrait of Gideon', *Revue des études juives* 152: 5-28.

The Scrolls and the Scriptures

Herbert, E.D.
　　1995　'A New Method for Reconstructing Biblical Scrolls, and its
　　　　　Application to the Reconstruction of 4QSam[a]' (Doctoral thesis, Uni-
　　　　　versity of Cambridge) [Used by permission].
Hess, R.S.
　　1996　*Joshua: An Introduction and Commentary* (TOTC, 6; Downers Grove,
　　　　　IL: IVP).
Tov, E.
　　1992　'The Contribution of the Qumran Scrolls to the Understanding of the
　　　　　LXX', in G. Brooke and B. Lindars (eds.), *Septuagint, Scrolls and
　　　　　Cognate Writings: Papers Presented to the International Symposium
　　　　　on the Septuagint and its Relations to the Dead Sea Scrolls and Other
　　　　　Writings (Manchester 1990)* (SBLSCS, 33; Atlanta: Scholars Press):
　　　　　11-47.
　　1995　'4QJosh[b]', in E. Ulrich *et al.* (eds.), *Qumran Cave 4: Deuteronomy,
　　　　　Joshua, Judges, Kings* (DJD, 9; Oxford: Clarendon Press): 153-60,
　　　　　plate XXXV.
Trebolle Barrera, J.
　　1989　'Textual Variants in *4QJudg[a]* and the Textual and Editorial History of
　　　　　the Book of Judges', *RevQ* 14: 229-45.
　　1991　'Édition préliminaire de 4QJuges[b]: Contribution des manuscrits qum-
　　　　　râniens des Juges à l'étude textuelle et littéraire du livre', *RevQ* 15: 9-
　　　　　100.
　　1992　'Light from 4QJudg[a] and 4QKgs on the Text of Judges and Kings', in
　　　　　D. Dimant and U. Rappaport (eds.), *The Dead Scrolls: Forty Years of
　　　　　Research* (STDJ, 10; Leiden: Brill): 315-24.
　　1995a　'4QJosh[a]', in E. Ulrich *et al.* (eds.), *Qumran Cave 4. Deuteronomy,
　　　　　Joshua, Judges, Kings* (DJD, 9; Oxford: Clarendon Press): 143-52,
　　　　　plates XXXII-XXXIV.
　　1995b　'4QJudg[a]', in E. Ulrich *et al.* (eds.), *Qumran Cave 4. Deuteronomy,
　　　　　Joshua, Judges, Kings* (DJD, 9; Oxford: Clarendon Press): 161-64,
　　　　　plate XXXVI.
　　1995c　'4QJudg[b]', in E. Ulrich *et al.* (eds.), *Qumran Cave 4. Deuteronomy,
　　　　　Joshua, Judges, Kings* (DJD, 9; Oxford: Clarendon Press): 165-69,
　　　　　plate XXXVI.
White, S.
　　1993　'Three Deuteronomy Manuscripts from Cave 4, Qumran', *JBL* 112:
　　　　　23-42.
Würthwein, E.
　　1979　*The Text of the Old Testament* (Grand Rapids: Eerdmans).

DISTINGUISHING THE LINGUISTIC AND THE EXEGETICAL: THE CASE OF NUMBERS IN THE BIBLE AND 11QT[a]*

John Elwolde

Although the Hebrew language employed in the Dead Sea Scrolls displays numerous striking discrepancies from the Hebrew of the Bible, scholars working on what the texts mean, from a theological, cultural, or historical perspective, usually come to the Scrolls armed with little more than a reasonable knowledge of Biblical Hebrew. This fact is reflected in (1) the absence of detailed linguistic analysis in most editions of the Scrolls—J.T. Milik on the Copper Scroll (DJD, 3) and E. Qimron on 4QMMT (DJD, 10) are notable exceptions—and in (2) the leaving aside of, or, perhaps, failure even to notice, linguistic difficulties, in translations and commentaries. In the following remarks, I attempt to show how linguistic considerations can cast light on our understanding of Qumran texts and how the Qumran writers might have arrived at the particular forms of expression they have bequeathed to us. In so far as there is an underlying or recurring theme to this study, it is the issue of how (and if) elements reflecting linguistic developments can be distinguished from features of an interpretative or stylistic nature. The analysis is based on texts from the Temple Scroll (11QT) that appear to make direct use of passages from the book of Numbers.[1]

---

* Hereafter designated simply as 11QT. This is a revised version of my Dead Sea Scrolls and the Bible lecture, concentrating exclusively on 11QT. An early form of the paper was delivered as part of a workshop at Leiden in 1995, but was not published in the corresponding proceedings: T. Muraoka and J.F. Elwolde (eds.), *The Hebrew of the Dead Sea Scrolls and Ben Sira: Proceedings of a Symposium held at Leiden University, 11-14 December 1995* (STDJ, 26; Leiden: Brill, 1997). I intend to examine citations of Numbers in Scrolls other than 11QT in a forthcoming article.

1. My assumption is that the author (or authors or scribe or scribes) had access to, or in mind, a text (written and/or oral) of the Bible that corresponded quite closely

1. *Numbers 9.3*

Num. 9.3	בְּאַרְבָּעָה עָשָׂר־יוֹם בַּחֹדֶשׁ הַזֶּה
11QT 17.6[2]	[בארב]עה עשר בחודש הראישון

a. [בארב]עה עשר[3] for בְּאַרְבָּעָה עָשָׂר־יוֹם. In the Pentateuch, only Lev. 23.5 has the formula without יוֹם 'day', and even there it is supplied by Sam (= Samaritan Peutateuch), LXX, Vulgate, and *Targ. Neof.* On the other hand, this formula, without יוֹם, is attested seven times outside the Pentateuch, once in Joshua, once in Ezekiel, and, significantly, five times in the late books of Esther, Ezra, and Chronicles.[4] Thus, the Qumran variant here appears to result from trends in contemporary phraseology rather than from any text-transmission or exegetical factor.

b. הראישון for הַזֶּה. 11QT's choice here is matched by that of the LXX (although not Sam, Vulgate, or *Targums*). Both בַּ/לַ/הַחֹדֶשׁ הַזֶּה '*this* month' and בַּ/לַ/הַחֹדֶשׁ הָרִאשׁוֹן 'the *first* month' are found seven times in the Pentateuch. However, whereas the זֶה formula occurs only once outside the Pentateuch (at Neh. 9.1), the רִאשׁוֹן formula is attested an additional fourteen times, once in Joshua, but the rest in Esther, Daniel, Ezra, and Chronicles—again, all late books of the Bible (as well as another nine times in the Scrolls themselves, including 11QT 17.6).[5] So, once more, the possibility of idiom influence seems attractive. In other words, the expression 'the first month' was so common among the Temple Scroll author's peers, that it tended to displace

to the Hebrew Bible as presented in *BHS* (from which the biblical texts cited in this article are extracted), not one that would have been more like a retroversion of the Septuagint, for example.

2. Y. Yadin, *The Temple Scroll*. II. *Text and Commentary* (Jerusalem: Israel Exploration Society, 1983), p. 73, seemed to regard this text as a reflection more of Lev. 23.5 than of Num. 9.3, although the word order favours the latter.

3. As Peshitta.

4. Checking just under ארבע/ארבעה in the new concordance (fascicle four) to B.Z. Wacholder, M.G. Abegg, and J. Bowley (eds.), *A Preliminary Edition of the Unpublished Dead Sea Scrolls* (4 fascicles; Washington: Biblical Archaeology Society, 1991–96), the consistent omission of יוֹם in dates, especially in 4QMishB[a] [4Q321], is striking; where יוֹם is used, it precedes the numeral (4QpGen[a] [4Q252] 1.1.8, 17).

5. The figure includes reconstructions from the new concordance (note 5 above).

similar phrases, such as 'this month'. However, going against this interpretation is the fact that הַחֹדֶשׁ הַזֶּה 'this month' also re-emerges in the Dead Sea Scrolls, despite its absence from the late books of the Bible. In fact, three of the four Qumran occurrences of הַחֹדֶשׁ הַזֶּה are found in 11QT (25.10 = Num. 29.7 and 17.10/27.10 = Num. 29.12), replacing each time the sequence month plus ordinal in the Pentateuch—in other words, the reverse of the phenomenon just described (not exactly, of course, as 'this' can replace any ordinal, whereas 'first' can only replace 'this'). Moreover, if the editors of 4QJub[a] [4Q216][6] are right in their reconstruction, a Jubilees text from Qumran almost gratuitously reads [לחודש ה[זה 'of *this* month' immediately after [בחוד[ש השל[ישי] 'the *third* month' has been specified, tending to indicate that the expression הַחֹדֶשׁ הַזֶּה was itself developing into a clichéd phrase.

Given that the evidence appears to point in opposite directions, we cannot safely claim that trends in contemporary language have affected the Qumran writings at this point (that is, at 11QT 17.6). Indeed, the reason for choosing הַחֹדֶשׁ הָרִאשׁוֹן 'the *first* month' here but הַחֹדֶשׁ הַזֶּה '*this* month' in the three other Temple Scroll passages (17.10; 25.10; 27.10) is probably of a much more practical nature, relating to the 'real world' for which the Qumran writings were legislating. For in the texts with זֶה, reference to the month occurs in a narrative unit that is already well-advanced, whereas when רִאשׁוֹן is used, the author is *introducing* the whole subject of passover and therefore requires a more precise indication of date. Indeed, this point is nicely demonstrated by the very passage we have examined, which starts off with 'on the fourteenth day of *the first* month' at 17.6, where the topic is introduced, and then continues, at l. 10, 'and on the fifteenth day of *this* month', the number of the month obviously no longer needing specification. In this particular case, then, linguistic considerations are overshadowed by matters of a more pragmatic nature.

c. רִאישׁוֹן for רִאשׁוֹן. The spelling with *aleph-yod* (אי) for רִאשֹׁנָה/רִאשׁוֹן is standard in Sam and also the most commonly-attested form in the Qumran writings, occurring 24 times (excluding CD). A variant of

---

6. 1.5 (= *Jub.* 1.1) according to J.C. VanderKam and J.T. Milik, 'The First *Jubilees* Manuscripts from Qumran Cave 4: A Preliminary Publication', *JBL* 110 (1991), pp. 243-70 (247), and in DJD, 13 (1994), pp. 1-22 (5-7), where the wording is compared with Exod. 19.1.

this spelling, *yod-aleph* (יא), is attested seven times and a plain *yod*, without *aleph*, 23 times. The biblical spelling with just *aleph* occurs fourteen times.[7] The various forms reflect an orthographic perspective that is at times more etymological (retaining the 'silent' *aleph* of the root form), at times *positively* phonetic (representing the vowels that are actually pronounced), and at times negatively phonetic, or *prophylactic* (attempting to avoid pronunciation as *reshon* or *rashon*).[8] The fact that on six occasions the Dead Sea Scrolls also evidence spellings with *nothing*, that is, neither *yod* nor *aleph*, for biblical *aleph* (that is רשון, etc.),[9] *and* that these different spellings or classes of spellings are not usually found within the *same* document,[10] suggests that the Qumran forms reflect not simply a trend towards phonetic spelling but apparently two different pronunciations or even dialects: *rishon* as against *reshon* or *rashon*. We have only to think of the various ways in which the lexeme ראש 'head' is phonetically realized across Semitic—Arabic *ras*, Aramaic *resh*, Hebrew *rosh*—as well as the geographical location of Qumran to realize how possible such a mixed-dialect situation is.

7.   These and subsequent figures are based on the concordance mentioned in note 5 and on that included in *The Historical Dictionary of the Hebrew Language, Materials for the Dictionary (Series I: 200 B.C.E.–300 C.E.)* (Jerusalem: Academy of the Hebrew Language, 1988). The biblical spelling occurs in 1QH (twice), 4QJub[a] [4Q216], 4QJub[d] [4Q219], 4QMishB[a] [4Q321] (3 times), 4QMishH [4Q330] (twice), 4QApocJos[b] [4Q372] (twice), 4Q387, 4Q389, and 4Q414.

8.   See E.Y. Kutscher, *The Language and Linguistic Background of the Isaiah Scroll (1QIsa[a])* (STDJ, 6; Leiden: Brill, 1974), pp. 20, 170-71, 176-78.

9.   Documents other than 4Q504 (see the next note) that employ the null spelling are 1QS (twice), 4QPrQuot [4Q503] (once), and 4QRitPur [4Q512] (three times). At the Leiden symposium, Professor E. Qimron made the point that the longer the word the more likely it is to be spelt defectively, thus, for example in 4QOtot [4Q319], the forms are always אות and אתות. In the Bible, compare דור, where, although דרות is the normal form of the construct plural (four times but at Gen. 9.12 דרת), a suffixed variant of this form occurs just once, דרותינו (Judg. 22.7), with suffixed forms of דרת being attested 42 times. (The form דורת- is not attested.)

10.   4Q321 exhibits one spelling with *aleph-yod* and two with just *aleph*. Related documents sometimes exhibit different forms. For example, 4QDibHam[a] [4Q504] uses the null form whereas 4QDibHam[c] [4Q506] uses *yod*. However the 4QD [4Q265–73] material, for example, always employs spellings from the *y* group (265: *aleph-yod*; 266: *yod*; 267: *aleph-yod*; 269: *aleph-yod*; 270: *yod*; 271: *yod-aleph*). In the case of ראשית 'beginning', null, *aleph*, and *yod* forms seem to be more freely distributed.

2. *Numbers 19.14a*

Num. 19.14a זֹאת הַתּוֹרָה אָדָם כִּי־יָמוּת בְּאֹהֶל
11QT 49.5 ואדם כי ימות בעריכמה

a. ואדם for זֹאת הַתּוֹרָה אָדָם. Note that both the LXX and Sam prefix the initial clause by 'and', which is perhaps reflected in 11QT's ואדם 'and/as for a person'. The omission of 'this is the law' would seem to be primarily due to the constraints of the Temple Scroll's narrative structure. However, the oddity of the biblical text may well have also played a part. The two other occurrences of זֹאת הַתּוֹרָה, pointed out by Licht,[11] at Lev. 7.37 and 14.54, are both followed by the preposition לְ 'of, concerning'; the Numbers text is, therefore, stylistically strange, and also contrasts with the formula of v. 2, which reads זֹאת חֻקַּת הַתּוֹרָה 'this is the *statute of* the law (that)'.[12] Vulgate (*lex hominis*) and Syr (*nāmusā de-nāshā*) also saw fit to ease the Bible's syntax by rendering הַתּוֹרָה as תּוֹרַת 'the law of/concerning (a person)', and *Targ. Ps.-J.* and *Targ. Neof.* harmonize with v. 2, 'this is the instruction of the law',[13] although the LXX and *Targ. Onq.* retain the grammar of the MT.

b. בעריכמה for בְּאֹהֶל. In this passage, the LXX employs οἶκος, which probably represents a kind of cultural adaptation ('tent' means 'house'),[14] evidenced as well by the use of בַּיִת in the very next clause

11. J. Licht, *A Commentary on the Book of Numbers [XI–XXI]* (Jerusalem: Magnes Press, 1991 [Hebrew]), p. 191.

12. As noted by Licht (*Commentary*), the Ḥizzequni (of Hezekiah ben Manoaḥ, a thirteenth-century commentator) also links v. 14 with v. 2 in a way that appears to separate הַתּוֹרָה זֹאת from what follows, and joins it, *inclusio*-like, with what precedes: זאת התורה, כלומר זאת שאמרנו בתחילת הפרשה היא חוקת התורה. '*This is the law:* in other words, that which we said at the beginning of the *parashah* is a statute of the law'.

13. *Targ. Ps.-J.*: דָּא אַחֲוֵית אוֹרָיְתָא (v. 2: דָּא גְּזֵרַת אַחֲוַת אוֹרָיְתָא); *Targ. Neof.*: דָּא גְזֵרַת אוֹרָיְתָה (the same as v. 2).

14. Abraham Ibn 'Ezra makes the same equation: באהל, והבית כאהל, רק הזכיר הכתוב האהל בעבור היות ישראל באהלים 'In the tent: and the house is like the tent—Scripture only mentioned the tent on account of Israel's being in tents [in the wilderness]'. See also Naḥmanides: ועוד מפני שהיו ישראל יושבי אוהלים במדבר ודיבר הכתוב בהווה כי המצוה מיד ולדורות, אבל הוא הדין לבית ולכל מאהילים 'Furthermore, the Israelites were tent-dwellers in the wilderness and Scripture spoke of the usual [circumstances at that time], because the commandments applied [both] immediately and for later generations; but the same law applies to a house and to everything that 'covers' [a corpse]' (C.B. Chavel, *Ramban [Nachmanides] Commentary on the*

of 11QT and at CD 12.18.[15] In fact, as Licht points out, the use of אֹהֶל 'tent' to mean 'home' (דִּירָה) is stylistically 'solemn and slightly anti-quated' even in the biblical passage itself and in such collocations as 'to your tents, O Israel', which Licht qualifies as 'half-frozen cliches', that is, as stereotyped expressions.[16] At Num. 19.14, then, the implicit contrast is simply between a person found dead in their home and a person found dead away from their normal residence,[17] in the country-side, etc. 11QT's version ('in your cities') represents not just *cultural* adaptation, from desert to urban life, but also a *halakhic* tendency to make biblical commandments more restrictive (not just in your houses, but in your cities as well).[18]

3. *Numbers 19.14b*

Num. 19.14b	כָּל־הַבָּא אֶל־הָאֹהֶל וְכָל־אֲשֶׁר בָּאֹהֶל יִטְמָא שִׁבְעַת יָמִים
11QT 49.6	כול אשר בבית וכול הבא אל הבית יטמא שבעת ימים

We have already discussed the use of בַּיִת for אֹהֶל. 11QT's ordering of the clauses differs from that of the Sam and LXX, which agree with the MT. In the light of the Qumran author's insertion of a sentence,

כול בית אשר ימות בו המת יטמא שבעת ימים

Any house in which a dead person has died will be impure seven days (11QT 49.5-6),

between the first and second halves of the verse as it stands in the Bible, the rationale for changing the order is probably *exegetical* in

---

Torah: Numbers [New York: Shilo Publishing House, 1975], p. 200). In fact, as Naḥmanides goes on to mention, the equivalence is not exact, as a house, being permanently attached to the ground, cannot contract impurity: שאין הבית מחובר מקבל טומאה בעצמו כלל. The use of 'house' for 'tent' is not evidenced (at Num. 19.14), however, in Sam, Vulgate, the *Targums*, or *Sifre*. L.H. Schiffman, 'The Impurity of the Dead in the *Temple Scroll*', in L.H. Schiffman (ed.), *Archaeology and History in the Dead Sea Scrolls: The New York University Conference in Memory of Yigael Yadin* (JSPSup, 8; Sheffield: JSOT Press, 1990), pp. 135-56, points out (p. 139) that Maimonides did *not* regard the tent as equivalent to a building here.

15. אשר עם המת בבית.

16. מַטְבְּעוֹת לָשׁוֹן קְפוּאוֹת לְמֶחֱצָה; בְּסִגְנוֹן חֲגִיגִי וּמְיוּשָּׁן מְעַט.

17. Yadin, *Temple Scroll*, p. 213, commented on the next clause: 'The intent of this sentence... is to stress that not only a tent is in question, but every dwelling'.

18. I am grateful to Professor M.Z. Kaddari for reiterating this point at the Leiden symposium.

intent, to work from objects to souls—the house itself, then its furniture, then its visitors. In this ordering of elements, the Temple Scroll has doubtless been influenced by Num. 19.18:

וְהִזָּה עַל הָאֹהֶל וְעַל כָּל הַכֵּלִים וְעַל הַנְּפָשׁוֹת

> And he is to sprinkle upon the tent and upon all the vessels and upon the souls.

Once again, though, it is perhaps a perceived *linguistic* difficulty in the Bible that has triggered the change. In the Bible, the ordering of the prepositions, אֶל 'to' followed by בְּ 'in', could support an interpretation that has human beings as the referent of כֹּל 'all' in both clauses: everyone who goes *up to* the tent, everyone who goes right *into* the tent.[19] Indeed, this is precisely the understanding not just of modern versions of the Bible, but also of *Targ. Neof.*[20] and Sifre.[21] However, from the wider context, there is a strong possibility that the first (biblical) clause referred to human beings and the second to objects, as

19. In their translations of 11QT, Yadin (*Temple Scroll*, p. 387) has 'everything …everyone' as does M.O. Wise, in '131. The Temple Scroll', in M.O. Wise, M.G. Abegg, Jr, and E.M. Cook (eds.), *The Dead Sea Scrolls: A New Translation* (London: HarperCollins, 1996), pp. 457-92 (479). J. Maier, *The Temple Scroll: An Introduction, Translation, and Commentary* (JSOTSup, 34; Sheffield: JSOT Press, 1985), p. 43, and F. García Martínez, *The Dead Sea Scrolls Translated: The Qumran Texts in English* (trans. W.G.E. Watson; Leiden: Brill, 1994), p. 169, have 'everything…everything', Schiffman, 'Impurity', p. 138, has 'anyone…anyone', and G. Vermes, *The Dead Sea Scrolls in English* (London: Penguin, 4th edn, 1995), p. 168, has 'whatever…whoever'.

20. A. Díez Macho, *Neophyti 1. Targum Palestinense Ms de la Biblioteca Vaticana*, IV: *Numeros* (Madrid: CSIC, 1974), p. 178, and M. McNamara, *The Aramaic Bible*, IV (Edinburgh: T. & T. Clark, 1995), p. 108, understand human beings as subjects in both clauses (although in a note McNamara accepts 'all that is in the tent' as a possibility in the second clause).

21. The fact that the second clause relates to human beings (as well as to objects) provides *Sifre* (§126.2) with a wonderful opportunity to invoke an עַד שֶׁלֹּא יֹאמַר יֵשׁ לִי בַדִּין argument, that is, 'without the Bible needing to have said it, I could have deduced the same thing through logical reasoning'; the second clause is superfluous to the extent that if a person is contaminated merely by coming up to a tent, then it follows they will also be contaminated if they come right inside the tent. The 'superfluous' text is there, though, because its presence avoids the need to impose a penalty merely on the basis of logical argument: see M. Pérez Fernández, *An Introductory Grammar of Rabbinic Hebrew* (trans. by J.F. Elwolde; Leiden: Brill, 1997), p. 210.

the LXX (ὅσα) and Vulgate (*universa vasa*) assume,[22] and it is pre-cisely this line of interpretation that the Qumran author is making more explicit. Note that in ll. 16-17, where in fact human beings are referred to in both a -בְּ clause and an אֶל clause, again in that order, the Qumran author makes doubly sure that readers/listeners are aware of this (1) by introducing the entire sentence with וְהָאדם 'and as for the person' and (2) by using the verb הָיָה 'to be' in the -בְּ clause rather than a verbless construction:

והאדם כול אשר היה בבית וכול אשר בא אל הבית

> And as for a person, whoever had been in the house and whoever had come to the house.[23]

4. *Numbers 19.19b*

Num. 19.19b	<div dir="rtl">וְחִטְּאוֹ בַּיּוֹם הַשְּׁבִיעִי וְכִבֶּס בְּגָדָיו וְרָחַץ בַּמַּיִם וְטָהֵר בָּעָרֶב</div>
11QT 49.19	<div dir="rtl">וביום השביעי</div>
11QT 49.20	<div dir="rtl">יזו שנית וירחצו ויכבסו בגדיהמה וכליהמה ויטהרו לערב</div> <div dir="rtl">מהמת</div>

a. <div dir="rtl" style="display:inline">לערב</div> for <div dir="rtl" style="display:inline">בָּעָרֶב</div>. The rendering '*by* the evening' of Yadin, Vermes, Maier, and Schiffman[24] as against '*in* the evening' of García Martínez,[25] gives an unusual interpretation to the preposition.[26] However, *by* is defensible as structurally closer (in semantic terms) to <div dir="rtl" style="display:inline">וְטָמֵא עַד־הָעָרֶב</div> 'and he will be impure *until* the evening' (and minor variations) at Num. 19.7-8 and 20-21 and, indeed, at v. 19, according to the LXX. On

22. Ibn 'Ezra thinks the reference of the second <div dir="rtl" style="display:inline">כל</div> is specifically garments, see-ing that vessels (<div dir="rtl" style="display:inline">כֵּלִים</div>) are dealt with in the next verse.

23. My interpretation here contrasts with that of Schiffman, 'Impurity', p. 140.

24. Not only in the work cited in note 15 but also in 'Pharisaic and Sadducean *Halakhah* in Light of the Dead Sea Scrolls: The Case of *Ṭevul Yom*', *DSD* 1 (1994), pp. 285-99 (293-94), where Schiffman highlights the stringency of 11QT's purity regulations, in comparison with those of the Mishnah.

25. See García Martínez, *Dead Sea Scrolls*, p. 168; 'a la tarde', in the Spanish original, *Textos de Qumrán* (Madrid: Trotta, 2nd edn, 1993). The English version badly misses the thrust of the Spanish idiom in the words that follow. Read: 'and, in the evening, they will have been [not 'they shall stay'] purified...'. The same con-struction is, however, rendered correctly throughout column 50. At 11QT 49.20, Wise, *Dead Sea Scrolls*, p. 480, has 'When evening comes'.

26. Note that L. Koehler and W. Baumgartner (eds.), *The Hebrew and Aramaic Lexicon of the Old Testament* (trans. M.E.J. Richardson; Leiden: Brill, 1994–), II, p. 508, does not list 'by' under §3 (temporal uses) of <div dir="rtl" style="display:inline">לְ</div>.

the other hand, the Qumran form here *could* simply reflect the preference, found notably in rabbinic literature, for the preposition -לְ to be used with future reference, thus לְעוֹלָם הַבָּא 'in [-לְ] the world to come' but בָּעוֹלָם הַזֶּה 'in [-בְּ] this world',[27] a semantic process that we already see developing in the late books of the Bible: contrast Ezra 3.3, לַבֹּקֶר וְלָעֶרֶב 'in [-לְ] the morning and in [-לְ] the evening', and Eccl. 11.6, בַּבֹּקֶר...לָעֶרֶב 'in [-בְּ] the morning [nearer to now]...in [-לְ] the evening [further from now]'.[28] If so, then the meaning of the preposition in 11QT is almost the same as that in the MT, except that the Qumran version marks the future *aspect* more clearly.[29] The difference between the Qumran text and the MT would, therefore, be linguistic, not exegetical, here.

b. וְחִטְּאוֹ בַּיּוֹם הַשְּׁבִיעִי ובניום השביעי יזו שנית for ('and on the seventh day they are to sprinkle a second time' for 'and he will purify him from sin on the seventh day'). The primary motive for the differences here probably relates to narrative flow rather than to a more strictly linguistic consideration. The phrase יזו 'they are to sprinkle' has already been employed in l. 18,[30] and l. 19 simply continues the sequence, with the use of the temporal adverb, שֵׁנִית 'a second time',[31] clarifying that a new action, rather than a specification of the earlier one, is denoted. But again, it seems clear that linguistic factors have played a part, for the Temple Scroll's version has the dual effect of (1), at the syntactic level, structuring out the *waw*-consecutive of the MT, in line

27. Pointed out to me by Professor Qimron at the Leiden symposium. See also, for example, Qimron in DJD, 10, p. 99, and in 'Le-Millonah shel Megillat ha-Miqdash', *Shnaton* 4 (1979–80), pp. 239-62 (245), where similar usages at 11QT 45.5 and 50.9 are also cited.

28. Qimron (in 'Le-Millonah') points out that this use of -לְ for -בְּ even occurs in early biblical texts (e.g. Gen. 49.27), but argues that it is restricted to poetry and set-phrases. My thanks to Martin Baasten of Leiden for his help in this matter and others.

29. In that case, of course, García Martínez's rendering, 'in the evening', is the most appropriate.

30. J. Milgrom, 'The Laws of Purity of the *Temple Scroll*', in Schiffman (ed.), *Archaeology and History*, pp. 83-99 (89-94), attempts an explanation as to why 11QT introduces bathing and laundering on the first and third days of the purification of corpse-contaminated persons (here and at 50.10-16), when they are not required by Scripture. See as well Schiffman, 'Impurity', p. 147.

31. Note the use of the biblical rather than rabbinic form, שְׁנִיָּה (see Pérez Fernández, *Grammar*, p. 86).

138 *The Scrolls and the Scriptures*

with the practice of the late biblical books, and (2), at the lexical level, removing the problem of the *piel* of the root חטא, in the sense of 'purify from uncleanness', attested only four times according to BDB[32] and not found in Ben Sira or the Scrolls in any meaning.

From a linguistic perspective, the use of plural verbs and suffixes ('*they* wash *their* clothes') from l. 17 onwards for the singular forms of the MT is probably intended to convey a generalized subject: 'one is to wash one's clothes'. Of course, this could have an exegetical aspect, converting instructions for occasional events in the desert into timeless *halakhah*. Distinguishing the linguistic and the exegetical is, again, difficult.

c. וכבסו בגדיהמה וכליהמה for וְכִבֶּס בְּגָדָיו. For the plural subject, see the last paragraph. The addition of כֵּלִים 'vessels' is an exegetical expansion designed to cover anything having contact with the body, but may also, once again, represent 'idiom influence': בֶּגֶד 'garment' and כְּלִי 'vessel' are found as a word-pair four times in the Bible (Num. 31.20; 2 Kgs 7.15; Ezek. 16.39; 23.26), so there is a possibility that the regular collocation of the two nouns has influenced the Qumran author at this point.[33] Note that in ll. 18-19 there is a similar construction, with סַלְמָה 'garment' in place of בֶּגֶד.[34]

32. At *m. Yoma* 5.5, P. Blackman, *Mishnayoth*. II. *Order Moed: Pointed Hebrew Text, English Translation, Introductions, Notes* (New York: Judaica Press, 2nd rev. edn, 1963), p. 296, agrees with H. Danby, *The Mishnah: Translated from the Hebrew with Introduction and Brief Explanatory Notes* (Oxford: Oxford University Press, 1933), p. 168, in rendering 'sprinkle', a semantic extension perhaps first attested in 'late Biblical Hebrew', at 2 Chron. 29.24 ('they are to sprinkle their blood against the altar', where חטא would appear to substitute for זָרַק 'scatter', which is frequently employed in this construction); otherwise, the sense would probably be 'purify from sin, exculpate' (six times in the Bible, according to BDB), rather than 'purify from uncleanness, make clean'. The two uses can only be distinguished by close attention to context; among biblical dictionaries I have consulted, only M.Z. Kaddari's *Thesaurus of the Language of the Bible*, II (ed. S.E. Loewenstamm and J. Blau; Jerusalem: The Bible Concordance Press, 1968), p. 115, makes the distinction as clearly as BDB does.

33. Elsewhere in the Dead Sea Scrolls, there are examples of biblical word pairs being 'lexicalized', or 'fossilized', into construct chains: see T. Muraoka, 'Notae Qumranicae Philologicae (2)', *Abr-Nahrain* 33 (1995), pp. 55-73 (55), and J.F. Elwolde, 'Developments in Hebrew Vocabulary between Bible and Mishnah', in Muraoka and Elwolde (eds.), *Hebrew of the Dead Sea Scrolls*, pp. 17-55 (42).

34. The underlying biblical text here is Exod. 19.10, according to Schiffman,

From an exegetical perspective, however, it could also be argued that the author is continuing to stress his insistence on the purification of כֵּלִים and their contents,[35] mentioned four times previously in this section;[36] in a parallel text at 50.14, where כֵּלִים are only mentioned *once* before in the section (concerning the purification of a woman who miscarries, 11QT 50.10-16), בְּגָדִים occurs on its its own, without כֵּלִים.

The change from *waw*-consecutive plus perfect (וְכִבֵּס) to *waw*-simple plus imperfect (ויכבסו) is a matter both of linguistic simplification in a general way and of the requirements of 11QT's narrative structure.

d. מהמת ...ויטהרו for וְטָהֵר. The expression טהר מהמת 'be cleansed of the dead person' is striking, as in the Bible the verb טהר 'be cleansed' (all *binyanim*) plus the preposition מִן 'of, from' is usually followed by an 'abstract' noun, denoting sin or impurity. This is still true in the Dead Sea Scrolls, although here we also find nouns denoting the *source* of impurity: זוֹב 'discharge' (11QT 45.15), מָקוֹר 'source', of ejaculation (4QOrd[c] [4Q154] 1.1.4), as well as מֵת 'corpse', here.[37] Almost certainly, this is a continuation of a process begun in the later biblical books, where, at Ezek. 36.25 and 2 Chron. 34.3, we find מִן טָהֵר before nouns denoting unorthodox cult places and objects. The process was doubtless aided by Hebrew's tendency to extend an abstract term for a particular impurity to the impure substance itself, or vice-versa, as, notably, with נִדָּה 'impurity, menses' (used after מִן טָהֵר at 4QTohA [4Q274] 1.1.7). In this respect, note the striking usage in another late biblical passage, Neh. 13.30, וְטִהַרְתִּים מִכָּל־נֵכָר 'and I purged them of

'Impurity', p. 148. Schiffman claims that the verb קָדֵשׁ earlier in the same verse has been understood by the author of 11QT in reference to washing (רָחַץ). Note also 11QT 49.16, ובגדים...כול כלים, and 50.16, כול הכלים ובגדים.

35. See especially 11QT 50.16-19 and the expansion of Num. 19.15 in 11QT 49.7-10; see Schiffman, 'Impurity', pp. 140-42, for a detailed analysis.

36. 11QT 49.14-21, actually the second half of a larger unit beginning at 49.5.

37. At 4QJub[d] [4Q219] 2.19 [= Jub. 21.19], [האדם] לְ[הטהר מדם 'to be purified of human blood' has been restored. Note also מִן טָהֵר followed by חַיָּה 'wild beast' in a collection of psalms (1.5) from the Cairo Genizah and dated by the Academy of the Hebrew Language (*Materials for the Dictionary*) to the second century BCE. Perhaps 4QpGen[b] [4Q253] 2.3, טהורים מן הבריאה, which G.J. Brooke, '4Q253: A Preliminary Edition', *JSS* 40 (1995), pp. 227-39 (231), renders 'pure things from creation', might have a similar force: 'purified of (any) creature'. (The מִן at Job 4.17 is agentive and so not relevant to our discussion.)

all foreignness' (i.e. of every foreigner). Perhaps some element of euphemism or avoidance of taboo forms is involved.

e. וְכִבֶּס בְּנָדָיו וְרָחַץ בַּמַּיִם for וירחצו ויכבסו בגדיהמה וכליהמה. The change in phrase order seems to be part of a stylistic grouping, so that the two verbs without stated objects (הִזָּה 'sprinkle', רָחַץ 'wash oneself, bathe') precede the one verb (כִּבֶּס 'launder, wash [clothes]') that does take an object. Stylistic reasons of a different order have led to the same reversal in the Vulgate, *lavabit et se et vestimenta sua*. In our Qumran text, the exegetical trend we noticed earlier, of working from objects to human beings, is now reversed.

However, the choice of word-order here could represent part of a more general stylistic-rhetorical structuring, which can be presented as follows:

> 49.17: wash in water and launder clothes
> 49.18: wash   and launder clothes
> 49.20: wash   and launder clothes and vessels
> 50.13: launder clothes and wash (in water)
> 50.14: launder clothes and wash
> 50.15: launder clothes and wash
> (The brackets at 50.13–14 indicate that what was written originally was
> ורחץ במים הראישון 'and he is to wash with water at first', from which the
> *mem* was struck out, leaving the sequence 'and he is to wash on the first
> day'.)

The striking reversal is perhaps indicative of a conceptual contrast: the impurity of the first passage derives from a person, assumed to be an adult, who has lived their life and then died in a house as normally understood; the second passage relates to impurity of a dead human being who in some way has never lived and whose 'house' is the flesh and blood of another human being.

From a semantic and lexical perspective, the absence of a prepositional phrase after the verb רָחַץ in our text might indicate that for the Dead Sea Scrolls רָחַץ has a predominantly 'middle' sense of 'wash oneself' (with material used semantically redundant), whereas in the MT it is 'active', 'clean' (with patient and/or material requiring specification). On the 18 occasions in the Bible that it follows רָחַץ, כִּבֶּס בְּנָדִים itself is *always* followed by בַּמַּיִם 'with water' (and on five occasions also takes an object). In the Dead Sea Scrolls, however, רָחַץ is followed by a prepositional phrase expressing material in only eight out of 28 occurrences (and by an object five times). The struck-out *mem* we noted at 11QT 50.14 could indicate that, whereas for stylistic reasons, the author felt it was necessary here to specify material, he also thought it could be dispensed with for reasons of lexical economy. Alternatively, of course, the erasure here could reflect a real *lapsus calami*, in which the writer meant to write בַּיּוֹם 'on the day' but, influenced by the prevalence of the expression רָחַץ בְּמַיִם, wrote the latter instead (and then corrected himself). Distinguishing linguistic from literary motives here is extremely difficult.

There is also a more complicated collocational matter here. In the Bible, we find that כִּבֵּס never follows רָחַץ, but on 19 occasions רָחַץ follows כִּבֵּס. In all but one of these instances (Lev. 17.16), כִּבֵּס takes בֶּגֶד as an object. In the Dead Sea Scrolls, of the seven times that the *qal* imperfect of רָחַץ occurs, it is followed on four of those occasions by כִּבֵּס. Of the 20 times that the perfect of רָחַץ occurs, it too is followed by כִּבֵּס four times. However, on eleven (out of 20) occasions רָחַץperfect is preceded by כִּבֵּס (usually—seven times—in the imperfect). Furthermore, whereas כִּבֵּס always takes בֶּגֶד as object on these eleven occasions, רָחַץ takes an object just once. In other words, the most frequent construction of the various elements at Qumran is יְכַבֵּס בְּגָדָיו וְרָחַץ 'he washes his garments and bathes' (not continued by בְּמַיִם).

What we appear to be seeing here is a set-phrase in the making. Even though (1) the elements are still reversible, (2) an object can still occasionally be inserted after רָחַץ when collocated with כִּבֵּס, and (3) כִּבֵּס itself can occasionally take an object other than בֶּגֶד or no object at all, the elements are clearly favouring a particular collocational structure, namely יְכַבֵּס בְּגָדָיו וְרָחַץ. This process of lexicalization, or, more accurately, idiomatization, is aided by the incorporation of a fossilized, archaic, feature, namely the *waw*-consecutive.

In the Dead Sea Scrolls, then, we may be witnessing two semantic processes. First, the biblical idiom was to some extent re-lexicalized (re-analysed), as demonstrated by the manipulation of elements in the collocation, and then re-idiomatized (re-synthesized), as indicated by the emergence of a dominant grammatical patterning of the collocational elements. Secondly, because of its frequent recurrence in this collocation, the meaning of רָחַץ developed so that in the Dead Sea Scrolls it tended to be used in the 'middle' meaning of 'wash oneself', a sense attested in the MT, but much less common there. Thus, the data represent collocation both in the unitary sense of 'set-phrase' but also in the generic sense of 'meaning by collocation'.

THE OLDEST OF ALL THE PSALMS SCROLLS:
THE TEXT AND TRANSLATION OF 4QPs[a]

Peter W. Flint and Andrea E. Alvarez

The purpose of this article is threefold: to briefly introduce the Psalms Scrolls, to examine the main features of 4QPs[a], and to present a facing Hebrew–English text of the manuscript. The English translation, which is a rare feature with respect to the biblical scrolls, is provided in order to make this material accessible to as wide a readership as possible.[1]

1. *The Psalms Scrolls*

Between 1947 and 1956, eleven caves were discovered in the region of Khirbet Qumran, about 1.6 km inland from the western shore of the Dead Sea and some 13 km south of Jericho and 30 km east of Jerusalem.[2] These caves yielded various artifacts, especially pottery, and almost 900 manuscripts written in Hebrew, Aramaic, and Greek.[3]

---

1.   Andrea Alvarez is mainly responsible for the English translation, as well as checking the final form of this article. The critical edition of this unpublished manuscript will appear in P.W. Skehan, E. Ulrich and P.W. Flint, 'The Cave 4 Psalms Scrolls', in E. Ulrich (ed.), *Qumran Cave IV. The Writings* (DJD, 16; Oxford: Clarendon Press, forthcoming).

2.   The distance from Jerusalem is between 25 and 32 kms, depending on the road that is travelled.

3.   Hartmut Stegemann previously indicated that 'about 814 scrolls…came to the museums' from Qumran ('Methods for the Reconstruction of Scrolls from Scattered Fragments', in L.H. Schiffman [ed.], *Archaeology and History in the Dead Sea Scrolls: The New York University Conference in Memory of Yigael Yadin* [JSPSup, 8; JSOT/ASOR Monographs, 2; Sheffield: JSOT Press, 1990], pp. 189-220, esp. 190, 208-209 n. 12). However, Stegemann has since pointed out that some manuscripts were listed together under a single Q number in certain editions, and now estimates the total number as closer to 900 (*Die Essener, Qumran, Johannes*

Although a few are well-preserved, most of the Scrolls are very fragmentary; a fair estimation is 100,000 pieces, with many no bigger than a postage stamp. Over 200 manuscripts are classified as 'biblical scrolls', since they contain material found in the canonical Hebrew Bible,[4] and constitute our earliest witnesses to the text of Scripture. Many of the (more than) 600 'non-biblical' documents are of direct relevance to early Judaism and emerging Christianity, since they anticipate or confirm numerous ideas and teachings found in the New Testament and in the Mishnah. The Qumran manuscripts, which were copied (many composed) between the third century BCE and 68 CE[5] in Palestine itself, have generated intense debate among scholars and wide interest among the general public. It is no exaggeration to state that the Dead Sea Scrolls constitute the most important archaeological find of the century, at least from the perspective of Judaism and Christianity. In addition to Khirbet Qumran, Psalms manuscripts were discovered at Naḥal Ḥever (1951[?]–60),[6] and Masada (1963–65) in the vicinity of the Dead Sea. The full listing of Psalms Scrolls is as follows:

(1) 1Q10. 1QPs^a	(9) 4Q91. 4QPs^j	(17) 4Q236. 4QPs89
(2) 1Q11. 1QPs^b	(10) 4Q92. 4QPs^k	(18) 4Q522. Work with Place Names
(3) 1Q12. 1QPs^c	(11) 4Q93. 4QPs^l	(19) 5Q5. 5QPs
(4) 2Q14. 2QPs	(12) 4Q94. 4QPs^m	(20) pap6Q5. pap6QPs
(5) 3Q2. 3QPs	(13) 4Q95. 4QPs^n	(21) 8Q2. 8QPs
(6) 4Q83. 4QPs^a	(14) 4Q96. 4QPs^o	(22) 11Q5. 11QPs^a
(7) 4Q84. 4QPs^b	(15) 4Q97. 4QPs^p	(23) 11Q6. 11QPs^b
(8) 4Q85. 4QPs^c	(16) 4Q98. 4QPs^q	(24) 11Q7. 11QPs^c

der Täufer und Jesus [Freiburg: Herder, 4th edn, 1994], p. 115). Martin Abegg (personal communication) arrives at a figure of 864 manuscripts for the Qumran material, which confirms Stegemann's higher estimate

4.   According to Stegemann, 'little more than twenty percent of all these Qumran manuscripts represent biblical books *sensu strictu*' ('Reconstruction from Scattered Fragments', p. 190). Eugene Ulrich (chief editor of the Cave 4 biblical scrolls) suggests (personal communication) a number of 'just on 200', while James VanderKam (*The Dead Sea Scrolls Today* [Grand Rapids: Eerdmans; London: SPCK, 1994], pp. 30-31) estimates the number at 202 biblical scrolls, with 19 more found at other sites in the Judaean desert.

5.   The *terminus ad quem* is the apparent destruction of the Qumran settlement by the Romans in the late Spring (April?) or early Summer (June?) of 68 CE.

6.   It was initially thought that some of this material came from Wadi Seiyal (Naḥal Ṣe'elim); however, these manuscripts were almost certainly found at Naḥal Ḥever (Wadi Khabra).

(25) 4Q86. 4QPs^d	(30) 4Q98a. 4QPs^r	(35) 11Q8. 11QPs^d
(26) 4Q87. 4QPs^e	(31) 4Q98b. 4QPs^s	(36) 11Q11. 11QPsAp^a
(27) 4Q88. 4QPs^f	(32) 4Q98c. 4QPs^t	(37) 5/6Hev-Se4 Ps
(28) 4Q89. 4QPs^g	(33) 4Q98d. 4QPs^u	(38) MasPs^a (M1039–160)
(29) 4Q90. 4QPs^h	(34) 4Q98e.(?) 4QPs^v(?)	(39) MasPs^b (M1103–1742)

Analysis of this primary material reveals many interesting features which are relevant for our understanding of the biblical book of Psalms and the issues that arise. Three examples may be given.

a. *Material Preserved*

Of the 150 canonical Psalms, 126 are at least partially extant in the thirty-nine Psalms Scrolls or other relevant manuscripts such as the *Pesharim*. The remaining twenty-four were most likely included, but are now lost due to the fragmentary state of most of the Scrolls. Of Psalms 1–89, nineteen no longer survive (3–4, 20–21, 32, 41, 46, 55, 58, 61, 64–65, 70, 72–75, 80, 87), and of Psalms 90–150 five are not extant (90, 108[?], 110, 111, 117).

b. *'Apocryphal' Pieces*

At least fifteen 'Apocryphal' Psalms or compositions are distributed among five manuscripts (4QPs^f, 4Q522, 11QPs^a, 11QPs^b, 11QPsAp^a). Seven of these were previously familiar to scholars: Psalms 151A, 151B, 154, 155, the Catena of Psalm 118 (possibly forming a single psalm with 136), David's Last Words (= 2 Sam. 23.1-7), and Sir. 51.13-30. The other nine were unknown prior to the discovery of the Dead Sea Scrolls: the Apostrophe to Judah, Apostrophe to Zion, David's Compositions, Eschatological Hymn, Hymn to the Creator, Plea for Deliverance, and three Songs against Demons.

c. *Major Disagreements with the Masoretic Psalter*

Twelve scrolls contain major variations in comparison with the Masoretic Psalter. Differences in the *order* of Psalms alone appear in seven manuscripts from Cave 4 (4QPs^a, 4QPs^b, 4QPs^d, 4QPs^e, 4QPs^k, 4QPs^n, 4QPs^q), while variations in *content* (i.e. the inclusion of compositions not found in the MT) occur in two scrolls from Cave 4 and another from Cave 11 (4QPs^f, 4Q522, and 11QPsAp^a). Differences in both *order* and *content* are present in two scrolls from Cave 11 (11QPs^a and 11QPs^b).

2. *The Main Features of 4QPs^a*

The chief purpose of this article is to present the text and translation of 4QPs^a, and to identify its most noteworthy features. Consequently, it is unnecessary to include details such as the physical description of each fragment, notes on the readings, or listings of all the ortho-graphic variants.

a. *Description and Contents*
4QPs^a (or 4Q83) was written on leather that is moderately thin and light brown in colour with honey tones. Unfortunately, the manuscript is badly damaged; only 23 fragments remain, some of which are quite large (for example frags. 7, 16, 17), while others (for example frags. 2, 10, 21–23) contain only a few letters. The number of letter-spaces (i.e. Hebrew letters plus spaces between words) generally averages 73 per line, although the column preserved on frags. 14 i and 16 has approximately 60. The columns of this scroll are thus exceptionally wide, as can be seen in the transcription and facing English translation in section 3 below. Reconstruction indicates that the complete manuscript must have contained a large amount of text following the last surviving fragment.[7] In view of the small writing and large columns, it seems possible that it originally contained a complete Psalter, but—because little or no text is actually preserved after Psalm 69 in frag. 17—no definite conclusion seems to be possible as to the shape of this Psalter.

On the basis of palaeography (analysis of the handwriting), the manuscript was copied in an 'early semiformal hand', which dates it to approximately the mid-second century BCE. The preserved contents

---

7.   On 8 August 1995, Stegemann examined the manuscript in the Rockefeller Museum, and the following day consulted the plates at the École Biblique in Jerusalem. He first observed that this scroll was rolled with the beginning on the outside, and the end on the inside (centre). Stegemann also detected a pattern of deterioration in specific fragments on the basis of their shapes and large holes or gaps in the leather. Such patterns in frag. 15 and the two large pieces 16 and 17 show that at this point one turn of the scroll measured c.14.8 cm. Using these data, P. Flint calculated that—with each successive turn towards the centre measuring 0.2 cm less than the previous one—the scroll contained another 31 turns after frag. 15, yielding a length of 7.604 m. from frag. 15 to the end of the complete manuscript.

range from Pss. 5.9 to 69.19, although not necessarly always in the order of the received MT:

Contents of 4QPs^a by Fragment and Column

Fragment	Passage	Fragment	Passage
1	5.9–6.4	10	47.2
2	25.8-12	11–12	53.2–54.6
3	25.15	13	56.4
4 i	31.23→33.1-12	14 i–15 (Col. I)	62.13–63.4 [5, reconstructed]
5	34.21–35.2	14 ii–19 i (Col. II)	[63.6–66.15, reconstructed]
6	35.13-20		66.16–67.8
4 ii	35.26–36.9	19 ii–20 (Col. III)	[68.1-36, reconstructed]
7-8	38.2-12		69.1-19
9	38.16-23 + 71.1-14		

b. *Noteworthy Aspects of the Scroll*

This manuscript has several features which render it of interest to the reader and of importance to scholarship.

1. *The oldest of the Psalms Scrolls.* Copied in approximately the mid-second century BCE this manuscript is older than all other Psalms Scrolls with the possible exception of 4QPs89, which has been variously dated between 175 and 125 BCE.

2. *Quantity preserved.* Although a few other Qumran manuscripts (such as 4QPs[b]) are larger in physical terms, some 123 verses are represented in 4QPs[a], making it second only to 11QPs[a] in terms of preserved content. The surviving fragments preserve parts of nineteen Psalms, while three more (64, 65, 68) may be confidently included on the basis of reconstruction (see the Table).

3. *Unique material.* Among all the Psalms Scrolls from Qumran and other Judaean sites, 4QPs[a] alone preserves material from Psalms 34, 38, 47, 54, 56, 62–63, 66–67, and 69, which means that our manuscript contains by far the oldest text that is available for these particular Psalms.

4. *Prose format.* A survey of all the Psalms Scrolls reveals that several are arranged stichometrically,[8] more are written in prose format,[9] and a few contain material in both formats.[10] These data are

---

8.   For example: 1QPs[a], 4QPs[b], MasPs[a].

9.   For instance, 1QPs[b], 2QPs, 4QPs[e], 11QPs[d].

10. For example, 11QPs[a].

significant for our understanding and definition of 'poetry' and 'prose' in the Second Temple period. As is obvious from the transcription and translation, 4QPs[a] presents its material in a prose arrangement.

5. *Superscriptions and* selah. Scholars agree that the superscriptions were not originally part of individual Psalms, but were added later. 4QPs[a] preserves part or all of five superscriptions (to Pss. 36, 54, 63, 67, 69) and two more by reconstruction (to Pss. 6 and 35), and shows that by the mid-second century many superscriptions were already attached to their Psalms. It is also interesting to note that, whatever its precise function was, *selah* is written as part of the running text at Ps. 67.5.

c. *Variant Readings*

Most readers of this article, as well as biblical scholars in general, will be keenly interested in 'variants' (that is, readings found in 4QPs[a] that disagree with other scrolls or the Masoretic Psalter). The third section of this article contains a full listing of variants in two forms: the first beneath the Hebrew transcriptions, and the second beneath the facing translations. The fact that 4QPs[a] contains one of the highest number of variants in proportion to its size suggests that earlier manuscripts such as this tend to preserve earlier forms of the Hebrew text.[11] It would not be profitable to discuss the many variants in this scroll one by one; it is essential that such readings be 'weighed rather than counted', since different types of variants exist, and some are more significant than others. The data may be profitably viewed according to four categories.[12]

1. *Orthographic and morphological variants.* The orthography (spelling) is expanded, with frequent use of *waw* and *yod* as vowel-

---

11. To state this assertion as a fact would involve a general assessment of the earlier biblical manuscripts, which is beyond the scope of the present article.

12. A more comprehensive view is offered by Ulrich ('Pluriformity in the Biblical Text', pp. 23-41 esp. 29; 'Double Literary Editions', pp. 101-16), who divides textual variations between manuscripts into three principal groups: (a) orthographic differences; (b) individual variant readings; and (c) variant literary editions. The last of these categories, a literary edition, is particularly significant and is defined by Ulrich as 'an intentional reworking of an older form of the book for specific purposes or according to identifiable editorial purposes' ('Pluriformity in the Biblical Text', p. 32; cf. 'Double Literary Editions', pp. 103-104. The longer Masoretic and shorter LXX versions of the David and Goliath story [1 Sam. 17–18] are two variant editions of the same passage).

letters. Two morphological features are the regular use of the long pronominal suffix *–hah* (הכ-), and the occurrence of *–tah* (תה-) at Ps. 69.6. This type of variant reading is not even listed in section 3 (below), since it has no effect on meaning and is analagous to the differences in British and American spelling in modern times.

2. *Macro-variants*. As was pointed out in section 1, twelve scrolls contain major disagreements in comparison with the Masoretic Psalter, whether in the order of adjoining psalms or in the presence or absence of entire compositions. A useful term for such large-scale variations is 'macro-variants'.[13] 4QPs[a] preserves two macro-variants: Psalms 31→33 (in frag. 4 i), and Psalms 38→71 (frag. 9 ii).[14] It is interesting to note that, for Psalms 1–89, these are the only preserved deviations from the order to be found in the Masoretic Text (31→33 also occurs in 4QPs[q]). Both deviations coincide with the rare absence of superscriptions in Books I to III of the Masoretic Psalter, which signals a correlation between stabilization and the presence of titles for Psalms 1–89. To explore this interesting issue further would exceed the scope of this essay.[15]

3. *Major variants*. While the dividing line between 'major' and 'minor' variants is not always clear, some readings in a scroll such as 4QPs[a] may be considered more significant than others.[16] Many major variants are to be found, but only two from Psalm 69 in col. II (frags. 19 ii–20) will be mentioned here. The first occurs in line 30, where the reading of 4QPs[a] ('But I struck my soul with fasting', cf. LXX) makes better textual sense than MT ('But I wept with fasting my soul'). The second example appears in l. 34, where the scroll's text ('Answer me according to the goodness of your lovingkindness') seems preferable to that of MT and LXX ('Answer me, O LORD, for your lovingkindness is good'); consider the parallelism in this verse, where the second half reads 'according to the abundance of your compassion turn to me'.

13. Cf. P. Flint, *The Dead Sea Psalms Scrolls and the Book of Psalms* (STDJ, 17; Leiden: Brill, 1997), pp. 153-55.

14. The siglum '→' denotes that one composition actually follows the one listed before it on the leather, as opposed to reconstruction or speculation on the part of scholars.

15. See Flint, *Dead Sea Psalms Scrolls,* Chapter 6 (pp. 135-49), esp. section 5 ('Superscriptions and Different Arrangements of Psalms') pp. 146-48.

16. For the category, cf. Flint, *Dead Sea Psalms Scrolls*, p. 234.

4. *Minor variants.* This category involves less important variants,[17] but it should be noted that these can be significant when evaluated together as a group. With our focus still on Psalm 69, l. 26 of 4QPs^a mentions 'a flowing stream' in v. 3, while MT and LXX prefix the copula ('and a flowing stream'). Another example is in l. 28, where in 69.7 our manuscript reads 'Let not those who wait for you be ashamed'. Here MT and LXX have a slightly longer text, adding 'through me'.

3. *Hebrew Transcription and English Translation*

While most elements of the transcription and facing translation are self-evident, two features require explanation. First, for virtually all fragments the Hebrew transcription is incomplete, with only some text being supplied for purposes of context. In contrast, the English translation is as comprehensive as possible, with missing material being translated from the MT. The effect is twofold: giving the reader access to the scroll's Hebrew text, and enabling its contents to be read as parts of entire Psalms or passages. Secondly, it is often impossible to determine where a specific line actually began and whether a particular verse commenced in that line or the next. While this presents no difficulty in the transcriptions, where only parts of lines are often presented (for example, frags. 2 and 3), the situation with respect to the translations is more complex. In frags. 2 and 3, for example, the verses involved may not have begun on the lines where they now stand. Thus comprehensiveness comes at the price of precision; but in this case the cost seems justified, since the reader can easily determine how accurately each fragment may be placed by consulting the transcription on the facing page.

17. Cf. Flint, *Dead Sea Psalms Scrolls*, p. 232.

Hebrew Transcription

Fragment 1
Psalms 5.9–6.4

[ ]°°°א(10)דֹ֒רככה[לפנֿי הושר שוררי למען בצדקתכה נחני יהוה ⁹ ביראתכה קדשכה [היכל   1

[יֿם]אלֹהֿ֒ הֹֿאשׁימו ¹¹חֿליקון[י לשונם גרונם פתוח קבר הוות קרבם נכונה בפיהו אין כי ⁽¹⁰⁾]   2

[נוֹ]ירֿנֿ לעולם בכה חֹסי כולע וֿישמחו ¹²מרובך כי הדיחמו פשעיהם ברב ממעצותיהם [יפלו   3

[וֹ]תעטרֿנֿ רצֹוֹן בצנה יהוה[כי צדיק תברך אתה ¹³כי שמכה אהבי בך ויעלצו עלימו [ותסך   4

[   ]   *v[a c a t*   ]   5

[סרני]חֿ בחמתכה ואל תוכי[חֹני באפכה אל יהוה ²לדוד מזמור השמינית על בנגינות ⁶·¹למנצח   6

[   ]מאֿ֒ד נֹבֿהֿלה[ונפשי ⁴עצמי נבהלו כי יהוה רפאני אני אמלל כי יהוה חֿני³[7

[   ]°°[   ]   8

VARIANTS
5.9-10   (1)   ᴍ₲; אֿין [כי אין] א°°° 4QPs^s
5.11   (2)   הֹֿאשׁימו [האשׁימם ᴍ₲
5.13   (4)   בצנה [כצנה ᴍ₲

Fragment 2
Psalm 25.8-12

[מֿ]אֿ[ים חטֿ   ] (9)   1

¹¹חֿיֿו[תיו וֿעדֿ]בֿר[   ]   2

דֿר[כֿו בֿדֿ] נֿ[יור   ]   3

Fragment 3
Psalm 25.15

יהוה אל[תמידֿ ¹⁵עֿיני]   ]   1

bottom margin?

English Transcription

Fragment 1
Psalms 5.9–6.4 (English 5.8–6.3)

1   9(8)[O LORD, lead me in your righteousness because of my enemies; make straight] your way [before my face]. *approximately 10 additional letters*

2   [. . . 10(9)For there is no steadfastness in their mouth; their heart is sheer destruction. Their throat is an open sepulchre; with their tongue they f]latter. 11(10) *Punish them*, O Go[d];

3   [let them fall by their own counsels. For the multitude of their transgressions thrust them out, for they have rebelled against you. 12(11)But let all those] who take refuge in you [rejoice]; let them ever shout [for joy,

4   and spread your protection over them. And let those who love your name rejoice in you. 13(12)For you will bless the righteous], O LORD; you will surround [him] with favour (as) *with a shield.*

5   [blank line between Psalms 5 and 6]

6   Ps. 6.1(6.0)[For the Music Director: on stringed instruments, set to 'Sheminith'. A Psalm of David. 2(1)O LORD, do not rebu]ke me [in your anger], and do not ch[asten me] in your wrath.

7   3(2)[Have mercy upon me, O LORD; for I am faint; heal me, O LORD, for my bones are stressed. 4(3)My soul also] is very troubled; [but as for you, LORD— how long?]

8   [   ] . . [   ]

VARIANTS

5.9-10   (1)   About 10 additional letters] For there is no faithfulness MT, LXX
5.11   (2)   Punish them (lit. "him")] Punish them (pl.) MT, LXX
5.13   (4)   (as) with a shield] like a shield MT, LXX

Fragment 2
Psalm 25.8-12

1   8[The LORD is good and upright; therefore he directs si]nners [in the way. 9He leads the afflicted in justice and he teaches the afflicted his way.

2   10All the ways of the LORD are lovingkindness and faithfulness, to those who keep] his [cove]nant and [his] testi[monies. 11For the sake of your name, O LORD, (also) forgive my iniquity, for it is great.

3   12Who is the type of man that fears the LORD? He will dire]ct him in the w[ay (that) he shall choose].

Fragment 3
Psalm 25.15

1   15My eyes are continually [towards the LORD, for he will release my feet from the snare].

bottom margin?

Fragment 4 col. i
Psalms 31.23-25 + 33.1-12

23ואני אמרתי בחפזי נגרזתי מנגד עיניכ]ה	]	3
24אהבו את יהוה כול חסידי]ו אמונ]ים נ]וצר	]	4
יהוה ומשלם על יתר עשה גאוה 25חזקו ויאמץ לבבכם כול המיחלים ליהוה] *vacat*		5
Ps 33.1 רננו צדיקים ביהוה לישרים נאוה תהלה 2הודו ליהוה בכנור בנבל]עשור זמרו לו	]	6
4כי ישר דבר יהוה וכול מעשהו]באמונה 5אהב	3]	7
6בדבר יהוה שמים נעשו וברוח פי]ו כול צבאם	]	8
8ייראו]ו מיהוה כול	7]	9
10יהוה הפיר]עצת גוים	] (9) 10
12אשרי]הגו]י	[ ] (11) 11

VARIANT

33.1 (6)   pr Ps 31 4QPs^q] pr Ps 32 𝔐𝔊[31]; cj. Ps 33 with Ps 32 𝔐^mss (cf 𝔊^mss)

Fragment 5
Psalms 34.21-35.2

[נשב]ר 22תמו]תת	]	1
[ ] *vacat* [	]	2
[Ps 35.1 לדוד ריבה יהוה את יריבי לחם את לחמי 2]החזק מג]ן וצנה		3

Fragment 4 col. i

Psalms 31.23-25 (English 31.22-24) + 33.1-12

3   [. . . for he has wonderfully shown his lovingkindness to me (when I was) in a besieged city. 23(22)But as for me, I said in my trepidation, 'I am cut off from your si]ght'.

4   [Even so you heard the sound of my supplications when I cried to you for help. 24(23)Love the LORD, all] his h[oly ones; the LORD ke]eps the faithf[ul,

5   and pays back in full the one who practices haughtiness. 25(24)Be strong and let your heart take courage, all those who wait for the LORD].

6   Ps 33.1[Give a ringing cry to the LORD, O you righteous ones; praise is fitting for the upright. 2Give thanks to the LORD with a lyre]; make music to him [on] a ten-stringed [harp.

7   3Sing to him a new song; play skillfully on the strings with a shout of joy. 4For the word of the LORD is upright, and all his work] takes place in faithfulness. 5He loves

8   [righteousness and justice; the earth is full of the LORD's lovingkindness. 6By the word of the LORD the heavens were made, and by the breath of] his [mouth] all their host.

9   7[He gathers the waters from the sea like a heap; he puts the deeps into store-houses. 8Let] all [the earth fe]ar the LORD;

10   [let all the inhabitants of the world stand in awe of him. 9For he spoke and it came into being; he commanded and it stood firm. 10The LORD foils] the plans of (the) nations;

11   [he thwarts the schemes of (the) peoples. 11The counsel of the LORD will stand forever, the plans of his heart from generation to generation. 12Blessed] is the nati[on] . . .

VARIANT

33.1 (6)   preceded by Psalm 31 4QPs^q] preceded by Psalm 32 MT, LXX[31]. Psalm 33 is joined directly with 32 in some Masoretic manuscripts (cf. some LXX manuscripts).

Fragment 5

Psalms 34.21–35.2 (English 34.20-35.2)

1   21(20)[He keeps all his bones, not one of them is brok]en. 22(21)[Evil] will sl[ay the wicked; and those who hate the righteous will be held guilty. 23(22)The LORD redeems the soul

2   of his servants, and none of these who seek refuge in him will be held guilty].

3   Ps. 35.1(35.0)[Of David. Eng 35.1Contend, O LORD, with those who contend with me; Do battle with those battling against me]. 2Take hold of a buck[ler and large shield, and rise up in my aid].

Fragment 6
Psalm 35.13-20

[[ואני בחלותם לבושי שק עניתי ב]צׄוׄם נׄ[פשי   (14)   1

[קדר שחותי ¹⁵ובצלעי שמחו נׄאׄסׄפׄוׄ ○[(16)   2

[מעוג חרקו עלי שנים ¹⁷אׄדׄוׄני כמה] תראה   (18)   3

[בקהׄלׄ]]רׄב בעם עצום אׄ[הללכׄ]הׄ] ¹⁹   (20)   4

[   ]ידבר]וׄ וׄאׄל רׄ[גׄע]יׄ ארׄיׄ[ן]   5

VARIANTS

35.15   (2)   נׄאׄסׄפׄוׄ ○[ ] נאספו נאספו 𝔐 𝔊; ונאספו נאספו 𝔐 𝔊; נספו] 4QPs^q

35.16   (3)   חרקו עלי שנים] חָרַק עלי שנימו 𝔐; ἔβρυξαν ἐπ᾽ ἐμὲ τοὺς ὀδόντας αὐτῶν 𝔊

35.20   (5)   וׄאׄל] ועל 𝔐 𝔊 וׄאׄל (cf. n. 20a in *BHK*)

Fragment 4 col. ii
Psalms 35.26–36.9

שמׄחי רעׄתׄ]יׄ   (27)   1

חׄפׄצי שלוׄםׄ] עבדו   2

[לׄ[מׄנׄצֵׄחׄ לעבד יהוהׄ לדויׄדׄ]^{Ps 36.1}   (2,3)   3

אלׄיׄו בעׄיׄניו למצׄוׄא עונו]לשׄנׄא ⁴   (5)   4

מׄשׄכבו יתעצ כולׄ דׄרך לׄ]וׄא טוב   5

⁶יהוה מהשמים חׄסׄדׄ]כה   (7)   6

בה תושיעׄ] יהוה ⁸   (9)   7

וׄנחל]עדניכה תשקם   8

Fragment 6
Psalm 35.13-20

1   ^13[. . . when they were sick, my clothing was sackcloth; I humbled mys]elf [with] fasting; [and my prayer turned back upon my bosom. ^14I went about (in mourning) as for my friend and as for my brother; as one who laments a mother],

2   I bowed down with gloom. ^15But at my stumbling they rejoiced, *they gathered together*; [they gathered together against me; smitten ones whom I did not know slandered me without ceasing. ^16Like godless] "cake-[mockers"]

3   they gnashed (their) *teeth* at me.^17 O LORD, for how long [will you look on? Rescue my life from their ravages, my only life from the lions. ^18I will give you thanks]

4   in the great congregation; in the mighty throng I [will praise y]ou. ^19[Do not let those who are wrongfully my enemies rejoice over me neither let those who hate me without cause wink the eye. ^20For they do not

5   spe]ak [peace], but *towards* tho[se who are qui]et in the land, [they devise words of deceit].

VARIANTS

35.15 (2)   they gathered together] and they gathered together MT, LXX; they have been swept away (but perhaps = MT, error in spelling) 4QPs^q

35.16 (3)   they gnashed (their) teeth at me] gnashing their teeth at me MT; they gnashed their teeth at me LXX

35.20 (5)   but towards] but against MT, LXX

Fragment 4 col. ii
Psalms 35.26–36.9 (English 35.26-28; 36.1-8)

1   ^26Let those who rejoice at [my] distress [be ashamed and confused together. Let those who exalt themselves against me be clothed with shame and dishonor. ^27Let those who delight in my vindication shout for joy and rejoice. And let them say continually, 'The LORD be magnified];

2   *my delight* is in the welfare of [his servant'. ^28And my tongue will declare your righteousness and your praise all the day long.

3   ^36.1(0)For] the Music Director. Of David, the servant of the LORD. ^2(1)[Transgression speaks to the wicked deep in my heart. There is no fear of God before his eyes. ^3(2)For he flatters]

4   himself in his own eyes, concerning the discovery of his iniquity and [hatred of it. ^4(3)The words of his mouth are wickedness and deceit; he has ceased to act prudently and do good. ^5(4)He plans wickedness]

5   upon his bed; *he conspires on every path* (that) is n[ot good; he does not reject evil].

6   ^6(5)[Your] lovingkindness, O LORD, *is from* the heavens, [your faithfulness is to the clouds. ^7(6)Your righteousness is like the mountains of God; your justice is like the great deep]; *by it* you deliver [both man and beast,

7.   [O LORD. ^8(7)How precious is your lovingkindness, O God! The children of men take refuge in the shadow of your wings. ^9(8)They drink of the abundance of your house.]

8   and (from) the river [of your delights you give them drink].

VARIANTS

35.27 (2) החפץ 𝔐 [חֶפְצִי (2°) 𝔊 (οἱ θέλοντες)

36.5 (5) ה\יתיצב 𝔊 (παρέστη πάσῃ ὁδῷ) [יתיצב על (דרך)] 𝔐; = (דרך) כל [ב] יתיע כול (דרך)

36.6 (6) מהשמים [בהשמים *sic!* 𝔐; = בש 𝔐^mss; ἐν τῷ οὐρανῷ 𝔊

36.7 (7) בה [> 𝔐 𝔊

Fragments 7–8
Psalm 38.2-12

[	³וּבֹחֹ[מֹתכֹה תֹ]יֹסרני	] (4) 1
[	⁵מֹ[פּני זעמכה ٥]יֹן שׁ[]לוֹם בעצמי מֹ[פּני חטאתי	] 2 f.8
[	⁶הבאיٰ[שׁוֹ וֹנמקוּ ח]בורו[תֹי מפני אולֹתֹ]י	] (7,8) 3
[	]٥[מֹתם בבשֹׂרֹי ⁹נפֹֹנֹא ٥] [٥]וֹ[	] 4
[	[ממכה לוֹא נסתֹר]	] (10,11) 5
[	מנֹ[גֹד רעי ומיוֹד]עֹי	] (12) 6

VARIANTS

38.6 (3) נמקו 𝔐 [וֹנמקוּ 𝔊
38.9 (4) נפֹֹנֹא[٥] 𝔐; ἐκακώθην 𝔊 [נפוגותי]
38.10 (5) נסתרה (fem.) 𝔐 [נסתֹר (masc.)
38.12 (6) ורעי מנגד נגעי יעמדו 𝔐; καὶ οἱ πλησίον μου ἐξ ἐναντίας μου ἤγγισαν καὶ ἔστησαν 𝔊 [רעי ומיוֹד]עֹי (מנֹ[גֹד) (cf. Ps 88.19; Job 19.13-14)

Fragment 9 col. i
Psalm ?

٥[	] 10
יֹ[	] 11
לֹ[	] 12

VARIANTS

35.27 (2) my delight, LXX (those who desire)] who delights MT
36.5   (5) he conspires on every path] he stations himself on a path MT; he stations himself on every path LXX
36.6   (6) from the heavens] in the heavens MT; = in heaven in some Hebrew manuscripts; LXX (in) the heaven
36.7   (7) by it (your righteousness?)] absent in MT, LXX

Fragments 7–8
Psalm 38.2-12 (English 38.1-11)

1   $^{2(1)}$[O LORD, Do not rebuke me in your wrath and in] your [bur]ning rage, ch[asten me not. $^{3(2)}$For your arrows have sunk into me, and your hand has pressed down on me.

2   $^{4(3)}$There is no soundness in my flesh be]cause of your indignation; [there is no he]alth in my bones be[cause of my sin. $^{5(4)}$For my iniquities have gone over my head; as a burden they weigh

3   too heavy for me]. $^{6(5)}$My w[oun]ds [grow foul] *and* fester because of [my] folly. $^{7(6)}$[I am bent over and greatly bowed down; all the day I go about mourning. $^{8(7)}$For my loins are filled

4   with burning and there is no] health in my body. $^{9(8)}$I am *XXX* [and greatly crushed; I groan because of the agitation of my heart. $^{10(9)}$O LORD, all my desire is known

5   to you and my sighing] *is not hidden* from you. $^{11(10)}$[My heart throbs, my strength fails me and (as for) the light of my eyes,

6   even they are not with me. $^{12(11)}$I have become a plague *bef]ore my companions and [my] acquaintanc[es,* and my kinsmen stand afar off].

VARIANTS

38.6   (3) and fester LXX] fester MT
38.9   (4) XXX meaning unclear] I am benumbed MT; I was afflicted LXX
38.10 (5) (my sighing) is not hidden (masc.)] my sighing is not hidden (fem.) MT
38.12 (6) before my companions and my acquaintances (cf. Ps. 88.19; Job 19.13-14)] (my friends) and companions stand aloof from my plague MT; (my friends) and my neighbours drew near before me and stood still LXX

Fragments 9 col. i
Psalm ?

10 [   ]
11 [   ]*nw*
12 [   ]*d*

Fragment 9 col. ii
Psalms 38.16-23 + 71.1-14

[ ] ○ [ ]	1

אדני אתה תעגני כי אלהׄיׄ [¹⁷אמרתי פן ישמחו לי במוט רגלי עלי]יׄגדילו ¹⁸כי אני לצׄ[לע נכון]   2

ומכאבי נגדי תמיד ¹⁹כה עונתי [אגיד] אדאג מן חׄטׄאותי ²⁰ואיבי חֿנם עֿצמֿו וֿרֿ[בו שנאי]   3

שקרי ²¹משלימי רעֿה תחת טובה ישׂטני תחת דבר טוב ²²אל תעזׄובני אלהׄ[י   [4

מֿ[מֿנׄי²³חישה לי לעזרתי אדני תשועתי ⁷¹·¹בכה יהוה חסיתי אל אֿבושה לעוֿ[לם ²בצדקתכה]   5

הצילני תפלטני הטה אלי אוזנכה הצילני ³היה לי לצור מעון לבי עדמׄ○[[6

כׄי סלעי ומצודתי אתה ⁴אלהי פלטני מיד רשׄע מכׄף מעול וֿחמוׄץ ⁵כׄי אֿ[תה תקוחי אדני]   7

[יׄ]הוה מבטחי מנעורי ⁶עליׄכֿה נסמכתׄי מֿ[בטן]ממעי אמֿי אֿתֿה עוזי בכהֿ[תהלתי תמיד]   8

כמופת הייתי לרבים ואתה מחסי עוז ⁸ימלׄא פׄיׄ תהלתכה כול היום תֿ[פארתכה]   9

⁹אל תשליכני לעת זקנה ככלות כוחׄי אל תעזׄ[בני] ¹⁰כׄי אמרו איׄבֿי לֿ[י ושמרי נפשי נועצו]   10

יׄחדׄו ¹¹לאמור אלהים עזבו רדפו תפֿ[שוהו כי אין מציל ¹²אׄ[ל]הׄיׄ[ם] אל תרחק ממני אלהי]   11

[לעׄ]זרתי חישה ¹³יבושו ויכל[ו] שטני נפשי יעטו חרפה וכלמה מבקשי רעתי ¹⁴ואני תמיד]   12

[אׄי]חֿל והוספתי על כול תֿ[הלתכה ¹⁵פי יספר צדקתכה כול היום תשועתכה כי לוא ידעתי]   13

bottom margin

Fragment 9 col. ii
Psalms 38.16-23 (English 38.15-22) + 71.1-14

1   [   ].[16(15)[For you, O LORD, do I wait]

2   O LORD, you will answer *me for (you are)* my God. 17(16)[I said, May they not rejoice over me] who *boast* [against me when my foot slips]. 18(17)For I am re[ady to fall]

3   and my pain is continually before me. 19(18)*Thus* [I confess] *my iniquities;* I am anxious because of *my sins.* 20(19)But those who are my enemies *without cause* are numerous, and ma[ny are those who hate me]

4   *by deceiving me.* 21(20)*Those who perform* evil instead of good, *plunder me (?) instead of a good thing.* 22(21)Do not forsake me *[my] God; [O LORD,* do not be far

5   fro]m me. 23(22) Make haste *for me* to help me, O LORD, my salvation. Ps. 71.1In you, O LORD, I have taken refuge; let me ne[ver] be ashamed. 2[With your righteousness]

6   *deliver me; rescue me,* incline your ear to me, *deliver me.* 3Be to me a rock of habitation; *my heart/a lion XXX* [   ];

7   for you are my rock and my fortress. 4O my God, rescue me from the hand of the wicked; from the palm of the unjust and *the ruthless.* 5For y[ou, O LORD, are my hope],

8   O LO[RD], my trust from my youth. 6Upon you, I have leaned from [birth]; you are *my protector* from my mother's womb. [My praise is continually of you].

9   7I have become as a wonder to many, but you are my strong refuge. 8My mouth is filled with your praise and with [your glo]ry all the day.

10   9Do not cast me off in the time of old age; do not fors[ake me] when my strength is spent. 10For my enemies have spoken concerning [me; those who lie in wait for my life have conspired]

11   together 11saying, "God has forsaken him; pursue him; *sei[ze* him, for there is no one to deliver (him).12O Go]d, [do not be far from me; O my God],

12   come quickly [to] my a[id]. 13May [the adversaries of my life] be ashamed *and consumed;* [may those who seek my injury be covered with reproach and disgrace. 14But as for me,

13   I] will ho[pe continually], and will pr[aise you] all the more. 15[My mouth will tell of your righteousness, (and) of your salvation all the day long, for I do not know the...].

bottom margin

VARIANTS

38.16	(2)	𝔐 ⅏ אתה תענה אדני] אדני אתה תענני
38.16-17	(2)	𝔐 ⅏ אלהי [17כי] כי אלהי
38.17	(2)	⅏ הגדילר] [י]נדלו
38.19	(3)	𝔐 ⅏ כי] כה
38.19	(3)	𝔐 ⅏ עוני] עונתי
38.19	(3)	𝔐 ⅏ מחטאתי] מן חטאותי
38.20	(3)	𝔐 ⅏ חיים] חנם (cf. 35.19; 69.5; note 20ᵃ in *BHS*)
38.20	(4)	𝔐 ⅏ שקר] שקרי
38.21	(4)	𝔐 ומשלמי] משלמי ⅏ (οἱ ἀνταποδιδόντες)
38.21	(4)	𝔐 ⅏ ישטמוני] שסני[י']
38.21	(4)	𝔐 רדופי] דבר
38.22	(4)	𝔐 ⅏ יהוה אלהי] אלה[י (transposed?)
38.23	(5)	𝔐 ⅏ > [לי
71.1	(5)	pr Ps. 38] pr. Ps 70 𝔐 ⅏[69]
71.2	(6)	𝔐 תצילני] הצילני ⅏ (ῥῦσαί με)
71.2	(6)	𝔐 ותפלטני] תפלמני 𝔐; = ⅏ ופלמני ⅏; > ⅏ᵐˢ(cf. 31.2)
71.2	(6)	𝔐 ⅏ והושיעני 2° (cf. 31.3) הצילני
71.3	(6)	לבית מצודות ⅏ (vid) ;𝔐 = לבוא תמיד (צויתי)] לבי עדמ[ם∘] (cf.. 31.3)
71.4	(7)	𝔐 ⅏ וחומץ] וחמֹץ (cf. Isa. 1.17)
71.6	(8)	𝔐 גוזי] עוזיʼ ⅏ (μου εἶ σκεπαστής)
71.11	(11)	𝔐 ⅏ ותפשוהו] תפ[שוהו
71.13	(12)	𝔐 יכלו] ויכלו ⅏ 𝔐ᵐˢˢ (καὶ ἐκλιπέτωσαν)

Fragment 10
Psalm 47.2

[הריעו לאלה]ים ב̇קול [רנה   ]   1

VARIANTS

38.16	(2)	O LORD, you will answer me] you will answer, O LORD.
38.16-17	(2)	for (you are) my God.] my God. ¹⁷For...MT, LXX
38.17	(2)	they will boast [against me]] they magnify themselves [against me] MT LXX
38.19	(3)	Thus] For MT, LXX
38.19	(3)	my iniquities] my iniquity MT, LXX
38.19	(3)	my sins] my sin MT, LXX
38.20	(3)	without cause] living MT, LXX
38.20	(4)	by deceiving me] wrongfully MT, LXX
38.21	(4)	those who perform LXX (those who repay)] and those who repay MT
38.21	(4)	(they) plunder me (?, meaning unclear)] they oppose me MT, LXX
38.21	(4)	(instead of a good) thing] because I follow (good) MT
38.22	(4)	my God; O LORD (transposed?)] O LORD; my God MT, LXX
38.23	(5)	for me] absent in MT, LXX
71.1	(5)	preceded by Psalm 38] preceded by Psalm 70 MT, LXX [69]
71.2	(6)	Deliver me (imperative) LXX] deliver me (imperfect) MT
71.2	(6)	Rescue me] and rescue me MT; = and deliver me LXX; absent in one manuscript LXX (cf. 31.2)
71.2	(6)	Deliver me 2° (cf. 31.3)] and save me MT, LXX
71.3	(6)	my heart/a lion (XXX, meaning unclear)] to come continually you have commanded MT; a strong fortress LXX (cf. 31.3)
71.4	(7)	and the ruthless (cf. Isa. 1.17)] and the (one who is) ruthless (partic.) MT, LXX
71.6	(8)	my protector LXX] the one who delivers me MT
71.11	(11)	seize him] and seize him MT, LXX
71.13	(12)	and (let them be) consumed MT manuscripts, LXX] (let them be) consumed MT

Fragment 10

Psalm 47.2

1   ²[shout to Go]d with the voice of [joy   ]

Fragments 11–12
Psalms 53.2–54.6

אין [עֹוֹשֵׂ]ה טֹוב ³	]	1
[כול סג יחדֹ]ו נאלחו⁴	]	2
אכל [ל]חם] אלהים לֹוא קרא	] (5)	3 f.12
מי י]תֹן ביום ציון⁷	⁶]	4
vacat [	]	5
הלוא דויד [מסתתר עמנו ³אלהים	⁵⁴·¹] (2)	6
כי] זרים קמו עלי]⁵	] (4, 6)	7
אד]וֹני בֹסֹמ]כי נפשי	]	8

VARIANTS
53.4   (2)   כָלּו 𝔐 [(הכל)] כול]𝔊(πάντες); cf. 14.3
53.5   (3)   לֹוא קרא] לא קראו 𝔊 𝔐
53.7   (4)   ביום ציון] מציון 𝔊 𝔐

Fragment 13
Psalm 56.4

[ויום אירא] אני אליכה אבטח	]	1
vacat / bottom margin?	]	2
]∘[	]	3

VARIANT
56.4   (1)   וֹיום] יום 𝔐 𝔊 (ἡμέρας); cf. ביום v. 10

Fragments 11–12
Psalms 53.2–54.6 (English 53.1-6 + 54.0-4)

1   2(1)[The fool has said in his heart, 'There is no God'. They are corrupt and commit grievous injustice; there is no one] who do[es good. 3(2)[God looks down from heaven on the sons of man to see if there

2   is any who understands who seeks after God]. 4(3)*All* have fallen away; togeth[er they have become morally corrupt; there is no one who does good, not even one.

3   5(4)Has he who works wickedness no knowledge, who eats up my people as he eats] br[ead], *and who does not call* upon God?

4   6(7)[There they were in great dread where there was no dread; for God scattered the bones of the one who encamps against you. You have put (them) to shame, for God has rejected them. 7(6)Oh that he may gr]ant [the deliverance of Israel] *on the day of Zion!* [When God restores the fortunes of his people, let Jacob rejoice, let Israel be glad].

5   [   ] *blank line*

6   Ps. 54.1(0)[To the Music Director: on stringed instruments. A Maskil of David. 2(0)When the Ziphites came and told Saul, 'Is not David] hiding among us?' 3(1)O God, [save me by your name, and vindicate me by your might.

7   4(2)O God, hear my prayer! Listen to the words of my mouth. 5(3)For] strangers have risen up against me, [and ruthless men seek my life; they do not set God before them. 6(4)Behold,

8   God is my helper; the LO]RD is with those who sust[ain my life].

VARIANTS
53.4   (2)   All LXX (= הכול); cf. 14.3] All of them MT
53.5   (3)   and who does not call] and they do not call MT, LXX
53.7   (4)   on the day of Zion] from Zion MT, LXX

Fragment 13
Psalm 56.4 (English 56.3)

1   [   ] 4(3) *And* the day when I am afraid [I will put my trust in you]
2   *blank space or bottom margin?*
3   [   ] [

VARIANT
56.4   (1)   and the day] the day MT, LXX; cf. in the day v. 10

Fragments 14 col. i–14 (Column I)
Psalms 62.13–63.4

כי אתה תשלם לאיש כמעש[הו	] 31	

va[cat] 32

²אלהים אלי אתה אשחרכה צמאה לכה נ[פשי   Ps. 63.1] 33

[³ כמה לכה בשדי באדץ ציה ועי]ף בלי מי[ם   ] 34   f.15

[⁴כי טוב חסדכה מחיים שפ[תי ישבחו]נכה   ] 35

bottom margin

Fragments 14 col. ii, 16–19 col. i (Column II)
Psalms 66.16–67.8

¹⁶לכ]ו ושמעו] ואספרה כול יראי[   ] 28   f.16
¹⁸א[ון אם ר[איתי בלבי לוא ישמע[אלהים](17) 29   f.14

אדני ¹⁹אכן [שמע אלהים הקשיב בקול תפלתי ²⁰ברוך אלהים א[שר לוא [הסיר תפ]לתי וחסד[ו]   30   f.17

[   ]   [   ]   [*vacat*   ] מ א ו ת י   31
[³ למנצח]Ps. 67.1 בנגינת מזמור שיר ²אלהים יחננו ויבר]כנו יאר פניו א[תנו סלה   32   f.18

⁴יודוכה עמים [אלהים יודוכה]   עמים כולם ⁵ישמחו וירננו לא[מ]ים   ] 33   f.19

[ולאמים בארץ תנח]ם סלה ⁶וידוכה [עמים אלהים   ] 34

[⁷ארץ נתנה יבולה יברכנו אלהים אלהי]נו ⁸יברכוכה אלהים]   35

bottom margin

VARIANTS
66.16   (28)   שמעו] ושמעו 𝔐 𝔊
67.6   (34)   יודוך °1] וידוכה[𝔐 𝔊
67.8   (35)   יברכנו] יברכוכה 𝔐 𝔊

Fragments 14 col. i, 15 (Column I)
Psalms 62.13–63.4 (English 62.12–63.3)

31    $^{13(12)}$[And to you, O LORD, belongs lovingkindness. For you will requite a
man according to] his [work.

32   [   ] bl[ank line

33   Ps. 63.1(0)[A Psalm of David, when he was in the Wilderness of Judah.
$^{2(1)}$O God, you are my God, I will seek you earnestly], my [so]ul

34   [thirsts for you; my body longs for you in a dry and wea]ry [land] without
wat[er. $^{3(2)}$Thus I have beheld you in your sanctuary, to look on

35   your power and your glory. $^{4(3)}$Because your lovingkindness is better than
life], my [li]ps will praise [you].

bottom margin

Fragments 14 col. ii, 16–19 col. i (Column II)
Psalms 66.16-20; 67.1-8 (English 67.0-7)

28   [^{16}Com]e *and hear*, all you who fear

29   God, [and I will tell what he has done for me ^{17}I cried to him with my mouth,
and he was exalted on my tongue]. ^{18}If [I] had che[rished wic]kedness [in my
heart], the LORD [would not have heard me].

30   ^{19}Surely [God has listened; he has given heed to the sound of my prayer.
^{20}Blessed be God w]ho has not [turned away] my [pra]yer or [his]
lovingkindness

31   from me.   [*blank   space*]   [   ]   [   ]

32   Ps.67.1(0)To the Music Director: [on stringed instruments. A Psalm, a song.
$^{2(1)}$May God be gracious to us and bless] us and make his face shine u[pon us
(Selah), $^{3(2)}$that your way may be known on the earth,

33   your salvation among all nations. $^{4(3)}$Let the peoples praise you], O God; let [all
the peoples] praise you. $^{5(4)}$[Let the na]tions [be glad and sing for joy,

34   for you will judge the peoples with uprightness and gui]de [the nations upon the
earth] (Selah). $^{6(5)}$*So let [the peoples] praise you,* [O God; let all the peoples

35   praise you. $^{7(6)}$The earth has yielded its produce; God], our [God, has blessed
us]. $^{8(7)}$*May they bless you,* O God; [let all the ends of the earth fear you].

bottom margin

VARIANTS

66.16   (28)   and hear] hear MT, LXX
67.6   (34)   So let the peoples praise you] Let the peoples praise you MT, LXX
67.8   (35)   May they bless you] May (God) bless us MT, LXX

Fragments 19 col. ii–20 (column III)
Psalm 69.1-19

[   ]   *vacat*   [   ]   24

[למנצח]עֵל שושׁנים לדויד 2הושׁ[יעני אלהים כי באו מים ע]ד֗ נפש 3טבעתי בין מצולה אין מ[עמד]   25

[באתי]במעמקי מים שבולת שׁ[טפתני 4יגעתי בקראי נחר גרונ]֗י כליו שני בחיל לאלהי יש[ראל   26

[5ר֗]בֿו֗ משערי ראשי שונאי חנם֗] עצמו מצמיתי איבי שקר אשר]לוֹא גזלתי֗ [אז אשיב 6אלהים]   27

אתה ידעת לוא לויתי ואשמותי֗] ממכה לוא נכחדו 7אל י֗]בושו קויכה א֗[דני יה]וֹה֗] צבאות אל]   28

[י֗]כלמו מבקשׁיכה אלהי ישראל 8כ]י ע]ל[יכה נ]שאתי חרפה כסת]ה֗ כלמה פני 9מי זר היית[י לאחי]   29

נכרי לבני אמי 10כי קנא[ת ביתכה] אכלתני וחרפ֗[ות חורפיכה נ]פֿלו עֵלֿי 11ואך בצום נפשי ות֗[הי]   30

לחרפות לי 12ואתנה לב[ושי]שֹק ותהי להם [למשל 13י]שיחו ישבי שער בי וֹנגֹנ֗ו [שו]תֹי֗   31

שכר 14ואני תפלתי למה] יהו֗]ה עתה רצון אלהֹ[ים ב]רב חסדכה ענני באמת ישעכה ○ [   ]   32

15הצי֗ליֿ֗ ממיט [ו]אֿל אטבעֿ[ה]ויקחני גזלי֗[ן הצ]ילני משנאי מעמקי מים 16אל תשטֹ[פני]   33

שבולת מ֗ים ואל תֹמבעני מצֹולה ואל ֹה֗[אטר על]֗י באֹר פי 17עני כטוב חסדכה כֹ֗[ב רחמיכה]   34

פנה אלי 18אל תסתֹר פניכה מעבדכה כי֗[צר לי מה]ֹרֹה ענני 19קרב על נפשי גאלה ל[מען]   35

bottom margin

Fragments 19 col. ii–20 (Column III)
Psalm 69.1-19 (English 69.0-18)

24   [   ] *blank space*   [   ]

25   Ps. 69.1(0)[To the Music Director]: according to 'Lilies'. Of David. 2(1)Sav[e
      me, O God! For the waters have come u]p to (my) neck. 3(2)I have sunk
      between the abyss, there is no fo[othold;

26   I have come] into deep waters, *a flowing stream* en[gulfs me. 4(3)I am weary
      with crying]; my [throat is parched]. *My teeth are consumed(?) in anguish for
      the God of Isr[ael.*

27   5(4)Ma]ny more than the *hairs* of my head are those who hate me without
      cause; [mighty are those who would annihilate me, who are wrongfully my
      enemies. What] I did not steal, [should I now restore? 6(5)O God],

28   you know *not my crown(?)* and [my] wrongs [are not hidden from you. 7(6)Let
      not] those who wait for you *be ashamed,* O L[ORD G]od [of hosts; let not]

29   [th]ose who seek you *be dishonoured,* O God of Israel. 8(7)Be[cause for]
      your sake [I have] bo[rne reproach], disgrace [has cover]ed my face. 9(8)*O that
      [I] would become a stranger* [to my brothers],

30   *an alien* to my mother's sons. 10(9)For zea[l towards your house] has
      consumed me, and the reproach[es of those who reproach you] have fallen
      upon me. 11(10)*But I struck* my soul with fasting, and it beca[me]

31   a reproach to me. 12(11)When I made sackcloth [my clo]thing, it (i.e. my
      soul) became [a byword] to them. 13(12)[Th]ose who sit at the gate talk against
      me; and the [dru]nkards play songs.

32   14(13)But as for me, *what is my prayer,* [O LO]RD? *Now is acceptable;* O
      Go[d, in] the greatness of your lovingkindness answer me with your saving
      truth. [   ]

33   15(14)Deliver me from the mire, [and] and do not let me sin[k], *nor let the
      one who seizes me conquer me. [Del]iver me* from those who hate me, *from the
      depths of the waters.* 16(15)Let not the stream of waters

34   en[gulf me], or the deep *sink me,* or the pit [close] *my mouth* [on] me.
      17(16)*Answer me according to the goodness of your lovingkindness;* according
      to the abun[dance of your compassion]

35   turn to me. 18(17)*Do not* hide your face from your servant; for [I am in
      distress, make] haste, answer me. 19(18)Draw near unto my soul, redeem it,
      [ransom me] be[cause of my enemies].

bottom margin

VARIANTS

69.3	(25)	בין] (or ?בון) 𝔐 𝔊
69.3	(25)	אין] ואין 𝔐 𝔊
69.3	(26)	שבולת] ושבלת 𝔐 𝔊
69.4	(26)	כליו שני] כלו עיני 𝔐
69.4	(26)	בחיל] מיחל 𝔐; = מיחל (or מיחל BHS) 𝔊
69.4	(26)	לאלהי יש[ראל (cf. v. 7; ישעי Mic. 7.7)] לאלהי 𝔐 𝔊
69.5	(27)	משערות (fem.)] משערי (masc.) 𝔐
69.6	(28)	לוא לויתי] לאולתי 𝔐 𝔊
69.7	(28)	י[בושו] + בי 𝔐 𝔊
69.7	(28–29)	[אל\י]כלמו] אל יכלמו בי 𝔐 𝔊
69.9	(29)	מי זר] מוזר hof. partic. 𝔐 𝔊
69.9	(30)	נכרי] ונכרי 𝔐 𝔊
69.11	(30)	ואך] ואבכה 𝔐; καὶ συνέκαμψα 𝔊
69.12	(31)	ואהי] ותהי (cf. v. 11) 𝔐 𝔊
69.13	(31)	י[שיחו ישבי שער בי] ישיחו בי ישבי שער 𝔐; cf. 𝔊
69.13	(31)	[שו]חתי ונגנו] ונגינות שותי שכר 𝔐; καὶ εἰς ἐμὲ ἔψαλλον οἱ πίνοντες τὸν οἶνον 𝔊
69.14	(32)	תפלתי למה] תפלתי לך 𝔐 𝔊
69.14	(32)	עתה] עת 𝔐 𝔊
69.15	(33)	[ו]אל אטבע[ה]] ואל אטבעה 𝔐 𝔊 (ויקחני גזלי >) וّיקחני גזלי
69.15	(33)	הצ[י]לני 2°] אנצלה 𝔐 𝔊
69.15	(33)	ממעמקי מים] מעמקי מים 𝔐 𝔊 (sg. καὶ ἐκ τοῦ βάθους τῶν ὑδάτων); cf. Ps. 130.1
69.16	(34)	תטבעני] תבלעני 𝔐 𝔊
69.16	(34)	פי] פיה 𝔐 𝔊
69.17	(34)	עני] + יהוה 𝔐 𝔊
69.17	(34)	כטוב חסדכה (cf. *BHS* note 17[a–a])] כי טוב חסדך 𝔐 𝔊
69.18	(35)	ואל 𝔐 𝔊[ms] (μή)] אל 𝔐[mss] 𝔊
69.19	(35)	קרב על] קרבה אל 𝔐

Unidentified Fragments

Fragments 21	Fragments 22	Fragments 23
]∘∘[	]∘[	[תרומ]
[באד]	] יהי[	
]∘[		

VARIANTS

69.3	(25)	between the abyss] in (the) deep mire MT, LXX
69.3	(25)	there is no] and there is no MT, LXX
69.3	(26)	a flowing stream] and a flowing stream MT, LXX
69.4	(26)	My teeth are consumed(?)] My eyes grow dim MT, LXX
69.4	(26)	in anguish] with/from waiting MT, LXX
69.4	(26)	for the God of Israel (cf. v. 7; the God of my salvation Mic. 7.7] for my God MT, LXX
69.5	(27)	hairs (masc.)] hairs (fem.) MT
69.6	(28)	(you know) not my crown(?)] (you know) my folly MT, LXX
69.7	(28)	be ashamed] + through me MT, LXX
69.7	(28–29)	not be dishonoured] + through me MT, LXX
69.9	(29)	O that I would become a stranger] I have become estranged MT, LXX
69.9	(30)	an alien] and an alien MT, LXX
69.11	(30)	But I struck my soul with fasting] But I wept with fasting my soul MT; but I bowed down my soul with fasting LXX
69.12	(31)	(and) it (i.e. my soul) became (cf. v. 11)] and I became MT, LXX
69.13	(31)	Those who sit at the gate talk against me] They talk against me, those who sit at the gate [different word-order] MT, LXX
69.13	(31)	and the [dru]nkards play songs] and the drunkards (make) songs MT; and the drunkards sang against me LXX
69.14	(32)	what is my prayer?] my prayer is to you MT, LXX (in my prayer...)
69.14	(32)	now is acceptable] an acceptable time MT, LXX
69.15	(33)	and do not let me sink, nor let the one who seizes me conquer me] and do not let me sink MT, so that I do not stick (in it) LXX
69.15	(33)	[Del]iver me] Let me be delivered MT, LXX
69.15	(33)	from the depths of the waters] and from the depths of the waters MT (cf. Ps. 130.1); LXX (and from the depth of the waters)
69.16	(34)	sink me] swallow me up MT, LXX
69.16	(34)	my mouth] its mouth MT, LXX
69.17	(34)	Answer me] + O LORD MT, LXX
69.17	(34)	according to the goodness of your lovingkindness (compare *BHS* note 17^a-a^)] for your lovingkindness is good MT, LXX
69.18	(35)	Do not MT (several manuscripts), LXX] and do not MT, LXX (one manuscript)
69.19	(35)	draw near onto] draw near to MT; dative case LXX

Unidentified Fragments

The following fragments are not on plate 43.027 nor on Inv. 1148

	Fragment 21	Fragment 22	Fragment 23
1	] .[	].[	].[ ].....[
2	]...[	]...[	]... [

THE BIBLE'S 'FESTIVAL SCROLLS' AMONG THE DEAD SEA SCROLLS

John Jarick

1. *Introductory Remarks*

To speak of 'the Bible's "Festival Scrolls" among the Dead Sea Scrolls' is something of an anachronism, not only because there is no final and fixed biblical canon evident at Qumran, but also because the grouping together of five small compositions in our Hebrew Bibles—namely the Song of Songs, Ruth, Lamentations, Ecclesiastes and Esther—and the designating of them as 'Festival Scrolls' reflects the Jewish liturgical practice of reading these books in public worship at five important festivals. I do not mean to imply, by using such a modern designation, that the same liturgical practice was already in place at the beginning of the Common Era, but I do see a number of ways in which it may be profitable to examine this particular 'sub-collection' of scrolls in connection with the discoveries at Qumran.

One aspect of possible interest has indeed to do with the festival connection of at least some of these five scrolls. Such a connection is explicit in the book of Esther, which claims to give the historical origins of the festival of Purim. It is also quite marked in the book of Lamentations, where the poetic mourning over the fall of Jerusalem has a decidedly 'ritual' feel about it, such that its eventual adoption into the 9th of Ab commemorations is a natural development. Less natural, though nonetheless understandable, are the associations of the Song of Songs (which makes considerable use of springtime imagery) with the spring festival of Passover, the book of Ruth (which includes scenes set amid the grain harvest) with the harvest festival of Weeks, and Ecclesiastes (which may suggest the approach of wintertime and darkness) with the autumn festival of Tabernacles. Perhaps the Dead Sea discoveries can shed some light on these festival or ritual connections.

Another aspect of possible interest in the consideration of these particular documents is the question of their place in the biblical canon. We know from the Talmud that all but one of them were the subject of some dispute concerning their scriptural credentials. The only one not mentioned in rabbinical discussions as having had its place in the canon questioned is Lamentations. By contrast the Song of Songs, Ecclesiastes and Esther were each the target of severe doubts about their fitness to be numbered among the biblical books, and Ruth also raised certain problems for the rabbis (all four of these scrolls are mentioned in one breath in the rabbinical discussion on the canon in *b. Meg.* 7a). It would seem that different sections of the Jewish community in the early days were not of one mind in embracing or refraining from embracing certain books. Perhaps the Dead Sea discoveries can contribute to a discussion about the perceived canonical credentials of these disputed works.

In looking, then, at these five particular biblical scrolls in the forms in which they appear among the Dead Sea Scrolls, let us consider them in the order of the festivals with which they are nowadays associated.

2. *Song of Songs*

Fragments of four manuscripts of the Song of Songs were found in the Qumran caves.[1] 47 verses are represented (7 of them in more than one manuscript), and together they constitute about two-fifths of the book in the Hebrew Bible.

They might have constituted more than that but for a curious phenomenon: two of the manuscripts from Cave 4 show evidence that the text has been deliberately shortened, by the omission of certain verses. For example, there is a fragment which for a time is faithfully following the description of the female lover's charms in the biblical ch. 4. Her eyes are like doves, her hair is like goats, her teeth are like ewes,

---

1. 4QCant[a] (= 4Q106, comprising Cant. 3.7-11; 4.1-7; 6.11-12; 7.1-7), 4QCant[b] (= 4Q107, comprising Cant. 2.9-17; 3.1-2, 5, 9-10; 4.1-3, 8-11, 14-16; 5.1) and 4QCant[c] (= 4Q108, comprising Cant. 3.7-8) are yet to appear in DJD; for a preliminary edition, see E. Tov, 'Three Manuscripts (Abbreviated Texts?) of Canticles from Cave 4', *JJS* 46 (1995), pp. 88-111, and see further his article, 'Excerpted and Abbreviated Biblical Texts from Qumran', *RevQ* 16 (1995), pp. 581-600. 6QCant (= 6Q6, comprising Cant. 1.1-7) was published by M. Baillet in DJD, 3 (1962), pp. 112-14.

her lips are like a crimson thread, her cheeks are like halves of a pomegranate behind her veil (4.1-3); and so the male lover invites her to come with him to Lebanon (4.8). But wait a moment: what has happened to the verses describing her neck like a tower and her breasts like fawns, and the complete flawlessness of her body (4.4-7)? It is not that the ravages of time have eaten away that part of the Dead Sea manuscript; it is quite intact at that point. And it is not scribal negligence, to be explained by the word at the end of one verse looking very much like the word at the end of the other, such that tired eyes moved back to the wrong place in the text during the copying process. No, the scribe knew what he was doing, and he has indicated it by leaving an open paragraph at the end of v. 3 and a large indentation at the beginning of v. 8, thus clearly marking the place at which some of the text before him has been omitted in the copy he produced. These spaces in the Qumran text also mean that we are most probably looking at a document which has been abbreviated from an earlier manuscript, rather than looking at an earlier version of the Song to which would be added the extra verses appearing in the biblical version.

But what might be the purpose of such a calculated omission? This example could lead us to suppose that a kind of censorship is the issue, namely a drawing of the veil over all parts of the woman's body below her face. But another of the Cave 4 manuscripts does include the verses about her neck and breasts from ch. 4, and all the body parts itemised again in ch. 7, yet leaves out other large segments of text, so if it was censorship at work then it has not been applied consistently to all copies of the Song of Songs.[2] The two manuscripts in fact sometimes include the same sections of text and sometimes omit different sections of text, so it does not look like a matter of

---

2. It may be noted, however, that we do not have an extant example of the description of the male lover's body (Cant. 5.10-16) in the Qumran texts. In discussion at the conference, Philip Alexander speculated whether, if there were 'censorship' of the text, it might have fallen on that passage, in view of Jewish interpretations of the male lover as God. Cf. G. Scholem, *Jewish Gnosticism, Merkabah Mysticism, and Talmudic Tradition* (New York: Jewish Theological Seminary of America, 2nd edn, 1965), pp. 36-42 and 118-26 (the latter section an appendix supplied by S. Lieberman); and M.S. Cohen, *The Shi'ur Qomah: Liturgy and Theurgy in Pre-Kabbalistic Jewish Mysticism* (Lanham, MD: University Press of America, 1983), esp. pp. 19-28, 111-12.

producing and copying one authoritative Qumran edition of the Song. But the fact that this particular composition has been shortened in more than one manuscript is a curious matter. It shows at least that the Song of Songs was the focus of some attention, and this was presumably in the context either of private study or communal worship.

If the Song was limited to personal reading or devotion, then it must have been felt that a kind of *'Reader's Digest* Song of Songs' would be more appropriate or useful in some way than the full article. Perhaps it was thought that the poetry in the Song was rather too repetitious as it stood, and that the contemplative soul could get all the nourishment he needed from an abbreviated version. Yet the scroll is hardly a long one even when it is set out as an unexpurgated document, and it is hard to imagine that the full 117 verses of appealing poetry would have struck its Qumran readers as being overly tedious.

The other possibility, then, is that we are dealing with excerpted texts for liturgical purposes. This is a phenomenon seen elsewhere among the Dead Sea Scrolls, or at least one which may be supposed in the cases of a number of Cave 4 manuscripts, containing sections of the Psalms or parts of Exodus or Deuteronomy. Thus the existence of two abbreviated texts of the Song of Songs may well imply that the Song was used in worship at Qumran. This is of course a long way from demonstrating any association with the Passover festival at that time, but it is a significant finding nonetheless.

3. *Ruth*

Fragments of four manuscripts of Ruth were found among the Dead Sea Scrolls.[3] 42 verses are represented (7 of them in more than one manuscript), and together they constitute about half of the book in the Hebrew Bible.

This means that we have a greater proportion of the book of Ruth available for scrutiny than for any of the other 'Festival Scrolls', but I propose to make fewer comments about this scroll than any of the others, merely noting that it is there, and that that presence is in itself

3. 2QRuth[a] (= 2Q16, comprising Ruth 2.13–3.8; 4.3-4) and 2QRuth[b] (= 2Q17, comprising Ruth 3.13-18) were published by M. Baillet in DJD, 3 (1962), pp. 71-75. 4QRuth[a] (= 4Q104, comprising Ruth 1.1-12) and 4QRuth[b] (= 4Q105, comprising Ruth 1.1-6, 12-15) are yet to appear in print.

of some significance. The document does after all run counter to a clear commandment in the Torah—namely, that no descendant of a Moabite shall be admitted to the assembly of the Lord, not even after ten generations (Deut. 23.3)—in that none less than David himself (after a mere three generations) and, by implication, also the Messiah, son of David (after a destined number of generations), are unmasked as being descended from Moab. Yet so far as we can tell prior to the publication of the Cave 4 fragments, on which the crucial verses labelling the heroine as a Moabite are preserved, the Qumran community did not suppress this embarassing information. It may be that they subscribed to the mishnaic double-standard, under which it is said that an Israelite woman may not marry a Moabite man but that an Israelite man may marry a Moabite woman (*Yeb.* 8.3), but such a solution can hardly stand alongside Ezra's and Nehemiah's absolute insistence that the descendants of marriages between Israelite men and Moabite women be removed from Israel (Ezra 9–10; Neh. 13.1-3), nor alongside the book of *Jubilees'* strict law prohibiting marriage with foreigners (*Jub.* 30.7-17). Nevertheless, the book of Ruth stands among the Dead Sea Scrolls.

4. *Lamentations*

Fragments of four manuscripts of Lamentations were found in the caves.[4] 60 verses are represented (5 of them in more than one manuscript), and together they constitute about two-fifths of the book in the Hebrew Bible.

Now four-fifths of the book of Lamentations happens to be made up of a set of four alphabetic acrostic poems, but in our Bibles there is a

---

4. 3QLam (= 3Q3, comprising Lam. 1.10-12; 3.53-62) was published by M. Baillet in DJD, 3 (1962), p. 95, while 5QLam[a] (= 5Q6, comprising Lam. 4.5-8, 11-16, 19-22; 5.1-13, 16-17) and 5QLam[b] (= 5Q7, comprising Lam. 4.17-20) were published by J.T. Milik in the same volume, pp. 174-78. 4QLam (= 4Q111, sometimes labelled '4QLam[a]', comprising Lam. 1.1-18; 2.5) is yet to appear in DJD; for a preliminary edition, see F.M. Cross, 'Studies in the Structure of Hebrew Verse: The Prosody of Lamentations 1.1-22', in C.L. Meyers and M. O'Connor (eds.), *The Word of the Lord Shall Go Forth: Essays in Honor of David Noel Freedman in Celebration of his 60th Birthday* (Winona Lake, IN: Eisenbrauns, 1983), pp. 129-55. See also D.R. Hillers's excursus, 'Study of the Text of Lamentations and 4QLam[a]', in his *Lamentations* (AB, 7A; New York: Doubleday, 2nd edn, 1992), pp. 41-48.

slight variation in the acrostic pattern: the first poem follows the order of the Hebrew alphabet as we know it, but in the other three poems the letter *pe* comes before the letter *ayin*. However, in the Qumran manuscript the first poem has the same order as the other three—that is, the verse beginning with *pe* always precedes the verse beginning with *ayin*. This consistency of order in the Qumran manuscript suggests that at least in some circles the Hebrew alphabet had a slightly different sequence to the one with which we are familiar. After all, part of the point of writing alphabetic acrostic poetry is presumably to facilitate the accurate memorization of that poetry. The scheme appears to have faltered somewhat in the case of the Masoretic text on account of the influence, during the text's transmission, of the more standard alphabetic sequence, though no attempt was made systematically to impose that sequence throughout the document.

In addition to the fragments of the biblical book of Lamentations that have been found among the Dead Sea Scrolls, it should be noted that fragments of two other poetic compositions of a similar style have also been discovered.[5] One of these, with the resounding cry '[How] solitary [lies] the city!' and the depiction of Jerusalem as a royal lady who now bitterly weeps at her fall, so characteristic of the first poem in the biblical book, is particularly worthy of the label 'Lamentations Apocryphon', while the other, with the urgent plea 'Give not our inheritance to strangers!' and the implied hope of restoration, has some affinity with the last poem in the canonical Lamentations. The most straightforward explanation for the existence of these compositions is that they have been inspired by the biblical book, although the possibility that both they and the canonical Lamentations have each drawn independently from a common ancestor cannot be ruled out. The manuscripts of these 'apocryphal Lamentations' have been dated to the last decades before the Common Era, and it is reasonable to surmise that the people of the Scrolls had liturgical use for all these compositions in some kind of commemoration of Jerusalem's destruction by the Babylonians, a commemoration which might also have been tinged with recognition of the Qumran community's own sectarian exile from the erstwhile royal city. Though Jerusalem was again at

---

5. 4QapLam (= 4Q179) was published by J.M. Allegro and A.A. Anderson in DJD, 5 (1968), pp. 75-77, while 4Q501 (sometimes labelled '4QLam[b]', though it is no more a copy of Lamentations than is 4Q179) was published by M. Baillet in DJD, 7 (1982), pp. 79-80.

least notionally in Jewish hands and a rebuilt temple was fully functioning towards the end of the pre-Common Era, from a Qumran perspective the city lay in the hands of apostates and wicked priests, administering an impure and illegitimate system, destined to be replaced in the fullness of time by a purified Jerusalem with a new and perfect Temple to which the exiled community could return.

Of all our 'Festival Scrolls', then, Lamentations seems to be the clearest contender for having had a liturgical use at Qumran. Whether it had a specifically 'festival' use, in the context of an annual commemoration of the 'fall' of Jerusalem, must remain speculative. Such a commemoration is obviously not one of the festivals handed down purportedly from time immemorial in 'the books of Moses', even if one includes *Jubilees* or the Temple Scroll, and so the various Dead Sea texts that are at pains to place the ancient festival cycle into the Qumran calendrical scheme do not list this decidedly post-Mosaic festival. If the people of the Scrolls were consistent in avoiding any festival not believed to have been instituted by Moses, then clearly they could not have marked a 'festival' of Jerusalem's fall, although some lesser form of acknowledgment of the occasion may not be out of the question. In any event, it is clear that Lamentations and cognate poetry on the fall of Jerusalem was used by the Qumran community, and quite plausibly in a communal way.

One further phenomenon with regard to Lamentations among the Dead Sea Scrolls should yet be mentioned, namely that in the as-yet-unpublished fragments from Cave 4 there is a manuscript in which Lamentations is apparently cited.[6] It will be interesting to see, when this document is published, whether it can provide a clear answer to the question, 'Was Lamentations regarded as authoritative at Qumran?', and perhaps some indication of how the book may have been interpreted. No doubt, in view of the extremely fragmentary nature of what remains to be published from Cave 4, the contribution of this particular fragmentary manuscript will be modest, but merely by citing the biblical book it is already more than we have for our other 'Festival Scrolls'.

---

6. 4Q241 is mentioned as 'fragments citing Lamentations' by E. Tov, 'The Unpublished Texts from the Judean Desert', in G.J. Brooke (ed.), *New Qumran Texts and Studies* (STDJ, 15; Leiden: Brill, 1994), pp. 81-88 (p. 87).

5. *Ecclesiastes*

Fragments of just two manuscripts of Ecclesiastes were found at Qumran.[7] 30 verses are represented, constituting about one-seventh of the book in the Hebrew Bible. As well as being the smallest find mentioned so far, this book also differs from the other scrolls under investigation in having been uncovered only in Cave 4, which might indicate that it was not as popular as, say, Lamentations.[8]

Nor was it treated in the excerpt style that we have seen for the Song of Songs. So far as we can tell, the manuscripts of Ecclesiastes were copied out verse after verse in the arrangement familiar to us from the Bible. And this may represent something of a blow to certain theories concerning the transmission history of this document, which proposed a number of stages in the copying of the scroll.[9] Typically, the theory ran along the lines that at first there had been only the unremittingly pessimistic observations of an original philosopher, but that in the course of copying the manuscript for later generations various additions were made to modify and even reverse the tone of the original work, first by a more optimistic soul who juxtaposed the opposite point of view to that held by the pristine Koheleth, then also by a wisdom teacher who contributed a number of more traditional

---

7. 4QQoh[a] (= 4Q109, comprising Qoh. 5.13-17; 6.1, 3-8, 12; 7.1-10, 19-20) and 4QQoh[b] (= 4Q110, comprising Qoh. 1.10-14) are yet to appear in DJD; for a preliminary edition of the former, see J. Muilenburg, 'A Qoheleth Scroll from Qumran', *BASOR* 135 (1954), pp. 20-28.

8. It may be worthy of note that none of the 'Festival Scrolls' was found in Caves 1 or 11, which presumably indicates that none of them was used in the allegedly more respectful way in which those scrolls (e.g., Genesis Apocryphon and Isaiah in Cave 1, Deuteronomy and Ezekiel in Cave 11) were used—though of course this observation holds true for most of the Hebrew Bible, since very few of the canonical books appear in those two caves. See the remarks concerning those caves' collections in George Brooke's '"The Canon within the Canon" at Qumran and in the New Testament', in this conference volume.

9. For the most extreme version of this theory, that of D.C. Siegfried in his *Prediger und Hoheslied* (HKAT, II [3/2]; Göttingen: Vandenhoeck & Ruprecht, 1898), English readers may consult G.A. Barton, *A Critical and Exegetical Commentary on the Book of Ecclesiastes* (ICC; Edinburgh: T. & T. Clark, 1908), p. 28. Also see Barton, pp. 25-26, for the dislocation theory mentioned below, as put forward by G. Bickell in his *Der Prediger über den Wert des Daseins* (Innsbruck, 1884).

wisdom sayings to the expanding scroll, and by a pious individual who redeemed the work still further through the judicious insertion of a number of orthodox sentiments.

Now it happens that Ecclesiastes, as manifested at Qumran, appears to be just as seamless a composition as it is in the Masoretic text. In the provisionally published fragments we can see a verse assigned under the theory to the wisdom glossator ('Wisdom gives strength to the wise more than ten rulers that are in a city', 7.19) sitting comfortably alongside a verse allegedly added by the pious glossator ('Surely there is no one on earth so righteous as to do good without ever sinning', 7.20), exactly as they do in the Bible. And it seems that in an as-yet-unpublished manuscript we will be able to observe the opening poem about generations coming and going, the sun rising and falling, all the streams running to the sea and so forth, sitting there in its accustomed position before the autobiographical narrative gets under way with the words 'I, Koheleth, was king over Israel in Jerusalem' (1.12). If we accept the dating of these Qumran Ecclesiastes manuscripts on paleographical grounds as about the middle of the second century BCE, then we would presumably need to push back the supposed lengthy process of accretions to considerably earlier generations. Certainly the proposal of the Herodian era as the time in which the process was completed is now untenable. But better to put aside such a theory altogether, as indeed most commentators have done in any case through a reappraisal of what an ancient Near Eastern wisdom composition can look like and a general suspicion about the postulating of complicated textual prehistories.

So too we should consign to the bin the inventive theory which held that the seeming twists and turns in Koheleth's train of thought were due to a logically-organized composition inscribed on several sheets having become broken up and disordered, and when a scribe endeavoured to put the work back together again he made a rather poor job of it and left succeeding generations with the allegedly topsy-turvey document that has come down to us. If such a scenario occurred, again it must now be placed well before the middle of the second century BCE, in a time when the use of a codex, upon which this theory would seem to depend (in view of the small amounts of text assigned to each sheet), is scarcely likely. For better or worse, Ecclesiastes now appears a more unified composition than some of our predecessors thought. That it was acceptable to the people at Qumran may owe much to the more orthodox side of the work, but the more heterodox side was there too, and there are no visible seams between them.

6. *Esther*

No fragments of Esther have emerged among the Dead Sea Scrolls. Indeed, Esther can lay claim to being the only book of the Hebrew Bible not preserved at Qumran. It is true that no fragment of Nehemiah has turned up either, but if one assumes that Ezra and Nehemiah were written on one scroll as a single work—as they appear in Hebrew Bibles—then the fragments of Ezra can be taken as pointing also to the presence of Nehemiah, which then leaves the book of Esther in a unique position.

Now it might be argued that this absence of Esther is merely accidental. Perhaps the book was in fact among the Dead Sea Scrolls, but by chance no fragment of it has survived the ravages of time. After all, it is not a lengthy work, and so one may imagine that such copies of it as existed in the caves disintegrated beyond recognition over the centuries. However, our survey has shown that fragments from several copies of each of the other 'Festival Scrolls' have survived, and it should be borne in mind that the Song of Songs, Ruth and Lamentations are all considerably shorter scrolls than is the scroll of Esther, while Ecclesiastes is only moderately longer. So the lack of a single scrap of Esther does seem to be significant.

It is not that nothing like Esther has appeared at Qumran. We do have several fragments of another ripping yarn set in the Persian court, this one revolving around a hero called Bagasraw.[10] Together with the various apocryphal stories of Daniel and other heroes, the existence of such manuscripts demonstrates that the Qumran community was happy to preserve at least some of the popular literature of the day, and even to take inspiration and encouragement from it. But it seems they were not happy with Esther.

What is there to be unhappy about in this book? After all, the

10. 4Q550 was published by J.T. Milik in 'Les Modèles Araméens du Livre d'Esther dans la Grotte 4 de Qumrân', *RevQ* 15 (1992), pp. 321-99, and is sometimes labelled '4QProto-Esther' or the like as a result of Milik's suggestion, but see the discussions in S. Talmon, 'Was the Book of Esther Known at Qumran?', *DSD* 2 (1995), pp. 249-67; and S.W. Crawford, 'Has Esther Been Found at Qumran? 4QProto-Esther and the Esther Corpus', *RevQ* 17 (1996), pp. 307-25.

wicked opponents of the Jewish people are thwarted, sorrow turns into gladness, and there is widespread rejoicing and feasting. Surely any Jewish movement that regarded itself as the true community of God, threatened for the moment by the wider impure world but destined to become triumphant over all opponents, could find in the story of Esther a tale which provided encouragement and assurance. It is true that in the story victory over the infidel is only achieved after the Jewish heroine has married outside the community of faith, and such a union of a daughter of Israel with a son of perdition could well be offensive to a fundamentalist community like that of Qumran. But in the story of Ruth several sons of Israel marry Moabite women, apparently unmindful of the deuteronomistic law mentioned earlier, and yet the scroll of Ruth was not barred from Qumran. Of course the character of Ruth calls upon the name of the Lord at the beginning of her story and at the end of that tale the divine name is blessed again (Ruth 1.17; 4.14), whereas nobody in the Esther story gives any thought to God at all. Although the Greek version of Esther remedies such an embarassing oversight on the part of the earlier storytellers by having the queen and her guardian pray to the God of Israel and having her husband the king similarly recognize the divine dimension to the inter-ethnic battle, the Hebrew text as we know it is entirely secular, which could have prevented it from becoming a text worthy of study in such a thoroughly religious community as Qumran. But there is no mention of God to be found in the Song of Songs, either, unless we are to find it poetically hidden towards the end in the expression *šalhebetyâ* ('a raging flame' or 'the flame of Yah'?) in 8.6, and yet the Song of Songs was deemed to be worthy of study at Qumran. Perhaps a community which had renounced the world might object to the fact that Esther does not hold back from putting on the royal robes and entering into the worldly excesses of palace life, thus presenting herself as a most unsuitable role-model. But there is no holding back from worldly excesses on the part of the experimenting monarch in the book of Ecclesiastes, and yet Ecclesiastes was not suppressed by the sectarians on that account.

The suspicion must therefore be that Esther was not in favour at Qumran on account of its role in putting forward the festival of Purim. The fact that it presents Purim unambiguously as a 'new' festival, in the sense that it was not enshrined in the laws of Moses but arose at a later time in Jewish tradition, might not necessarily be a decisive mark against it, since there is some evidence that the Qumran community observed certain minor festivals in addition to the major ones listed in 'the books of Moses',[11] and we have already noted the possibility that the scroll of Lamentations and its apocryphal variations may have been used in a commemoration of the fall of Jerusalem, which would similarly be an innovation beyond the festivals decreed of old. But the real difficulty in a Qumran context for Purim and the scroll which champions it comes near the end of the scroll, where Mordecai is recorded as sending letters to Jews everywhere, 'enjoining them that they should keep the fourteenth day of the month Adar and also the fifteenth day of the same month, year by year, as the days on which the Jews gained relief from their enemies, and as the month that had been turned for them from sorrow into gladness and from mourning into a holiday; that they should make them days of feasting and gladness, days for sending gifts of food to one another and presents to the poor' (Est. 9.20-22). The problem is that the 14th of Adar is a sabbath day in the fixed 364-day calendar at Qumran, a calendar which is at pains to ensure that no particular holy day (except of course in the case of week-long festivals) and no dated event in scriptural tradition falls on any of the 52 sabbaths. Given that the scroll of Esther recounts how the Jews of Susa worked energetically at killing three hundred of their enemies on precisely one of those sabbath days, and moreover calls upon all Jews to work at feasting and gift-giving on that sabbath every year from then on, the lack of copies of such a scroll in the Dead Sea caves becomes understandable.

It may be said that the lack of this particular scroll among the discoveries in the Judaean desert is more than compensated for among other Jewish communities for whom the Qumran calendar is of no consequence. In the Cairo Genizah there were more fragments of Esther than of any other book outside the Pentateuch, while in the Talmud and in mediaeval and modern Judaism the scroll of Esther is '*the* Scroll'. This makes its absence from Qumran all the more noteworthy.

11. See J.T. Milik, 'Le travail d'édition des manuscrits du désert de Juda', in *Volume du Congrès: Strasbourg 1956* (VTSup, 4; Leiden: Brill, 1957), pp. 25-26. This reference, and the following argument on the calendar, stem from R. Beckwith, *The Old Testament Canon of the New Testament Church and its Background in Early Judaism* (London: SPCK, 1985), p. 292.

7. *Concluding Remarks*

The situation regarding Esther is the clearest result in this short survey: while its absence from the Dead Sea caves is just possibly accidental, it is more likely that the scroll and its festival were not honoured among the Qumran community. On the other hand the indications are strong that both Lamentations and the Song of Songs found honoured places in the liturgical life of the community, perhaps even a festival use in the case of Lamentations. And of course Ruth and Ecclesiastes, too, received their own places of honour in the collection of scrolls, despite the difficulties raised by some of their words.

Apart from Esther, each of the Bible's 'Festival Scrolls' has been found to exist in either three copies (in the case of Ecclesiastes) or four copies (in the cases of the Song of Songs, Ruth, and Lamentations) among the Dead Sea discoveries. While these numbers fall well short of the 36 copies of Psalms, 29 copies of Deuteronomy and 21 copies of Isaiah, they nevertheless outdo the two copies of Joshua and Proverbs and the one copy of Ezra–Nehemiah and Chronicles, and they are on a similar standing in this respect to the three copies of Judges and Kings and the four copies of Samuel and Job. These small scrolls must be acknowledged, then, as by no means least among the writings of Judah.

DAVID IN THE DEAD SEA SCROLLS

Craig A. Evans

The heroic and paradigmatic status of David is amply attested in the Scriptures of Israel and the early Church. He is the founder of Israel's greatest royal dynasty,[1] is favored with a covenant with God (2 Samuel 7; Psalm 89),[2] and becomes the inspiration for a good deal of the messianic hopes that both Jews and Christians would later entertain.[3] Ancient Israel's king takes his place alongside venerated

1. See R.A. Carlson, *David, the Chosen King* (Stockholm: Almqvist, 1964); A.M. Cooper, 'The Life and Times of David according to the Book of Psalms', in R.E. Friedman (ed.), *The Poet and the Historian: Essays in Literary and Historical Biblical Criticism* (HSS, 26; Chico: Scholars Press, 1983), pp. 117-31; S.J. De Vries, 'Moses and David as Cult Founders in Chronicles', *JBL* 107 (1988), pp. 619-39; D.M. Gunn, *The Story of King David* (JSOTSup, 6; Sheffield: JSOT Press, 1978); T. Ishida, *The Royal Dynasties in Ancient Israel* (BZAW, 142; Berlin: de Gruyter, 1977); L. Rost, *The Succession to the Throne of David* (Historic Texts and Interpreters in Biblical Scholarship, 1; Sheffield: JSOT Press, 1982).

2. See J. Coppens, *Le messianisme royal: Ses origines, son développement, son accomplissement* (LD, 54; Paris: Cerf, 1968); O. Eissfeldt, 'The Promises of Grace to David in Isaiah 55.1-5', in B.W. Anderson and W. Harrelson (eds.), *Israel's Prophetic Heritage* (London: Harper & Brothers, 1962), pp. 196-207; Ishida, *The Royal Dynasties in Ancient Israel*, pp. 81-117; E.T. Mullen, 'The Divine Witness and the Davidic Royal Grant: Ps 89.37-38', *JBL* 102 (1983), pp. 207-18; H. Ringgren, *The Messiah in the Old Testament* (SBT, 18; London: SCM Press, 1956); N. Sarna, 'Psalm 89: A Study in Inner Biblical Exegesis', in A. Altmann (ed.), *Biblical and Other Studies* (Brandeis University Studies and Texts, 1; Cambrige, MA: Harvard University Press, 1963), pp. 29-46; P.E. Satterthwaite, 'David in the Books of Samuel: A Messianic Hope?', in P.E. Satterthwaite *et al.* (eds.), *The Lord's Anointed: Interpretation of Old Testament Messianic Texts* (Exeter: Paternoster Press; Grand Rapids: Baker, 1995), pp. 41-65; T. Veijola, *Die ewige Dynastie* (Annale Academiae Scientiarum Fennicae, 193; Helsinki: Academia Scientiarum Fennica, 1975).

3. See K. Berger, 'Die königlichen Messiastraditionen des Neuen Testament', *NTS* 20 (1973–74), pp. 1-44; G.L. Davenport, 'The "Anointed" of the Lord in

worthies like Abraham, the great patriarch from whom the people of Israel sprang, and Moses, the great lawgiver.

Now that all of the Dead Sea Scrolls are available,[4] scholars may

Psalms of Solomon 17', in G.W.E. Nickelsburg and J.J. Collins (eds.), *Ideal Figures in Ancient Judaism* (SBLSCS, 12; Chico: Scholars Press, 1980), pp. 67-92; D.C. Dulling, 'The Promises to David and their Entrance into Christianity—Nailing down a Hypothesis', *NTS* 20 (1973), pp. 55-77; A. Hultgård, 'The Ideal "Levite", the Davidic Messiah, and the Savior Priest in the Testament of the Twelve Patriarchs', in Nickelsburg and Collins (eds.), *Ideal Figures in Ancient Judaism*, pp. 93-110; S.E. Johnson, 'The Davidic-Royal Motif in the Gospels', *JBL* 87 (1968), pp. 136-50; E. Lohse, 'Der König aus Davids Geschlect—Bemerkungen zur messianischen Erwartung der Synagoge', in O. Betz *et al.* (eds.), *Abraham unser Vater: Juden und Christen im Gespräch über die Bibel* (Festschrift O. Michel; AGJU, 5; Leiden: Brill, 1963), pp. 337-45; G. Kuhn, 'Röm 1,3 f und der davidische Messias als Gottessohn in den Qumrantexten', in C. Burchard and G. Theissen (eds.), *Lese-Zeichen für Annelies Findreiß zum 65. Geburtstag am 15. März 1984* (Heidelberg: Carl Winter, 1984), pp. 103-13; J.L. McKenzie, 'Royal Messianism', *CBQ* 19 (1957), pp. 25-52; T.N.D. Mettinger, *King and Messiah* (ConBOT, 8; Lund: Gleerup, 1976); S. Mowinckel, *He that Cometh* (Oxford: Basil Blackwell; Nashville: Abingdon, 1956); K.E. Pomykala, *The Davidic Dynasty Tradition in Early Judaism: Its History and Significance for Messianism* (SBLEJL, 7; Atlanta: Scholars Press, 1995); J.J.M. Roberts, 'The Old Testament's Contribution to Messianic Expectations', in J.H. Charlesworth (ed.), *The Messiah: Developments in Earliest Judaism and Christianity* (Philadelphia: Fortress Press, 1992), pp. 39-51; S. Talmon, 'The Concepts of *mašîaḥ* and Messianism in Early Judaism', Charlesworth (ed.), *The Messiah*, pp. 79-115; S. Talmon, 'Types of Messianic Expectation at the Turn of the Era', in *idem*, *King, Cult, and Calendar in Ancient Israel: Collected Studies* (Jerusalem: Magnes, 1986), pp. 202-24.

4.   Besides the fifteen or so volumes published to date in the DJD series (Oxford: Clarendon Press), see B.Z. Wacholder and M.G. Abegg, Jr, *A Preliminary Edition of the Unpublished Dead Sea Scrolls: The Hebrew and Aramaic Texts from Cave Four* (4 fascicles; Washington: Biblical Archaeology Society, 1991–96). The fourth fascicle concords this material. A multi-volume work which will provide the Hebrew, Aramaic, and Greek text of all of the Scrolls, with English facing pages, is in preparation under the direction of J.H. Charlesworth (Tübingen: Mohr [Paul Siebeck]; Louisville: Westminster/John Knox). For photographic plates, see G.J. Brooke (ed.), *The Allegro Qumran Photograph Collection* (Leiden: Brill, 1996); R.H. Eisenman and J.M. Robinson (eds.), *A Facsimile Edition of the Dead Sea Scrolls* (2 vols.; Washington: Biblical Archaeology Society, 1991); E. Tov (ed.), *The Dead Sea Scrolls on Microfiche* (Leiden: Brill, 1993). The most comprehensive English translations of the Scrolls available are by F. García Martínez, *The Dead Sea Scrolls Translated: The Qumran Texts in English* (Leiden: Brill, 1994 [Spanish edn, 1992]), and M.O. Wise, M.G. Abegg, Jr, and E.M. Cook, *The Dead Sea Scrolls: A*

begin comprehensive assessments of the data. The present study limits itself to a survey of these data and offers a modest assessment of their contribution to first century messianic ideas, especially those that appear to have been taken up by Jesus and the New Testament writers.[5] The references to David and Davidic tradition fall into three some-times overlapping categories: (1) references to the historical man and his times, (2) appeals to David as an ideal figure, and (3) employment of the Davidic tradition for eschatology and messianism. These references will be surveyed and briefly commented upon, then in the last part of the paper attention will be drawn to interpretive traditions that may be distinctive to the Dead Sea Scrolls and what their potential relevance for first-century messianism might be.

1. *References to the Historical David*

Historical references to David (sometimes cast as 'prophecies' by various Old Testament worthies) are infrequent when compared to figures like Moses or Aaron. But there is a sufficient number to give us an idea of how the covenanters of Qumran viewed David. In fact, several of the references to David occur in the writings that are recognized as sectarian (for example, the Damascus Document, The War Scroll, and 4QMMT). The references to him found in other writings, which may or may not be sectarian, appear to be consistent with the references in the sectarian writings.

In what was probably supposed to be a prophecy of the birth and reign of David and of his plans to build the Temple, we read: 'For, behold, a son is born to Jesse [כי הנה בן נולד לישי], son of Perez, son of Ju[dah...he will choose] [4]the rock of Zion and drive out from there all the Amorites from [Jerusalem...][5] to build the house for the Lord, God of Israel' (4Q522 frag. 1, col. ii, ll. 2-5). The reference to David's birth is reminiscent of the oracle of Isa. 9.4 (English v. 5): 'For to us a child is born, to us a son is given [כִּי־יֶלֶד יֻלַּד־לָנוּ בֵּן נִתַּן־לָנוּ]; and the government shall be upon his shoulder'.

The War Scroll alludes to what was probably David's greatest personal military triumph, his defeat of Goliath:

New Translation (London: HarperCollins, 1996). The latter translation will often be followed in this paper.

5. The only survey of the data since 1991 of which I am aware is E. Jucci, 'Davide a Qumran', *RSB* 7 (1995), pp. 157-73.

[1]Truly the battle is yours, and by the strength of your hand their corpses have been broken to pieces, without anyone to bury them. Indeed, Goliath the Gittite, a mighty man of valor, [2]you delivered into the hand of David, your servant, because he trusted in your great name and not in sword and spear. For the battle is yours (1QM 11.1-2).

The Damascus Document criticizes the religious rivals for their practice of divorce and remarriage. The criticism is then buttressed with Scripture: 'Concerning the leader it is written: "He shall not multiply wives to himself" [Deut. 17.17]'. The trouble is, King David had had several wives. What to do? Fortunately for David, Deuteronomy was not in circulation in his day: 'But David had not read the sealed book of the Law [3]in the Ark; for it was not opened in Israel from the day of the death of Eleazar' (CD 5.1-3 = 4Q273 frag. 5, l. 1-3). David may be excused, because he had not had access to the 'sealed book of the Law'. It seems that sometimes ignorance of the Law is a valid defense after all.

The Damascus Document goes on to say that the book of the Law remained unopened until the days of Zadok the High Priest. Despite its unavailability, 'David's deeds were all excellent', we are told—'except for the murder of Uriah, [6]but God forgave him for that' (CD 5.5-6).

In the Works of the Law Document (4QMMT), which has aroused a great deal of debate, readers are reminded of David who 'was delivered from many troubles and was forgiven' (4Q398 frag. 2, col. ii, ll. 1-2 = 4Q399 frag. 1, col. i, ll. 9-10). The document goes on to speak of the blessings that were bestowed on the people during the reign of David's son Solomon (4Q398 frag. 1, l. 2).

The Psalms Scroll from Cave 11 provides a delightful summary of David's life, drawing upon 1–2 Samuel, certain Psalms, and various intertestamental traditions.[6] It reads (11QPs[a] [= 11Q5] 27.2-11):

Now David the son of Jesse was wise and shone like the light of the sun, a scribe [3]and man of discernment, blameless in all his ways before God and men. The Lord gave [4]him a brilliant and discerning spirit, so that he wrote: psalms, 3,600; [5]songs to sing before the altar accompanying the daily [6]perpetual burnt-offering, for all the days of the year, 364; [7]for the sabbath offerings, 52 songs; and for the New Moon offerings, [8]all the festival days and the Day of Atonement, 30 songs. [9]The total of all the

6. See the transcription of text, translation, and helpful notes in J.A. Sanders, *The Psalms Scroll of Qumrân Cave 11 (11QPs[a])* (DJD, 4; Oxford: Clarendon Press, 1965), pp. 91-93.

songs that he composed was 446, not including [10]four songs for charming the demon-possessed with music. The sum total of everything, psalms and songs, was 4,050. [11]All these he composed through prophecy given him by the Most High.

Other texts contain hymnic addresses, so familiar in the Psalter (for example, 4Q177 frags. 5–6, ll. 6-7; 11QPs[a] [= 11Q5] 28.3).

Yet another Psalm[7] summarizes the life and virtues of Israel's famous king (11QPs[a] [= 11Q5] 28.3-11):

> [3]Hallelujah! A psalm of David, son of Jesse. I was smaller than my brothers, youngest of my father's sons. So he made me a [4]shepherd for his sheep, a ruler over his goats. My hands fashioned a pipe, my fingers a lyre, [5]and I glorified the Lord. I said to myself, 'The mountains do not testify [6]to him, nor do the hills proclaim'. So—echo my words, O trees, O sheep, my deeds! [7]Ah, but who can proclaim, who declare? Who can recount the deeds of the Lord? God has seen all, [8]heard and attended to everything. He sent his prophet to anoint me, even Samuel, [9]to raise me up. My brothers went forth to meet him: handsome of figure, wondrous of appearance, tall were they of stature, [10]so beautiful their hair—yet the Lord God did not choose them. No, he sent and took me [11]who followed the flock, and anointed me with the holy oil; he set me as prince to his people, a ruler over the children of his covenant.

There are other probable historic references to David, but the texts are so fragmentary that it is difficult to know what is being narrated. For example, in 4Q457, we find: 'David was glad to return [שמח דויד להשיב]...the Most High will make in the heavens...' (frag. 1, col. ii, l. 2). 4Q479 speaks of 'servitude...the seed of David...David went forth' (frag. 1, l. 4).

2. *Texts that Emphasize David's Virtues*

One cannot draw a sharp line between historical references and idealizing references; the distinction is blurred, for the two often go together. We find, among other things, a tendency to exculpate David (much as the Chronicler does in his retelling of the books of Samuel and Kings). We observe also that much of the key language has been drawn from Scripture.

According to a passage in the Damascus Document already cited, 'the deeds [מעשי] of David were all excellent [ויעלו]' (CD 5.5).[8] The

---

7. See Sanders, *The Psalms Scroll*, pp. 54-64.
8. On עלה meaning 'were excellent', see Deut. 28.43; Prov. 31.29.

claim is remarkable, given that in l. 2 the author had to admit that David was a polygamist and that in ll. 5-6 he was a murderer. The polygamy is excused on the grounds of ignorance—the book that taught against it was not in circulation—and the murder of Uriah is mitigated by noting that God had forgiven David. The positive view of David compels the author to overlook these faults and to speak of the excellence of his deeds.

The idea of the excellence of David's deeds may have enjoyed some scriptural warrant: 'And Jonathan spoke well of David to Saul his father, and said to him, "Let not the king sin against his servant, against David; because he has not sinned against you, and because his deeds [מַעֲשָׂיו] have been very good toward you"' (1 Sam. 19.4).

The passage in the War Scroll already cited said that Goliath had been 'delivered into the hand of David, (God's) servant, because he trusted [בטח] in (God's) great name and not in sword and spear' (1QM 11.2). The reference here to David's trust in God recalls the opening words of Psalm 26, a Psalm of David: 'Judge me, O Lord, for I have walked in my integrity: I have trusted [בָּטַחְתִּי] also in the Lord without wavering' (Ps. 26.1). The reference to 'sword and spear' is drawn from the story of David's battle with Goliath (1 Sam. 17.45, 47 ['the Lord saves not with sword and spear']).

The Works of the Law Document, which also has already been cited, describes David as 'a man of kindnesses' (4Q398 frag. 2, col. ii, l. 1 = 4Q399 frag. 1, col. i, l. 9). This epithet translates איש חסדים. Martin Abegg has translated these words 'a pious man'.[9] This is not a bad translation, but it tends to obscure what kind of piety is in mind. The plural of the word חסד in the Hebrew Bible almost always means 'kind/merciful deeds' (for example Gen. 32.10; Isa. 63.7; Pss. 17.7; 89.49; 106.7; 2 Chron. 6.42), as opposed to cultic piety (such as prayer, sacrifice, sabbath observance, etc.) or moral disposition. The singular can have this meaning also (for example Gen. 24.12; 39.21). Almost always it is the Lord who has done these good deeds. But a few times it is a human who has done the 'good deeds'. For example, Nehemiah prays to God: 'Remember, O my God, concerning this, and do not wipe out my good deeds that I have done for the house of God and for his service' (Neh. 13.14). The Chronicler says of king Hezekiah: 'Now the rest of the acts of Hezekiah, and his good deeds, behold, they are

9.   M.G. Abegg, Jr, 'A Sectarian Manifesto', in Wise, Abegg, Cook, *The Dead Sea Scrolls*, p. 364.

written in the vision of Isaiah' (2 Chron. 32.32). The Chronicler says the same thing of king Josiah (2 Chron. 35.26). This is probably the point that is being made here in 4QMMT. But where is David remembered as a man of kind deeds? The story of his mercy shown to surviving relatives of the late king Saul immediately comes to mind. David asks: 'Is there yet any that is left of the house of Saul, that I may show him kindness for Jonathan's sake?' (2 Sam. 9.1). The story goes on to tell of David's kindness to the son of Jonathan (2 Sam. 9.7; see also 2 Sam. 10.2, where David shows kindness to the new king of the Ammonites). We should think also of Isa. 55.3, where God promises Israel: 'and I will make with you an eternal covenant, even the sure acts of kindnesss to David [הַחְסְדֵי דָוִד הַנֶּאֱמָנִים]'. The implication here is that God will bestow on Israel kind deeds for David's sake, perhaps in the sense of reciprocity.[10]

Finally, the clause, 'he was delivered [נצל] from many troubles', is reminiscent of David's testimony moments before taking on the giant: 'And David said, "The Lord who delivered me [הִצִּלַנִי] out of the paw of the lion, and out of the paw of the bear, will deliver me [יַצִּילֵנִי] out of the hand of this Philistine"' (1 Sam. 17.37; see also 2 Sam. 22.1).

In the Words of the Heavenly Lights (4Q504–506) the election of Jerusalem, the people of Israel, especially the tribe of Judah, and of the Davidic monarchy is recalled. The author reminds God: 'You have established [הקימותה] your covenant [בריתכה] with David, so that he would be [7]like a shepherd, a prince over your people, and would sit upon the throne of Israel before you [8]forever' (4Q504 frag. 1, col. ii, ll. 6-8). This language recalls Psalm 89, where again God is reminded of having promised David: 'I have made a covenant [כָּרַתִּי בְרִית] with my

10. The meaning of the text is admittedly uncertain. The RSV translates: 'I will make with you an everlasting covenant, my steadfast, sure love for David'. The ASV translates: 'I will make an everlasting covenant with you, even the sure mercies of David'. The former is much more paraphrastic. חסד, modified by עולם, appears in Isa. 54.8: 'with eternal lovingkindness will I have mercy on you'. See also Isa. 63.7 and Ps. 89.50 (English v. 49). These texts potentially support the understanding adopted here. See also Eissfeldt, 'The Promises of Grace to David in Isaiah 55.1-5', pp. 196-207; Mowinckel, *He that Cometh*, p. 170. The חסד that David showed in 2 Samuel 9 illustrates the king's faithfulness in keeping his vow to show mercy toward Jonathan (cf. 1 Sam. 20.12-17), even though, in the case of Saul's surviving relative Mephibosheth, it ran counter to his earlier refusal to permit the blind and crippled to enter his house (cf. 2 Sam. 5.6-9). On this interesting question, see S. Vargon, 'The Blind and the Lame', *VT* 46 (1996), pp. 498-514.

chosen, I have sworn to David my servant' (Ps. 89.4 [English v. 3]). The Chronicler puts it this way: 'The Lord would not destroy the house of David, because of the covenant [הַבְּרִית] that he had made with David' (2 Chron. 21.1). The promise to be 'established' is another important component in the Davidic covenant. David's son Solomon is told: 'If you will walk in my statutes, and execute my ordinances, and keep all my commandments to walk in them; then will I establish [וַהֲקִמֹּתִי] my word with you, which I spoke to David your father' (1 Kgs 6.12); and 'I will establish [וַהֲקִמֹתִי] the throne of your kingdom over Israel for ever, according as I promised to David thy father' (1 Kgs 9.5). In these texts 'established' renders the *hiphil* of קוּם. This term is relatively rare compared to the more common כון, which is frequently used in reference to the Davidic covenant (for example 2 Sam. 7.12, 13, 16, 24, 26).

In the Cave 11 Psalms Scroll cited above we read that David testified: God 'anointed me with the holy oil [וימשחני בשמן הקודש]' and 'set me as a prince to his people, a ruler over the children of his covenant' (11QPs^a [= 11Q5] 28.11). This language once again echoes Psalm 89, where we read: 'I have found David, my servant; with my oil I have anointed him [בְּשֶׁמֶן קָדְשִׁי מְשַׁחְתִּיו]' (Ps. 89.21 [English v. 20]). The addition of the adjective 'holy' in the Psalms Scroll enriches the recollection by adding an element that is consistent with its priestly orientation. This language also parallels other fragmentary texts from Cave 4. In 4Q458 we read of a figure 'anointed with the oil of the kingdom of [משיח בשמן מלכות]...' (frag. 2, col. ii, l. 6). David is not mentioned in this fragment, but this anointed person 'will swallow up all the uncircumcised' (l. 4). Fighting the 'uncircumcised' largely characterized David's reign (see 1 Sam. 17.26, 36). He may also be the 'first born' mentioned in 4Q458 frag. 15, l. 1. Given the fact that David is also called in Ps. 89.28 (English v. 27) God's 'first born' it could very well be that the anointed person of 4Q458 is David, or perhaps a messianic figure modeled after him.

This Dead Sea Scroll psalm also says that God set David up 'as prince [נגיד] to his people, a ruler [מושל] over the children of his covenant'. In Scripture David is recognized as both נגיד (2 Sam. 6.21; 7.8) and מושל (2 Sam. 23.3). This terminology may enable us to identify the person described in 4Q369 as David himself or as a David-like future king: '^{5}and you have made clear to him your good judgments [...] ^{6}in eternal light. And you made him for yourself a first-b[orn] son [...] [7]like him, a prince and ruler [שר ומושל] in all Your earthly land...' (4Q369 frag. 1, col. ii, ll. 5-7).[11] The perspective of this text is uncertain; we may have historical reminiscence, or we may have the anticipation of a future prince.[12]

Finally, the other psalm from the Cave 11 Psalms Scroll delineates several virtues of David. We are told that the 'son of Jesse was wise and shone like the light of the sun [כאור השמש]...' (11QPs[a] [= 11Q5] 27.2-11). The wise woman of Tekoa describes David as having 'wisdom like the wisdom of an angel of God' (2 Sam. 14.20). We are also once again reminded of David's song: 'He shall be as the light [כְּאוֹר] of the morning, when the sun [שֶׁמֶשׁ] rises' (2 Sam. 23.4). David is said to be 'literate' (cf. 1 Chron. 27.32, where David's uncle is said to be literate and a scribe). David is 'discerning' (cf. 1 Sam. 16.18), 'blameless in all his ways' (cf. 2 Sam. 22.24, 26, 33), possesses a 'brilliant and discerning spirit' (cf. 2 Sam. 23.2), and is musically gifted (cf. 1 Sam. 16.12-23), which derives from prophecy given to him by God (cf. 1 Sam. 16.13; 2 Sam. 23.1-7; 1 Chron. 25.1; Josephus, *Ant.* 6.8.2 §166; Acts 2.29-30). Some of the songs that David composed are said to aid the stricken, by which is probably meant to 'charm the demon-possessed' (cf. 1 Sam. 16.16-23; 18.10; 19.9; all of these passages refer to David's music that soothes Saul and drives away the evil spirit).

3. *Eschatological Use of the Davidic Tradition*

The Davidic tradition contributes significantly to the messianic expectation of the Dead Sea Scrolls, just as it does to that found in the Old Testament prophets. Not all of the eschatology of the Scrolls is messianic, nor is all of the messianic material Davidic, but it is clear that the Davidic tradition is the single most important factor. The following passages make explicit reference to 'David' or to a descendant of 'Jesse'. Many other texts could be cited that probably also draw upon the Davidic tradition, but no name appears and the text is usually poorly preserved.

11. שר ('prince' or 'captain') is used here, instead of נגיד ('prince'); but see 1 Sam. 18.13, where king Saul makes David שר of a thousand troops.

12. On this question, see C.A. Evans, 'A Note on the "First-Born Son" of 4Q369', *DSD* 2 (1995), pp. 185-201.

The citation of passages from Amos in the Damascus Document makes for an interesting beginning:

> '...and the foundation of your images beyond the tents of Damascus' [Amos 5.27]. The books of the Law are the tents [16]of the king, as it says, "I will re-erect the fallen tent of David" [Amos 9.11]. The king [17]is <the Leader of> the nation and the "foundation of your images" is the books of the prophets...' (CD 7.15-16 = 4Q269 frag. 5, l. 1-2).

The same passage from Amos 9 is cited in Acts 15.14-18 in reference to the ingathering of Gentiles into the young Christian Church. The fallen tent, or booth, of David is said to be in the process of being set up once again. Is it the rule of David, or his descendant, that is being restored? Or, does the 'tent of David' refer to Jerusalem, perhaps as the eschatological religious center of the world?

The meaning of the appeal of Amos 9.11 to the 'fallen tent of David' becomes clear in the later interpretation found in CD 7.17-21. The prophecy of Amos anticipates the appearance of the Davidic messiah who will, along with the 'star' who interprets the Law, rise as the 'staff' foretold in Num. 24.17 and 'shatter the sons of Sheth', that is, Israel's enemies. Although there is nothing explicitly Davidic about the prophecy in Numbers 24, its association here with Amos 9 suggests that it was so understood by the author of the Damascus Document. The appeals elsewhere to Numbers 24 in the Scrolls adds further support and clarification to this line of interpretation.

4Q174 preserves a similar interpretation:

> ... 'I will establish the throne of his kingdom [11][fore]ver, I will be a father to him, and he will be my son' [2 Sam. 7.12-14]. This passage refers to the 'Branch of David', who is to arise with [12]the Interpreter of the Law, and who will [arise] in Zi[on in the La]st Days, as it is written, 'And I shall raise up the booth of David that is fallen' [Amos 9.11]. This passage describes the fallen 'Branch of [13]David', [w]hom he shall raise up to deliver Israel (4Q174 3.10-13).

The epithet 'Branch of David' alludes to Jer. 23.5, 33.15, and Ps. 132.17, passages which look to the day when God will raise up for Israel a new Davidic king.

An important commentary on Gen. 49.10 adds:

> 'A ruler shall [no]t depart from the tribe of Judah' when Israel has dominion. [2][And] the one who sits on the throne of David [shall never] be cut off, because the 'ruler's staff' is the covenant of the kingdom, [3][and the thous]ands of Israel are 'the feet', until the righteous Messiah, the

'Branch of David', has come. [4]For to him and to his seed the covenant of the kingdom of his people has been given for the eternal generations, because [5]he has kept [...] the Law with the men of the community (4Q252 frag. 1, col. v, ll. 1-6).

Another commentary, this one concerned with Isa. 10.34–11.5, sees the future in a similar way:

['A rod will grow from] Jesse's stock, a sprout [will bloom] from his [roots]; upon him wi[ll rest] the spirit of [16][the Lord: a spirit of] wisdom and insight, a spirit of good coun[sel and strength], a spirit of true know[ledge] [17][and reverence for the Lord, he will delight in reverence for] the Lord. [He will not judge only] by what [his eyes] see, [18][he will not decide only by what his ears hear]; but he will rule [the weak by justice, and give decisions]...' [Isa. 11.1-5]... [22][This saying refers to the 'Branch of] David', who will appear in the Las[t Days,...] [23][...] his enemies; and God will support him with [a spirit of] strength [...] (4Q161 frags. 7–10, ll. 15-23).

Although the text is fragmentary, the gist of it seems pretty clear.

It is in the light of this commentary on Isaiah that we should understand the controversial War Rule Scroll, whose fifth fragment reads:

'...felled with an axe, and Lebanon with its majestic trees w]ill fall, A shoot shall come out from the stump of Jesse [3][and a branch shall grow out of his roots' [Isa. 10.34–11.1]. This is the] 'Branch of David'. Then [all forces of Belial] shall be judged, [4][and the king of the Kittim shall stand for judgment] and the Leader of the nation—the Bra[nch of David]—will have him put to death. [5][Then all Israel shall come out with timbrel]s and dancers, and the [High] Priest shall order [6][them to cleanse their bodies from the guilty blood of the c]orpse[s of] the Kittim. [Then all the people shall...] (4Q285 frag. 5, ll. 2-6).

There are several references to David that cannot be classified and cannot be interpreted due to the fragmentary and incomplete contexts in which we find them.[13] This concludes this survey of the Qumran documents.

4. *Importance of the Davidic Tradition in the Scrolls*

Should we survey other intertestamental Jewish literature as well as early Christian literature, we would find that the Davidic tradition in

---

13. See 4Q177 frags. 12–13, col. i, l. 2; 4Q422 frag. 9, l. 5; 6Q9 frag. 22, l. 4; 11QPs[b] 1.2; 11QAp[a] 4.4; 11Q14 frag. 3, l. 2.

the Dead Sea Scrolls is not remarkable. We find several historical references, but almost all of them are cited for moral lessons, proof texts, or support for eschatological expectations. Although Davidic tradition plays a role in eschatology, especially messianism, concern with this subject cannot be said to dominate the Scrolls.

An important caveat at this point is in order. It is necessary to guard against the danger of synthesizing ideas found in texts generated by different persons in different periods of time and then thinking we know what *the* messianism is of the Scrolls. The same caveat applies to other bodies of literature, even to the New Testament, though in its case there is a fairly consistent messianism centered on one figure.[14]

On the other hand, when we find certain texts, such as Isa. 10.34–11.5, Gen. 49.10, and Num. 24.17, appealed to in many texts, within the Dead Sea Scrolls and without, it is necessary to assume that many Jews in different times and places did hold to some of the same basic concepts of messianism.[15]

The Dead Sea Scrolls' use of the Davidic tradition contains no truly big surprises. The much debated 'two messiahs' observation, not discussed in this paper, is probably little more than the diarchism implicit in parts of the Old Testament. The idea of an anointed king of Israel serving alongside an anointed priest finds expression in the history of Israel and in some of the idealism that fed into the messianic streams of expectation (as in Zechariah, for example).[16] At some point

---

14. For books that emphasize the diversity of messianic ideas in late antiquity, see J. Neusner *et al.* (eds.), *Judaisms and their Messiahs at the Turn of the Christian Era* (Cambridge: Cambridge University Press, 1987); Charlesworth (ed.), *The Messiah*.

15. This point is well taken in J.J. Collins, *The Scepter and the Star: The Messiahs of the Dead Sea Scrolls and Other Ancient Literature* (ABRL, 10; New York: Doubleday, 1995); *idem*, 'Jesus and the Messiahs of Israel', in H. Cancik *et al.* (eds.), *Geschichte–Tradition–Reflexion: Festschrift für Martin Hengel zum 70. Geburtstag*. Band III: *Frühes Christentum* (Tübingen: Mohr [Paul Siebeck], 1996), pp. 287-302; Pomykala, *The Davidic Dynasty*, pp. 180-216. On the coherence of interpretation of Isa. 10.34–11.5 in various bodies of literature, see R.J. Bauckham, 'The Messianic Interpretation of Isa. 10.34 in the Dead Sea Scrolls, 2 Baruch and the Preaching of John the Baptist', *DSD* 2 (1995), pp. 202-16.

16. Qumran's diarchic messianism was probably based on Zechariah. This claim appears to enjoy a measure of support in 4Q254, a fragmentary commentary on Genesis 49, where in interpreting the blessing upon Judah (Gen. 49.8-12), Zech. 4.14 ('the two sons of oil') is cited. The implication is that the two sons of oil are the

in Israel's ancient history the older office of 'judge' split into the two offices of king and priest. The last of these legendary figures— Samuel—functioned as priest, prophet, and *de facto* king. But with the establishment of the royal monarchy, alongside the priest, a form of diarchic government emerged in ancient Israel, with David the king and Zadok the high priest setting the benchmark by which their successors would be measured and by which those who were expected to fulfill the prophecies of salvation would also be measured.

Does Qumran shed light on the New Testament? It does in several ways. For one, the Davidic tradition in the Dead Sea Scrolls sheds light on the broad range of its usage by the authors of the New Testament. These writers view David as a prophet, a righteous man, and an exemplary figure. For another, the tradition of the Scrolls clarifies the nature of Davidic messianism in the time of Jesus. The traditional notion of the expectation of a militant messiah who, like David of old, would lead Israel to a military victory over her enemies, especially the Romans,[17] seems well established. It could be for this reason that Jesus does not exploit the Davidic element in his understanding of messianism. Although known as the son of David (cf. Mk 10.46, 47; Rom. 1.3)—a datum not likely invented by the early Church, but grounded in genealogical fact[18]—Jesus makes little of it. The only reference to it (in Mk 12.35-37) is to challenge a point of scribal interpretation. Jesus seems concerned to claim that he is no mere 'son of David'. His consistent appeal to the mysterious human figure of Daniel 7 (the 'son of man') reflects in part his avoidance of Davidism—at least popular expressions of it.

For Jesus research, perhaps the most significant feature of the

royal descendant of Judah and the priestly descendant of Levi. See C.A. Evans, '"The Two Sons of Oil": Early Evidence of Messianic Interpretation of Zechariah 4.14 in 4Q254 4 2', in D. Parry and E. Ulrich (eds.), *The Provo International Conference on the Dead Sea Scrolls* (STDJ; Leiden: Brill, forthcoming).

17. See, for example, E. Schürer, *The History of the Jewish People in the Age of Jesus Christ* (3 vols.; rev. and ed. by G. Vermes *et al.*; Edinburgh: T. & T. Clark, 1973–87), II, pp. 526-29; M. Hengel, *The Zealots: Investigations into the Jewish Freedom Movement in the Period from Herod I until 70 A.D.* (Edinburgh: T. & T. Clark, 1989), pp. 302-10.

18. See R.E. Brown, *The Birth of the Messiah: A Commentary on the Infancy Narratives in the Gospels of Matthew and Luke* (ABRL, 1; New York: Doubleday, 2nd edn, 1993), pp. 505-12; J.P. Meier, *A Marginal Jew: Rethinking the Historical Jesus* (ABRL, 3; Garden City, NY: Doubleday, 1991), pp. 216-19.

description of David in the Scrolls is his portrait as a Spirit-empowered prophet and exorcist (as seen especially in 11QPs[a] 27.10-11). It is highly significant that Jesus, hailed 'son of David' (Mk 10.47)[19] and welcomed as bringer of the 'kingdom of our father David' (Mk 11.10), performed deeds consistent with this portrait. Jesus, regarded as a prophet (Mk 6.4, 14-15; 8.28; 14.65), was well known as an exorcist (Mk 1.27-28, 32, 39; 3.22). In at least one context, comparison with Solomon, the son of David, follows on the heels of controversy surrounding his exorcistic activity (Mt. 12.22-45).[20] It seems, then, that being recognized as a prophet and exorcist in no way competes with a Davidic identity.

The portrait of David as a prophet and as endowed with the Spirit is emphasized in the New Testament and other early Christian literature. In appealing to Ps. 110.1 Jesus says that David uttered his words 'in the Spirit' (Mk 12.36). Luke tells us that the disciples appealed to David, through whom the Holy Spirit spoke previously, when it became necessary for them to replace Judas Iscariot (Acts 1.16). Opposition to the early Church is also explained by an appeal to the words of Scripture, given 'by the Holy Spirit, by the mouth of our father David' (Acts 4.25). In the *Epistula Apostolorum* Jesus quotes Ps. 3.1-8, which he introduces as 'the prophecy of the prophet David concerning my death and resurrection' (§19). The reference to the 'prophecy' of David is reminiscent of 11QPs[a] 27.11. Later in the *Epistula Apostolorum* Jesus again appeals to the 'prophet David', quoting (LXX) Pss. 13.3, 49.19b, 18, 20, 21b to describe the 'deceivers and enemies' of the Church (§35). Finally, one Gnostic writing casts this tradition in a sinister light when it claims that David and his son Solomon dwelt with demons who assisted in the building of Jerusalem and the Temple (cf. *Test. Truth* IX 70.3-11). Accusing David of being in league with demons roughly parallels the charges thrown at Jesus in order to explain away his success in exorcism (cf. Mk 3.22-30).

The tradition in the Scrolls, however, antedates these early

19. See J.H. Charlesworth, 'The Son of David: Solomon and Jesus', in P. Borgen and S. Giversen (eds.), *The New Testament and Hellenistic Judaism* (Aarhus: Aarhus University Press, 1995), pp. 72-87; C.A. Evans, *Jesus and his Contemporaries: Comparative Studies* (AGJU, 25; Leiden: Brill, 1995), pp. 447-56. David's prophetic gifts are embellished in the Targums.

20. See D.C. Duling, 'Solomon, Exorcism, and the Son of David', *HTR* 68 (1975), pp. 235-52.

Christian traditions and reflects ideas in circulation in Israel in the time of Jesus. The Scrolls therefore fill in an important gap between the teaching of Jesus and the Davidic messianic expectations many of his contemporaries entertained. Ongoing work in the Scrolls will probably clarify additional aspects of messianism and the way Jesus was viewed in his time.[21]

21. I would like to thank Professor Stanley E. Porter and his colleagues of Roehampton Institute London for organizing a splendid conference and for the generous hospitality accorded to all participants. My paper benefited from many helpful comments, especially those offered by George Brooke.

'SON OF GOD' AS 'SON OF MAN' IN THE DEAD SEA SCROLLS? A RESPONSE TO JOHN COLLINS ON 4Q246

James D.G. Dunn

John Collins has put us all considerably in his debt by his excellent recent study of messianic expectation in Second Temple Judaism in the light of the Dead Sea Scrolls.[1] His thesis that royal messianism—the hope of a warrior king who would destroy Israel's enemies and institute an era of unending peace—was the common core of Jewish messianism around the turn of the eras[2] is generally persuasive. It nicely counters both the wilder speculations based on partial readings of the texts, and what for some time had seemed to be the growing consensus, that Jewish messianic expectation was either too disparate or too vague for us to speak appropriately of a dominant or coherent messianic expectation for the period. The fact that the Dead Sea sect seems to have cherished an expectation of two messiahs, a priestly as well as a royal messiah,[3] is a variation of the more common view, not a departure from it.

I

The one point at which I find myself less persuaded by Collins's overall presentation is with regard to his well known thesis regarding the man-like figure in the famous vision of Daniel 7 (7.13—'one like a son of man'). Collins is now the principal proponent of the view that the figure in Daniel's vision was understood or should be understood[4] 'as a heavenly individual, probably the archangel Michael, rather than

---

1. J.J. Collins, *The Scepter and the Star: The Messiahs of the Dead Sea Scrolls and Other Ancient Literature* (ABRL; New York: Doubleday, 1995).
2. Collins, *Scepter*, p. 68.
3. Collins, *Scepter*, p. 5.
4. Is it the same thing?

as a collective symbol'.[5] Once that claim is accepted it is but a small step to the further deduction that this heavenly individual was understood by some at the turn of the eras as the or a 'heavenly messiah'. Hence Collins's fuller thesis that within the Judaism of the time there were 'four basic messianic paradigms (king, priest, prophet, and heavenly messiah), (though) not equally widespread'.[6]

Without rehearsing the full argumentation on the much disputed issue of the significance of the Danielic 'one like a son of man', I should perhaps briefly indicate the basic reasons why I part company with Collins at this point. They are threefold.

(1) First, the sequence of visions in Daniel 7 itself strongly suggests that the man-like figure is a symbolic representation. As the rather bizarre beast-like creatures represent the nations hostile to Israel, so the man-like figure probably represents Israel itself.

Collins argues, in contrast, that 'the apparition of the "one like a human being" is separated from the beasts in the text by the description of the Ancient of Days' and subsequently, unlike the beasts, is not interpreted by the angel. 'If an argument is drawn from the nature of the symbolism, then, it should favour the view that the "one like a human being" is a symbol of the same order as the Ancient of Days—a mythic-realistic depiction of a being who was believed to exist outside the vision'.[7]

But does Collins give enough consideration to the parallelism between what is granted to the man-like figure (7.14) and what is granted to the saints of the Most High (7.18, 22, 27)? Here we should note that the subsequent use made of Daniel's vision by *4 Ezra* 13 certainly assumed that the man-like figure of the vision was the same kind of symbol as the beasts. For whereas in Dan. 7.2-3 only of the beasts is it said that they 'came up out of the sea', in *4 Ezra* 13.3 it is 'something like the figure of a man' which 'comes up out of the heart of the sea' (as well as the eagle in the preceding vision—12.11). The implication is obviously that the man-like figure was seen to be like the four beasts in symbolic character and resonance. However *4 Ezra* goes on to interpret the figure, it *presupposes* that the man-like figure

---

5. Collins, *Scepter*, p. 176; earlier, J.J. Collins, *The Apocalyptic Vision of the Book of Daniel* (Missoula, MT: Scholars Press, 1977), pp. 144-46; also *Daniel* (Hermeneia; Minneapolis: Fortress Press, 1993), pp. 304-10.

6. Collins, *Scepter*, p. 12.

7. Collins, *Daniel*, p. 305.

was to be (and had been) understood as a symbolic figure analogous to the beasts.

Moreover, I remain impressed by the allusion to the creation narrative which seems to me obvious in Daniel 7. That is, as man was the climax of creation after the beasts, so the man-like figure is obviously the climax of the vision in Daniel 7 in succession to the beasts; and as man was given dominion over the beasts (Gen. 1.26-28), so the saints of the Most High are given dominion over the other nations. In other words, Daniel 7 is a classic re-statement of a fairly common theme in Jewish writing which understood Israel as the crown and point of creation.[8]

Against such considerations I find little in the text to commend the argument of Collins that Daniel's man-like figure would have been more obviously associated with the differently formulated descriptions of angels subsequently in Daniel (8.15; 10.5; 12.7).[9] The logic of Daniel 7 seems to be sufficiently coherent within itself as not to require us to look beyond Daniel 7 for its interpretation. Moreover, if the man-like figure was intended to be distinct from 'the people of the saints of the Most High' ('one like a son of man' = an angelic being) and not just to be identified with them ('one like a son of man' = the people/saints), it is odd that the angelic individual does not appear in the interpretation of 7.18, 22, 27.[10]

(2) Secondly, the 'son of man' motif within the Jesus tradition undoubtedly goes back to Jesus himself, or at the very least to the earliest phase of Christian reflection regarding Jesus—that is, to the 30s CE. What has always struck me about the Jesus tradition at this point is that it reflects no awareness of a prior interpretation of the Danielic 'one like a son of man' as a saviour figure or heavenly individual within Second Temple Judaism. That is to say, within the Jesus tradition we find no question such as: 'Are you the (well known) Son of Man?' Within the Jesus tradition we find no confessional identification: 'You are the Son of Man'. On this point the contrast with other forms or titles used of Jesus is very striking. On the evidence of the Jesus

8. For details, see particularly D. Goh, *Creation and the People of God: Creation and the Boundaries of the Covenant in Second Temple Jewish Writings and in Paul's Letter to the Galatians* (doctoral thesis, Durham University, 1994).

9. 8.15—'one having the appearance of a man (כמראה גבר)'; 10.5 and 12.7—'a man (איש) clothed in linen'.

10. J. Goldingay, *Daniel* (WBC, 30; Dallas: Word Books, 1989), p. 172.

tradition and early Christian usage we can certainly speak of titles or concepts of 'Messiah', 'Son of God', 'Lord'.[11] The silence with regard to 'son of man' at this point is eloquent. It is hard to conclude from this evidence other than that there was no such interpretation of Daniel 7 then current—that is, no current belief in or expectation of a heavenly figure identified as the son of man or with the man-like figure of Daniel 7.[12]

It remains a puzzle for me why this evidence (or lack of evidence) is given so little weight in scholarly discussions at this point. I can only assume that the whole Jesus and early Christian tradition is bracketed out of the discussion of Jewish expectation as in effect inadmissable evidence. But that material is a vital part of the total deposit of literature reflecting Jewish thought in the final phase of Second Temple Judaism. Indeed, the Jesus tradition is the only material about whose origin in the first half of the first century of the Common Era we can be wholly confident. To exclude its evidence as to the understanding of 'son of man' and influence of Daniel's man-like figure within Judaism at the time of Jesus is to ignore one of our primary witnesses.

When we do include the Jesus tradition, its testimony is clear and the conclusion rather compelling: that the identification of the Danielic 'son of man' as an individual may first have appeared in Judaism in the Jesus tradition's own use of Daniel's imagery to describe the exaltation (and parousia?) of Jesus himself.

(3) Thirdly, as is generally agreed, the earliest evidence of an interpretation of Daniel 7 in individual terms, apart from the Jesus tradition, appears in the *Similitudes of Enoch* and in *4 Ezra* 13. There is no dispute that the latter originated after the fall of Jerusalem in 70 CE. The former is variously dated, but the arguments for dating it prior to 50 CE are at best slender. My own suspicion is that, like *4 Ezra* 13, it reflects an enhanced interest in Daniel 7's vision which the crisis of the 60s and early 70s brought to Judaea.[13] At any rate, it

---

11. See, e.g., Mk 8.29; Heb. 4.14; Rom. 10.9.

12. Worth noting is the development in Barnabas Lindars's views on the matter between his 'Re-Enter the Apocalyptic Son of Man', *NTS* 22 (1975–76), pp. 52-72, and his *Jesus Son of Man: A Fresh Examination of the Son of Man Sayings in the Gospels* (London: SPCK, 1983), Chapter 1 'The Myth of the Son of Man'.

13. See further my *Christology in the Making* (London: SCM, 1980; 2nd edn, 1989), pp. 77-78 and n. 79.

would be very unwise to assume that the *Similitudes* should be dated prior to the 30s.

What I find to be most significant at this point, however, is that both the *Similitudes* and *4 Ezra* 13 seem to be making what they regarded as a new or fresh interpretation of Daniel's vision (cf. *4 Ezra* 12.10ff.), and that they do so without any obvious awareness of each other (or of the Jesus tradition). That is to say, the argument that the two documents can be taken to indicate earlier reflection on Daniel's vision simply does not work. For neither document shows any awareness of such earlier reflection. In both cases the interpretation is introduced and explained with all the air of a new insight into or exposition of an old text.[14]

In short, the evidence for the thesis that there was a 'Son of Man' theology or the hope of a heavenly messiah framed on Daniel 7 within the Judaism of Jesus' day is markedly lacking.

II

Collins, however, thinks that 4Q246 provides just that evidence and may even be the earliest case of an individual and messianic interpretation of the man-like figure in Daniel's vision.[15]

The fragment is in two columns, the beginning of the first (right

---

14. *1 En.* 46.1-3: 'And there I saw one who had a head of days, and his head was white like wool; and with him there was another, whose face had the appearance of a man... And I asked one of the holy angels... about that Son of Man, who he was, and whence he was, and why he went with the Head of Days. And he answered me and said to me, This is the Son of Man who has righteousness, and with whom righteousness dwells...' (M.A. Knibb, in H.F.D. Sparks [ed.], *The Apocryphal Old Testament* [Oxford: Clarendon Press, 1984]). *4 Ezra* 13.1-3: 'After seven days I dreamed a dream in the night; and behold, a great wind arose from the sea so that it stirred up all its waves. And I looked, and behold, this wind made something like the figure of a man come up out of the heart of the sea. And I looked, and behold, that man flew with the clouds of heaven...' (M.E. Stone, *Fourth Ezra* [Hermeneia; Minneapolis: Fortress Press, 1990], p. 381). See further M. Casey, *Son of Man: The Interpretation and Influence of Daniel 7* (London: SPCK, 1979), Chapter 5.

15. Collins, *Scepter*, Chapter 7; in an earlier form as 'The *Son of God* Text from Qumran', in M.C. De Boer (ed.), *From Jesus to John: Essays on Jesus and New Testament Christology* (Festschrift M. de Jonge; JSNTSup, 84; Sheffield: JSOT Press, 1993), pp. 65-82.

hand) column having been torn away. The text of the second column, which is of the most immediate relevance, is clear and well pre-served,[16] which makes the delay in publication all the more frustrating.[17]

ברה די אל יתאמר ובר עליון יקרונה כזיקיא	1
די חזותא כן מלכותהן תהוה שני[ן] ימלכון על	2
ארעא וכלא ידשון עם לעם ידוש ומדינה למדי[נ]ה	3
vac עד יקו/ים עם אל וכלא ינו/יח מן חרב	4
מלכותה מלכות עלם וכל ארחתה בקשוט ידי[ן]	5
ארעא בקשט וכלא יעבד שלם חרב מן ארעא יסף	6
וכל מדינתא לה יסגדון אל רבא באילה	7
הוא ועבד לה קרב עממין ינתן בידה וכלהן	8
ירמה קדמוהי שלטנה שלטן עלם וכל תהומי	9

[1]Son of God he will be named and son of the Most High they will call him. Like sparks [2]of the vision, so will their kingdom be; they will rule for years on [3]the earth and trample on everything; people will trample on people, and province on province [4](blank) until the/a people of God arises and everyone rests from the sword. [5]Its kingdom will be an eternal king-dom, and all its paths shall be in truth/righteousness. It will jud[ge] [6]the earth in truth and all will make peace. The sword will cease from the earth, [7]and all the provinces will pay it homage. The great God is its

16. The photo of 4Q246 is reproduced by E. Puech, 'Fragment d'une Apocalypse en araméen (4Q246 = pseudo-Dan[d]) et le "Royaume de Dieu"', *RB* 99 (1992), pp. 98-131 (facing p. 108) and by J.A. Fitzmyer, '4Q246: The "Son of God" Document from Qumran', *Bib* 74 (1993), pp. 153-74 (facing p. 168). For the first column, see the detailed discussion in Puech, 'Fragment', pp. 109-14, and Fitzmyer, '4Q246', pp. 157-61. In reproducing only col. ii I follow the advice of G. Vermes, 'Qumran Forum Miscellanea I', *JJS* 43 (1992), pp. 299-305 (302), that in view of the broken state of col. i and the necessity for conjectural completion if sense is to be made of it, we ought to focus on col. ii.

17. According to J.A. Fitzmyer, 'The Contribution of Qumran Aramaic to the Study of the New Testament', *NTS* 20 (1973–74), pp. 382-407 (391), reprinted in *A Wandering Aramean: Collected Aramaic Essays* (Missoula, MT: Scholars Press, 1979), pp. 85-113, with an *Addendum* (pp. 102-107 [90-91]), it was conveyed to J.T. Milik in 1958, who lectured on it at Harvard in December 1972, on which occasion he 'passed out a tentative English translation of the text and exposed the Aramaic text'. In this early article Fitzmyer reproduced only ll. 1-4 of col. ii; see his further explanation in '4Q246', pp. 153-54 (he reproduces the text in full on p. 155). Even in the reproduction of a 1983 paper in 1992, F. García Martínez, 'The Eschatological Figure of 4Q246', in *Qumran and Apocalyptic: Studies on the Aramaic Texts from Qumran* (Leiden: Brill, 1992), pp. 162-79, was able only to produce a few words from ll. 5-9.

strength. [8]He will make war for it; peoples he will deliver into its hand and all of them [9]he will cast before it. Its dominion will be an eternal dominion, and all the depths of. . .

The obscurities of the text are frustrating and leave several issues tantalizingly unclear.

(a) Who is the 'son of God', 'son of the Most High'—a historical personage (presumably a king),[18] or an eschatological agent from heaven or sent by God?[19] The preceding (broken) line does not help much—'great will he be called and he will be designated by his name' (col. i, 1. 9).

(b) What is his relation to the following sequence—as one caught up in the turmoil and disasters envisaged in ll. 2-3, or as one who brings it to an end? It is particularly noticeable that the description of the internecine warfare follows the hailing of the 'son of God'; the recognition of the 'son of the Most High' does not mark the end of the troubles. Moreover, the final victory is gained, it would appear, by 'the great God' (col. ii, ll. 7-9).

(c) How does the 'son of God' relate to ll. 4-5? Line 4 could be translated either: 'until there arises (יקום) the people of God', or 'until he raises (יקים) the people of God'.[20] In turn the מלכותה in l. 5 could

18. Milik suggested Alexander Balas, son of Antiochus Epiphanes (according to Fitzmyer, 'Qumran Aramaic', p. 392 [= *Wandering Aramean*, p. 92; '4Q246', pp. 167-68]); Puech recognizes the possibility of such a reference ('Fragment', p. 127); Vermes suggested 'the last ruler of the final world empire. . . a usurper of the "son of God" title' ('Qumran Forum', p. 303); Fitzmyer originally envisaged 'the son of some enthroned king, possibly an heir to the throne of David' ('Qumran Aramaic', p. 392 [= *Wandering Aramean*, pp. 93, 106]), and in his further study of the text concludes that what is in view is 'a coming Jewish ruler, perhaps a member of the Hasmonean dynasty, who [will] be a successor to the Davidic throne, but who is not envisaged as a Messiah' ('4Q246', pp. 173-74). Fitzmyer also points out that this is the earliest attested use of the phrase/title 'son (singular) of the Most High' (cf. [LXX] Sir. 4.10; Mk 5.7) (*Wandering Aramean*, p. 106).

19. There have been several suggestions here: Antichrist (D. Flusser, 'The Hubris of the Antichrist in a Fragment from Qumran', in *Judaism and the Origins of Christianity* [Jerusalem: Magnes Press, 1988], pp. 207-13; but see Fitzmyer, '4Q246', pp. 168-69); Melchizedek, Michael (García Martínez, 'Eschatological Figure', pp. 173-78, referring particularly to 1QM col. xiii, 1. 10, col. xvii, ll. 5-8 and 11QMelch); Danielic son of man (S. Kim, *The "Son of Man"' as the Son of God* [WUNT, 30; Tübingen: Mohr, 1983], pp. 21-22; Collins, *Scepter*, pp. 158-60 [more hesitantly]); messiah (Puech, 'Fragment' [on balance]; Collins, *Scepter*).

20. The ' and the ו are virtually indistinguishable in the text.

be translated as 'its kingdom' (the kingdom of the 'people of God') or 'his kingdom' (the kingdom, presumably, of the 'son of God'). The decision made with regard to l. 5 would then carry through the rest of col. ii—'his/its paths'; 'he/it will jud[ge]'; 'pay him/it homage'; 'his/its strength'; 'for him/it'; 'his/its hand'; 'cast before him/it'; 'his/its dominion'. Opinion is divided here too. Most prefer to read יקום,[21] but Puech notes that יקים would find parallels in 4QBenPat 1 1.3-4, *Pss. Sol.* 17.21, 24-26 and Zech. 9.10 (LXX)—the advent of the messiah as the turning point in the conflict.[22] As to whether the main subject of col. ii, ll. 5-9 is 'the son of God' ('his kingdom') or 'the people of God' ('its kingdom'), Puech, Fitzmyer, Collins and García Martínez[23] favour the former, and Flusser and Vermes the latter.

Through these questions of disputed readings and renderings Collins drives a clear line:

(a) The individual named as 'son of God', 'son of the Most High', is unlikely to be a historical king (or eschatological Antichrist);[24] the honorific language used of the figure makes such interpretations unlikely.

(b) The following description of persecution and chaos wrought by (a) kingdom(s) which are temporary and violent seems to reflect the portrayal of Dan. 7.7, as indicated particularly by the verb דוש ('trample on, crush') in l. 3.

(c) The kingdom (ll. 5-9) which is then contrasted with these kingdoms is likely to be the kingdom of the individual mentioned in l. 1. In particular, l. 5 is a close verbal echo of Dan. 7.27 (מלכותה מלכות עלם), as is l. 9 of Dan. 7.14 (שלטנה שלטן עלם).

On the basis of these echoes of Daniel 7 (b and c) Collins suggests that the one named as 'son of God, son of the Most High' (a) may be identified with the 'one like a son of man' in Daniel 7.13-14.[25] The key consideration here seems to be that the sequence of lines in col. ii parallels the sequence in Daniel 7 where the kingdom is first given to

21. Flusser, 'Hubris', p. 208; Fitzmyer, '4Q246', pp. 155, 163-64; Collins, *Scepter*, p. 155; García Martínez, *The Dead Sea Scrolls Translated* (Leiden: Brill; Grand Rapids: Eerdmans, 2nd edn, 1996), p. 138; G. Vermes, *The Dead Sea Scrolls in English* (Harmondsworth: Penguin Books, 4th edn, 1995), p. 332.

22. Puech, 'Fragment', p. 117.

23. Already in 'Eschatological Figure', p. 170.

24. See above n. 19.

25. Collins, *Scepter*, pp. 158-60.

the man-like figure of Daniel's vision (Dan. 7.14) and then to 'the saints of the Most High' (Dan. 7.18, 22, 27). So in 4Q246 the initial talk of the 'son of God' (col. ii, l. 1) is followed by talk of the people of God and his/its kingdom.

However, I have some problems with this.

(a) If an allusion to the man-like figure of Daniel 7 was intended, it is remarkable that it is not clearer. The two features which everywhere else indicate such an allusion are the man-likeness/humanness of the figure, and his heavenly transport on clouds. When echoes of Daniel 7 are otherwise so notable in 4Q246 col. ii, it is odd to find them lacking at just this point. Collins is well aware of these weaknesses in his thesis,[26] as also of the fact that the title 'son of God' is nowhere attributed to the principal angel variously referred to elsewhere in the Dead Sea Scrolls (Michael, Melchizedek, or whoever).[27] 'Nonetheless', he concludes with surprising confidence, 'it is difficult to avoid the impression that the author had Daniel's figure in mind'.[28]

(b) Line 3 does indeed seem to echo Dan. 7.7, and the term דוש is used in the restatement of 7.7 in 7.23.[29] However, there is no indication in ll. 1-3 that Israel is particularly the victim of this persecution (as in Dan. 7.20), a central feature of Daniel 7. If anything, the echo is of the internecine warfare within the Syrian empire ('people on people, province on province') which enabled the Maccabees and Hasmonaeans to arise and establish their independent kingdom (cf. col. ii, ll. 6-9).

(c) This suggests in turn that יקום is indeed the correct reading and that the text is framed with the success of the Maccabees and Hasmonaeans in mind ('until the people of God arises and makes everyone rest from the sword').[30] The more natural reading thereafter

26. *Scepter*, p. 167.
27. *Scepter*, pp. 161, 163.
28. *Scepter*, p. 167.
29. The verb is used elsewhere in the Old Testament for the image of nations being trampled under foot (see, for example, H.F. Fuhs, *TDOT*, III, pp. 183-84) including Israel (Isa. 21.10).
30. Milik dated the fragment to the last third of the first century BCE (Fitzmyer, 'Qumran Aramaic', p. 391). Puech suggested that it was contemporary with Daniel ('Fragment', p. 129). Collins prefers a date in the first century BCE, but prior to the advent of Rome (*Scepter*, p. 167). If the comments made in the text are to the point, a date in the late second century BCE would be appropriate.

is in reference to this kingdom: 'its kingdom...' Three considerations may strengthen the case.

First, the awkwardness of the English translation ('its kingdom') should not be counted against this rendering; Vermes quite properly translates the references thereafter to 'people' as to a corporate noun ('their kingdom', 'their paths', 'they will judge' etc.). Collins objects that 'judgment is a royal function'; 'in no case...is the function of judgment given to the people collectively'.[31] But if the people are given royal authority (kingdom and dominion) then that would carry with it judicial authority. This may be already implicit in Dan. 7.18. It is certainly noticeable that the thought of the saints sitting in judgment is soon articulated within the apocalyptic tradition (Rev. 20.4); it is already referred to in 1 Cor. 6.2 as something well known, and is part of the Jesus tradition (Mt. 19.28/Lk. 22.29-30; implicit in Mk 10.37 and parallels).

Secondly, the echo of Dan. 7.27 in l. 5 strengthens the implication that the reference is to 'its/their kingdom', since the sequence is closely similar in both documents:

> The kingdom and dominion... shall be given to the people of the saints of the Most High; their kingdom shall be an everlasting kingdom (עלם מלכותה מלכות)... (Dan. 7.27).
> Until the people of God arises and makes everyone rest from the sword. Their kingdom shall be an everlasting kingdom (מלכותה עלם מלכות)... (col. ii, ll. 7-9).

The fact that the people owe this success to 'the great God' (col. ii, ll. 7-9) further strengthens the parallel: as in Dan. 7.27, the kingdom has been given to them by God.

Thirdly, the fact that the final echo of Daniel 7 is to 7.14 can be taken two ways. In Dan. 7.14 שלטנה שלטן עלם has to be rendered, 'His dominion is an everlasting dominon', the reference being to the dominion given to the 'one like a son of man'. Would that be enough to swing all the preceding ambiguous phrases back to a reference to a single individual ('his kingdom')? More likely we should see in the twofold echo of Dan. 7.27 and 14 an early recognition that the 'one like a son of man' was to be understood as a symbolic representation

---

31. *Scepter*, pp. 159, 161, referring to Ps. 72.1-2; Isa. 11.4; 4QpIs[a] col. iii frag. 7.26; *Pss. Sol.* 17.29; cf. Fitzmyer, '4Q246', p. 164.

of 'the people of the saints of the Most High'.[32] What was given to the people of Israel was what was given to the man-like figure in Daniel's vision.

In short, the case for seeing a deliberate echo of Daniel 7 in 4Q246 col. ii is strong enough to provide the basis for further reflection regarding its significance. But the echo seems to be most strongly of the triumph predicted for the people of the saints of the Most High, with the historical allusion to the triumph of the Maccabaean/ Hasmonaean kingdom in the decline of the Syrian empire more clearly sketched in than it could have been in Daniel 7 itself.

III

Where then does this leave the question regarding the identity of the 'son of God', 'son of the Most High' in 4Q246 col. ii, l. 1? Collins's suggestion, that the figure is intended as an allusion to the man-like figure of Dan. 7.13-14, has proved less than convincing. A reference to the dominion given to the man-like figure there might be (col. ii, l. 9; Dan. 7.14), but not as a reference to an individual figure distinguishable from the people themselves. If anything, the double/parallel echo of Dan. 7.27 and 7.14 strengthens the inference that the man-like figure was understood as indeed a visionary symbol of the people of the saints of the Most High. The absence of what elsewhere are the sure allusions to the Danielic 'one like a son of man'—the use of the phrase itself ('the/that son of man') or consciousness that the phrase meant simply 'man', and/or the talk of one 'coming with clouds'— suggests more strongly that 4Q246 col. ii, l. 1 had no intention of evoking the humanness or heavenly arrival of the Danielic 'man'.

Who then is the 'son of God, son of the Most High' in l. 1 of 4Q246 col. ii? Given the sequence of the fragmentary col. i and of col. ii, the most plausible hypothesis is still that a human king is in view, one who made claims for himself and who was hailed by others as 'son of God' and 'son of the Most High'. Such a figure is almost standard in such traditional polemic (the king of Babylon, Isa. 14.12-14; the king of Tyre—Ezek. 28.12-15; the lawless one, 2 Thess. 2.4).[33] The text then envisages this figure emerging (col. ii, l. 1) within the course of

32. Vermes, 'Qumran Forum', p. 303.
33. The 'honorific language', on which Collins bases his objection to such an interpretation, provides no real basis at all.

turmoil such as marked the decline of the Syrian empire (col. ii, ll. 2-4), prior to the rise of 'the people of God' (col. ii, ll. 2-5).

If, however, it was a question of recognizing an association between one called 'son of God' and talk of an 'everlasting kingdom', the most obvious echo would be of 2 Sam. 7.13-14:[34]

וכננתי את כסא ממלכתו עד עולם:
אני אהיה לו לאב והוא יהיה לי לבן

I will establish the throne of his kingdom forever.
I will be a father to him and he shall be a son to me.

The possibility that such an echo was intended is strengthened by the fact that 4Q174 (4QFlor) col. i, ll. 10-11 cites just this passage:

והכינותי את כסא ממלכתו [לעול]ם:
אני [א]ה[י]ה] לוא לאב והוא יהיה לי לבן

Moreover, in 4Q174, the quotation of 2 Sam. 7.13-14 is part of a more extended exposition beginning, so far as our text is concerned, at 2 Sam. 7.10, where the emphasis is on the promise of divinely given cessation from affliction by others: 'I will give you rest from all your enemies' (7.11; 4Q174 col. i, l. 7). The similarity to 4Q246 col. i, ll. 4-7 is noticeable.

The possibility, then, cannot be excluded that 4Q246 col. ii is something of an amalgam of expectations born of 2 Sam. 7.10-14 and Daniel 7. That is to say, the 'son of God' of 4Q246 col. ii, l. 1 may indeed be a way of referring to the hoped for messiah, 'son of God' of 2 Sam. 7.14.[35] In which case, it would provide further evidence that the thought of the royal messiah as God's son was familiar to the Qumran community. What seems to be lacking, however, is any obvious allusion to the 'one like a son of man' of Dan. 7.13-14. Consequently, whatever we make of 4Q246 col. ii, l. 1, we must conclude that the identification of the 'son of God' of 4Q246 with the 'one like a son of man' of Dan. 7.13-14 goes beyond the evidence, and that

34. Fitzmyer, '4Q246', p. 162: 'It (ii 1) is probably inspired by 2 Sam. 7.14...' Nevertheless Fitzmyer remains unpersuaded by a messianic interpretation of 4Q246 col. ii, l. 1 (pp. 170-71).

35. Oddly enough, Collins is so captivated by the possibility that 4Q246 col. ii, l. 1 is a reference to Dan. 7.13-14 that he does not consider the possibility of a more immediate allusion to 2 Sam. 7.14, even though he refers to it in this discussion (*Scepter*, p. 164).

4Q246 provides no support for the thesis that the Danielic man-like figure was understood as an individual being, messiah or angel, in the period prior to Jesus.

THE THRONE-THEOPHANY OF THE BOOK OF GIANTS: SOME NEW LIGHT ON THE BACKGROUND OF DANIEL 7

Loren T. Stuckenbruck

1. *Introduction*

Ever since 1971 the scholarly world has generally known about the existence of the *Book of Giants* among the fragments of Qumran.[1] At that time, it was Josef T. Milik who, having been assigned the publications of the fragments corresponding to parts of *1 Enoch* from Cave 4, had identified a set of Enochic fragments from Cave 4 not found in any extant part of *1 Enoch*. The basis of his identification of these materials with the *Book of Giants* rested ultimately on two further criteria: (1) the fragments in question contain details which were uniquely shared with fragments from the Manichaean *Book of Giants* published during the 1940s by W.B. Henning[2] and (2) the fragments

1. J.T. Milik, 'Turfan et Qumran: Livre des géants juif et manichéen', in G. Jeremias, H.-W. Kuhn, and H. Stegemann (eds.), *Tradition und Glaube: Das frühe Christentum in seiner Umwelt* (Göttingen: Vandenhoeck & Ruprecht, 1971), pp. 117-27; and 'Problèmes de la littérature hénochique à la lumière des fragments araméens des Qumran', *HTR* 64 (1971), pp. 333-78 (esp. pp. 366-72). See also Milik's *The Book of Enoch: Aramaic Fragments from Qumrân Cave 4* (Oxford: Clarendon Press, 1976), esp. pp. 4, 6-7, 57-58, 230, 236-38, and 298-339.

2. See W.B. Henning, 'The Book of Giants', *BSOAS* 11 (1943–46), pp. 52-74 (a publication of readings and translations of fragmentary materials in Middle Persian, Parthian, Uygur, Sogdian, and Coptic). A significant later publication of a Manichaean fragment, and too late for Milik to take into account, is by W. Sundermann, *Mittelpersische und partische kosmogonische und Parabeltexte der Manichäer* (Berliner Turfantexte, 4; Berlin: Akademie Verlag, 1973), pp. 76-78 (MS 'M 5900'), and *idem*, 'Ein weiteres Fragment aus Manis Gigantenbuch', in *Orientalia J. Duchesne–Guillemin emerito oblata* (Acta Iranica, 23 [and Second Series, 9]; Leiden: Brill, 1984), pp. 491-505 (frag. 'L'). For the most thorough recent treatment of the Manichaean sources for the *Book of Giants*, see J.C. Reeves, *Jewish Lore in Manichean Cosmogony: Studies in the Book of Giants Traditions* (Monographs of the Hebrew Union College, 14; Cincinnati: Hebrew University College Press, 1992).

show a specific interest in the offspring of the 'sons of God' and the 'daughters of humankind' whose birth as giants (LXX, γίγαντες; in the Hebrew, called נפילים and נבורים) is narrated in Gen. 6.1-4. Unlike the *1 Enoch* materials and like the Manichaean sources, these fragments give specific names to the giants: for instance, Mahaway, 'Ohyah, Hahyah, Ahiram, Hobabish, and Gilgamesh.[3]

In 1976, as part of his publication of the Aramaic fragments from extant parts of *1 Enoch*, Milik decided to publish the *Book of Giants* fragments from one manuscript with photographs (4Q203), while offering some readings (without photographs) from other as yet unknown manuscripts and re-identifying some previously published materials with the work.[4] As a result of his studies and the subsequent ones of other scholars, it seems clear that the *Book of Giants* at Qumran is represented by seven manuscripts at the very least (4Q203; 4Q530, 531, 532; 1Q23; 2Q26; and 6Q8),[5] with the very real possibility that three more should be included (4Q206 frags. 2–3; 4Q556; and 1Q24).[6] This attestation, whether the manuscripts derive from one

In addition Milik observed that portions of the *Book of Giants* seem to correspond to the so-called *Midrash of Shemhazai and 'Aza'el*, for which he provides a collation of four mediaeval Hebrew MSS in *The Books of Enoch*, pp. 321-39.

3. Mahaway (1Q23 frag. 27, l. 2; 4Q203 frag. 2, l. 4; 4Q530 col. ii, l. 20; col. iii, ll. 6-7; 6Q8 frag. 1, ll. 2, 4); 'Ohyah (1Q23 frag. 29, l. 1; 4Q203 frag. 4, l. 3; frag. 7A, l. 5; 4Q530 col. ii, ll. 1, 15; frag. 12, l. 2; 4Q531 frag. 17, l. 9; 6Q8 frag. 1, ll. 2, 4); Hahyah (4Q530 col. ii, ll. 7-12 is probably his dream-vision; 4Q203 frag. 4, l. 3; frag. 7A, l. 5); Ahiram (4Q531 frag. 4, l. 1); Hobabish (4Q203 frag. 3, l. 3); and Gilgamesh (4Q530 col. ii, l. 2; 4Q531 frag. 17, l. 12). See also the incomplete name אדכ.[in 4Q203 frag. 3, l. 3.

4. So in *The Books of Enoch*.

5. See especially F. García Martínez, 'The Book of Giants' in *idem, Qumran and Apocalyptic: Studies on the Aramaic Texts from Qumran* (STDJ, 9; Leiden: Brill, 1992), pp. 97-115 and, further, Chapter 2 in my forthcoming volume on *The Book of Giants from Qumran: Text, Translation, and Commentary* (TSAJ, 63; Tübingen: Mohr [Paul Siebeck], 1997).

6. Far less plausible are the proposals to assign the following manuscripts to the *Book of Giants*: 4Q533 (so initially Jean Starcky; see E. Tov with S.J. Pfann [eds.], *The Dead Sea Scrolls on Microfiche: Companion Volume* [Leiden: Brill, 1993], p. 47); 4Q534 (J.A. Fitzmyer, 'Qumran Aramaic in the New Testament', in *idem, A Wandering Aramean: Collected Aramaic Essays* [SBLMS, 25; Chico, CA: Scholars Press, 1979], p. 101); 1Q19 and 6Q14 (K. Beyer, *Die aramäischen Texte vom Toten Meer* [Göttingen: Vandenhoeck & Ruprecht, 1984], pp. 229 n. 1, 268); 4Q535–536 (K. Beyer, *Die aramäischen Texte vom Toten Meer: Ergänzungsband* [Göttingen:

or more groups, may reflect a relative popularity of the *Book of Giants* during the Second Temple period.

While there is no question that Milik has made a real contribution by calling attention to the existence of a new work among the Qumran caves, his work was far from exhaustive. For instance, a number of fragments from manuscripts 4Q530, 4Q531, and 4Q532, some of these significant, were not included in his discussion. This is understandable due to the fact that these materials had been assigned to Jean Starcky for publication. Even more frustrating in his monograph on the *Books of Enoch*, however, was Milik's inexact allusions to *Book of Giants* manuscripts, which has resulted in contradictory interpretations by subsequent scholars concerning the nature of his references.[7]

2. *Consequences of Interpreting an Unpublished Text: The Case of 4Q530 col. ii, ll. 17-19*

Perhaps one of the best examples of a significant text which Milik did not choose to discuss comes from 4Q530 col. ii, ll. 17-19. This part of the *Book of Giants* contains the dream-visions of two giants, the brothers Hahyah and 'Ohyah. In the narrative of the work, the meaning of their ominous visions is not readily understood by the giants, who resort to sending one of their own (the giant Mahaway) to Enoch

---

Vandenhoeck & Ruprecht, 1994], pp. 125-26); and 4Q537 (Reeves, *Jewish Lore*, p. 110).

7. See especially his statement in *The Books of Enoch*, p. 309: 'Up to the present I have located six copies of the Book of Giants among the manuscripts of Qumrân: the four manuscripts cited above (1Q23, 6Q8, 4QEnGiants[b,c]), a third manuscript from the Starcky collection, and 4QEnGiants[a] published below. There are also five other manuscripts too poorly represented to allow a sufficiently certain identification of the fragments: En[e] 2–3 (above, pp. 236-38), 1Q24 (DJD, 1, p. 99 and pl. IX), 2Q26 (DJD, 3, pp. 90-91 and pl. XVII; see below, pp. 334-35), and two groups of small fragments entrusted to the Starcky edition.' Milik's vague references here to a 'third manuscript' and 'two groups of fragments' from the lot assigned to Starcky have been capable of incompatible interpretations. The 'third manuscript' is 4QEnGiants[e] in Fitzmyer (*The Dead Sea Scrolls: Major Publications and Tools for Study* [SBLRBS, 20; Atlanta: Scholars Press, 1990)], pp. 52-53), while it is taken as a reference to 4QEnGiants[a] by Beyer (*Die aramäischen Texte*, pp. 259-60) and García Martínez ('The Book of Giants', pp. 104-105 and *The Dead Sea Scrolls Translated*, p. 505. In Milik's 'two groups of fragments' these authors have seen '4QEnGiants[d,f]' (Fitzmyer), '4QEnGiants[f,g]' (Beyer), and '4QGiants[e] ar?' and '4QEnGiants[e]' (García Martínez).

for an interpretation (col. ii, l. 21 to col. iii l. 11). Through Enoch the giants' worst fears are confirmed: the dreams of Hahyah and 'Ohyah herald God's imminent judgment of the giants for the atrocities they have committed on earth during the ante-diluvian period. As a whole the *Book of Giants* thus emphasizes that the giants will not be able to escape the consequences of their activities.[8] The lines in question belong to 'Ohyah's dream, the second of these visions.

Having cited most of the rest of the column (ll. 3-12, 14-16, 20-23), Milik was content with merely summarizing the content of ll. 17-19, which according to him are a description of divine judgment 's'inspiré de Dan 7,9-10'.[9] It was apparent from this statement alone that the text, to the extent that it is legible, would be of particular significance, since the early interpretation of Daniel 7's vision of the Ancient of Days and of one like a son of man has been a matter of interest for students of both the Hebrew Scriptures and the New Testament alike. Nevertheless, Milik's allusive comment provided all one could know about the text until its photographic evidence was made available in 1991 through Robert Eisenman and James Robinson's *Facsimile*

8. If there is a polemical edge to the *Book of Giants*, then, it may be found within the context of conflicting views among early Jewish works concerning the fate of the ante-diluvian giants in relation to the great flood. The view represented in the *Book of Giants*, the *Book of Watchers* (cf. *1 En.* 10 and 15–16), and other early Jewish documents (so CD col. ii, ll. 17-21; *Sir.* 16.17a; and *Wis.* 14.6-7) contrasts with the motif of the giants' survival of the flood preserved in Eusebius, *Praep. Evang.* 9.17.1-9 and 9.18.2. These passages cited a work *On the Jews of Assyria* by the first century BCE Alexander 'Polyhistor', who in turn has preserved traditions attributed, respectively, to a 'Eupolemus' and to 'anonymous' (ἀδέσποτοι) authors. For all their differences, these fragments—often referred to together as 'Pseudo-Eupolemus'—share a common perspective in that they (1) link Abraham and the γίγαντες to the transmission of Babylonian astrological science; (2) associate the building of a tower with a giant (passage 2) or giants (passage 1); and (3) relate an *escape* by giants from some form of destruction. In 9.17.1-9 the giants are said to have been 'saved from the deluge' (οἱ διασωθέντοι ἐκ τοῦ κατακλύσμου) and in 9.18.2 one of them, Belos, escapes death and lived in Babylon. The motif of the giants' escape may have been read out of LXX Gen. 10.9 (Nimrod = γίγας) and Num. 13.33 (נפילים = Anakim) and is picked up in rabbinic stories which identify the kings Sihon and Og as giants surviving the flood (*b. Zeb.* 113b and *b. Nid.* 61a; cf. *Targ. Ps.-J.* to Deut. 2.2 and 3.11). The *Book of Giants* denies such survival to the evil giants.
9. 'Turfan et Qumran', p. 122. See also *The Books of Enoch*, p. 305.

Edition[10] and in 1992 in Emanuel Tov's *Dead Sea Scrolls on Microfiche*.[11] Finally, on the basis of these photographic editions, Klaus Beyer then published his readings of these lines in the *Ergänzungsband* to his *Die aramäischen Texte vom Toten Meer* in 1994.[12]

In the meantime, however, Milik's description of the unpublished text betrayed a tradition-historical judgment about the background of the *Book of Giants* text: that is, it implied that the text from the *Book of Giants* is dependent on Daniel 7. Of course, without access to the photographs themselves, there was no way of knowing in the meantime what is actually to be read in the text. In the absence of evidence, Beyer (in 1984)[13] and Reeves[14] were thus wise to mention the mere similarity between ll. 17-19 and the throne-theophany in Dan. 7.9-10.

The tradition-historical implication of Milik's comments, however, was more influential on Florentino García Martínez's discussion of the *Book of Giants*,[15] more particularly on the matter of dating the composition. García Martínez was rightly calling into question Milik's dating of the *Book of Giants* to sometime between 128 BCE (his date for the composition of *Jubilees*) and 100 BCE (for him the latest possible date for the composition of the Damascus Document), especially since (1) the dates themselves are debatable;[16] (2) it is precarious to assume that *Jubilees* would have cited the *Book of Giants* had it been in existence; and (3) it is doubtful that the Damascus Document actually cites the *Book of Giants*.[17] In his alternative proposal, García Martínez proposed a way forward by focusing on the significance of the relationship between the unpublished text in 4Q530 col. ii, ll. 17-19 and the text of Dan. 7.9-10. He reasoned that if Milik's claim of literary dependence on the Danielic text could be substantiated, then

10. R. Eisenman and J. Robinson, *A Facsimile Edition of the Dead Sea Scrolls* (2 vols.; Washington, DC: Biblical Archeology Society, 1991).

11. See bibliography in n. 6 above.

12. Bibliography in n. 6 above.

13. *Aramäischen Texte*, p. 264 n. 1.

14. *Jewish Lore*, p. 92.

15. 'The Book of Giants', p. 104.

16. See Reeves's excellent critique in *Jewish Lore*, pp. 53-54.

17. So correctly García Martínez, 'The Book of Giants', p. 115. The passage in question is CD col. ii, ll. 18-19 which describes the sons of the Watchers as those 'whose height was as the height of cedars'. However, this description, according to García Martínez, is better understood as a 'poetic extension' of a previous phrase ('his height like the height of cedars') which itself is taken from Amos 2.9.

the composition of the *Book of Giants* is to be assigned to an 'upper limit by the middle of the 2nd century BC'.[18] Despite García Martínez's *proviso* that a literary dependence on Daniel would need to be confirmed, the validity of his proposal for a date was nevertheless based on the correctness of Milik's passing tradition–historical judgment.

3. *Comparison between 4Q530 col. ii, ll. 16-19 and Daniel 7.9-10*

It is now becoming clear that Milik's claim of a literary dependence on Daniel 7 in 'Ohyah's dream-vision is untenable. This is borne out by a comparative analysis of the two Aramaic texts. After providing a reading of the Aramaic text for 4Q530 col. ii, ll. 16b-19 below, its translation is compared with a translation of Dan. 7.9-10 (correspondences between the texts in vocabulary and/or sense are given in *italics*):

ה]א שלשלטן שמיא לארעא נחת	16
וכרסון יחיטו וקרישא רנא יתנ]ב מאה מ]אין לה משמשין אלף אלפי לה	17
[פלחין כ]ל] ק]דמוהי הוא קאמין וארון ספרן]ין פתיחו ודין אמיר ודין	18
[רבא בכתב כ]תיב וברשם רשים].]לכל חיא ובסרא ועל	19

	Book of Giants		**Daniel 7.9-10**
(16b)	Be]hold,		
		(9)	(a) I was looking until
	the ruler of the heavens descended to the earth,		
(17a)	and *thrones* *were erected* (*yhytw*)		(b) *thrones* *were set up* (*rmyw*)
(17b)	and the Great Holy One *sat d[own.*		(c) and an Ancient of Days *sat down*
			(d) His clothing (was) like snow-white.
			(e) and the hair of his head (was) like white wool.
			(f) His throne (was) flames of fire;
			(g) its wheels (were) a burning fire.

18. García Martínez, 'The Book of Giants', p. 115. García Martínez determined his *terminus ante quem*, the 'end of the 2nd century BC', on the basis of Milik's claim that the manuscript 4QEnoch[c] relies on an earlier manuscript from the second century BCE in which the Enochic writings were already being collected.

Book of Giants		Daniel 7.9-10
		(10) (a) a river of fire flowed (b) and went forth from before it.
(17c)	A hundred hu]ndreds (were) *serving him;*	
(17d-18a)	*a thousand thousands* [(were) worshiping?] him.	(c) *A thousand thousands served him,*
(18b)	[A]ll stood *[be]fore him.*	(d) and a myriad myriads *stood before him.*
(18c-d)	And behold [*books*]s *were opened,* and judgment was spoken;	(e) The court sat down, (f) and books *were opened.*
(18e-19a)	and the judgment of [the Great One] (was) [wr]itten [in a book] and (was) sealed in an inscription... [	
(19b)	]for every living being and (all) flesh and upon [	

Based on this comparison, the two passages may be said to correspond in the following four ways: First, the conjunctions excepted, the passages have at least eight vocabulary items in common: כרסה (throne), יתב (sit down), שמש (serve), אלף (thousand), ספר[19] (book), קדם (before), and קום (arise, stand). Secondly, it is significant to note that of these eight terms seven appear in an identical grammatical form: כרסון (abs. pl.), יתב (*qal* 3rd masc. sing. pf.), ספרין (abs. pl.), פתיחו (*qal* pass. 3rd com. pl.), קדמוהי (prep. with 3rd masc. pl. suff.), יקומון (*qal* 3rd masc. pl. impf.), אלף (abs. sing.), and אלפים/ן (abs. pl.). Under this category one might also wish to include the *qal* passive third person plural perfect forms for רמיו and יחיטו in the respective parallel texts of Daniel and *Book of Giants*. Thirdly, the sequence of the phraseology in both is remarkably similar. The *Book of Giants* has five successive phrases (so 17a, 17b, 17c-d, 18b, and 18c) which correspond exactly to the order of the parallel phrases in Daniel 7 (cf. vv. 9b, 9c, 10c, 10d, and 10f). Fourthly, the five parallel phrases preserve a

---

19. In view of the context and the similarity with Dan. 7.10, ספר[ין is the most probable restoration in 4Q530 col. ii, l. 18c.

common sequence for their parts (17a = 7.9b; 17b = 7.9c; 17c = 7.10c [substantive + verb]; 18b = 7.10d; and 18c = 7.10-11).

These similarities demonstrate sufficiently that a tradition-historical dependence between the texts is likely. Without further analysis, however, one is not in a position to consider the nature of this source-critical relationship. If there is a literary connection of some sort, then several explanations for this are possible: (a) the *Book of Giants* has adapted the Daniel text (as suggested by Milik's comment); (b) Daniel has adapted and extended the text in the *Book of Giants*; (c) both the *Book of Giants* and Daniel draw upon a prior independent tradition. Under (c) two further possibilities may be considered: Daniel preserves a prototype of the tradition used in the *Book of Giants*[20] or the *Book of Giants* preserves a prototype of the tradition used in Daniel. Whereas alternatives (a) and (b) may be closely bound up with the dating of both compositions in relation to each other, (c) envisions the possibility of dependence on a more faithfully preserved form of a tradition underlying one or the other passage.

In order to evaluate the viability of these options, it is necessary to consider the main differences between the passages. First, whereas in the *Book of Giants* the subject of the theophany is designated 'the Great Holy One', Dan. 7.9 (and vv. 13, 22) refers to an 'Ancient of Days'. Secondly, the *Book of Giants* text describes the theophany as an advent—or better, 'descent' (נחת)—to the earth. In the Daniel text, there is no attempt to locate the theophany, though its interest in the details of the divine throne (see *1 En.* 14.18-22) suggests that the vision is concerned with the execution of judgment in a *heavenly* court. Thirdly, 'Ohyah's vision uses three verbs to describe the worship activity before the divine throne ('serving', ['worshiping'], and 'standing'), while Daniel makes use of two verbs ('serving' and 'standing'). Fourthly, while the *Book of Giants* text only describes 'the Great and Holy One' as taking a seat, Daniel attributes 'sitting' to both the 'Ancient of Days' (v. 9c) and the heavenly court (v. 10e). Fifthly, and perhaps significantly, the texts differ in their respective numbers of worshippers: while the *Book of Giants* refers to 'hundreds' and 'thousands' (17c-d), Daniel has 'thousands' and 'myriads' (7.10c-d). Finally, and sixthly, if the literary contexts of the visions are taken into

---

20. That is, the *Book of Giants* is not directly inspired by the text of Daniel but by a proto-Daniel tradition.

account, the *Book of Giants* vision, unlike Daniel, makes no reference to a 'son of man' figure.

4. *Evaluation and Conclusion*

As a whole, the differences listed here suggest that the giant's vision in the *Book of Giants* is structurally and theologically less complicated than its counterpart in Daniel. Except for the motif of a theophanic advent, the only clear instance in which the vision of 'Ohyah is longer than that of Daniel occurs near the end: the judgment, which has been pronounced, is both written and sealed (19a). Within the context of the *Book of Giants* the solemnity and finality of the court decision functions as a guarantee that the giants, despite their false hopes, will be destroyed because of the evil deeds they have perpetrated.[21] Thus this part of the vision, which correlates so well with the larger narrative context of the *Book of Giants*, may reflect the way the author(s) appropriated the theophanic tradition. In other respects, however, it seems that it is Daniel—and not the *Book of Giants*—which preserves the more well-developed of the two visions. It seems more likely that the Daniel vision has added speculative details concerning the seated figure, his throne, and the 'son of man' figure than to suppose that the form in the *Book of Giants* represents a redactor's removal of them. In the case of Daniel, a number of scholars have explained the presence of these details on the basis of an author's use of the merkabah vision in Ezekiel 1.[22] Furthermore, if one is allowed to suppose that details of such traditions tend to inflate rather than undergo a scaling down, then it is probable that the 'hundreds' and 'thousands' of worshippers in the giant's vision would have been transformed into

21. See n. 8. above.
22. This point has been emphasized, most notably, by C. Rowland, *The Influence of the First Chapter of Ezekiel on Judaism and Early Christianity* (doctoral thesis, University of Cambridge, 1975); *idem*, *The Open Heaven* (New York: Crossroad, 1982), pp. 95-113 (see esp. p. 98); J. Lust, 'Daniel 7,13 and the Septuagint', *ETL* 54 (1978), pp. 62-69 (esp. pp. 67-68); D. Halperin, *Faces of the Chariot: Early Jewish Responses to Ezekiel's Vision* (TSAJ, 16; Tübingen: Mohr [Paul Siebeck], 1988), pp. 74-78; and L.T. Stuckenbruck, '"One like a Son of Man as the Ancient of Days" in the Old Greek Recension of Daniel 7,13: Scribal Error or Theological Translation?', *ZNW* 86 (1995), pp. 274-75. In addition, details from Dan. 7.9d, f-g and 10a-b, which are not in the *Book of Giants*, may have been derived from the tradition in *1 En.* 14.19-20, 22.

'thousands' and 'myriads' in Daniel rather than the other way around.

This line of reasoning suggests that Milik's comment that the *Book of Giants* text 's'inspiré de Dan 7,9-10' is misleading. Neither is one, on the other hand, to suppose that the *Book of Giants* must therefore have antedated Daniel 7.[23] The comparative analysis offered here does, however, make it likely that the *Book of Giants* preserves a theophanic tradition in a form which has been expanded in Daniel. If this thesis is correct, then the recently available text from 4Q530 col. ii brings contemporary scholarship closer than ever to identifying the kinds of traditions which the author(s) of Daniel 7 had to hand when recording the theophany involving an 'Ancient of Days' and one 'like a son of man'.[24]

23. For a full argumentation concerning the question of dating the *Book of Giants*, see Chapter 1 of my forthcoming book, *The Book of Giants from Qumran*.

24. It is important, then, to distinguish between the religio- and traditio-historical backgrounds for Daniel 7. In emphasizing the importance of the former, J.J. Collins, in his commentary on *Daniel* (Hermeneia; Minneapolis: Augsburg Fortress, 1993), pp. 280-94, has tried to underscore the literary unity of the chapter, not least by associating the visions of the 'Ancient of Days' in vv. 9-10, the beast in vv. 11-12, and the one 'like a son of man' in vv. 13-14. It is instructive here to review Collins's thesis briefly. In rejecting possible backgrounds in Babylonian and Iranian mythologies, Collins appeals to a Canaanite myth as attested among the Ras Shamra materials at Ugarit since they depict Ba'al, 'a rider of the clouds', as subordinate to 'El who is perhaps described as 'father of years'. Ba'al, in turn, slays the beast 'Lôtân' and 'Yamm' (= the sea). If Canaanite mythology is to be understood as having played a formative role in the structure and characters in Daniel's vision, this insight is now to be weighed against the tradition-historical considerations brought to bear on the text through the theophany in the *Book of Giants*. I do not think it necessary to discount a mythological background in favour of the question of sources. However, the vision in 4Q530 col. ii, ll. 16-20 demonstrates that the theophanic vision of the kind found in Dan. 7.9-10 may have circulated independently before it was adapted and integrated into a more complicated vision of larger proportions. It would not be misleading if we suppose that traditions such as the *Book of Giants* theophany, *1 Enoch* 14 and Ezekiel 1 provided the author(s) of Daniel 7 with some of the raw materials for the vision. If this hypothesis is accepted, then it is possible to reconsider the significance of Canaanite mythology for Daniel: provisionally, it would seem to have formed part of a mythological *Vorverständnis* and/or an organizing principle through which independent traditions, whether the author(s) were conscious of this background or not, were welded together to create a new composition. The *Book of Giants* tradition, therefore, may well open up the need for a further exploration of the background for Daniel 7.

THE BOOK OF THE TWELVE, AQIBA'S MESSIANIC INTERPRETATIONS, AND THE REFUGE CAVES OF THE SECOND JEWISH WAR

Brook W.R. Pearson

1. *Introduction: Studying the Bar Kokhba Revolution*

Beyond a few LXX fragments and some unidentifiable Greek fragments found at Qumran,[1] those interested in Greek documents from the Dead Sea region are, for the most part, limited to those from the era of the Bar Kokhba revolution (132–35 CE). For biblical scholarship, this introduces the further difficulty that the Bar Kokhba revolution, beyond the potential significance of the messianic pretensions of its leader, is not viewed as relevant to New Testament studies.[2]

In fact, before the dramatic finds in the 1950s and early 1960s[3] of several caves and their contents which had been occupied by refugees from the Bar Kokhba revolution, this period was a very dimly-lit area of study indeed. Bar Kokhba was, and in many ways, despite the new evidence, still is a semi-legendary figure. He is not dissimilar to the figure of King Arthur in the history of England—we know he existed

---

1. See E. Tov, *The Greek Minor Prophets Scroll from Nahal Hever (8HevXIIgr)* (DJD, 8; The Seiyâl Collection, 1; Oxford: Clarendon Press, 1990), p. 25, for a list of most of the Greek scrolls or fragments found at Qumran. Also see C.P. Thiede, *The Earliest Gospel Fragment? The Qumran Fragment 7Q5 and its Significance for New Testament Studies* (Exeter: Paternoster Press, 1992), and the response to that in G.N. Stanton, *Gospel Truth? New Light on Jesus and the Gospels* (London: HarperCollins, 1995).

2. Notable exceptions to this include R.A. Horsley, 'Popular Messianic Movements around the Time of Jesus', *CBQ* 46 (1984), pp. 491-94; and, more recently, C.A. Evans, *Jesus and his Contemporaries: Comparative Studies* (AGJU, 25; Leiden: Brill, 1995), pp. 183-211.

3. Perhaps the furthest ranging survey of the contributions that these finds made to the study of the second revolt can be found in J.A. Fitzmyer, 'The Bar Cochba Period', in his *Essays on the Semitic Background of the New Testament* (SBLSBS, 5; Missoula, MT: Scholars Press, 1974), pp. 305-54.

in one form or another, his legend is near and dear to the heart of England, but we also know that the legends which have grown up around him are greatly enhanced. Bar Kokhba, by comparison, was the last figure in the history of the Jewish people to rule over a Jewish state, until the formation of the modern state of Israel in 1948. The stories about him in rabbinic literature range from denigration of him as a pretender to the leadership of Israel, to fantastic records of his prowess,[4] but his significance as a national hero to modern Israel goes far beyond these texts.[5]

However—unlike Arthurian scholarship—since the finds of the early 1960s, Bar Kokhba scholarship has leapt forward. Old texts have been reassessed, and the new documents and archaeological remains have allowed a much more accurate and full picture to be drawn of the revolt and its aftermath. This does not, by any means, mean that all, or even most, of our questions surrounding this period have been answered, but it does mean that there is much more with which to work than before.

One of the most frustrating things about this new evidence, however, is the very fact that, though it is so tantalizingly primary, it allows us only a dim glance into the events of the revolution, and an even more poorly-lit glance into the beliefs of the revolutionaries. Of course, even this glance is much more than we have had access to in the past. Items such as the uniqueness of the appellation of 'brother' in several letters and administrative documents,[6] the proto-Masoretic nature of the biblical documents that have been found at the various sites, the existence of fragments of phylacteries,[7] Jewish bronze ritual

4. For denigration of Bar Kokhba, see *Midr. Lam.* 2.2 §§2, 5, in which he is castigated for the murder of Rabbi Eleazar. For a particularly fantastic story, see *y. Taan.* 4.8, where Bar Kokhba is recorded as catching Roman siege stones hurled by catapult and flinging them back, killing many Roman soldiers. For discussion of these and other sources, see R.G. Marks, 'Dangerous Hero: Rabbinic Attitudes toward Legendary Warriors', *HUCA* 54 (1983), pp. 181-94.

5. A thorough discussion of the ideological element in the study of Bar Kokhba can be found in B. Isaac and A. Oppenheimer, 'The Revolt of Bar Kokhba: Ideology and Modern Scholarship', *JJS* 36 (1984), pp. 33-60. This study does not, however, fail to fall into an ideological position of its own.

6. See B. Lifshitz, 'The Greek Documents from the Nahal Seelim and Nahal Mishmar', *IEJ* 11 (1961), pp. 60-61, for a discussion of this appellation.

7. P.Mur. 4 and two fragments from Cave 34 of the Nahal Seelim (see

vessels (especially those converted from Roman/pagan origin),[8] sug-gestive symbolism on coins minted by the revolutionaries,[9] and the correlation of archaeological evidence with previously known infor-mation about Jewish customs and rituals—all have allowed us paint a picture of a fairly conservative, even reactionary, group of Jewish revolutionaries. However, these remains have not allowed us more than a glimpse into the specific beliefs and aspirations of this group. Perhaps this explains why most of the scholarly reconstruction of the beliefs of the rebels is still based on rabbinic sources, coupled with the few classical and early Christian sources which we have had available to us for many centuries.[10]

Y. Aharoni, 'The Expedition to the Judean Desert, 1960: Expedition B', *IEJ* 11 [1961], pp. 22-23).

8.   Y. Yadin ('The Expedition to the Judean Desert, 1960: Expedition D', *IEJ* 11 [1961], p. 39) discusses the find of several bronze vessels in the famous Cave of Letters. The most fascinating aspect of this cache is the fact that several of the vessels have pagan mythological scenes or figures on them which have been defaced, so as to make them kosher for Jewish use.

9.   For thorough discussion of the numismatic material from the Bar Kokhba period, see L. Mildenberg, *The Coinage of the Bar Kokhba Revolt* (Zürich: Schweizerische Numismatische Gessellschaft, 1984).

10.   So, for instance, in his lengthy survey of the revolt, H. Mantel refers to the Dead Sea Scrolls only once ('The Causes of the Bar Kokba Revolt', *JQR* 58 [1968], pp. 224-42, 274-96; reference to the Scrolls is in part 1, p. 241); and A. Oppenheimer, in a similar article fourteen years later, by which time it can be assumed the finds were sufficiently disseminated that they would be generally available, mentions them only twice ('The Bar Kokhba Revolt', *Immanuel* 14 [1982], pp. 58-76; references to the Scrolls and the caves on pp. 64 and 71). S. Applebaum's original *Prolegomena to the Study of the Second Jewish Revolt (AD 132–135)* (BARSup, 7; Oxford: British Archaeological Reports, 1976), and the follow-up article in response to the publication of P. Schäfer's *Der Bar Kokhba Aufstand: Studien zum zweiten jüdischen Krieg gegen Rom* (TSAJ, 1; Tübingen: Mohr [Paul Siebeck], 1981) ('The Second Jewish Revolt [AD 132–135]', *PEQ* 116 [1984], pp. 35-41), also make very little reference to the Scrolls and archaeology from around the Dead Sea; and Schäfer himself, in his 'Rabbi Aqiva and Bar Kokhba' (in W.S. Green [ed.], *Approaches to Ancient Judaism: Essays in Religion and History*, II [Chico, CA: Scholars Press, 1980]), makes only a single reference to the material (pp. 118-19).

The rabbinic sources are too numerous to list here, especially as those most impor-tant for this paper are discussed later on, but a brief list of those extra-rabbinic sources illustrates the paucity of texts connected with the history of the second Jewish revolt. Christian sources: Justin, *Apology* 1. 31.6, in which he uses Βαρ-χοχεβας as the proper name for the leader of the revolt, and records that Bar Kokhba

In fact, while many histories of the revolt have been and continue to
be written, there has not been much of an attempt on the part of
scholars to use these widely divergent pieces of information—rabbinic
and non-rabbinic sources, archaeological evidence, as well as the Dead
Sea Scrolls pertinent to the era—to reconstruct something of what the
Bar Kokhba revolutionaries believed. This may be because of the
absence of texts such as those discovered at Qumran which at least
seem to be full of explicit information about the beliefs of that particular community. Scholars are understandably leery of stretching
themselves too far, and ending up writing fanciful fiction instead of
solid history. Or, it could be that, as no such sectarian texts have been
discovered amidst the administrative, legal, and biblical documents
found at the Bar Kokhba sites, scholars simply think that, though
fairly conservative, the revolutionaries' religious beliefs must have
been relatively mainstream, and not worth much comment. The only
area of dispute regarding the beliefs of the rebels seems to revolve
around the messianic pretensions of the leader, and the support he
may or may not have enjoyed among the Rabbis and religious leaders
of the time. The presence of the name 'Eleazar the priest' on some of
the coins from the period has fascinated many,[11] but the most tenden-
tious issue in the study of the Bar Kokhba uprising continues to be the
relationship or lack thereof between Rabbi Aqiba, one of the most

was especially concerned with the persecution of Christians, 'unless they would
deny Jesus and utter blasphemy', which presumably means that the Christians were
to admit that Bar Kokhba was the messiah, in place of Jesus; Eusebius, *H.E.* 4.6
(§§311–313 LCL), in which he refers to Bar Kokhba as Βαρ-χωχεβας, which he
says means 'star', and gives other details about the revolt and its leader; Eusebius,
Chron. 2148; Jerome, 'Apology to Rufinius', in which he refers to Βαρ-χοχεβας as
the leader of this revolt, mocking him for the performance of false signs and wonders; *Apocalypse of Peter*—R. Bauckham ('*The Apocalypse of Peter*: A Jewish
Christian Apocalypse from the Time of Bar Kokhba', *Apocrypha* 5 [1994], pp. 7-
111, esp. pp. 24-43) makes a very convincing argument that this document does
come from the time of Bar Kokhba's persecution of the Christians in Palestine.
Classical source: Dio Cassius, *Rom. Hist.* 69.12-14 (actually an epitome of Dio
Cassius by Xiphilin, an eleventh-century monk), the most complete account of the
second revolt (see M. Gichon, 'New Insight into the Bar Kokhba War and a
Reappraisal of Dio Cassius 69.12-13', *JQR* 77 [1986], pp. 15-43). For further discussion of sources available for the study of Bar Kokhba, see Evans, *Jesus and his
Contemporaries*, pp. 183-211.

11. See Mildenberg, *Coinage, passim.*

important tanaitic Rabbis, and the leader of the revolution, Simeon Bar Kokhba.

2. *The Relationship between R. Aqiba and the Bar Kokhba Revolution in Recent Scholarship*

> R. Simeon b. Yohai taught, 'My teacher Aqiba used to expound, "There shall step forth a star out of Jacob [Num 24.17]—thus Koziva steps forth out of Jacob!"'
>
> 'When R. Aqiba beheld Bar Koziva, he exclaimed, "This is the king Messiah"'. R. Yohanan b. Torta retorted, 'Aqiva, grass will grow between your cheeks and he still will not have come'.
>
> (*y. Taan.* 4.8)

> R. Yohanan said, 'My teacher used to expound, "There shall step forth a star out of Jacob [Num 24.17]—thus, read not *kokab* [star], but *kozeb* [liar]"'. 'When R. Aqiva beheld Bar Koziva, he exclaimed, "This is the king Messiah".'
>
> R. Yohanan b. Torta retorted, 'Aqiva, grass will grow between your cheeks and he still will not have come'.
>
> (*Lam. R.* 2.4)

This story, in its three versions (a further parallel can be found in *Lam. R.* 101 [ed. Buber]), has become one of the most contentious aspects of Bar Kokhba studies. Peter Schäfer's 1980 article on the relationship between Aqiba and Bar Kokhba, following his earlier book on the subject, examines these and other passages that have been at issue for examining the relationship between the two figures. He sub-divides the material into six categories: (1) Aqiba's journeys, (2) his proclamation of Bar Kokhba as messiah, (3) his messianic expectations, (4) his dialogues with Tineius Rufus (the governor of Judaea at the time of the revolt), (5) his imprisonment, and, finally, (6) his martyrdom, death, and burial. Early on, Schäfer sets the tone for his article with a statement of his attitude toward past scholarship in the area: 'There is little point in discussing in detail the literature on the subject of Rabbi Aqiba and Bar Kokhba; for the most part it is fanciful and not critically sound'.[12] This attitude, while reflecting well Schäfer's bias that almost none of the rabbinic material on Aqiba has historical value, does not do justice to the general opinion in the field. There were, indeed, many fanciful so-called 'studies' in a previous era

---

12. Schäfer, 'Rabbi Aqiva and Bar Kokhba', p. 113.

of scholarship, which do not bear mentioning here, but there have also been several of note. Some of these are in Schäfer's list of baseless works, but Schäfer's sceptical stance has not been without its own detractors.[13]

Schäfer's and others'[14] scepticism has, however, had a significant influence on subsequent scholarship. For instance, Hugo Mantel's 1968 survey of the causes for the second revolt, simply assuming the connection between the two figures, is prepared to take many of the statements about Aqiba's journeys throughout the Diaspora at face value, interpreting them as preparations for the revolt (the traditional interpretation). This assumption of the validity of these sources is completely missing, however, from such a study as Louis Finkelstein's 1990 article on the subject.[15] Finkelstein wishes to allow for the connection between the figures, but, in the prevailing atmosphere of scepticism concerning the role of Aqiba in the revolt, cannot believe that the connection was a strong one, and so goes to great lengths to see Aqiba's words proclaiming Bar Kokhba as the messiah[16] in a different light:

> [Aqiba] was not in favor of the Bar Kochba rebellion...
>
> After Bar Kochba's initial victories, when it appeared that there was a chance that he might succeed, naturally Rabbi Akiba did all he could to encourage the resistance to Rome. It was too late to warn people to desist. Rabbi Akiba knew only too well what would happen if the rebellion failed and he did his best to prevent its failure. So he said a few words which are ascribed to him, praising Bar Kochba as the Messiah. What else could he do but hope that despite everything the rebellion would succeed?[17]

13. Although Applebaum, 'Second Jewish Revolt', p. 35, does suggest that Schäfer's approach is hyper-sceptical, H.L. Strack and G. Stemberger (*Introduction to the Talmud and Midrash* [trans. M. Bockmuehl; Edinburgh: T. & T. Clark, rev. edn, 1991], pp. 69, 79) also point out the difficulty of writing anything but hagiography about Aqiba, on the basis of the rabbinic material about him.

14. L. Ginzberg's 'Akiba ben Joseph' (*JewEnc*, I, pp. 304-308), in which he seeks to prove that Aqiba could not have been an important figure in the second revolt, seems to be the most notable sceptical influence apart from Schäfer. See also G.S. Aleksandrov, 'The Role of Aqiba in the Bar-Kokhba Rebellion', *REJ* 132 (1973), pp. 65-77, for a similar view.

15. 'Rabbi Akiba, Rabbi Ishmael, and the Bar Kochba Rebellion', in J. Neusner (ed.), *Approaches to Ancient Judaism, New Series* (Atlanta: Scholars Press, 1990), I, pp. 3-10.

16. *y. Taan.* 4.7, 68d. See above, p. 225.

17. Finkelstein, 'Akiba, Ishmael, and Bar Kochba', pp. 6-7.

Finkelstein's reasoning here is somewhat dubious, but claims to be based on 'direct evidence':

> There is direct evidence that Rabbi Akiba had no part in the rebellion of Bar Kochba. In *Mekilta Mishpatim* par. 18, p. 313, we are told that when Rabbi Simeon and Rabbi Ishmael were executed, Rabbi Akiba spoke the following eulogy over them to his pupils:

> Prepare yourselves for suffering, for if good prospects were before us no one would be more worthy to receive them than Rabbi Simeon and Rabbi Ishmael. But He who spoke and the world came into being knows that great suffering is in store for our generation and He took them away from us.

> Apparently Rabbi Akiba spoke these words to discourage his pupils from participation in the effort which had been initiated by Rabbi Simeon and Rabbi Ishmael, namely the Bar Kochba rebellion. Normally, one did not recite eulogies for people executed by the government [*b. Sanh.* 11a], for obvious reasons. To do so would be to court trouble. The fact that Rabbi Akiba recited a public eulogy for Rabbi Ishmael and Rabbi Simeon indicates that he was not in favor of the Bar Kochba rebellion. The Roman government would not object to what he said. Indeed, they would even be grateful for his discouragement of the rebellion.[18]

This is not direct evidence, indeed falling under Schäfer's category of 'not critically sound'.[19] Three things can be pointed out with regard to this supposed evidence. First, the fact that Aqiba is purported to have spoken this eulogy at all shows that, rather than trying to discourage his students, he may well have been honouring the memory and actions of the two Rabbis in question (even more surprising when one realizes that Rabbi Ishmael and Rabbi Aqiba were generally portrayed in rabbinic literature as being opposed to each other on many interpretative matters, to the point of open and frequent disagreement).[20] Nothing in the tone of his reported speech smacks of disapproval, and

18. Finkelstein, 'Akiba, Ishmael, and Bar Kochba', p. 6.
19. Schäfer, 'Rabbi Aqiva and Bar Kokhba', p. 113.
20. However, Strack and Stemberger (*Introduction*, pp. 270-71) show that the exegetical differences typically ascribed to the two figures are not actually present until Amoraic times—before then, it is possible to see Aqiba practising the methods typically ascribed to Ishmael, and *vice versa*. The later tradition concerning their quarrels with each other may stem from a variety of factors, either early, from their lifetimes (that is, personal differences that came to be expressed in the later bifurcation between their exegetical approaches), or later, after they were gone (as a handy way to categorize what later became opposing exegetical camps).

his admonition for preparation could even be seen as an overt suggestion that he knew more about what was coming than his students. Secondly, the argument that one did not recite eulogies over those executed by the government, supported by a rabbinic passage or not, means nothing if one assumes that Aqiba was in support of the rebellion. (One does not *normally* foment armed rebellion against the government either, but this did not, apparently, stop the revolution in 132 CE.) Thirdly, the assertion that this is a 'public' eulogy is not supported by the text, as even Finkelstein admits; it says that the eulogy was *to his students*. It is assumed that, although Rabbis' words may have got back to the Romans on occassion,[21] Aqiba's students probably would not have run out and reported him to the governor. This sort of argumentation does not prove that Aqiba was uninvolved in the revolt or its preparations, and may even indirectly supply further evidence that, as traditional scholarship has always assumed, Aqiba may well have been quite heavily involved.

In the light of the evidence, a complete break between Aqiba and Bar Kokhba is unwise. Even Schäfer freely admits that, although he would not accept much of the rabbinic material as evidence, he is more than willing to admit that the connection between Bar Kokhba and Aqiba, while still an unknown quantity, was a strong part of the tradition from fairly early on.[22] Schäfer does qualify this, as we can see with his judgment of the Num. 24.17 interpretation. He thinks that, even if it does go back to Aqiba, it

> is by no means a solemn proclamation of Bar Kokhba as the Messiah nor does it support any of the other dramatic actions with which biographers of Aqiva or Bar Kokhba may care to connect it; it provides no information about the real relationship between Bar Kokhba and Aqiva or about any active support the latter may have given the rebellion.[23]

However, he is willing to give more credence to other texts, some of which we will examine below.

---

21. Finkelstein records such an instance ('Akiba, Ishmael, and Bar Kochba', pp. 8-9), but unfortunately does not give a source.
22. Schäfer, 'Rabbi Aqiva and Bar Kokhba', p. 119.
23. Schäfer, 'Rabbi Aqiva and Bar Kokhba', p. 119.

3. The Remains of the Bar Kokhba Revolutionaries
from the Dead Sea Area

The central issue of this paper, in so far as the beliefs of the Bar Kokhba revolutionaries are concerned, is the possible relationship which existed between Bar Kokhba and his followers and Rabbi Aqiba. We have seen that many of the references in rabbinic literature have been cast into doubt, and that, outside of these, there is no evidence of a direct link between Bar Kokhba and Aqiba. As noted, the only specifically religious 'texts' that have been found—the biblical documents, the coins with their confusing imagery, and the phylactery fragments—tell us relatively little about the group's beliefs. It has been noted on more than one occasion that the biblical manuscripts of the Dead Sea Scrolls from the Bar Kokhba period are almost all of the family of biblical manuscript loosely known as 'proto-Masoretic'.[24] They represent a phase in the regularization of the Hebrew Scriptures that we could previously only conjecture and infer from the writings of such a Church Father as Justin. His quotations from the Greek text of the Old Testament often seem to be from a version of the LXX which is much closer to the MT than to other versions of the LXX.[25] This fascinating evidence contributes to our understanding of the process of editing, revising and collecting the various documents of the Hebrew Bible or the LXX, and we should not be surprised that this regularizing tendency should be present in the biblical documents of a group of revolutionaries which we can characterize as, at the very least, fiercely nationalistic. As can be inferred from some of the letters from the various sites, and coins of the period,[26] they were

24. For a thorough, if somewhat unwieldy, examination of the various relationships between the LXX, 8HevXIIgr, and the MT, see Tov, *Greek Minor Prophets Scroll*, pp. 99-158. Less complicated discussions can be found in D. Barthélemy, 'Redécouverte d'un chaînon manquant de l'Histoire de la Septante', *RB* 60 (1953), pp. 18-29; *idem, Les devanciers d'Aquila* (VTSup, 10; Leiden: Brill, 1963); also B. Lifshitz, 'The Greek Documents from the Cave of Horror', *IEJ* 12 (1962), pp. 201-207.

25. See P. Katz, 'Justin's Old Testament Quotations and the Greek Dodekapropheton Scroll', in *Studia Patristica* 1 (TU, 63; Berlin: Akademie Verlag, 1957), pp. 343-53; and Barthélemy, *Les devanciers d'Aquila*, pp. 203-22.

26. All of which, as mentioned, have traditionally Jewish, if sometimes unclear, symbolism on them, and are inscribed with paleo-Hebrew characters, which would

probably also quite conservative and religiously traditional. However, is there anything else which these biblical documents can tell us?

The answer to that question must first take issue with an unfortunate trend in Dead Sea Scrolls studies—the interpretation of documents without reference to their archaeological surroundings. If these documents are documents not likely intended to be permanent, even if the material within them had permanent value,[27] then interpreting them must include determining why they continue to exist, and what that information could add to our knowledge and understanding of the documents themselves. Qumran studies has dealt with the question of why the documents placed in the caves were placed there in the first place, but this is not of primary concern to most. When the information available is as sparse as it is for Bar Kokhba research, however, it becomes of paramount importance that we pay as much attention to the surroundings in which the documents were found as we do to the documents themselves.

One of the most important biblical manuscripts of the Bar Kokhba period, the Twelve Prophets scroll written in Greek, was found in Cave 8 in the Nahal Hever (or, in its Arabic form, the Wadi Habra)— the so-called 'Cave of Horror'. Its official publication in the DJD series, however, virtually ignores this information. Rather than follow the examples of earlier volumes of documents from the Bar Kokhba period (such as the publication of the archaeological findings and texts from the Wadi Murabba'at),[28] this volume spends almost all of its

presumably have been unintelligible to those not familiar with, or indeed steeped in, Jewish tradition.

27. The difference between the actual material upon which texts are written and the texts themselves is an important distinction, drawn out by R.S. Bagnall (*Reading Papyri, Writing Ancient History* [AAW; London: Routledge, 1995], pp. 9-10) in his discussion of papyrus: '"papyrus" here is taken... to represent a class of written artefacts, not all actually involving papyrus as a material. The ancient societies that used papyrus also used pieces of broken pottery (called ostraka), parchment, wooden tablets and labels, and bone for the same kind of purposes for which papyrus was employed. What these materials generally have in common is that they were used for written artefacts with no particular pretensions to permanence. The *texts* written on these materials might or might not have been thought of by their authors as possessions for all time; we may imagine that most authors of what we call literature shared Thucydides hopes. But the particular embodiment of a text on a physical medium was endowed with no such expectation...'

28. P. Benoit, J.T. Milik, and R. de Vaux, *Les Grottes de Murabba'at*

commentary on discussion of the text itself. Archaeological information about the site of the text is given in less than half of a page, with the reader being pointed to preliminary documentation of its provenance. The discussion then proceeds to tell the reader that this document comes from the Cave of Horror in the Nahal Hever, giving no explanation of this graphic name, and the reader is left to his own devices to discover what this means. Robert Kraft's section on the actual state of the manuscript[29] does deal with some of the questions of archaeology and the actual place where the document was found (although leaving out vital details, to be discussed below), but he draws some untenable conclusions. These could possibly have been avoided by paying closer attention to the archaeological material published by Yigael Yadin.[30] However it may be treated by those publishing the texts themselves, this information is anything but unimportant.

Early in 1955, rumours had been passed to the (then) Israeli Department of Antiquities that Tammireh Bedouin had been seen excavating in the caves of the Nahal. The fear was that, if the caves were left unexcavated by the authorities, there would be nothing left to excavate. The Cave of Horror and the Cave of Letters (which was excavated and named by Yadin in 1960 and 1961) are a matched pair of caves in the opposite walls of the Nahal. They are both approximately 80-100 m down the cliff faces, and are reachable only by the most treacherous of climbs. They were well chosen by the revolutionaries as refuge caves in all but one respect: the lack of water. As hiding places, they were wonderful, but, when discovered, they were perhaps some of the easiest caves to siege. The remains of this siege are probably what led the Bedouin to the caves in the first place. On the top of the cliff on either side of the Nahal are two Roman camps, one for each group of refugees. The caves, although stocked in advance against this possibility, were turned into slow death traps. There is evidence in the Cave of Letters that the inhabitants were forced to drill holes in the pits of the olives they had previously eaten in an attempt to eke out the last remaining nutritional and moisture

---

(2 vols.; DJD, 2; Oxford: Clarendon Press, 1961).

29. R.A. Kraft, 'Description of the Materials and their State of Preservation', in Tov, *Greek Minor Prophets Scroll*, pp. 14-19.

30. In its popular form, Y. Yadin, *Bar Kokhba* (New York: Random House, 1971), or, for more detailed archaeological reports, Yadin, 'Expedition D'. We discuss this further, below.

value of the kernel inside the pit.[31] The Cave of Horror received its
name when members of Aharoni's 1955 expedition found the remains
of several bodies (some with skin and hair still attached) in the back of
the cave. The approximately eighteen skeletons that remain are almost
exclusively those of women, children, and infants. According to
Aharoni, they

> showed no signs of violence. It may be assumed, then, that they died of
> hunger and thirst during a long siege... The number of skeletons found
> almost certainly does not reflect the number of inhabitants... [b]ut the
> small number of male skeletons is probably not accidental. It is reasonable
> to assume that most of the men were killed in battle outside the cave in
> desperate attempts to bring food and water to the besieged women and
> children.[32]

4. Possible Connections? Aqiba's Messianic Interpretations of the Book of the Twelve and Tomb Genizahs near the Dead Sea

The conditions under which the inhabitants of this cave died are
almost too horrific to consider. One can imagine the fight going completely out of the people as they slowly died, the weakest first, those
wounded in battle, the children. The depression of having lost the
war, their hard won freedom, and their loved ones must have set in
quickly. It boggles the mind to imagine both their mental state and
physical conditions in those last days.

However, there are aspects of these last days which we are hard put
to explain. In the re-examination of the Cave of Horror during the
1961 expedition to the Judaean desert (after the dramatic finds of the
1960 season in the Cave of Letters), Aharoni and his people discovered signs that there appears to have been an intense fire in the middle
of the cave in which the occupants of the cave may very well have
destroyed any documents that they had brought with them.[33] Three
scraps of papyrus were found, torn and left in the part of the cave in
which the fire took place, along with glass vessels which show signs of
having been warped in intense heat.[34] Judging from the documents

---

31. Y. Aharoni, 'The Caves of Nahal Hever', *'Atiqot 3* (1961), p. 155.

32. Aharoni, 'Caves of Nahal Hever', p. 161.

33. Y. Aharoni, 'The Expedition to the Judean Desert, 1961: Expedition B—The Cave of Horror', *IEJ* 12 (1962), p. 195.

34. Aharoni, 'Expedition B [1962]', p. 195. Although Kraft would like to posit

found in the nooks and crannies of the Cave of Letters across the Nahal, these would have been in three classes: (1) documents of an important religious nature, (2) personal documents of importance to one or more of the individuals hiding in the cave, and (3) documents of importance to the administration of the revolutionary state itself. Destroying these would potentially save the lives of those who had escaped the vengeful attention of the Romans, or, at the very least, give the Romans no return for all their efforts during the siege. As Aharoni puts it in the original archaeological report:

> These fugitives met their deaths in the cave, though the absence of any signs of injury on the bodies shows that the place was not taken by force of arms. This was only to be expected, since the inaccessibility of the caves made any such conquest almost impossible... The reserves of water and food in the cave dwindled inexorably, until the besieged were faced with the choice of surrendering or dying of hunger and thirst. The graves in the Cave of Horror show that the siege was of considerably long duration and that the occupants did not surrender even when death had begun to take its toll of them. The dead were buried in the innermost parts of the cave, apparently with traditional religious rites...
>
> The human skeletons in the Cave of Horror bear mute witness to its occupants' choice of death rather than surrender. From the archaeological finds made in the cave it would seem possible to learn something of the last moments of the besieged. Most of the utensils were found broken into pieces in the debris from the great fire in the middle of the cave; and how intense the heat of this blaze was, can be seen from the warped glass bowl.

that this bonfire was a Roman action after the cave had been cleared of the revolutionaries ('Description of the Materials', p. 18), a casual perusal of the descriptions of the excavations of these caves (such as Yadin, *Bar Kokhba*) would show that the air supply in these caves is a serious issue. The lighting of any smoke-producing and air-depleting fire would have to be a desperate measure, one which would make no sense for the Romans, as they had no real reason to so thoroughly destroy the documents of the revolutionaries—in fact, as will be argued below, they could even be seen as wanting to use whatever was in the administrative documents and letters against those who may have escaped the Romans' attentions in the aftermath of the revolt. It is this reason which I assume was the motivation for the fire in the first place, but on the part of the revolutionaries, not the Romans. The Romans certainly could not have assaulted the cave while it was occupied (the approach being simply impossible for such an action), and would simply have been able to throw anything they wished to destroy out of the mouth of the cave, rather than light a fire which could, potentially, have had seriously harmful ramifications for them, as there would not have been any possibility of escaping the smoke from the fire within the cave.

> The Cave of Horror is not a large one like the Cave of Letters, so that
> there was no chance of concealing the articles in it where they would not
> have been found by the victorious Romans. The besieged occupants there-
> fore evidently decided to make a great bonfire in the middle of the
> cave...[35]

The Twelve Prophets scroll, mentioned above, was originally published by D. Barthélemy as coming from an unknown location.[36] It
was assumed that this unknown location was within the borders of
Jordan at the time when the Bedouin brought this document to
Barthélemy, but scholars were unsure as to its exact provenance.
During the excavation of the burials in the rear portion of the Cave of
Horror in 1961, however, fragments of this important scroll (which
had obviously broken off when the Bedouin absconded with it) were
uncovered.[37] There was evidence that there had been other scrolls
with it, but none of these have been identified, or even, perhaps, come
to light.[38] It is tempting to imagine that these other scrolls would also
have been biblical, but it is impossible to tell.

Barthélemy records that the document was already well used when
placed in its final resting place.[39] This, coupled with the facts that the
document both (1) survived the conflagration that was likely intended
by the occupants of the cave to destroy all their documents, and (2) was
interred[40] with the dead, may suggest two further things. First, this

35. Aharoni, 'Expedition B [1962]', pp. 198-99.
36. Barthélemy, 'Redécouverte', p. 19.
37. Lifshitz, 'Greek Documents from the Cave of Horror', pp. 201-202.
38. Kraft, 'Description of the Materials', p. 19. See J.C. Greenfield, 'The Texts
from Nahal Se'elim (Wadi Seiyal)', in J.T. Barrera and L.V. Montaner (eds.), *The
Madrid Qumran Congress: Proceedings of the International Congress on the Dead
Sea Scrolls* (STDJ, 2; Leiden: Brill, 1992), for a discussion of the provenance of all
of the different fragments which we know as 8HevXIIgr.
39. Barthélemy, *Les devanciers d'Aquila*, p. 163.
40. It is, of course, unclear by exactly what process the document came to be
amongst the dead found at the back of this cave. Was it placed there in a burial near
to the beginning of the time in the cave? Was it placed there by the last remaining
survivors of the cave, or could it even have been placed there by survivors of the
revolution who came back to re-inter the dead found in the caves (as we see in the
Cave of Letters across the Nahal [see Yadin, 'Expedition D', esp. pp. 37-38])?
Because of the disturbed nature of the archaeological strata, as a result of Bedouin
digging, it is impossible to tell exactly what happened in the last days of the refugees'
lives, althought the original archaeological report seems to suggest that the document
was buried while the occupants were still in the cave (Aharoni, 'Expedition B

document was highly valued. Those of us familiar with the love that religious Jews and, later, Christians, have always had for their Scriptures are probably not too surprised by that. However, together all these factors suggest that it may have had extra-special value to the people who went to the trouble of bringing it to the cave, and later burying it with their dead. Secondly, the burial of this manuscript may, in fact, be an example of a tomb genizah. The only other possible tomb genizah of this period, the admitted earliest of its kind, was found at Murabba'at.[41] The only document found in this burial (P.Mur. 88) also happens to be a copy of the Twelve Prophets, this time in Hebrew. Is this entirely coincidental? Of course, until someone unearths a videotape of the events surrounding this revolt, we are unlikely to know for sure. Still, it is highly suggestive that, in two sites of revolutionary refuge from the Romans, two burials would take place ensconcing the same text from the Jewish Scriptures with the dead.

This is not, however, the end of the chain of evidence. Two passages in rabbinic literature serve to illustrate a possible link between these two texts of the Twelve Prophets, the beliefs of the Bar Kokhba revolutionaries, and the teachings of Rabbi Aqiba.

Aqiba 'pleads for an extraordinarily short messianic period'[42] of only about 40 years, and this is usually interpreted as being the natural expected lifetime of Bar Kokhba.[43] However, his calculations did not end there. *B. Sanh.* 97b has the following passage:

> It has been taught: R. Nathan said, 'This verse pierces and descends to the very abyss: For there is yet a vision for the appointed time; and at the end it will come in breathless haste, it will not fail. If it delays, wait for it; for when it comes will be no time to linger [Hab 2.3]. Not as our

[1962]', p. 198). Regardless of who placed it, or when it was placed with the bodies in the rear of the cave, it is still highly suggestive that it was found with the dead. The strongest indication from the evidence is that these were people who died while the cave was inhabited, before, perhaps, the remaining survivors decided to burn their belongings and die, rather than surrender.

41. This single burial, found in a cave very near the rest in the Wadi Murabba'at, is discussed in Benoit, Milik, and de Vaux, *Les Grottes de Murabba'at*, p. 50, and its status as the most ancient example of a tomb genizah is discussed in J.T. Milik, *Bib* 31 (1950), pp. 505-509.

42. Schäfer, 'Aqiva and Bar Kokhba', p. 120.

43. The prediction is found in *Pesiq. R.* 4a, with parallels in *b. Sanh.* 99a and *Midr. Ps.* 90.17.

Masters...nor as R. Simlai...nor as R. Aqiva, who expounded [the verse] One thing more: I will shake heaven and earth [Hag 2.6].

This is one text to which Schäfer is prepared to give great credence:

We may not know Aqiva's actual interpretation, but we can say from the context (see also Hag 2.7: *I will shake all nations*) that he is definitely one of those who calculated the end... and whose calculations, in the opinion of the author or editor, proved incorrect and even detrimental... There can hardly be any doubt that the actual historical background to these words is the Bar Kokhba rebellion, and that Aqiva's messianic expectations that related to this rebellion are condemned.[44]

With regard to this passage, predictions about the forty year reign of the messiah, and other texts which 'number the days', Mantel states that all 'of these statements wish to bring conformity between the Messianic period and their own times, namely, the beginning of Bar Kokba's revolt and the establishment of his kingdom'.[45]

Is it simply coincidence that the interpretations in *b. Sanh.* 97b are based on two different texts from the Twelve Prophets? Maybe it is. Given the nature of the evidence, there is simply no way to be conclusive about this question, but the congruence at least needs to be recognized, and left for future studies to examine. Briefly, however, we must consider three other traditions which seem to find the material in Habakkuk and Haggai significant both messianically and eschatologically. The *pesher* on Habakkuk from Qumran (1QpHab) interprets the same passage as Aqiba does (Hab. 2.3), but suggests that

[Concerning v. 3a.] Interpreted, this means that the final age shall be prolonged, and shall exceed all that the prophets have said; for the mysteries of God are astounding. [Concerning v. 3b.] Interpreted this concerns the men of truth who keep the Law, whose hands shall not slacken in the service of truth when the final age is prolonged. For all the ages of God reach their appointed end as he determines for them in the mysteries of His wisdom.[46]

The commentary on Habakkuk only extends to the material in the first two chapters, but is not, according to those who have edited the document, incomplete.[47] The entire two chapters are given an

44. Schäfer, 'Aqiva and Bar Kokhba', p. 120.

45. Mantel, 'Causes of the Revolt', p. 276.

46. G. Vermes, *The Dead Sea Scrolls in English* (Sheffield: Sheffield Academic Press, 4th edn, 1995), p. 342.

47. M. Burrows, *The Dead Sea Scrolls of St Mark's Monastery*, I (New Haven,

eschatological interpretation, all concerning the various figures of note in the Qumran literature: the Teacher of Righteousness, the Wicked Priest, the Kittim (usually interpreted to be the Romans), etc. Obviously this material held special significance for the community that produced the *pesher*.[48]

In the New Testament, the writer of Hebrews, long recognized as especially influenced by Hellenistic Judaism, also seems to find eschatological significance in the material from Habakkuk 2. In Heb. 10.37-39, the author quotes Hab. 2.3-4, then, following on from his previous discussion about perserverance for the sake of God's (eschatological) promises, suggests that the readers are not of those who 'shrink back and are destroyed, but of those who have faith and keep their souls'. In Heb. 12.25-29, the author also makes eschatological and messianic use of the same material from Haggai as Aqiba is reported to have used to interpret the Habakkuk passage:

> See that you do not refuse him who is speaking. For if they did not escape when they refused him who warned them on earth, much less shall we escape if we reject him who warns from heaven. His voice then shook the earth; but now he has promisd, 'Yet once more I will shake not only the earth but also the heaven. [Hag 2.6]' This phrase, 'Yet once more', indicates the removal of what is shaken, as of what has been made, in order that what cannot be shaken may remain. Therefore let us be grateful for receiving a kingdom that cannot be shaken, and thus let us offer to God acceptable worship, with reverence and awe; for our God is a consuming fire (RSV).

The third tradition which deserves brief mention is that from *Targum Jonathan* to the prophets. His interpretative translation of Hab. 2.4, especially of the term 'righteous ones', has a definite messianic slant. As Pinkhos Churgin states with regard to 'Jonathan's' interpretation of this phrase: 'The Messianic tone is made audible...in the prominence given in his exegesis to the "righteous ones". In a good many instances [of which Hab. 2.4 is one] no other reason except to give Messianic sense to a phrase, is evident.'[49] Of course, as with all targumic mate-

CT: American Schools of Oriental Research, 1950), p. xix: 'The commentator clearly concluded his exposition at the end of what we know as chapter 2 of the book of Habakkuk, for at that point our document appears quite complete, and there are less than four lines of writing in the last column'.

48. See Vermes, *Dead Sea Scrolls*, pp. 34-46 for discussion of this topic.

49. P. Churgin, *Targum Jonathan to the Prophets* (New Haven: Yale University Press, 1927), p. 80.

rial, it is impossible to determine exactly the date of this particular interpretation, but it is still safe to say that, even if the material post-dates Bar Kokhba and Aqiba, it still shows a continuing strain of eschatological or messianic interpretation of this verse and its surrounding context.

In the earliest forms of the Bar Kokhba tradition, Aqiba is connected with Bar Kokhba. His messianic interpretations—however many of them one takes to be legitimate—are undoubtedly to be connected to Bar Kokhba, and some of those interpretations were based on texts from the Twelve Prophets. Because the Bar Kokhba revolutionaries who fled to the Judaean Desert seem to have held copies of the Twelve Prophets in a special position of honour and respect, it seems reasonable to make at least a circumstantial argument that the Book of the Twelve was not simply revered by the Bar Kokhba revolutionaries as a part of the Jewish Scriptures, but as a specially significant group of writings with specific messianic significance. The existence of other traditions of a roughly contemporary nature which also interpret eschatologically and messianically the passages which Aqiba is reported to have interpreted as such lends further credence to this view.

The status of Bar Kokhba as the messiah, and the nature of that messiahship, are topics for another paper, but one point needs to be made for those who follow the reasoning that, as there is no messianic tone to the Bar Kokhba correspondence which has been found, he could not have seen himself as the messiah. There is, of course, no place in rabbinic literature where Bar Kokhba is seen as claiming to be the messiah—all messianic appellations are given by others. There may very well have been no specific self-understanding on the part of Bar Kokhba that he was the messiah. It is inferable that, on the basis of the passage in Eusebius (see above, n. 10), Bar Kokhba was not keen on messianic competition, forcing Christians to 'blaspheme', presumably meaning that they had to switch their messianic allegiance. This would, potentially, have had more to do with securing loyalty than anything else, and does not necessarily mean that Bar Kokhba saw himself, for instance, in the same way that Jesus is characterized in the New Testament as having seen himself, or in the way in which the early Church saw him. One must not forget the multiplicity of messianic beliefs in the milieu of early Judaism.

Of course, the strongest evidence that Bar Kokhba was seen as the messiah is the very fact that he is denigrated as a false messiah after the revolt. As Adele Reinhartz puts it, 'The denunciation of Bar Kosiba as a false messiah...is irrefutable proof of the popularity of the identification of Bar Kosiba as the true Messiah'.[50] Perhaps the Book of the Twelve provided a special impetus for this identification.

5. *Special Scriptures and Lost Causes: The Rebuilding of History*

The papyrologist Roger Bagnall, in the conclusion to his *Reading Papyri, Writing Ancient History*, states that, in the creative kind of research which he advocates, 'even the failures are likely to be enlightening, and in reality most "failures" may be so only by inappropriate standards'.[51] It is hoped, even if this study has not, and indeed, *could* not incontrovertibly prove the connection between 8HevXIIgr, P.Mur. 88, and the beliefs of the Bar Kokhba revolutionaries, that this is at least a step in the right direction. It remains to further studies to continue the argument, as it is only in this way that we may hope to wring as much information from texts which simply do not provide us with clear pictures of life in the revolution.

---

50. A. Reinhartz, 'Rabbinic Perceptions of Simeon Bar Kosiba', *JSJ* 20 (1989), p. 177. For further discussion of the messianic character of the Bar Kokhba revolt, see Fitzmyer, 'Bar Cochba Period', pp. 312-16.

51. *Reading Papyri*, p. 116. Inspiration for the approach taken in this paper has been drawn largely from Bagnall's methodological study in the field of papyrology. He puts forward a challenge to those in his field to take the next step, as it were, and, moving beyond simple restoration of the texts, use the papyri as the raw material from which to write history. Of course, the kind of history which we think of as 'history' is not the kind that can easily be found in the papyri, nor, as we have seen above, in the documents from the Bar Kokhba period (of course, this distinction between the two corpuses is unrecognizable to any but biblical scholars—'the papyri' essentially means 'anything written in the Greco-Roman world on materials not meant to be permanent'). As Bagnall states in his introduction to the chapter of the book entitled 'Asking Questions', 'In this chapter I shall look at some examples of questions that do not come entirely from the papyri "themselves", studied in [the] philological tradition, but that are raised at least partly outside it, with the papyri then brought in to help test hypotheses formulated from other disciplines or sources' (p. 91). It may be that it is this sort of questioning which will be able to unlock any further secrets which the Bar Kokhba texts are hiding from us.

Part III

THE SCROLLS AND EARLY CHRISTIANITY

'THE CANON WITHIN THE CANON' AT QUMRAN AND IN THE NEW TESTAMENT

George J. Brooke

1. *Introduction*

It is necessary to begin by clarifying what this paper is about. It is not concerned directly with the extent and contents of the canon of the Hebrew Bible as that may be evident in the Dead Sea Scrolls and the New Testament. Nor is it concerned directly with the processes by which one book rather than another becomes authoritative and normative, nor with how groups of books also come to take priority over others. To this extent no apologies need be offered for using the word 'canon', even in inverted commas, since it is clearly both anachronistic and out of place.[1] Furthermore, to focus on how canons of writings emerge is naturally to describe negative matters, since canons are usually formed in a reactionary way, against other people's preferences. It is no accident that the firmest delimitations of the canon in Christian circles, even the earliest uses of the word in a technical sense, come at the same time as the creeds are emerging: authoritative texts are produced to protect and project orthodoxy against what are perceived as the wild assertions of heresy.

The subject matter of this paper is altogether more positive, for to speak of a 'canon within a canon' is to focus on those writings or books, or parts of them, which a community considered especially important for one reason or another. The term 'canon within a canon' is used loosely to assert that within the range of books which were

---

1. For a useful summary treatment of technical terminology in relation to the canon of the Old Testament and for views on the place of the Old Testament in the early churches, see E.E. Ellis, 'The Old Testament Canon in the Early Church', in M.J. Mulder (ed.), *Mikra: Text, Translation, Reading and Interpretation of the Hebrew Bible in Ancient Judaism and Early Christianity* (CRINT 2/1; Assen: van Gorcum; Philadelphia: Fortress Press, 1988), pp. 653-90.

emerging as authoritative in a general way, for some groups a few works were especially significant, and not just whole books, but parts of them. Against a backdrop of the canonical process proper,[2] the purpose of this study is to ask in a very preliminary way why certain books were being cherished and used at the centre of the life of various communities, not to worry about whether a particular document was deemed to be part of a canon, thought to be divinely inspired, or considered to control one's lifestyle.

With regard to the scrolls found in the eleven Qumran caves two other preliminary matters need to be made clear immediately. First, it will be assumed in this study that the collection of nearly nine hundred manuscripts found between 1947 and 1956 in the eleven caves near to the Qumran settlement and in the adjoining foothills form some kind of collection. It may certainly be true that some caves had distinctive purposes: the manuscripts in Cave 1 were neatly wrapped in linen and placed in jars almost like a genizah or time capsule, those in Cave 7 were all in Greek, not all those in Cave 4 could have been in the dozen or so jars of which fragments were found, and so on. Nevertheless, there is a coherence in the collection from three aspects. (1) There are no copies of clearly non-Jewish literature, such as any of the Greek classics, nor are there any copies of particular Jewish texts which we have good reason to think were in circulation in Palestine in the first century BCE, such as 1 and 2 Maccabees or Judith. (2) In the three caves which have produced most manuscripts (1, 4, and 11), there is an evenness of distribution, both in proportion, about 30% biblical, 30% sectarian, and 40% other materials,[3] and also in the way in which

2.   This canonical process has been delineated suitably by E. Ulrich, 'The Canonical Process, Textual Criticism, and Latter Stages in the Composition of the Bible', in M. Fishbane and E. Tov (eds.), *'Sha'arei Talmon': Studies in the Bible, Qumran, and the Ancient Near East Presented to Shemaryahu Talmon* (Winona Lake, IN: Eisenbrauns, 1992), pp. 267-91, see esp. p. 274: 'Prior to the end of the first century, we do not have a canon in either Judaism or Christianity. We have a canon-in-the-making, but we do not have a canon. We have, well documented by practice, the concept of authoritative sacred books which are to be preserved very faithfully. And we have a "canonical process", that is, the activity by which books later to become accepted as the canon were produced and treated as sacred and authoritative. But we do not have a canon or a canonical text before the end of the first century.'

3.   This has been pointed out most clearly by D. Dimant, 'The Qumran Manuscripts: Contents and Significance', in D. Dimant and L.H. Schiffman (eds.), *Time to Prepare the Way in the Wilderness: Papers on the Qumran Scrolls by*

the same composition recurs in the various caves, such as the *Serek ha-Yaḥad* (Community Rule), the War Scroll, and the *Hodayot* being found in Caves 1 and 4, the Temple Scroll or its sources in Caves 4 and 11, and *Jubilees* and the New Jerusalem text in Caves 1, 4 and 11; some of these compositions are found in other caves as well. (3) There is a consistency amongst the compositions concerning the calendar; not that only one calendar is known, but it seems as if only one calendar was normative.

The second assumption regarding the Qumran collection concerns its relationship to the Qumran settlement. It is most plausible to suggest that the caves and their scrolls are to be associated with the site, so that in discussing the Scrolls from the eleven caves, it is reasonable to talk about the community and the wider movement of which it was probably a part. If the recently discovered ostracon is being read correctly,[4] then there is some evidence from very near the site itself that the *yaḥad* lived there, but even if not, it must be recalled that the only way to some of the caves was through or past the site itself.

2. *'The Canon within the Canon' at Qumran*

a. *Establishing 'the Canon within the Canon' at Qumran*
Given the assumptions just outlined, and in the hope that the evidence from the Qumran caves to be described is not distorted unduly by the accidents of preservation and survival, it is possible to move directly to describe 'the canon within the canon' at Qumran. There are four ways to establish such a 'canon within a canon'; these four ways must be taken together.

(1) Notwithstanding the ravages of insects and earthquakes, it is possible to count up the number of extant copies of particular compositions to see what kind of popularity they might have had amongst the group which preserved them. There is naturally some uncertainty about whether a particular fragment has been correctly identified[5] and

---

Fellows of the Institute for Advanced Studies of the Hebrew University, Jerusalem, 1989–1990 (STDJ, 16; Leiden: Brill, 1995), pp. 23-58, esp. p. 58.

4.   See now F.M. Cross and E. Eshel, 'Ostraca from Khirbet Qumran', *IEJ* 47 (1997), pp. 17-28.

5.   A small fragment containing what looks like a biblical text could belong to a composition which is explicitly citing Scripture. Even some manuscripts, such as 4QDeut[n], which contain nothing but biblical material can be better understood as

so statistics, as always, are susceptible to economical truth, but a rough guideline can be presented as follows. When the various compositions from the Qumran caves are counted up, there are more than twenty copies of Genesis, Deuteronomy, Isaiah, and the Psalms. There are approximately seventeen copies of Exodus and at least fifteen of the book of *Jubilees*, so these come a close second. Then still in double figures we have Leviticus, the *Hodayot* and the Community Rule.[6]

(2) The second way to discern the popularity of any work is to see how many times it is referred to in other compositions. Here we are faced with a problem, because certain genres lend themselves to being quoted explicitly, and certain types of writing may be more inclined to quote explicitly than implicitly. Thus a legal text may more readily quote another authority explicitly, whereas a hymnic composition is likely only to allude implicitly to a poetic source. No detailed comprehensive analysis of the use of Scripture in the compositions found at Qumran has yet been completed.[7] For explicit quotations a basic starting point can be found in J.A. Fitzmyer's classic study of the forty-three quotations in the Community Rule, the War Scroll, the Damascus Document, and 4Q174.[8] These texts contain a variety of

---

excerpted texts: see the large number of such manuscripts listed and described by E. Tov, 'Excerpted and Abbreviated Biblical Texts from Qumran', *RevQ* 16 (1993–95), pp. 581-600.

6.   With some minor adjustments in light of recent volumes in the Discoveries in the Judaean Desert series, these figures are worked out on the basis of the manuscripts as listed by F. García Martínez, *The Dead Sea Scrolls Translated: The Qumran Texts in English* (Leiden: Brill; Grand Rapids: Eerdmans, 2nd edn, 1994), pp. 467-519. Helpful lists of the biblical manuscripts and their contents can be found in U. Gleßmer, 'Liste der biblischen Texte aus Qumran', *RevQ* 16 (1993–95), pp. 153-92; E. Ulrich, 'An Index of the Passages in the Biblical Manuscripts from the Judean Desert (Genesis–Kings)', *DSD* 1 (1994), pp. 113-29; *idem*, 'An Index of the Passages in the Biblical Manuscripts from the Judean Desert (Part 2: Isaiah–Chronicles)', *DSD* 2 (1995), pp. 86-107.

7.   The most helpful recent index of scriptural passages in the scrolls is that produced by J. Maier, *Die Qumran-Essener: Die Texte vom Toten*, III (UTB, 1916; Munich: Ernst Reinhardt, 1996), pp. 161-82. However, it is difficult to know how to use the information in Maier's index without attempting to classify it somehow; explicit quotations are listed alongside rewritten texts and implicit allusions without any differentiation.

8.   J.A. Fitzmyer, 'The Use of Explicit Old Testament Quotations in Qumran Literature and in the New Testament', *NTS* 7 (1960–61), pp. 297-333; reprinted in J.A. Fitzmyer, *Essays on the Semitic Background of the New Testament* (London:

genres and the quotations are used for a variety of purposes; indeed Fitzmyer offers a preliminary classification of uses ('literal', 'modernized', 'accommodated', 'eschatological'). These four compositions may all be identified closely with the Qumran community and its wider movement. Of the forty-three citations eleven are from the Twelve Minor Prophets, nine from Deuteronomy, seven from Isaiah, five from Numbers. Only one comes from Genesis, none from the Psalms.

Alongside these explicit allusions, one should put a work that because of its genre, is using Scripture in a more intricate implicit fashion. For want of a more accessible way into this, we may take the index of scriptural allusions in S. Holm-Nielsen's analysis of the Cave 1 version of the *Hodayot* (1QH).[9] He counts forty-eight passages from the Psalms to which there are clear allusions in 1QH,[10] some of them more than once, and ninety-seven passages from the Psalms which may be alluded to but about which there cannot be any certainty.[11] For Isaiah, there are sixty-eight clear allusions and fifty-three uncertain ones.[12] There are also thirty-one passages from the Twelve Minor Prophets (together with eighteen uncertain ones),[13] eighteen passages from Jeremiah (together with thirteen uncertain ones),[14] and ten from Job (together with twenty-one uncertain ones).[15] For the Pentateuch, Holm-Nielsen notes seven passages from Genesis (together with eight uncertain allusions), six from Exodus (together with seven uncertain allusions), none from Numbers (but five uncertain allusions), and seven from Deuteronomy (together with four uncertain allusions); the

Geoffrey Chapman, 1971), pp. 3-58 (republished in *The Semitic Background of the New Testament* [Grand Rapids: Eerdmans, 1997]).

9. S. Holm-Nielsen, *Hodayot: Psalms from Qumran* (Acta Theologica Danica, 2; Aarhus: Universitetsforlaget, 1960). Holm-Nielsen's chapter on 'The Use of the Old Testament in the Hodayot' (pp. 301-15) is especially important, since he justifiably concludes that the use of Scripture in the *Hodayot* does not depend on previously existing collections of extracts.

10. Maier lists 26 allusions to the Psalms in 1QH, not all of which correspond with Holm-Nielsen's identifications.

11. He also notes 10 passages where phrasing from a biblical psalm could be used suitably to make a restoration in the scroll.

12. Maier lists 31 passages of Isaiah to which there are clear allusions in 1QH.

13. Maier lists 8 passages in the Twelve Minor Prophets to which allusion is made in 1QH.

14. Maier lists 13 passages from Jeremiah to which there is allusion in 1QH.

15. For 1QH Maier lists 3 passages from Job.

poets who composed the *Hodayot* do not seem keen to cite Leviticus![16] Other biblical books are also alluded to but only a very few times. Thus amongst one collection of the community's poetry the Psalms, Isaiah and the Twelve seem to be particularly influential.

(3) The third way to appreciate which compositions are significant for the Qumran community and its wider movement is to take any one composition and assess its dependence on other texts in detail. Let us briefly take the Damascus Document as an example. If one looks at the explicit quotations of Scripture in the Damascus Document, at least forty citations can be isolated: two from Genesis, four from Leviticus, four from Numbers, nine from Deuteronomy, one from 1 Samuel, six from Isaiah, three from Ezekiel, twelve from the Twelve Minor Prophets, and one from Proverbs.[17] Deuteronomy, Isaiah and the Twelve are clearly significant, but so too are Leviticus, Numbers and Ezekiel. However, when one turns to consider the dominant implicit allusions, even in the section of the Admonition alone, then the picture changes somewhat. In his detailed study J.G. Campbell has been able to point out the principal uses of Scripture in CD 1–8 and 19–20.[18] Deuteronomy is evidently the most important of the books of the Torah, especially sections of Deuteronomy 27–32, and Leviticus, especially ch. 26, is also prominent. The number of allusions to Isaiah is almost equalled by the number to Ezekiel. Citations of or allusions to Hosea and Micah also feature prominently in almost all the sections of the Admonition. Most significantly, however, the Psalms are also important, especially Psalms 37, 78, and 106, a fact that one cannot recognize from concentrating on explicit quotations alone.[19]

Thus in any particular work various scriptural passages may play a part; some of these may be used explicitly, some implicitly. An overall study of the use of the biblical books in all the Scrolls has yet to be undertaken, but each composition from the Qumran caves, whether sectarian or not, even though part of the overall Qumran

16. Maier's index of citations lists 2 for Genesis, 3 for Exodus, and 4 for Deuteronomy.

17. See G. Vermes, 'Biblical Proof-Texts in Qumran Literature', *JSS* 34 (1989), pp. 493-508.

18. J.G. Campbell, *The Use of Scripture in the Damascus Document 1–8, 19–20* (BZAW, 228; Berlin: de Gruyter, 1995).

19. See especially the chart in Campbell's book, *The Use of Scripture in the Damascus Document 1–8, 19–20*, pp. 179-82.

collection, may have patterns of scriptural exegesis which are distinctive. So, for the Damascus Document, Genesis plays only a small role,
whilst parts of Leviticus, Deuteronomy, Isaiah, Ezekiel, the Twelve,
and a few select Psalms are all significant. By taking note of one composition in this way, even though only briefly, the limitations of generalizations become all too apparent.

(4) The fourth way to appreciate which compositions are significant
for the Qumran community and its wider movement is to consider
briefly the number of compositions which seem to be dependent in
some way on earlier models. The process of evaluation here is much
more subjective, but amongst the matters to be considered are the
following. Only since all the Scrolls have become generally available
has it become apparent just how significant the traditions contained in
Genesis and the first part of Exodus were for the community. There
are dozens of texts which retell, rework, rewrite, and comment on
Genesis in particular. Foremost amongst these is the book of *Jubilees*,
a second century BCE composition which is dependent on Genesis and
Exodus for the most part but which contains other traditions as well;
there are apparently at least fifteen copies of this work in the Qumran
caves.[20] Furthermore there are compositions very like it, known as
Pseudo-Jubilees, and importantly for our purposes *Jubilees* seems to
be cited as some kind of authority, both in the well-known section of
the Damascus Document ('And the explication of their times, when
Israel was blind to all these; behold, it is specified in the Book of the
Divisions of the Times in their Jubilees and in their Weeks'; CD 16.2-
4) and also in 4Q228 which has even come to be known as the 'Work
with citation of Jubilees' ('For thus it is written in the Divisions';

---

20. For the copies from Caves 1, 2, 3 and 11, see J.C. VanderKam, *Textual and
Historical Studies in the Book of Jubilees* (HSM, 14; Missoula, MT: Scholars Press,
1977); for the Cave 4 manuscripts, see J.C. VanderKam and J.T. Milik, 'Jubilees',
in H. Attridge *et al.* (eds.), *Qumran Cave 4. VIII: Parabiblical Texts, Part 1* (DJD,
13; Oxford: Clarendon Press, 1994), pp. 1-140. VanderKam and Milik do not
include the three fragments of 4Q176 identified as from the book of *Jubilees* by
M. Kister, 'Newly-Identified Fragments of the Book of Jubilees: Jub 23,21-23. 30-
31', *RevQ* 12 (1985–87), pp. 529-36; these fragments were probably written by the
same scribe who copied 4QJub^f. In addition 4Q482 and 4Q483 may be copies of the
book of *Jubilees*: see M. Baillet, *Qumran Cave 4. III. (4Q482–4Q520)* (DJD, 7;
Oxford: Clarendon Press, 1982), pp. 1-2.

frag. 1, col. i, l. 9).[21] In addition to these *Jubilees* manuscripts, one should associate with Genesis in some way the *Enoch* manuscripts (4Q201–12; also 4Q247), the Book of Giants (1Q23; 1Q24; 2Q26; 4Q530–33; 6Q8), those which concern Noah (1Q19; 1Q19bis; 4Q534–36), the Admonition based on the Flood (4Q370), the Aramaic retelling of Genesis in the Genesis Apocryphon (1QapGen^ar), the Genesis–Exodus paraphrase (4Q422), the Reworked Pentateuch manuscripts (4Q158; 4Q364–67) which also form some kind of biblical paraphrase, the compositions associated with various patriarchal figures (1Q21; 3Q7; 4Q213–15; 4Q369; 4Q371–73; 4Q464; 4Q537; 4Q538–41), the Ages of Creation (4Q180–81), and last but not least, the Genesis Commentaries (4Q252; 4Q253; 4Q254; 4Q254a). In addition several of the wisdom and poetic texts allude to various materials in Genesis.

For Deuteronomy, a similar list of secondary uses of the work can be summoned up. There are rewritings such as in the Reworked Pentateuch manuscripts already mentioned, and parts of the Temple Scroll (4Q524; 11Q19; 11Q20). There are at least two manuscripts which have adapted sections of Deuteronomy probably for liturgical purposes (4QDeut^n, q). Furthermore, there are a significant number of phylacteries that have survived from the caves; these generally contain Deuteronomy 5. There are several apocryphal texts which can be associated with Moses (1Q22; 1Q29; 2Q21; 4Q374–77; 4Q385a; 4Q387a; 4Q388a; 4Q389–90). More obliquely, Deuteronomy may be envisaged as providing the framework for key community texts like MMT (4Q394–99) and the Community Rule. It is also certainly the case that the paraphrases of Joshua (4Q378–79) and various admonition texts weave into their presentations the ideology and the phraseology of Deuteronomy.

For the Psalms, the same is the case. The Scrolls are replete with hymnic compositions (for example, 4Q380–81, as well as all the copies of the *Hodayot*, 1QH; 1Q35–39; 4Q427–33), some of which copy out large chunks of what we would identify as biblical psalms or which use hymnic compositions which appear elsewhere in the Scriptures. The commentaries on the Psalms (4Q171; 4Q173) are also evidence of the importance of these texts. The Psalms probably also played a key role in the structure of exegetical texts like 4Q174 and

21. J.C. VanderKam and J.T. Milik, '4QText with a Citation of Jubilees', in Attridge *et al.* (eds.), *Qumran Cave 4*. VIII, pp. 177-85.

177, as well as 11QMelch. In addition there are many liturgical compositions which echo the Psalms, sometimes quite explicitly (for example, 11QApPs^a).

The story with the Prophets is rather different. We have noticed in the previous two points that both Isaiah and the Twelve have featured significantly, both with respect to the number of manuscripts and in the number of times they are quoted in particular community texts. However, for neither Isaiah nor the Twelve are there any rewritten forms as there are for the Pentateuch, the Psalms, and both Jeremiah and Ezekiel. It is even the case that it is likely that some manuscripts are best understood as reworked forms of the lives of other prophets, especially Elijah and Elisha. But Isaiah and the Twelve have escaped such treatment. Conversely it is remarkable that to date nothing resembling the formal pesher kind of commentary has been found in which Jeremiah and Ezekiel are exegeted in a consistent running fashion. Yet such commentaries are found on both Isaiah and on half of the books of the Twelve (Hosea, Micah, Nahum, Habakkuk, Zephaniah, Malachi).

Taking the four criteria together, it seems evident that 'the canon within the canon' at Qumran is formed from the biblical books of Genesis, Deuteronomy, Isaiah and the Psalms, although in certain compositions other scriptural texts also play a role.[22] Together with Genesis, one should include all the various forms of its traditions and also the pre-Sinaitic parts of Exodus. Together with Deuteronomy, one should include the various rewritten forms of the text and those compositions which are controlled by its structure and ideology. Together with the Psalms proper, one should leave open the question of whether there was more than one Psalter at Qumran, but one should also include a wide range of poetic compositions which depend on the Psalms for their inspiration. Together with Isaiah, one should associate the Twelve Minor Prophets. The two collections seem to be treated in a similar way by the Qumran community and may have had similar functions.

22. This means that the standard view that it is Deuteronomy, Isaiah and the Psalms which are the most favoured biblical books at Qumran needs adjustment; see, for example, J.G. Campbell, *Deciphering the Dead Sea Scrolls* (London: Fontana, 1996), p. 41.

b. *The Significance of Qumran's 'Canon within the Canon'*

What does this fourfold 'canon within the canon' signify for the better understanding of the developing community which copied and preserved these texts?

(1) For Genesis and pre-Sinaitic Exodus several issues seem to be at stake. First, as with many contemporary groups in the Hellenistic world, there is a concern with antiquity. An appeal to the covenant at Sinai was clearly considered important, but it was felt necessary by some to look back before Sinai to explain the movement's unique place in the divine scheme of things. From a certain perspective the community and its wider movement viewed itself as established by God to be for him what he had originally intended for humanity as a whole. Those who hold fast to the sure house which God has established in Israel 'are destined to live for ever and all the glory of Adam shall be theirs' (CD 3.20). Or, put another way, God has commanded 'that a sanctuary of Adam be built for himself, that there they may send up, like the smoke of incense, the works of thanksgiving' (4Q174 3.6-7).[23] The community's *Endzeit* experience is to be an *Urzeit* realization.

But the appeal to Genesis does more than this. It raises acutely the problem of the inadequacy of the preaching and practice of the priestly tradition which finalized its form and passed it on. To read the creation accounts solely as presented in the Pentateuch is to be forced to admit human inadequacy. Humanity's only dessert is to be expelled from the garden; there is no escaping human responsibility for the state of things. However, here is a movement that wants to say that it qualifies for a place in the garden once again; it even thinks of itself as the garden replanted.[24] Whilst the individual may confess his own wrongdoings, responsibility for the overall sorry state of things is thought to lie elsewhere. Hence much of the interest in the traditions in Genesis is with those parallel attempts to handle the problem of evil (Gen. 6.1-4) that reduce the role of human inadequacy and present a myth of angelic responsibility for the chaos around. Here the Watchers play a significant role as the first to go astray and lead others with them (CD 2.17-19). Those who continue to sin have fallen prey to the

---

23. Using the column and line numbering of the edition of 4Q174 by A. Steudel, *Der Midrasch zur Eschatologie aus der Qumrangemeinde (4QMidrEschat$^{a.b}$)* (STDJ, 13; Leiden: Brill, 1994), pp. 23-29.

24. Cf. 1QH 14[6].16-17; 16[8].20-22.

snares of Belial. Thus in several texts found at Qumran there is a concern to remythologize or represent the old myths which allow for the possibility that humanity, that is, the community, may once again have a place in the garden, become truly *homo horticultor*.

As a corollary to this remythologization of the Genesis narratives, the whole book comes to be recognized as a text, not of history per se, so much as of the actualization of divine blessing and curse in history. The interest in the Qumran collection in the narratives of Genesis and in the fortunes and fates of various patriarchs exemplifies this. In particular there is an interest in Noah, Abraham, Jacob and Levi—all those to whom particular promises were made or divine blessings given. It is salutary to recall David Clines's recognition of this in the Pentateuch as a whole:

> The theme of the Pentateuch is the partial fulfilment—which implies also the partial non-fulfilment—of the promise to or blessing of the patriarchs. The promise or blessing is both the divine initiative in a world where human initiatives always lead to disaster, and a re-affirmation of the primal divine intentions for man.[25]

For the Qumranites, this was how and why Genesis and Deuteronomy were to be read: as partially fulfilled blessings and, of course, curses. What remained to be fulfilled was being completed in the life and times of the community itself and its immediate future.

Part of the blessings of Genesis involves the replacement of those things which have distorted the order of the cosmos as God intended it and a reaffirmation of the harmony of creation in its sabbatarian balance. With regard to Genesis, especially the first creation account, mention should also be made of the community's concern for the right calendar and its strict sabbath-keeping which is a reflection of its concern to imitate the intended created order.[26]

---

25. D.J.A. Clines, *The Theme of the Pentateuch* (JSOTSup, 10; Sheffield: JSOT Press, 1978), p. 29.

26. Many texts could be cited under these headings. On keeping the right calendar, note especially 1QS 10.1-8 and the calendrical sections of the Temple Scroll and MMT[a] (4Q394); note too, amongst many calendrical compositions, Astronomical Enoch (4Q208–11); Genesis Commentary A on dating the events of the flood (4Q252 1.4–2.4); Phases of the Moon (4Q317); the Otot Text (4Q319); calendrical documents (4Q320–30); astronomical fragments (4Q335–37). On the Sabbath, see especially CD 10.14–11.18; concern with the right observance of the Sabbath is also

(2) With Deuteronomy, the appeal rests in several matters. First, if Genesis provides the ideology of Paradise regained, then Deuteronomy provides the ideology of place for the localization of the garden. The several descriptions of the atonement of the land in the community texts disclose how important the suitable occupation of the land is for the community.[27] The gift of the land to Abram is a promise that has been actualized and so the land is a reality to be protected and restored. Whether or not the Temple Scroll is a community composition, its preservation in the caves, probably both Caves 4 and 11, shows that it was studied there with some attention. The use of Deuteronomy 12–22 in cols. 51-66 is based on the understanding that these chapters define the law that should be applied in the land.[28] The correct practice of the king is paramount.

Indeed many scholars have noted how the so-called 'Law of the King' in the Temple Scroll (11QT[a] 56.12–59.21) serves a useful purpose in helping to date the period of the text's compilation, but it is worth juxtaposing this law with a section of MMT which also discusses kingship. There two things are said about the place of the addressee (a ruler?). On the one hand he is to take to heart the way '[the blessings have (already) befallen in...] in the days of Solomon the son of David. And the curses [that] have (already) befallen from the days of Jeroboam the son of Nebat and up to when Jerusalem and Zedekiah King of Judah went into captivity'; thus all leaders are to 'think of the kings of Israel and contemplate their deeds: whoever among them feared [the To]rah was delivered from troubles'.[29] On the other he is to 'think of David who was a man of righteous deeds and who was (therefore) delivered from many troubles and was

a dominant feature of the book of *Jubilees* which is represented in the Qumran collection in at least fifteen copies.

27. Note especially 1QS 8.6: 'They shall be witnesses to the truth at the Judgement, and shall be the elect of Goodwill who shall atone for the Land and pay to the wicked their reward' (trans. G. Vermes, *The Dead Sea Scrolls in English* [Harmondsworth: Penguin Books, 4th edn, 1995], p. 80); cf. 1QS 8.10; 4Q265 frag. 7, col. ii, l. 9.

28. On the Temple Scroll and the land, see M.O. Wise, *A Critical Study of the Temple Scroll from Qumran Cave 11* (Studies in Ancient Oriental Civilization, 49; Chicago: Oriental Institute of the University of Chicago, 1990), esp. pp. 200-201.

29. 4Q398 11-13, 18-19, 23-24; trans. E. Qimron and J. Strugnell, *Qumran Cave 4. V. Miqṣat Maʿaśe ha-Torah* (DJD, 10; Oxford: Clarendon Press, 1994), p. 61.

forgiven'.[30] With the exception of David and one or two others, the Deuteronomistic view of Israel's history is to be taken seriously. Indeed, that the period from Solomon to the exile is so bad may account for why the books of Kings and Chronicles are largely absent from the Qumran library; little or none of the history of that period could be construed as normative in any way for those who were the members of the renewed covenant.

In addition to Deuteronomy providing the law for the land, it also reveals two tendencies which were avidly taken up in the community's writings. The first is that it offers permission for the rewriting of normative texts, and perhaps in some cases the model for how such rewriting should be done. The order of the books in the Pentateuch as we now know it was also known at least in the third century BCE.[31] The narrative of Deuteronomy itself places it after that of Exodus in any case. Thus it was recognized that Deuteronomy was a re-presentation of much of the material in the earlier books of the Pentateuch. This permission to rewrite was exploited to the full. It was not an innovation amongst the Qumranites. The author of the book of *Jubilees* took the same opportunity and others may have done as well, depending upon how the relationship of texts is viewed.[32] The Temple Scroll, in its overall representation of material from Exodus 34 to Deuteronomy 22, has been labelled a sixth book of the Torah;[33] whatever it is generically, it contains rewritten biblical material. J. Strugnell, in his revised pronouncements on MMT,[34] has drawn attention to the Deuteronomic structure of the non-calendrical parts of the work, opening with phrasing that resembles Deut. 1.1 and closing with recollections of blessings and curses. Even the Community Rule

30. Qimron and Strugnell (trans.), *Qumran Cave 4*, V, p. 63.

31. And is reflected in some of the Qumran biblical manuscripts (4QGen–Exod[a]; 4QpaleoGen–Exod[l]; 4QExod–Lev[f]; 4QLev–Num[a]) as well as the Reworked Pentateuch (4Q158; 4Q364–67).

32. For example, it has yet to be finally determined how the relationship between Genesis and the *Books of Enoch* is to be best understood; for what they have in common, both may contain reworked traditions from earlier sources.

33. H. Stegemann, 'Is the Temple Scroll a Sixth Book of the Torah—Lost for 2,500 Years?', *BARev* 13 (1987), pp. 28-35.

34. J. Strugnell, 'MMT: Second Thoughts on a Forthcoming Edition', in E. Ulrich and J.C. VanderKam (eds.), *The Community of the Renewed Covenant: The Notre Dame Symposium on the Dead Sea Scrolls* (Christianity and Judaism in Antiquity Series, 10; Notre Dame: University of Notre Dame Press, 1994), pp. 62-70.

in its 1QS form, in part another collection of laws, begins with an appeal based on the Shema: 'The Master shall teach the saints to live according to the Book of the Community Rule, that they may seek God with a whole heart and soul'.

The second tendency which Deuteronomy encourages is that of the toughening of laws. For example, whilst the Law at Sinai according to Exodus clearly prohibits idolatry, Deuteronomy goes into more detail and extends the severity of the Law; in Deut. 13.7-12 (English 13.6-11) whoever even attempts to entice another into idolatry, even if it is a close relative, shall surely be put to death. So it is that in many of the texts found at Qumran the legislation of some parts of the Pentateuch is extended or made more severe. For example, the Sabbath laws in CD 10.14–11.18 are both a clarification and an extension of scriptural Law: work must cease well before sunset on the sixth day (CD 10.14-16) so as to avoid any risk of working on the Sabbath; or again, the ban on handling any kind of tool on the Sabbath was strictly promulgated so that even if a person should be in danger of death, no implement should be used to save them (CD 11.16-17). Of the laws of purification in the Temple Scroll, Y. Yadin writes, 'The laws of the scroll are very harsh here, in diametrical opposition to the definitive rabbinic laws on the matter'.[35] Many more cases of such severity could be cited.

A last issue arises especially in Deuteronomy and is of interest in relation to how the community and its wider movement determined the correct interpretation, application, and extension of the Law. It is Deuteronomy which deals most explicitly with the status of Moses. He is obviously recognized as the mediator of the Law, not as priest or lay leader, but as prophet. Thus Deuteronomy becomes a key indicator for how the hidden law should be revealed in the community. Such revelation is a matter of prophetic activity: 'This is the interpretation of the Law which God commanded through Moses to observe, according to everything that is revealed from time to time, and as the prophets have revealed by his holy spirit' (1QS 8.15-16). Moses is a type of the prophet to come, as Deut. 18.15-18 itself claims.[36] The corollary to this is that there are texts which clearly define the nature of false prophecy (4Q375), and even provide us with a list of the

35. Y. Yadin, *The Temple Scroll*, I (Jerusalem: Israel Exploration Society, 1983), p. 333.
36. Deut. 18.15-18 is important in 4Q175 5-8.

worst false prophets in Israel's history (4Q339). The relationship between the law-giver and the prophet is an intimate one: through both, God makes known his will and his mysterious purposes. With strictness, through God's prophets, humanity is called to obey; Deuteronomy helps make humanity *homo oboediens*.

(3) The motif of prophecy links Deuteronomy both with the Psalms and with Isaiah and the Twelve. The Psalms are considered prophecy: the account of David's compositions in 11QPs[a] 27.2-11 concludes that David composed 4,050 psalms and songs, and 'uttered all these through prophecy which was given him from before the Most High' (cf. Acts 2.30). As prophetic texts they can be exegeted through the form of commentary peculiar to the Qumran community, that which describes the interpretation proper as pesher. Pesher is reserved for the interpretation of unfulfilled blessings, curses, visions and auditions. The Psalms belong in the category of texts which inform the community of the meaning of its own history and its imminent completion.

The prophetic activity of David is a particular concern of the 11QPs[a] scroll, but this is just one facet of the significance of David for the community. He is the prophetic poet *par excellence*, but he is also the one figure whose behaviour needs to be squared with the Law: with regard to polygamy 'David had not read the sealed book of the Law which was in the ark, for it was not opened in Israel from the death of Eleazar and Joshua, and the elders who worshipped Ashtoreth' (CD 5.1-5). He also plays a key role, perhaps in later compositions only,[37] as the progenitor of the messiah, who is occasionally described as the shoot of David. The unique role of David in these three respects is highlighted when one considers the almost total absence of any influence of Solomon in the Scrolls: not only are his Proverbs extant in only two very fragmentary manuscripts, but there is only one explicit reference to the book in the entire corpus (Prov. 15.8 in CD 11.21). Furthermore there is some ambiguity in the passages which actually use his name.[38]

---

37. As is the thesis of K. Pomykala, *The Davidic Tradition in Early Judaism: Its History and Significance for Messianism* (SBLEJL, 7; Atlanta: Scholars Press, 1995).

38. Solomon features in 4Q398 (MMT) frags. 11-13, l. 1 ('in the days of Solomon the son of David'); also in 11QApPs[a] the opening of col. i is unclear: '...] of Solomon, and he will invoke [...]'; it is quite likely that this collection of Psalms

But the Psalms and their numerous related poetic and liturgical texts are important not just for their association with David, but for another reason too. In light of the use of Deuteronomy in the Scrolls and its strict interpretation, the modern commentator might be tempted to conclude that the covenanters were a group of hard-liners. One should reserve judgment on such matters until one has read all the poetic texts which seek to encourage and inspire readers to place themselves before God with confidence; though confession is common, as in the biblical Psalms, the salvific power of God is recognized again and again. This is an oft-repeated motif in the *Hodayot*.

Through the sabbath songs arranged in a group of thirteen, and the list of David's compositions stating clearly that he composed three hundred and sixty-four songs for the daily offering throughout the year,[39] the worship of the community reflects a deep concern with the way things are, with the reality of the presence of God and his angels, to which the only adequate response is praise and adoration according to the right calendar. Thus all the poetry of the Psalms serves to realize what is contained in the blessings of Genesis and Deuteronomy, that the worshipping community is the location of God's mercy, and praise is the activity of the moment which combines heaven and earth. Humanity adjusted aright is also *homo laudans*.

(4) And what of the prophets, especially Isaiah and the Twelve? More of these texts was of concern to the community than might be thought at first. The pesharim allow us to see that for the most part, like the Psalms, or some of them at least, Isaiah and the Twelve were taken seriously in their entirety. Perhaps the preservation of the whole of a copy of the book of Isaiah (1QIsa[a]) and a partial copy of a second (1QIsa[b]) in Cave 1, in which the scrolls seem to have been placed with particular care, signals a reverence for the whole text. However, a minority of the pesharim also shows us that the commentator could at

---

was considered Davidic, like 11QPs[a] and others, and so the mention of Solomon is incidental. He appears lastly in a fragment of 4Q385 which seems to describe the end of David's reign and that Solomon was his successor, though perhaps something is taken from his hand (frag. 13, l. 4).

39. On the Qumran Psalter (11QPs[a]) as in some way reflecting a solar calendar, see M. Chyutin, 'The Redaction of the Qumranic and the Traditional Book of Psalms as a Calendar', *RevQ* 16 (1993–95), pp. 367-95. For another view, see R.T. Beckwith, *Calendar and Chronology, Jewish and Christian: Biblical, Intertestamental and Patristic Studies* (AGJU, 33; Leiden: Brill, 1996), Chapter 6.

times work through selected portions of the text (4QpIsa[b]). Another surprising feature of the handling of Isaiah and the Twelve in the *pesharim* is that the two are somewhat interdependent. In 4QpIsa[c] we have the rare phenomenon of the secondary quotation of Zech. 11.11 (frag. 21, ll. 7-8) and Hos. 6.9 (frag. 23, col. ii, l. 14); conversely in 1QpHab 6.11-12 there is a virtual quotation of Isa. 13.18. The implication of this is that both Isaiah and the Twelve seem to have been considered as mutually informative of the covenanters' experiences. Knowledge and use of the majority of the pericopae in Isaiah and the Twelve show that the covenanters were able to handle both judgment and consolation, the former for those outside the community, the latter for those inside.

As mentioned, it is not the past history of Israel with which the covenanters identified. The history of which they considered themselves a part—that they thought God was making actual in their own time and in their very experiences—was that foretold in the prophets. This needed to be exposed by gifted and learned interpreters, such as the Teacher of Righteousness, 'through whom God made known all the secrets of his servants the prophets' (1QpHab 7.4-5). Such comforting exegesis could make sense of abuse and persecution and could counter the dissonance resulting from a sense of being in the right but not in power. Thus despite circumstances, Isaiah and the Twelve allowed the community to think of itself as consisting of *homo electus*.

3. *'The Canon within the Canon' in the New Testament*

a. *Establishing 'the Canon within the Canon' in the New Testament*
Material on the use of the Old Testament in the New is voluminous.[40] There is neither space nor reason to rehearse it all again here, not even in as much detail as for the Qumran scrolls. However, three matters can be described in outline: the range of texts to which reference is made, the manner of such use, and the likely date when such usage might have begun.

(1) First, the overall array of texts that are cited with some authority by the authors of the various books of the New Testament is not

---

40. Amongst many other items reference might be made to D.A. Carson and H.G.M. Williamson (eds.), *It is Written: Scripture Citing Scripture* (Cambridge: Cambridge University Press, 1988), Chapters 11–19; E.E. Ellis, 'Biblical Interpretation in the New Testament Church', in Mulder (ed.), *Mikra*, pp. 691-725.

that dissimilar from that found in the compositions discovered at Qumran. No selection of biblical manuscripts as kept by some early Christian community has yet been unearthed, nor for the first century CE is there any vast selection of pseudo-biblical Christian materials, so the primary resource for discovering the early Christian 'canon within the canon' is the New Testament itself, both its explicit quotations of and its implicit allusions to other works.

The explicit quotations can be listed readily. As in the Scrolls, citations from texts deemed to carry some weight are often introduced by some kind of technical formula. The fourth edition of the United Bible Societies' Greek New Testament $(UBSGNT^4)^{41}$ has two indices concerning the use of the Old Testament in the New Testament as its editors have understood it. One index lists supposed explicit quotations. Two viewpoints need to be set side by side, a straightforward enumeration of the quotations and a preliminary appreciation of their selectivity. For the Pentateuch, twenty-six texts of Genesis are quoted, thirty from Exodus, eight from Leviticus, three from Numbers, and thirty-six from Deuteronomy. The explicit references to the history books are almost non-existent either as Joshua–Kings or as Chronicles and Ezra–Nehemiah, apart from 2 Samuel 7 and 1 Kings 19 (Rom. 11.3-4), both prophetic items. For the prophets proper including Daniel, there are fifty-four texts from Isaiah, four from Jeremiah, two from Ezekiel, twenty-four from the Twelve Minor Prophets, and one from Daniel. Fifty-eight texts from the Psalms are quoted, some several times; for the rest of the Writings there are only five references from Proverbs and two from Job. On this basis Isaiah and the Psalms are the runaway favourites with Genesis, Exodus, and Deuteronomy featuring respectably, together with the Twelve Minor Prophets.

In addition to simply counting the number of explicit quotations it is important to note something of where the quotations are taken from. It is noticeable, for example, that in terms of the explicit citation of Genesis there is nothing from the Noah cycle, almost nothing from the Jacob traditions, and nothing from the Joseph cycle. As for Deuteronomy most of the passages cited are from the Decalogue and the Shema, from Deuteronomy 18 on the prophet who is to come, and from the Song of Moses. Quotations from the Psalms are spread

41. B. Aland *et al.*, *The Greek New Testament* (Stuttgart: United Bible Societies, 4th edn, 1993).

throughout all five books, but chief amongst those which are quoted more than once are Psalms 2, 16, 69, 110, and 118, the relevant sections of each of which can be understood as referring to an individual, anointed or otherwise. For Isaiah, the Twelve, and Daniel, as with the Psalms, the majority of passages cited can be taken as having to do with an individual figure, whether Emmanuel (Isaiah 7), the servant (Isaiah 40, 42, 49, 52–53), the son of man (Daniel 7), son (Hosea 11), David (Amos 9), or the king (Zechariah 9).

As for allusions and other verbal parallels, the index in the *UBSGNT*[4] is very extensive. The proportions for various books of the Old Testament are similar to the proportions already enumerated for the explicit quotations. It is necessary, however, to be aware that the profile of passages to which allusion is made is somewhat different than with the explicit quotations, at least for certain books of the New Testament. This makes it necessary to nuance how various traditions may have been of influence, at least for some authors and audiences, if not more generally throughout all the churches. So, for example, whereas in the whole New Testament there are no explicit quotations of Leviticus concerning sacrifice, there are several allusions to such passages, not only in the letter to the Hebrews in which Leviticus 16 plays a major role, but also in the letters of Paul and Luke–Acts.[42] Or again, though there are no explicit quotations of the Former Prophets in the Gospels and Acts, there are many important allusions to them in a range of different genres, in the genealogies, in the poetry of Luke's infancy narrative, in the miracle stories, and in the speeches of Peter and Paul in Acts. For another example, the very restricted explicit use of Jeremiah and Ezekiel in the New Testament, almost limited for the former to the new covenant passage and for the latter to Ezek. 20.34, 41 and 37.27 in 2 Cor. 6.16-17, is replaced by a wealth of allusions to both prophetic books, most notably in Revelation.[43] A range of other works also features, almost exclusively from the Apocrypha and *1 Enoch*, but with no hint of *Jubilees*.

(2) Secondly, bearing in mind the ideological points which the particular use of certain books of Scripture in the scrolls found at Qumran suggests, what can be said about the manner in which the

---

42. See esp. Lev. 3.17 in Acts 15.20, 29; Lev. 6.16, 26 in 1 Cor. 9.13; Lev. 7.6, 15 in 1 Cor 10.18.

43. Amongst many others, see especially M.D. Goulder, 'The Apocalypse as an Annual Cycle of Prophecies', *NTS* 27 (1981), pp. 342-67.

books of the New Testament use their selected Old Testament passages? Some aspects of the use of Scripture in the New Testament are similar to that found in the Scrolls. For example, though the subject matter is Jesus, as Son or as the Word, there is some attempt in the appeal to the Scriptures in some sense to argue for the antiquity of what the Christ event might mean (for example, Heb. 1.1-4; Jn 1.1-14). The appeal to earliest times, to creation itself, does three things: it suggests that what God had originally intended is somehow comprehensible for the reader, that what God had intended all along was only partially known to intervening generations, and that therefore what is now to be understood is superior to that which was recognized by previous generations. All these matters can be seen in the Scrolls' handling of the scriptural traditions about the earliest times.

In another matter, to do with the use of Genesis in particular, there is a similarity between the Scrolls and the New Testament. In the Scrolls, appeal to the patriarchs is a matter both of providing pre-Mosaic examples for particular insights and matters of obedience, and also of providing typological models for expressing contemporary understandings and aspirations.[44] In the New Testament, too, there is both exemplary usage of patriarchal figures and others,[45] and there is also a wide-ranging typological use of figures such as Adam and Abraham, Sarah and Hagar, and Jacob. In both the Scrolls and the New Testament these types are used to present a similar *Urzeit und Endzeit* fulfilment, and to argue that the Mosaic covenant is in constant need of interpretation. However, as soon as one passes from method to content, then differences between the two corpora emerge, as the scriptural types in the New Testament are almost exclusively related to Jesus Christ and the new era he has inaugurated.[46] Furthermore in relation to promise and fulfilment the New Testament authors focus on universalist aspects of unfulfilled blessings given to the patriarchs and thereby creatively redirect the particularism of the Mosaic covenant: both the blessings and curses are read as referring to

44. For example, in some texts the community describes itself as 'the House of Judah' (1QpHab 8.1; 4QpPs^a frags. 1–10, col. ii, l. 14); in others the movement aspires to 'all the glory of Adam' (1QS 4.23; CD 3.20).

45. See especially the appeal to the exemplary faith of Abel, Enoch, Noah, Abraham and others in Heb. 11.4-40.

46. Similarity between the Scrolls and the New Testament is most obvious in how both communities variously claim to be the true Israel.

all people. The physical shift away from Palestine to the dispersion
and into the Gentile world also means that this universalism is not
generally expressed in the particular alternative mythologies available
within Palestinian Jewish tradition, but, for example, through appeal
to conscience and aspects of natural law. Thus allusions to Enoch are
largely restricted to texts which belong to or reflect Palestinian Jewish
Christian communities, notably Jude 14.

The universalist reading of Genesis also controls the reading of
Deuteronomy. Here the differences between the Scrolls and the New
Testament become all the more apparent. The use of Deuteronomy in
the New Testament is in no way tied to the gift of the land which
needs to be lived out appropriately, nor is it read as the true guide
to strict obedience. There is much appeal to the Decalogue of
Deuteronomy 5 and a few other pertinent laws[47] as a way of providing an effective summary of the Law for Christians. Deuteronomy
18.15-18 on the status of Moses as a prophet recurs in several places,
and as such is a key concept in understanding the various portrayals of
the figure of Jesus. The blessings of the Song of Moses are also set in
contexts of universal fulfilment.

The christological use of parts of Deuteronomy is reflected in the
dominant way in which the text of Isaiah is handled in the New
Testament. Whereas in the Scrolls it is difficult to specify which sections of the book were of key importance to the community and its
wider movement, in the New Testament Isaiah is explicitly used
overwhelmingly because of the messianic readings in Isaiah 7, 9 and
11 and the individualistic significance of the Servant Songs. Judgment
is retained through the use of Isa. 6.9-10 in several places and one or
two other passages. Rather than providing a sense of election for the
community, the book of Isaiah is searched for texts that relate to one
specific elect individual.

As for the Psalms, their use is primarily in line with the Scrolls'
view of them as prophetic texts in need of fulfilment. Especially is this
the case in the passion narratives, but also the overall structure of the
argument of Hebrews has been seen to be based on Psalms 95, 110 and
40. However, Psalms 2, 110, 118 and others are both cited and alluded
to often, confirming the particularist interest of the New Testament

47. Notably the rule against bribery in Deut. 10.17 based on the impartiality of
God himself which is alluded to in several New Testament passages: Acts 10.34;
Rom. 2.11; Gal. 2.6; Eph. 6.9; Col. 3.25; 1 Tim. 6.15; Rev. 17.14; 19.16.

authors in searching the Scriptures for texts that could be used christologically of Jesus. Furthermore, it is noticeable that those psalms in the New Testament which are almost certainly Jewish compositions slightly adapted, such as the canticles in Luke's infancy narrative, are indeed replete with implicit allusions to the Psalms, but only very occasional are hints of the Psalms to be found in the newly composed hymns such as are found in Philippians 2, Colossians 1 or scattered through the book of Revelation. Again, the christocentricity of early Christian worship has provoked a break with long-standing traditions of how God is suitably worshipped.

(3) The third matter to focus on in the prevalence of this quartet of scriptural books in the New Testament concerns the likely date of and reason for their predominance. Three examples follow in the next section of this paper. They are all taken from the earliest layers of the New Testament, from the source common to Matthew and Luke, from Mark, and from a pre-Pauline hymn which Paul probably adapted. These examples show that the four leading biblical books, Genesis, Deuteronomy, Isaiah and the Psalms, were prominent in the earliest layers of the tradition and are not the result of generations of reflection. The question to ask, then, is whether the similar pattern of the canon within the canon in the New Testament as in the Scrolls results from the dependence of one upon the other, or whether it is merely the case that eschatologically oriented, perhaps somewhat marginalized, forms of Judaism tended to look to the same Scriptures for their self-understanding. Though from the time of John the Baptist onwards some of those responsible for the copying and preservation of the Scrolls may indeed have joined the Jesus movement or the early Christian communities in Palestine and elsewhere, the subtle differences—in which parts of the favourite scriptural books were chosen and in the ways in which much of the handling of the texts occurred— suggest that the differences in content should be noted as much as the similarities in method. One suspects that for these kinds of Judaism 'the canon within the canon' was a fairly obvious matter.

b. *The Working and Significance of 'the Canon within the Canon' in the New Testament*
In this short section, three examples of the early Christian use of Old Testament texts will be given. Though selected to illustrate the prominence of Genesis, Deuteronomy, Isaiah and the Psalms, the texts discussed could be substituted with many others.

(1) *Luke 7.22-23 (Matthew 11.4-6)*. The disciples of John the Baptist have come to Jesus to enquire about whether Jesus was the expected one. Jesus' answer to them is a combination of scriptural allusions. The precise phraseology of 'the blind see' combines the language of Isa. 35.5 with Isa. 61.1; 'the lame walk' is partly Isa. 35.6; 'lepers are cleansed' may allude to Lev. 14.2-3 or 4 Kgdms 5.3; 'the deaf hear' is Isa. 35.5 again; 'the dead are raised' may allude to Deut. 32.39[48] or Isa. 26.19;[49] 'the poor have good news preached to them' is a form of Isa. 61.1. Here is a combination of Isaianic passages with some hints of motifs to be found in the Law. The passages are associated with the anointed prophet of the last days and so in their New Testament context exemplify how scriptural promises are fulfilled through Jesus. Some of these ideas are also portrayed in 4Q521 in relation to divine activity in the time of his anointed one, but there Isa. 61.1 is expanded through reference to Ps. 107.9 and 146.7.[50] Since this saying is shared between Luke and Matthew it may well come from a common source and possibly even stem in some form from Jesus himself.

(2) *Mark 12.1-12 (Matthew 21.33-36; Luke 20.9-19)*. Elsewhere it has been argued that combination of the parabolic use of the vineyard material from Isa. 5.1-7 and the proof-text concerning the cornerstone from Ps. 118.22-23 was a natural juxtaposition of texts, and in something like the form of the tradition as presented in Mark 12 and parallels may have originated with Jesus himself.[51] The details of that argument need not be rehearsed here. It is only important to notice that two other scriptural matters are commonly discussed in relation to the parable. First, two items of Genesis need to be noted. The term 'beloved' (Mk. 12.6; Lk. 20.13) is to be understood against a back

---

48. As pointed out for the parallel in 4Q521 by E. Puech, 'Une apocalypse messianique (*4Q521*)', *RevQ* 15 (1990–92), p. 493.

49. As claimed, for example, by J.A. Fitzmyer, *The Gospel according to Luke I–IX* (AB, 28; Garden City, NY: Doubleday, 2nd edn, 1983), p. 668.

50. For comments on the relationship between 4Q521 and Lk. 7.22-23, see G.J. Brooke, 'Shared Intertextual Interpretations in the Dead Sea Scrolls and the New Testament', in M. E. Stone and E. Chazon (eds.), *The Scrolls and the Interpretation of Scripture* (STDJ; Leiden: Brill, forthcoming).

51. G.J. Brooke, '4Q500 1 and the Use of Scripture in the Parable of the Vineyard', *DSD* 2 (1995), pp. 268-94.

ground of scriptural passages, foremost amongst which is Gen. 22.2.[52] The words of the tenants, 'Come, let us kill him', are also the words of Joseph's brothers in Gen. 37.20. Secondly, if the parable should be interpreted with respect to the laws and practices concerning inheritance, then clearly with regard to what the vineyard symbolizes the many references to the land as Israel's inheritance in Deuteronomy readily come to mind. Thus, in this pericope there is a subtle combination of themes from Genesis, Deuteronomy, Isaiah and the Psalms; furthermore, the particular usage of the material from Genesis and Psalm 118 is focused on Jesus. The selection of scriptural passages according to their christological potential is evident. Nevertheless all four books of 'the canon within the canon' are represented. A general allusion to the Twelve may also be present in the sending of the servants, one after the other, just as the prophets had also been sent, some of whom are explicitly called 'servant' (Amos 3.7; Zech. 1.6).

(3) *Philippians 2.6-11.* This early Christian hymn, either composed or more probably adapted by Paul, is replete with scriptural allusions. Often pointed out are the references to Genesis 1–3: in the contrast between the form of God and the form of a slave, in the temptation to be like God, implicitly in the contrast between Christ's obedience and Adam's disobedience, and in Christ's acceptance of Adam's lot, mortality, for himself, so that through his exaltation, glory could once again become visible.[53] Alongside the Genesis allusions are also some motifs from Isaiah: the precise word for 'servant' is used of Israel in Isa. 49.3 and 5; the motif of kenosis in Phil. 2.7 may be a suitable rendering of Isa. 53.12, 'he emptied out his life to death'; most obviously Isa. 45.23 is poetically adapted in Phil. 2.10-11. Allusions to Deuteronomy can also be recognized in the passage: the Decalogue (Deut. 5.6-21) and the Shema (Deut. 6.4-5) both insist on the singularity of God and that nothing should be made in his likeness, and the name of God is not be taken in vain (Deut. 5.11). The Shema also insists on the importance of obedience, and the glory of God is revealed as the Decalogue is given (Deut. 5.24). Furthermore, Paul seems aware of these Deuteronomic allusions as he sets the hymn within the context

52. The epithet also occurs in Mk 1.11 and parallels; it may also reflect the description of Israel in Isa. 44.2.

53. See esp. J.D.G. Dunn, *Christology in the Making: A New Testament Inquiry into the Origins of the Doctrine of the Incarnation* (London: SCM Press, 1980), pp. 114-21.

of an exhortation to obedience (Phil. 2.12) with fear and trembling
(cf. Exod. 15.15-16) endorsed by his own self-sacrifice (Phil. 2.17).
As mentioned earlier, there are few allusions, if any, to the Psalms in
these new early Christian hymns.[54] Nevertheless, here once again are
Genesis, Isaiah and Deuteronomy combined through an obvious christological purpose with universalist implications.

4. *Conclusion*

Four scriptural books and their extras were particularly popular
amongst those connected with the Scrolls and the various New
Testament authors: Genesis, Deuteronomy, Isaiah and the Psalms. To
both groups these books in various ways guaranteed the antiquity of
their claims, allowed them to justify their positions as the true repre-
sentatives of Israel, strongly suggested they were living at the time of
the fulfilment of God's promises, that his blessings were theirs despite
persecutions and misunderstandings.

The covenanters of the Scrolls thought of how in them humanity
was restored, that through God's mercy correct obedience was possible, and that in purity they could join the worship of the angels; God
was about to complete his consolation of them. For many of the early
Christians too, humanity seemed restored; God's mercy enabled correct response and thanksgiving became a community characteristic.
For the covenanters the interpretative myths associated with these four
authoritative books were shattered when the land was irretrievably
occupied and the locus of worship destroyed; for the Christians the
interpretative myth, somewhat similarly based, came to reflect a continuing reality because it was made of universal significance through
the recollection of the death of one man.

---

54. There is a possibility that Phil. 2.10 contains an allusion to Ps. 67.15 (LXX)
in which Shaddai is rendered by the very distinctive 'heavenly one'. The context in
the Psalm describes God as at Sinai.

QUMRAN AND THE FOURTH GOSPEL: IS THERE A CONNECTION?

Richard Bauckham

It seems to have become quite widely accepted that the parallels between the Johannine literature of the New Testament (the Gospel and Epistles of John) and those texts from Qumran which most likely express the community's own theology are probably the most impressive parallels between the New Testament and Qumran, and are so impressive as to require an historical connection closer than could be provided merely by the common Jewish milieu of late Second Temple Judaism. The hypothesis of some kind of influence from Qumran on John is widely accepted, whether this is regarded as indirect (for example, R.E. Brown[1]) or direct (for example, K.G. Kuhn,[2] J.H. Charlesworth,[3] J. Ashton[4]). In my view this hypothesis is mistaken. It arose from a natural enthusiasm about parallels between the Scrolls and the New Testament when the Scrolls were first published,[5] but the parallels in this case have not been assessed with sufficient

---

1. R.E. Brown, 'The Qumran Scrolls and the Johannine Gospel and Epistles', in *idem*, *New Testament Essays* (New York: Paulist Press, 1965), pp. 102-31; *idem*, 'The Dead Sea Scrolls and the New Testament', in J.H. Charlesworth (ed.), *John and the Dead Sea Scrolls* (New York: Crossroad, 1990), pp. 7-8; *idem*, *The Community of the Beloved Disciple* (New York: Paulist Press, 1979), pp. 30-31.

2. K.G. Kuhn, 'Die in Palästina gefundenen hebräischen Texte und das neue Testament', *ZTK* 47 (1950), pp. 192-211.

3. J.H. Charlesworth, 'A Critical Comparison of the Dualism in 1QS 3.13–4.26 and the "Dualism" Contained in the Gospel of John', in Charlesworth (ed.), *John and the Dead Sea Scrolls*, pp. 76-106.

4. J. Ashton, *Understanding the Fourth Gospel* (Oxford: Clarendon Press, 1991), pp. 232-37.

5. Cf. B. Lindars, *John* (NT Guides; Sheffield: JSOT Press, 1990), p. 49: 'Initial enthusiasm overstressed the importance of these similarities'. For a minimalist view of the significance of the Scrolls for understanding John, see C.K. Barrett, *The Gospel according to St John* (London: SPCK, 2nd edn, 1978), p. 34.

methodological rigour.[6] I do not think they amount to a case for influence or for any particular historical connection between John and Qumran. Given the limitations of space, I shall focus here on the evidence for a connection to which most weight is usually given: the expression of dualistic thinking in *light and darkness imagery* in both the Qumran texts and the Fourth Gospel.[7]

The extent of the similarity between the dualism of the Qumran texts and the dualism of the Fourth Gospel has been debated, but even those who emphasize dissimilarities more than others seem to agree that the extensive use of light/darkness imagery to express a dualistic worldview in both cases represents a very striking similarity.[8] In assessing the hypothesis of a Qumran origin for Johannine dualism, it is therefore very useful to focus on precisely how this imagery of light and darkness is used in each case. This will enable us to avoid conducting a comparison at too high a level of abstraction from the way the theology of the texts is actually expressed in them.

The dualism of the Fourth Gospel is expressed in two sets of images. One is the imagery of light and darkness (1.4-9; 3.19-21; 8.12; 9.4-5; 11.9-10; 12.35-36, 46; cf. 1 Jn 1.5-7; 2.8-11). The other is the spatial imagery which appears in the terms 'from above' and 'from below' (8.23), 'not from this world' and 'from this world' (8.23; 18.36), 'not from the world' and 'from the world' (15.19; 17.14, 16). The further

6. This is also true of those scholars who conclude that these same parallels show John's dependence on first-century Jewish forms of thought which Qumran exemplifies but which had wider currency (for example, J. Painter, *The Quest for the Messiah* [Edinburgh: T. & T. Clark, 2nd edn, 1993], pp. 50-52). Here too there is no sufficiently careful assessment of the alleged parallels themselves, as well as of the relationship of the Qumran texts, on the one hand, and of John, on the other, to comparable material in other Jewish literature.

7. For a survey of other similarities, see Brown, 'The Qumran Scrolls'. In what follows, material in 1 John will be noticed only in passing: limitations of space preclude adequate discussion of the use of light/darkness imagery in 1 John here.

8. Charlesworth, 'A Critical Comparison', pp. 100-101, after stressing the differences in the dualistic theologies of 1QS 3.13–4.26 and John, writes: 'After full account is taken of all the dissimilarities in theological perspective, we must ask whether in the realm of symbolism and mythology there exists between John and the Rule an underlying interrelationship of conceptual framework and literary expression. We may reasonably hold that the dualistic opposition between light and darkness is not something each developed independently, but rather something that betokens John's dependence on the Rule.'

contrasting phrases 'from God' and 'from the devil' (8.42-44, 47) and 'from God' and 'from humans' (12.43) are easily associated with the spatial imagery, since God is above and the devil and humans are below. The two sets of images therefore are the light/darkness opposition and the above/below and God/world opposition. It is very important to notice that these two sets of images never combine or overlap in the Fourth Gospel. Each is kept distinct from the other. (When 'the world' appears in connection with the image of light [1.9; 3.19; 8.12; 12.46], it has the neutral sense of the created world, never the pejorative sense of the world opposed to God which it has in the God/world dualistic passages.)

Of these two sets of images, the Qumran texts provide parallels only to the light/darkness opposition, which, of course, is found also in other Jewish texts. For the distinctively Johannine use of 'the world' and 'this world' in a pejorative sense, and the distinctively Johannine contrast of 'from above' and 'from below' the Qumran texts provide no parallel at all.[9] This in itself makes implausible the view that Johannine dualism as such derives from Qumran dualism. It would surely be hard to argue that the light/darkness imagery is the primary expression of Johannine dualism and the above/below and God/world opposition a secondary development. The latter plays just as important a role in the Gospel as the former. Consequently, even if the Johannine use of light/darkness imagery derives from Qumran, this could not easily be understood to mean that Johannine dualism as such derives from Qumran.

But can the Johannine use of light/darkness imagery plausibly be held to derive from the Qumran texts? We should first recall two evident facts. First, the contrast of light and darkness is the most obvious of dualisms observable in the natural world, and has therefore acquired the metaphorical meanings of knowledge and ignorance, truth and error, good and evil, life and death, in most (perhaps all) cultural traditions. Secondly, these metaphorical uses of the light/darkness imagery occur relatively often in the Hebrew Bible and in Second Temple Jewish literature, and so were readily available in the Jewish

---

9. It has rarely been noticed that the best parallels to these Johannine usages are in James (1.17, 27; 3.15, 17). Since there are no other resemblances between James and the Johannine literature, these parallels are best explained by common dependence on a Jewish terminology which does not seem to have been preserved in extant Jewish texts.

tradition to the authors of both the Qumran texts and Johannine literature. To establish a special connection between these it is not sufficient
to point out that none of the other Jewish texts emphasize the
light/darkness imagery to the extent that 1QS and the Fourth Gospel
do.[10] In fact, this is not strictly true, since the sustained use of the
metaphor of light and darkness for good and evil, truth and error
through some 132 verses of the apocalypse of the clouds in *2 Baruch*
(chs. 53, 56–72) represents a more extensive use of the imagery than
do the sixteen verses of the Fourth Gospel which use the imagery. But
in any case, the mere fact that both 1QS and the Fourth Gospel make
more prominent use of this imagery than most Jewish texts proves
very little. If the imagery was available in the Jewish tradition, it
would not be especially surprising to find two authors independently
developing it more extensively than most other Jewish texts do. Only
if the development in the two cases exhibited extensive similarities not
attributable to common roots in the common Jewish tradition would
there be any reason to postulate a connexion. If, on the other hand,
there were extensive dissimilarities in the two developments, and if
the distinctive development in each case could be plausibly explained
as a development of elements in the common Jewish tradition, then to
postulate a connection between the two developments would be unnecessary and implausible.

   In the rest of this paper, I shall argue, first, that the use of the light/
darkness imagery in the Fourth Gospel, on the one hand, and in the
Qumran texts, on the other, exhibits far more impressive dissimilarities than have been noticed in the scholarly enthusiasm for drawing
conclusions from the comparatively unimpressive similarities. While
this considerably weakens the case for influence from Qumran on
John, it does not necessarily disprove it. The dissimilarities might
result from John's creative adaptation of the basic motif he borrowed
from the Qumran texts. In order to disprove this possibility, I shall
show that the distinctively Johannine uses of the light/darkness imagery,
which cannot be paralleled in the Qumran texts, can be paralleled to a
significant extent in other Second Temple Jewish literature, and can
very plausibly be understood as rooted in biblical texts predominantly
different from the biblical texts which influenced the uses of the light/
darkness imagery in the Qumran texts. Since what is distinctive in the

---

10. Cf. Charlesworth, 'A Critical Comparison', p. 100.

Johannine use of the light/darkness imagery finds parallels in other Second Temple Jewish literature and sources in the Hebrew Bible, what the Johannine use has in common with the Qumran use is much more plausibly attributed to common dependence on the Hebrew Bible and general Jewish tradition than to any closer relationship between John and Qumran.

Among the Qumran texts, the light/darkness dualism occurs predominantly in the Rule of the Community (1QS), the War Rule (1QM, 4QM), and the fragmentary text known as 4QVisions of Amram (4Q543–548).[11] Since the most impressive parallels with John have been seen in the passage about the two spirits in 1QS 3.13–4.26, I shall focus on this passage, but add references to relevant material in the War Rule. The passage in the Rule of the Community uses synonymously the three pairs of opposites: light and darkness, truth and deceit, justice and injustice. It depicts two angelic beings, the Prince of Lights and the Angel of Darkness, the spirit of truth and the spirit of deceit, who are the sources of good and evil in the world. Both were created by God, though God loves one and hates the other, and has destined the one for triumph and the other for destruction. Meantime, they contend with each other in human hearts. Depending on the dominance of either, human beings are divided into the sons of light, truth or justice and the sons of deceit. The influence of the two spirits in human life is correlated with the image of the two ways drawn from the wisdom tradition: people walk either in the paths of light or in the paths of darkness. These two ways lead to different destinies at the eschatological judgment, again described partly in the imagery of light and darkness: the light of glory in eternal life, and the darkness of the nether regions in which the wicked are punished and destroyed. The War Rule uses the light/darkness dualism not in this psychological and individual way, but to depict the eschatological war in which Michael, his angels and the sons of light will defeat Belial, his angels and the sons of

11. Cf. also 4QSongs of the Sage[b] (4Q511); 11QApocryphal Psalms[a] (11Q11). The light/darkness dualism does not appear in the *Hodayot*, or in the Damascus Rule (though the title 'the Prince of Lights' is used for Michael in CD 5.18, as in 1QS 3.20). For other significant occurrences of light/darkness imagery in the Scrolls which seem more distant from the way this imagery is used in 1QS and 1QM, see 4Q462 9-10; 1QMysteries (1Q27) 1.5-6; 4QMysteries[a] (4Q299) 5.1-3; 4QCryptic A (4Q298) 1.1; 4Q471 4.5.

darkness. The same cosmic dualism appears in different aspects in the two works.

I will now outline some noteworthy differences in the use of the light/darkness imagery in the Fourth Gospel and the above mentioned Qumran texts.

(1) These Qumran texts exhibit a stereotyped and elaborate dualistic *terminology*, in which each term has its corresponding opposite: the spirit of truth and the spirit of deceit, the sons of light and the sons of darkness, the paths of light and the paths of darkness, and so on (see the Appendix for a table of terminology). Apart from the terms light and darkness themselves, only one of these terms—'the sons of light'—appears in those passages of the Fourth Gospel which use the light/darkness imagery (12.36). This single coincidence of terminology between John and Qumran is misrepresented by Charlesworth when he claims that 'the expression "sons of light" is characteristic only of Qumran and John'.[12] It is no more characteristic of John than of Luke, Paul and the author of Ephesians, each of whom, like John, uses the expression just once (Lk. 16.8; 1 Thess. 5.5; Eph. 5.8). The list of terminological parallels should not be expanded to include phrases which occur in John outside the passages which use the light/darkness imagery, especially not when these are such commonplace expressions as 'the holy Spirit', 'eternal life' and 'the wrath of God',[13] but not even in the case of the distinctively Johannine term 'the Spirit of Truth', which in John has no relationship to the light/darkness imagery.[14] It is hardly credible that, if the Qumran use

12. Charlesworth, 'A Critical Comparison', p. 101.

13. The first two of these three phrases are included by Charlesworth, 'A Critical Comparison', pp. 101-102, in his 'four shared linguistic formulae which suggest a strong correlation between John and 1QS 3.13-4.26', while the third occurs in his 'seven additional shared literary expressions'. For a few additional parallels, see C.A. Evans, *Word and Glory: On the Exegetical and Theological Background of John's Prologue* (JSNTSup, 89; Sheffield: JSOT Press, 1993), p. 147.

14. The coincidence in the use of this term 'the Spirit of Truth' in both 1QS (3.18-19; 4.21, 23; cf. 'all the spirits of truth' in 1QM 13.10) and John (14.17; 15.26; 16.13; cf. 1 Jn 4.6) has attracted much attention and deserves a full discussion, which should not, however, be confused by conflating John's use of this term with his use of light/darkness imagery, with which it has no textual connexion. The coincidence is far less remarkable than often thought, since genitival phrases combining 'spirit' and an abstract noun are a standard way, in Jewish literature and in the New Testament, of specifying the effect of the 'spirit'. When the 'spirit' is the divine

of the light/darkness imagery influenced John, the highly distinctive terminology which virtually *constitutes* the Qumran use of the light/darkness imagery should have left such minimal traces in John.[15]

(2) Conversely, expressions which characterize the Johannine use of the light/darkness imagery have no parallel in the Qumran texts: 'the true light' (1.9; cf. 1 Jn 2.8), 'the light of the world' (8.12; 9.5), 'to have the light' (8.12; 12.35-36), 'to come to the light' (3.20-21), 'to remain in the darkness' (12.46; cf. 1 Jn 2.9), and the contrast of 'day' and 'night' (9.4; 11.9-10).

(3) Several important features of the way the light/darkness imagery functions in the Qumran texts are entirely absent from John. For example, essential to the Qumran usage are the two spirits of light and darkness, the Prince of Lights and the Angel of Darkness, Michael and Belial in the War Rule. They do not appear in John's use of the

Spirit, as is the case in John, such expressions specify one particular effect of the divine Spirit (for example Exod. 28.3; Deut. 34.9; Isa. 11.1; *1 En.* 49.3; 62.2; Rom. 1.4; 8.2, 15; 2 Cor. 4.13; Eph. 1.17; 2 Tim. 1.7; Heb. 10.29; 1 Pet. 4.14). The term 'spirit of truth' is just one such natural formation, not confined to 1QS and John (cf. *Jub.* 25.14; *Jos. Asen.* 19.11). Its occurrence in both these texts is an aspect of the prominence of the term 'truth' in both.

15. Of the other 'shared literary expressions' listed by Charlesworth, 'A Critical Comparison', p. 102, only three deserve mention: (1) 'to walk in the paths of darkness' (1QS 3.21; 4.11) and 'to walk in darkness' (Jn 8.12; 12.35; cf. 1 Jn 1.6; 2.11); (2) 'the light of life' (1QS 3.7; Jn 8.12); (3) 'blindness of eyes' (1QS 4.11) and 'the eyes of the blind' (Jn 10.21; cf. John 9).

On these the following comments should be made: (1) Both expressions are biblical: 'to walk in the paths of darkness' (Prov. 2.13), 'to walk in darkness' (Ps. 82.5; Eccl. 2.14; Isa. 9.2[1]). 1QS uses the former twice (1QS 3.21; 4.11) and the latter once (1QS 11.10), whereas John uses only the latter (Jn 8.12; 12.35; cf. 1 Jn 1.6; 2.11). The difference is significant. The usage in 1QS derives from the wisdom tradition (in 1QS 3.21; 4.11 the phrase corresponds verbatim to Prov. 2.13) and is part of the picture of the two ways. By contrast the two ways terminology makes no appearance in the Fourth Gospel, whose use of light/darkness imagery seems uninfluenced by the wisdom tradition. Its use of the expression 'to walk in darkness' probably derives from Isa 9.2[1] (see below). (2) The phrase 'the light of life' is a biblical expression (Job 33.30; Ps. 56.13[14]), which also occurs in later Jewish literature (*1 En.* 58.3). In 1QS 3.7 it derives from Job 33.30, in Jn 8.12 probably from Ps. 56.13[14]. (3) The phrase 'blindness of eyes' (1QS 4.11) occurs in the following list: 'blasphemous tongue, blindness of eyes, hardness of hearing, stiffness of neck, hardness of heart'. Clearly blindness here has no particular connexion with light and darkness, as it does in John 9.

light/darkness imagery, where Christ himself is the light, but the devil, who in other parts of the Gospel is 'the ruler of this world' (12.31; 14.30; 16.11) and 'the father of lies' (8.44), is never related to darkness.[16] Secondly, neither the conflict of light and darkness within the heart of the individual nor the conflict between the two categories of humanity, the sons of light and the sons of darkness, appears in John, where 1.5 is the only verse to make any use at all of the image of conflict between light and darkness. Thirdly, the use of light and darkness to characterize the alternative eschatological destinies of the two classes of humanity is absent from John,[17] even though this was common in Jewish eschatological imagery (for example *1 En.* 92.3-5; 108.11-15).

(4) Although John's use of the light/darkness imagery is flexible and not wholly consistent, the central image is that of a great light coming into the world, shining in the darkness of the world, giving light to all people, so that they may come out of the darkness into the light, and be able to walk in this light instead of stumbling in the darkness (see 1.5, 9; 3.19; 8.12; 11.9-10; 12.35, 46). This dominant image of a great light shining in the darkness is not at all the dominant image in the Qumran texts' use of light/darkness imagery. Once the spirit of truth is said to enlighten the heart of the individual (1QS 4.2), while the War Rule envisages the time when, following their defeat of the Kittim, the sons of light will shine in all the edges of the earth, giving light until the end of all the periods of darkness, when God's own glory will shine for eternity (1QM 1.8). These seem to be the only instances of the image of light shining in and dispelling darkness. They are subsidiary to the dominant image of conflict between light and darkness, where very often the metaphorical force of the words light and darkness seems to have been largely lost and they function simply as names for opposing cosmic principles, interchangeable with truth and deceit, justice and injustice. In the Fourth Gospel the light/darkness imagery is always used to convey specific visual images of light and darkness, of which the central and dominant one, the great

16. Contrast 1 Cor. 6.14-15 and Acts 26.18, both of which are closer than John to Qumran usage.

17. In Jn 8.12 (cf. 12.35) 'walk in darkness' refers to living in ignorance and error, not to eschatological destiny.

light shining in the darkness of the world, finds a parallel at Qumran only in one line of the War Rule.[18]

(5) Finally, the difference in the imagery corresponds to a difference in the meaning conveyed by the imagery. In the Fourth Gospel the central image of the light shining in the darkness has christological and soteriological significance. Christ is the light of the world, come into the world so that people may come out of the darkness into the light. At Qumran, on the other hand, the imagery of light and darkness is used to portray a conflict between cosmic hierarchies of good and evil, which contend in the heart of the individual and on the heavenly and earthly battlefield of the eschatological war. There is no thought of people moving from 'the lot of darkness' into light.

In summary, then, the similarity between the use of light/darkness imagery in the two cases is almost entirely limited to the basic symbolism: light and darkness symbolize truth and error operating on a cosmic scale. The particular development of this symbolism in each case diverges widely. Characteristic terminology, dominant imagery and theological significance all differ to such an extent as to make the influence of Qumran on the Fourth Gospel unlikely.

I shall now show how the use of light/darkness imagery in the Fourth Gospel has its own sources in the Hebrew Bible and parallels in Second Temple Jewish literature which explain precisely the ways in which it diverges from the Qumran texts' use of such imagery and make the hypothesis of influence from Qumran on John entirely redundant.

(1) The opening verses of the prologue to the Gospel are an exegesis of the opening verses of Genesis, and the first appearance of the light/darkness imagery in the Gospel (1.4-5) constitutes an interpretation of the light and darkness of the first day of the Genesis creation narrative

---

18. Cf. also 1QMysteries (1Q27) 1.5-6: 'When those begotten of iniquity are delivered up, and wickedness is removed from before righteousness, as darkness is removed from before light, and just as smoke ceases and is no more, so wickedness will cease forever; and righteousness will be revealed as the sun throughout the measure of the world' (trans. D.J. Harrington, *Wisdom Texts from Qumran* [London: Routledge, 1996], p. 70). But here light and darkness appear as a *simile,* alongside the alternative simile of smoke, not in the way they appear in the dualistic light/darkness language of 1QS and 1QM. This text shows no other trace of light/darkness dualism. The passage in 1.5-6 is close to the imagery in *1 En.* 58.5-6 (and cf. 4Q541 frag. 9, col. i, ll. 3-5; *T. Levi* 18.2-4), and so provides general Jewish, not specifically Qumran, background to 1 Jn 2.8.

(Gen. 1.3-5). It is possible that when the Qumran Rule of the Community says that God 'created the spirits of light and of darkness' (1QS 3.25) it also reflects the Genesis creation account (though allusion to Isa. 45.7 is also possible),[19] but, even if this is the case, there are much better parallels in other Jewish literature. The Johannine prologue belongs to a Jewish tradition of theological exegesis of the Genesis creation narrative, which often devoted particular interest and speculation to the work of the first day and to the primordial light which appeared on that day (for example, *4 Ezra* 6.40; *LAB* 28.8-9; 60.2; 4Q392 1.4-7; *2 En.* 24.4J; 25; Aristobulus, *ap.* Eusebius, *Praep. Evang.* 13.12.9-11; Philo, *Op. Mund.* 29–35). Most instructive for our purposes is *Jos. Asen.* 8.9, which addresses God

> who gave life to all (things)
> and called (them) from the darkness to the light,
> and from the error to the truth,
> and from the death to the life.

This shows that to associate the contrast of light and darkness in the Genesis creation narrative with the contrasts of truth and error, life and death, as the Johannine prologue implicitly does, one did not need to be influenced by Qumran (since influence from Qumran in *Joseph and Aseneth* is unlikely[20]).[21]

(2) The image of a great light shining in the darkness of the world in order to give light to people, which as we have seen is marginal in the Qumran texts but central and dominant in the Fourth Gospel's use of the light/darkness imagery, has several kinds of sources in the Hebrew Bible and parallels in Second Temple Jewish literature. I note first the image of a prophet or teacher as a light who by his teaching of truth gives light. For example, Samuel is described as a light (*LAB* 51.4), not only 'for this nation', but even 'to the peoples' (51.6,

---

19. See 11QApocryphal Psalms[a] (11Q11) 1.12-13, for an explicit allusion to Gen. 1.4 in connexion with the light/darkness dualism.

20. Against alleged affinities between *Joseph and Aseneth* and the Essenes, see R.D. Chesnutt, *From Death to Life: Conversion in Joseph and Aseneth* (JSPSup, 16; Sheffield: JSOT Press, 1995), pp. 186-95.

21. *Gen. R.* 3.8 interprets the light and darkness of Gen. 1.3 as the deeds of the righteous and the deeds of the wicked. This later passage again shows how a Jewish exegete did not need to be influenced by Qumran in order to find good and evil symbolized by the light and darkness of the creation narrative.

echoing Isa. 51.4).[22] The Aramaic *Levi* text from Qumran (a pre-Qumran work[23]) depicts the teaching of the ideal priest of the future as an eternal sun which will shine to the ends of the earth, such that darkness will vanish from the earth (4Q541 frag. 9, col. 1, ll. 3-5; cf. *T. Levi* 18.2-4). That John was aware of such usage is proved by his depiction of John the Baptist as 'a burning and shining lamp' (5.35).[24]

(3) Familiar in Jewish literature is the image of the law as a light which shines to give light in which people may walk. This has biblical sources (Ps. 119.105; Prov. 6.23; cf. Isa. 2.3, 5; 51.4). Two points are worth noticing about this image. First, it seems particularly prominent in Jewish literature contemporary with the Fourth Gospel (*LAB* 11.1; 19.4; 33.3; 4 *Ezra* 14.20-21; 2 *Bar.* 17.4; 18.2; 59.2). 2 *Baruch*, in the context of extensive use of light and darkness as symbols of good and evil, truth and error (53, 56–72), says that 'the lamp of the eternal law which exists for ever and ever illuminated those who sat in darkness' (59.2), while 4 *Ezra* says that without the law 'the world lies in darkness, and its inhabitants are without light' (14.20). Secondly, when this image is used, the law is sometimes said to be a light for the world (Wis. 18.4; *LAB* 11.1; cf. Isa. 2.3, 5; 51.4). This language about the law is remarkably close to what the Fourth Gospel says about Jesus Christ as the light of the world, paralleling the central image in the Gospel's use of light/darkness imagery in a way that the Qumran texts so notably fail to do. It therefore seems likely that the Fourth Gospel deliberately claims for Jesus what the Jewish literature of its time claimed for the law. Just as Jesus is the true bread from heaven, by comparison with the bread Moses gave (6.32), and just as Jesus is the true vine, by comparison with Israel as the vine (15.1), so he is the true light (1.9), by comparison with the law given by Moses.

(4) If John's image of Christ as the light of the world parallels the Jewish image of the law as the light of the world, it is more directly a form of messianic exegesis of passages in Isaiah, whose prophecies have influenced this Gospel in many ways. John's image reflects Isaiah

22. Cf. also Sir. 24.32; 2 *Bar.* 18.2.

23. Cf. now R.A. Kugler, *From Patriarch to Priest: The Levi-Priestly Tradition from Aramaic Levi to Testament of Levi* (SBLEJL, 9; Atlanta: Scholars Press, 1996).

24. The second half of this verse is strikingly similar to 2 *Bar.* 18.2: 'did not rejoice in the light of the lamp' (that is, the lamp of the law which Moses lighted).

9.1[2] ('The people who walked in darkness have seen a great light; those who lived in a land of deep darkness—on them light has shined': cf. Jn 1.5; 8.12; 12.35), the references to the Servant of the Lord as 'a light to the nations' (Isa. 42.6-7: 'a light to the nations, to open the eyes that are blind, to bring out the prisoners from the dungeon, from the prison those who sit in darkness'; Isa. 49.6; cf. John 9), and the picture of the light which will rise over Zion, in the midst of the darkness that covers the earth, and attract the nations to its brightness (Isa. 60.1-3; Tob. 13.11).[25] These passages, which play no part in the light/darkness dualism of the Qumran texts, readily supply the central Johannine image of the great light shining in the darkness of the world to give light to people, as well as the christological-soteriological significance which this image bears in the Fourth Gospel.

(5) In setting Jesus' declaration 'I am the light of the world' (8.12) at the Feast of Tabernacles (7.2), John associates it with the light symbolism of the festival, just as Jesus' invitation to drink (7.37-39) relates to the water symbolism of the festival. The great lamps which blazed all through the night in the temple at Tabernacles (*m. Sukk.* 5.2-4) symbolized the perpetual light which God himself would be for his people in the eschatological age (Isa. 60.19-20; Zech. 14.7; cf. *1 En.* 58.6; Rev. 21.23-24).

In summary, the dominant picture of light and darkness in the Fourth Gospel results from a creative exegetical fusion of Jewish speculation about the primordial light of the first day of creation and messianic interpretation of the prophecies of eschatological light.[26] This understanding of the sources of the light/darkness imagery in John accounts for its actual character and significance in a way that the hypothesis of influence from Qumran cannot do. It proves to be a development of Jewish light/darkness imagery quite different from that which is distinctive to Qumran.

It was the publication of Qumran texts which effected a shift in Johannine scholarship towards recognizing the thoroughly Jewish

---

25. These passages are interpreted messianically and applied to Jesus in Lk. 1.79; 2.32; Acts 26.23; Rev. 22.16; *Barn.* 14.6-8.

26. According to one rabbinic interpretation of Gen. 1.3, recorded in *Gen. R.* 3.6, the light created on the first day is not the ordinary light of day but 'has been stored away for the righteous in the age to come' (with reference to Isa. 30.26). This shows another Jewish exegete connecting the primordial and eschatological light as John did.

character of Johannine theology. In retrospect this appears to have been a case of drawing the correct conclusion from the wrong evidence. There is no need to appeal to the Qumran texts in order to demonstrate the Jewishness of the Fourth Gospel's light/darkness imagery. This can be done more convincingly by comparison with other Jewish sources, which were already available long before the discovery of the Dead Sea Scrolls.

APPENDIX

The Terminology of Light/Darkness Dualism at Qumran

(Terms and references in 1QS are in Roman type; *terms only in 1QM are in italics.*)

Michael (1QM 17.6)	Belial (1QS 1.18 etc; *1QM*)
Prince of Lights (3.20; CD 5.18)	Angel of Darkness (3.20-21)
Prince of Light (1QM 13.10)	
the spirit of truth (3.19; 4.21, 23)	the spirit of deceit (3.19; 4.9, 20, 23)
all the spirits of truth (1QM 13.10)	all the spirits of his lot (3.24)
	the spirits of his lot (1QM 13.4,12)
the men of God's lot (1QS 2.2; *1QM 1.5*)	the men of Belial's lot (1QS 2.4-5; *1QM 1.15*)
	the lot of darkness (1QM 1.11; 13.5)
the lot of your truth (1QM 13.12)	
the sons of light (2.16; 3.24, 25; *1QM)* *	the sons of darkness (1.10; *1QM*)
the sons of truth (4.6)	the sons of deceit (3.21)
the sons of your truth (1QM 17.8)	
the sons of justice (3.20, 22; *1QM 1.8*)	
the paths of light (3.20)	the paths of darkness (3.21)
the paths of truth (4.17)	the paths of darkness and evil cunning (4.11)
the paths of justice and truth (4.2)	the paths of wickedness (4.19)
wisdom (4.24)	folly (4.24)

(*New Testament occurrences: Lk. 16.8; Jn 12.36; 1 Thess. 5.5; Eph. 5.8.)

MIDRASH PESHER IN THE PAULINE LETTERS

Timothy H. Lim

Since the *editio princeps* of the Habakkuk Pesher (IQpHab) was published in *The Dead Sea Scrolls of St Mark's Monastery* in the 1950s,[1]
there have been several studies on the use of explicit biblical quotations in the pesharim and Pauline letters. Prominent among this
research is E. Earle Ellis's view that identifies 'midrash pesher' as the
interpretative genre which Paul adopted.[2] Thus, Ellis argues that
scriptural quotations in the Pauline *Hauptbriefe* are conformed to the
context of the New Testament by the conflation of prooftexts, adjustment of the grammar of the biblical citations, and selection of variant
readings from known texts or the targumim, and by the creation of *ad
hoc* interpretations.

Ellis's views have not gone unchallenged.[3] Matthew Black, in his

1. M. Burrows, J.C. Trever and W.H. Brownlee (eds.), *The Dead Sea Scrolls
of St Mark's Monastery* (2 vols.; New Haven: American Schools of Oriental
Research, 1950).

2. *Paul's Use of the Old Testament* (London: Oliver & Boyd, 1957); 'Midrash
Pesher in Pauline Hermeneutics', *NTS* 2 (1955–56), pp. 127-33, which was repub-
lished in *Prophecy and Hermeneutics in Early Christianity: New Testament Essays*
(Tübingen: Mohr [Paul Siebeck], 1978), pp. 173-81; 'Midrash, Targum and New
Testament Quotations', in E.E. Ellis and M. Wilcox (eds.), *Neotestamentica et
Semitica: Studies in Honour of Matthew Black* (Edinburgh: T. & T. Clark, 1969),
pp. 61-69; 'Biblical Interpretation in the New Testament Church', in M.J. Mulder
(ed.), *Mikra: Text, Translation, Reading and Interpretation of the Hebrew Bible in
Ancient Judaism and Early Christianity* (Assen: Van Gorcum; Philadelphia: Fortress
Press, 1988), pp. 691-726; and *The Old Testament in Early Christianity: Canon and
Interpretation in Light of Modern Research* (Tübingen: Mohr [Paul Siebeck], 1991),
pp. 68-70.

3. See recently James Barr's criticism of Ellis's handling of the Septuagint, in
'Paul and the LXX: A Note on Some Recent Work', *JTS* 45 (1994), pp. 593-601, but
this is not our concern here.

1970 presidential address to the Societas Novum Testamentum Studiorum in Newcastle-upon-Tyne, dismissed Ellis's theory by stating that the genre of 'midrash pesher' was a modern invention 'probably best forgotten'.[4] Others, with less candour than Black, have also expressed their reservations about Ellis's thesis, but these have been less sharp and focused.[5]

The view that Paul was using techniques of a genre of 'midrash pesher' continues today, and is in fact entertained, if not openly supported, by some distinguished New Testament scholars.[6] Qumran scholarship, for the most part,[7] has ignored this apparently New Testament studies issue, and has concentrated its attention on the interpretative methods of the pesharim themselves.

What I would like to do in this paper is to raise again the relationship between the pesharim and Pauline letters in the light of some recently released and published texts from Cave 4. I shall confine my comments to the supposed titular use of the term 'midrash' in the Scrolls and its putative reference to a genre of Bible interpretation called 'midrash pesher'.[8]

It is undoubted that some of the exegetical techniques of the pesharim resemble those enumerated in the 7, 13 or 32 *middot* of Hillel, Ishmael

---

4. 'The Christological Use of the Old Testament in the New Testament', *NTS* 18 (1971), p. 1.

5. See, for example, R.B. Hays, *Echoes of Scripture in the Letters of Paul* (New Haven: Yale University Press, 1989), p. 11, who gently and obliquely criticizes Ellis's approach.

6. See, for example, C.K. Barrett, 'The Interpretation of the Old Testament in the New', in *Cambridge History of the Bible*, I (Cambridge: Cambridge University Press, 1970), p. 392; M. McNamara, *Palestinian Judaism and the New Testament* (Wilmington, DE: Michael Glazier, 1983), pp. 232-33; M.D. Hooker's description of 2 Corinthians 3 as 'midrash pesher' (*From Adam to Christ: Essays on Paul* (Cambridge: Cambridge University Press, 1990), pp. 141, 150-51; and J.A. Sanders, 'Habakkuk in Qumran, Paul and the Old Testament' (revised), in C.A. Evans and J.A. Sanders (eds.), *Paul and the Scriptures of Israel* (Sheffield: JSOT Press, 1993), p. 107.

7. Exceptionally, G.J. Brooke, *Exegesis at Qumran: 4QFlorilegium in its Jewish Context* (Sheffield: JSOT Press, 1985).

8. Earlier discussions of genre turned on content, but this has now shifted to matters of method. See G.J. Brooke's review of scholarship in 'Qumran Pesher: Towards the Redefinition of a Genre', *RevQ* 10 (1979–80), pp. 483-503. On the basis of structural features, Brooke himself has argued for the classification of the pesher as 'Qumran midrash' in its broad but titular sense.

or Eliezer ben Yose ha-Gelili respectively,[9] but it may be questioned as to how far these practices correspond to the actual exegesis of the rabbinic midrashim.[10] Moreover, Philip Alexander has argued that the midrashim may be formally distinguished from the pesharim by the lack of markers that separate the biblical lemmata from the commentary as is evident in the pesherists' use of interpretative formulae (פשר הדבר, פשרו, etc.).[11]

The issues involved in a comparison of the pesharim with the Pauline letters are, of course, much more complex than what can be discussed here. How does one know that the pesherists and Paul modified their biblical texts in the first place, given that there is now a greater recognition of the plurality of text-types prior to the standardization of the biblical texts? Are variant readings in the biblical quotations the result of exegetical modifications or textual divergences? Or again, are the hermeneutical principles followed by the pesherists and Paul comparable? Were they bibliocentric or did their hermeneutical centre lie elsewhere?[12]

1. *Titular Use of Midrash*

The suggestion that there is a genre called 'midrash pesher' in Paul arose from the discovery and publication of the Qumran scrolls. In 4Q174 or 4QFlorilegium, a text now thought to belong to an 'Eschatological Midrash',[13] it states in col. iii, l. 14:

---

9. See Brooke, *Exegesis at Qumran*, pp. 283-92.

10. P.S. Alexander, 'Midrash and the Gospels', in C.M. Tuckett (ed.), *Synoptic Studies: The Ampleforth Conferences of 1982 and 1983* (Sheffield: JSOT Press, 1984), p. 9, states that 'these obscure lists are beset by a host of historical and literary problems, and suffer from the fundamental drawback that they do not correspond all that closely to the actual practice of the *darshanim*'.

11. Alexander, 'Midrash', p. 3.

12. I have written on these topics in *Holy Scripture in the Qumran Commentaries and Pauline Letters* (Oxford: Oxford University Press, 1997), where readers are referred for detailed discussions.

13. A. Steudel, *Der Midrasch zur Eschatologie aus der Qumrangemeinde (4QMidrEschat[a.b]): Materielle Rekonstruktion, Textbestand, Gattung und traditionsgeschichtliche Einordnung des durch 4Q174 ('Florilegium') und 4Q177 ('Catena A') repräsentierten Werkes aus den Qumranfunden* (Leiden: Brill, 1994).

מדרש מאשרי האיש אשר לוא הלך בעצת רשעים פשר הדב]ר המ]ה סרי מדרך]

a midrash of *blessed is the man who does not walk in the counsel of the wicked* (Ps. 1.1). The interpretation of the ver[se: the]y are those who turn from a way [

Ostensibly, the difficulty of the verse lies in the apparently redundant occurrence of two interpretative prescriptions, a heading with the term 'midrash' and the characteristic pesher-formula following the biblical quotation.

Brownlee, in his commentary on the Habakkuk Pesher, renders the line as 'A midrash of "Blessed is the man who walks not in the counsel of the wicked"',[14] and suggests that l. 14 serves both as a heading of Psalms 1–2 and the first verse selected for interpretation. In his understanding, then, the formula פשר הדב]ר] 'the intepretation of the ver[se]', is not redundant, but is the regular formula signalling that what follows is an interpretation. The first word 'midrash', consequently, is not an interpretative formula as such, but is part of the *incipit* that describes this whole section. 'Midrash' here is understood in its titular sense. Brownlee then relates this understanding to the Habakkuk Pesher and concludes that '1QpHab is indeed a midrash; and if one wishes to characterize it further, he may qualify it appropriately as midrash pesher'.[15]

Ellis has appealed directly to Brownlee's work in identifying midrash pesher in the Pauline letters,[16] so it is important that this text be examined for what it can and cannot tell us. Does 'midrash' here refer to a specific genre of biblical exegesis, or should it be understood more generally to mean 'interpretation of' or 'instruction of'? Phrased differently, is the exegetical forerunner of the rabbinic midrashim embedded here in 4Q174?

What does 'midrash' mean? Brownlee is surely correct in grammatically linking 'midrash' with Ps. 1.1; it is 'a midrash of' (מדרש מן) the psalmist's declaration that the man who rejects wicked counsel is blessed. The commentary, introduced by the formula פשר הדב]ר] 'the intepretation of the ver[se]', however, ignores the biblical figure of the

---

14. W. Brownlee, *The Midrash Pesher of Habakkuk* (Missoula, MT: Scholars Press, 1979), p. 23.

15. Brownlee, *Midrash Pesher*, p. 25.

16. *Paul's Use of the Old Testament*, pp. 139-47.

beatified, but rather singles out the wicked ones whose counsel the blessed man is to avoid. The wicked are further identified with those who stray from the way, by the proof of two other biblical texts from Isa. 8.11 and Ezek. 44.10. By contrast, the sons of Zadok are the faithful ones who abide by the council of the Community. Psalm 2.1 is then cited and interpreted in ll. 18-19 as referring to the chosen ones at the end of days.

Is 'midrash' used here in the titular sense of defining a literary genre? The verbal root דרש 'to seek, investigate' occurs numerous times in Qumran literature, both with the positive connotation of seeking God's will and his Torah, or negatively as a reference to the act of those 'seeking smooth things', דורשי חלקות (cf. Isa. 30.10b), who are plausibly identified with the Pharisees.

The masculine substantive מדרש occurs twice in the Hebrew Bible in 2 Chronicles, referring once to the source from which the Chronicler drew his account of Abijah ('in the *midrash* of the prophet Iddo'; במדרש הנביא עדו, 13.22) and the second time to the many oracles against Joash and the acts of his sons which, though not included in his work, 'are written in the *midrash* of the book of the kings' (כתובים על מדרש ספר המלכים, 24.27). Much scholarly attention has been trained on these first two occurrences of 'midrash', and while it is recognized that they are titles of extant sources, it is generally agreed that the rabbinic usage of 'midrash' does not govern its meaning in the Hebrew Bible.[17] The former is commonly translated as 'in the story of the prophet Iddo' and the latter 'in the commentary (meaning the non-specific sense of interpretation) of the book of the kings'.

In the apocryphal wisdom of Ben Sira, 51.23 also attests to the Hebrew term 'midrash' when the sage admonishes the unlearned to lodge 'in my house of learning' (MS B: בבית מדרשי).[18] This is the earliest attestation of a house of instruction as *beth midrash*, the meaning of which is further illuminated in v. 29 by the reference in

---

17. S. Japhet, *I & II Chronicles: A Commentary* (London: SCM Press, 1993), pp. 699-700 and 854.

18. For the Hebrew text, see *The Book of Ben Sira: Text, Concordance and an Analysis of the Vocabulary* (Hebrew) (Jerusalem: The Academy of the Hebrew Language and the Shrine of the Book, 1973). The Greek (ἐν οἴκῳ παιδείας) and the Syriac (*bet yulpana*) seem to translate מוסר rather than מדרש (cf. P.W. Skehan and A.A. Di Lella, *The Wisdom of Ben Sira* [New York: Doubleday, 1987], p. 575).

the original Hebrew[19] to the *yeshibah*[20] in which the sage's soul delights
(תשמח נפשי בישיבתי).

The term 'midrash' occurs up to eight times in the Qumran scrolls:
four times in the Rule of the Community, possibly three times in the
Damascus Document, and once on the verso of 4Q249 Midrash Sepher
Moshe (MSM).[21] Sectarian usage is assured in the Rule of the Community and the Damascus Document, but is debatable in 4Q249.[22] The
meanings of 'midrash' may be grouped into four broad categories.

a. *Communal Study*

In 1QS 8.14-16, there is the well-known interpretation of Isa 40.3, 'in
the wilderness prepare the way (דרך) of the Lord; make straight in
the desert a highway (מסלה) for our God'.

היאה מדרש התורה אשר צוה ביד מושה לעשות ככול הנגלה עת בעת

It is the *midrash* of the Torah which he [namely, God] commanded by the
hand of Moses to do according to all that is revealed from time to time.

For the Qumran community the preparation of the way of the Lord in
the wilderness and levelling of a highway in the desert for God are
equated with Torah-study. היאה may be understood as a demonstrative
pronoun ('this alludes to'),[23] or as a reference to 'highway' (מסלה) or

---

19. That the Hebrew is not a retranslation, see my 'Nevertheless these were men
of piety (Ben Sira XLIV 10)', *VT* 38 (1988), p. 341 n. 1.

20. The Greek seems to be translating a different Hebrew original בישועתי (so G.H.
Box and W.O.E. Oesterley, 'Sirach', in R.H. Charles [ed.], *The Apocrypha and
Pseudepigrapha of the Old Testament* [Oxford: Clarendon Press, 1913], p. 517 n. 29).

21. Many thanks to George Brooke for drawing my attention to this cryptic text
and discussing parts of my presentation with me. Even though we disagree on various points, the cordial exchange of views was most welcome and instructive.

22. 4Q249 has not been edited, but see P.S. Alexander in G. Vermes *et al.* (eds.),
History of the Jewish People in the Age of Jesus Christ (175 B.C.–A.D. 135), III.1
(Edinburgh: T. & T. Clark, 1986), pp. 364-66; S. Pfann, '4Q298: The Maskîl's
Address to All Sons of Dawn', *JQR* 85 (1994), pp. 203-35; and M. Kister, 'Com-
mentary to 4Q298', *JQR* 85 (1994), pp. 237-49, for discussions of sectarian use of
cryptic A script. It is unclear, however, that a text is *necessarily* sectarian because it
uses a particular script. Surely the presence of letters from this script in 1QIsa[a] (see
E. Tov, 'Letters of the Cryptic A Script and Paleo-Hebrew Letters used as Scribal
Marks in Some Qumran Scrolls', *DSD* 2 [1995], pp. 330-39) does not make the
composition of the Great Isaiah Scroll sectarian!

23. P. Wernberg-Møller, *The Manual of Discipline: Translated and Annotated
with an Introduction* (Leiden: Brill, 1957), p. 34.

more likely to the 'way' (דרך),[24] given the importance of two ways tradition at Qumran. It is the study of the Torah according to the ongoing revelation of God that prepares for the eschatological end. The scriptural passage of 'the study of the Torah' appears to be Ezra 7.10, where the 'skilled scribe' is described as having set his mind 'to study the Torah of YHWH (לדרוש את תורת יהוה), to observe (it), and to teach in Israel the statute and judgment'. The origin of the Qumran Community, then, was characterized by assiduous attention to sacred Scriptures, and it was this fulfillment of the Isaianic prophecy that defined its formative period.

A similar use of 'midrash' to mean 'communal study' is found some ten lines later, in 1QS 8.26. The context is now of community discipline and while the deliberate (ביד רמה) and negligent (ברמיה) transgressor (יעבר דבר מתורת מושה) will be permanently banished, the one who sins inadvertently (בשגגה יעשה) will be allowed to return[25] when his way is perfect 'in session, *in study* and in the council [accord]ing [t]o [the] many' (במושב במדרש ובעצה [ע]ל [פ]י [ה]רבים).

b. *Inquiry*
A second meaning of 'midrash' is found in 1QS 6.24, where the term occurs in construct state with יחד 'community'.

ואלה המשפטים אשר ישפטו בם במדרש יחד על פי הדברים

And these are the judgments with which they will judge in an inquiry of (the) community (במדרש יחד) concerning these matters (or cases).

Apparently the whole community participates in the judgment of infractions, the most serious of which are blasphemy (1QS 7.1-2), slander (1QS 7.16), grumbling against the many (1QS 7.17), and apostasy after ten years of membership (1QS 7.22-24) which are all punishable by permanent banishment. In 1QS 9.7, judgment is reserved for the sons of Aaron alone (רק), and such a discrepancy in the document may be explained by the undoubted composite character of 1QS.

24. Understood as a feminine noun as in Exod. 18.20. So also M. Knibb, *The Qumran Community* (Cambridge: Cambridge University Press, 1987), pp. 128, 134-35.

25. The variant reading in 4QSᵈ makes this explicit when the consonants במושב are otherwise divided: ם[. ושב במדרש. See E. Qimron's transcription in J.H. Charlesworth (ed.), *Rule of the Community and Related Documents* (The Princenton Theological Seminary Dead Sea Scrolls Project, 1; Tübingen/Louisville: Mohr [Paul Siebeck]/Westminster John Knox, 1994), pp. 38 and nn. 263 and 78.

Nonetheless 'the midrash of the community' appears to be based upon the root notion of 'delving or investigating': a judicial inquiry conducted by the community into cases of indiscipline.

c. *Communal Regulation*

A similar, though distinct, use of 'midrash' in the sense of investigation is found in CD 20.6. The man who joins the community, but shrinks from the observance of the upright precepts (ישרים ויקוץ מעשות פקודי) is temporarily banished from the congregation. No member of the congregation shall have any dealings with him 'when his deeds become apparent according to the *midrash of the Torah* in which the men of perfection walk' (בו אנשי תמים ובהופע מעשיו כפי מדרש התורה אשר יתהלכו).[26] 'Midrash' here has the sense of communal regulation based upon the content of the Torah. Torah is the source of the precepts which are to be observed by anyone joining the men of perfect holiness. A miscreant's deeds, then, are revealed by the authoritative interpretation of the law that regulates the life of the community.

The notion that the authoritative interpretation of the Torah underpins the whole communal regulation appears to be supported also in the summation of the Damascus Document. In 4QD[a] (4Q266), frag. 18, col. v, ll. 18-20, it is stated that the exposition[27] of the judgments (פרוש המשפטים) is based upon 'the [m]idrash of the Torah' ([מ]דרש התורה). The corresponding portion in 4QD[e] (4Q270), frag. 11, col. ii, ll. 11-15, moreover attests to the reading 'midrash of Moses' (מדרש [מ]ושה). Unfortunately these texts are badly mutilated precisely where the technical term occurs[28] and a degree of caution should be exercised.[29]

---

26. Photograph and transcription in M. Broshi, *The Damascus Document Reconsidered* (Jerusalem: Israel Exploration Society/The Shrine of the Book, 1992), pp. 46-47. See now J.M. Baumgarten (ed.), *The Damascus Document 4Q266–273* (DJD, 18; Oxford: Clarendon Press, 1996), *non vidi*.

27. For פרוש as 'specifics', see A.I. Baumgarten, 'The Name of the Pharisees', *JBL* 102 (1983), pp. 417-28.

28. Both passages are based upon J.T. Milik's transcription as reconstructed in B.Z. Wacholder and M.G. Abegg, Jr (eds.), *A Preliminary Edition of the Unpublished Dead Sea Scrolls. Fascicles 1 and 2* (Washington: Biblical Archaeology Society, 1991), pp. 22 and 47. My own examination of the photographs confirms the reading of מדרש followed by a badly mutilated word in PAM 43.298 and the tops of possibly מדרש התורה in PAM 43.277.

29. E.M. Cook translates as 'This is the exposition of the regulation...[All of]

d. *Authoritative Interpretation*

Finally, 'midrash' is used in its titular sense in two manuscripts of 4QS and apparently also in the text called 'Midrash Sepher Moshe' (4Q249).

In 4QS^d (4Q258) frag. 1, col. i, l. 1, 'midrash' is the title of a set of instructions which the Maskil is to impart to those men of the Torah who dedicate themselves to turn from their wicked ways,

מדרש למשכיל על אנשי התורה המתנדבים מכל רע

a midrash for the Maskil concerning the men of torah who volunteer to turn from all evil.

This titular use of 'midrash' is also attested in the fragmentary 4QS^b (4Q256), frag. 5, col. i, l. 1. Although there are differences between 4Q258 and 4Q256, the two copies of 1QS show a number of affinities and more importantly read 'a midrash for the Maskil' as their titles.

But 'midrash' here does not refer to a genre of biblical exegesis, but 'instruction' or 'rule' which the Wise Teacher will impart to the sectarians. It is not study of the Torah as such, but the instructions and regulations, grounded in Torah to be sure, that all observant members of the community must follow.

The corresponding passage in 1QS, which is the longer recension of the Rule of the Community, makes this understanding explicit,

וזה הסרכ לאנשי היחד המתנדבים לשוב מכול רע

And this is the rule for the men of the community who volunteer to turn from all evil.

In the longer recension of 1QS, then, סרך 'rule' is used as a synonym of 'midrash'.

The closest parallel to the use of 'midrash' as a genre of Bible interpretation is to be found in 4Q249, a text with apparently a title page called 'The midrash of the book of Moses' (מדרש ספר מושה).[30] The recto of this papyrus manuscript is written in a coded script, now known as cryptic A, and on the verso the phrase 'midrash sepher moshe' is written in square Aramaic script. The mixing of scripts is attested in 4Q298, where the title '[Word] of a Maskil which he spoke

this is on the basis of the most recent interpretation of the Law' (M.O. Wise, M.G. Abegg, Jr, and E.M. Cook [eds.], *The Dead Sea Scrolls: A New Translation* [London: HarperCollins, 1996], p. 74).

30. Mentioned in passing by J.T. Milik in 'Milkî-sedeq et Milkî-resa' dans les anciens écrits juifs et chrétiens', *JJS* 23 (1972), p. 138.

to all Sons of Dawn' is written in square Aramaic script followed by an admonition penned in ciphers.[31] If 4Q249 is likewise understood, then, it too may be plausibly seen as a sectarian composition and it could be interpreted as referring to a form of biblical interpretation.[32]

So far as I am aware 4Q249 has not yet been edited,[33] but several considerations already present themselves. First, it may be asked whether this alleged title on the verso relates to the text on the recto, which is described by Milik as a 'pesher' on Genesis.[34] On some manuscripts the same text is written on the recto and verso of the papyrus or skin (for example, Phylactery A, B, D-K, M, O-R), but others appear to have different texts (for example, 4Q414 Baptismal Liturgy is on the verso of 4Q415 Sapiential Work A d).[35]

Secondly, there are precedents for the use of title pages. 1Q28 apparently served as the title page of 1QS, and while it was not written on the verso of col. i, the attached sheet of skin would have been turned to its reverse side so that it would be readable when the manuscript is rolled up.[36]

Thirdly, the use of 'sepher moshe' as a referrence to the Pentateuch is attested in 4QMMT frag. C, 1.10 (cf. ll. 11, 17 and 21).[37] Similarly, the phrase בספר התורה 'in the book of the Torah' in CD 5.2 is a reference to the mosaic authorship of the first five biblical books ('Moses said', CD 5.8) accompanied by explicit quotations from

---

31. Pfann, '4Q298: The Maskîl's Address to All Sons of Dawn'.

32. Milik, 'Milkî-sedeq et Milkî-resa'', p. 138, describes it as a 'pesher' ('j'ai à publier des fragments de quatre pesharim au moins, dont un, écrit en alphabet cryptique, porte au titre, tracé en caracterères du IIe siècle avant notre ère, מדרש ספר מושה...').

33. Menahem Kister and Stephen Pfann are the editors (see E. Tov, 'The Unpublished Qumran Texts from Caves 4 and 11', *JJS* 43 [1992], p. 114).

34. 'Milkî-sedeq et Milkî-resa'', p. 138.

35. A search of 'verso' in the database, *The Dead Sea Scrolls Electronic Reference Library* (Oxford: Oxford University Press; Leiden: Brill, 1997), registered hundreds of 'hits' of scrolls with writing on the reverse. Not all of these are relevant (for example, the mirror images of the Temple Scroll), but there remain numerous examples where two different texts are written on either side of a fragment.

36. See J.T. Milik in *Qumran Cave 1* (DJD, 1; Oxford: Clarendon Press, 1955), pp. 107-108, plate XXII: [סר]ך היחד ומן.

37. E. Qimron and J. Strugnell, *Qumran Cave 4. V. Miqṣat Maʿaśe ha-Torah* (DJD, 10; Oxford: Clarendon Press, 1994), pp. 59-60.

Genesis (CD 4.21), Deuteronomy (CD 5.2) and Leviticus (CD 5.8-9).[38] If 'midrash sepher moshe' is indeed the title of 4Q249, then it may be a long work commenting on (sections of) the Pentateuch.

And, finally, what does 'midrash' mean here? The text is badly mutilated (see PAM 43.408-14) and it is unclear that this is 'a pesher', as Milik has described it, or 'a midrash' in the rabbinic and technical sense of the term. A better rendering may well be that it is a reference to the authoritative interpretation of Genesis or the Pentateuch that forms the basis of the Qumran Community's regulations. Just as the Damascus Document concludes by stating that the exposition of the *mishpatim* is based upon an authoritative 'interpretation', so 'midrash' here may well mean the same. Interestingly when the variants [מ]דרש התורה of 4Q266 and מדרש [מ]ושה of 4Q270 are taken together, they form a near equivalent to מדרש ספר מושה.

With the possible exception of 4Q249, then, other instances of 'midrash' in the Qumran scrolls do not refer to a genre of biblical exegesis, but either have a specific referent in the theological preparation of the way in the wilderness (1QS8.16) or more generally refer to study as an act in which the community participates (1QS 8.26). The term could also refer to an inquiry or investigation (1QS 6.24) or to an instruction and rule based upon the authoritative interpretation of the Torah (4QS$^{d, b}$; 1QS 5.1; 4QD$^{a, e}$; and 4Q249).

If we take the semantic range of these sources as a guideline, then 'midrash' in l. 14 of col. iv of 4Q174 should not be understood as a reference to a specific genre of biblical exegesis. It would mean something like 'a study of' or 'an instruction deriving from an interpretation of' Ps. 1.1. Presumably, the moral lesson to be drawn is that men of the community, the sons of Zadok, are blessed because they did not walk in the counsel of the wicked.

2. *Redundancy*

There remains the problem of the apparently double occurrence of the prescriptions, one introducing the lemma itself and the other the interpretation.

Redundancy in the use of interpretative formulae is not unprecedented. In the pesharim, the most common formulae include the

---

38. Cf. ספרי התורה in CD 7.15 and [ס]פרים חומשים in 4Q30.

technical term פשר, but independent pronouns by themselves or with a demonstrative pronoun and/or אשר can also serve this function (for example, 4QpIsa^b 2.6-7 אלה הם אנשי הלצון 'these are they, the men of scoffing').[39]

It is notable, then, that in 4QpNah frags. 3–4, col. ii, ll. 1-2 the formula introducing the interpretation of Nah. 3.1 includes both פשר and היא.

פשרו היא עיר אפרים דורשי החלקות לאחרית הימים

Its interpretation, it is the city of Ephraim, the seekers of smooth things at the end of days.

Moreover, the use of formulae before a quotation, followed by an interpretative formula and a comment, is also found. Thus, for example, in 1QpHab 10.1-2, a formula, ואשר אמר, precedes the recitation of Hab. 2.10, after which פשרו הוא ('its interpretation, it') introduces the comment.

But I have not found any clear case that is precisely the same as 'midrash' and 'pesher' in 4Q174. 4QpHos B, frag. 10, col. xxvi, l. 1 appears to introduce Hos. 6.9 for the first time with ואשר,[40] followed by the interpreted formula פש[ר]. Unfortunately, the text is very fragmentary and not too much weight should be placed upon it.

3. Conclusions

This examination of the semantic range of 'midrash' shows that the term is best translated in 4Q174 as 'a study of' or 'an instruction deriving from' Ps. 1.1 rather than as a reference to a genre of biblical exegesis that is the direct precursor of the rabbinic midrashim. Although there is no exact parallel to the dual occurrence of 'midrash' and 'pesher' in 4Q174, there are similar usages of formulae in the pesharim to be found.

The view that there is a genre called 'midrash pesher' in Qumran sectarian literature rests on some questionable assumptions which have been discussed. The degree of uncertainty increases proportionately

39. For a full listing of the variety of interpretative formulae, see M.P. Horgan, *Pesharim: Qumran Interpretations of Biblical Books* (Washington: The Catholic Biblical Association of America, 1979), pp. 239-43.

40. See also Horgan, *Pesharim*, p. 243.

when it is thought that Paul consciously used such an exegetical genre in his letters where no such term is used.[41]

41. The Greek translation of פשר in Qoh. 8.1 is λύσιν, a term which Paul used once in 1 Cor. 7.27 to mean a 'dissolution of marriage' or 'divorce'. For the semantic overlap between τοῦτ' ἔστιν and פשר, see my 'Paul, Letters of', in *The Encyclopaedia of the Dead Sea Scrolls* (Oxford: Oxford University Press, forthcoming).

THE GREEK PAPYRI OF THE JUDAEAN DESERT
AND THE WORLD OF THE ROMAN EAST

Stanley E. Porter

The vast majority of the Greek documentary papyri[1] were found in Egypt during the last century and the first half of this century.[2] Of the estimated 75,000 documents found (with another approximately 8000 literary papyri), almost half have now been published, with the first consistent serialized publication beginning in 1887 and continuing to the present.[3] Enough major and significant texts have been in

---

1. As per current parlance, I use the term papyrus to refer to the ephemeral documents written on any of a number of surfaces, including papyrus, parchment, pottery, wood, etc. See R.S. Bagnall, *Reading Papyri, Writing Ancient History* (London: Routledge, 1995), pp. 9-10. On papyrus, see M.L. Bierbrier (ed.), *Papyrus: Structure and Usage* (London: British Museum, 1986), esp. pp. 1-23 and 90.

2. A good history of the discovery and publication of the papyri is found in E.G. Turner, *Greek Papyri: An Introduction* (Oxford: Clarendon Press, 1968), pp. 17-41. An early account is found in F.G. Kenyon, *The Palaeography of Greek Papyri* (Oxford: Clarendon Press, 1899), esp. pp. 34-55, with many plates.

3. See P. van Minnen, 'The Century of Papyrology (1892–1992)', *BASP* 39 (1993), pp. 5-18 for a brief history and these statistics (are these numbers correct? I cannot help but think that the number of documentary papyri may be well over one hundred thousand). For a chronological list of the major publications, see J.F. Oates *et al.*, *Checklist of Editions of Greek Papyri and Ostraca* (Atlanta: Scholars Press, 3rd edn, 1985), pp. 51-54. A serious omission in van Minnen's article is mention of Carl Wessely, the great Viennese papyrologist. See Turner, *Greek Papyri*, 22-23, who notes this neglect. Although van Minnen rightly gives recognition to BGU and to the work of Grenfell and Hunt, he fails to mention that it was Wessely from whom Grenfell and Hunt learned their papyrology during time spent in Vienna. I am thankful to Professor Dr Hermann Harrauer for this, as well as many other important insights regarding Wessely, in personal conversation at the Papyrussammlung of the Österreichische Nationalbibliothek in Vienna. See C. Wessely, *Aus der Welt der Papyri* (Leipzig: Haessel, 1914) for his introduction to papyri, among many other important volumes.

circulation for New Testament scholarship to have gained immensely from what these documents have revealed. One of the first and most important scholars to make insightful connections was not, strictly speaking, a papyrologist but was the biblical scholar Deissmann, first in his *Bible Studies* and then his *Light from the Ancient East*, followed by others such as Moulton.[4] Rather than being forced to make judgments about the complexities of the Graeco-Roman world simply on the basis of more literary texts, as valuable as they have been, with the documentary papyri we have an invaluable resource revealing the language of everyday life. The result has been a phenomenal increase in knowledge in numerous areas—not only the language of the Hellenistic world and its use in epistolary discourse, but the customs and conventions of the time, along with its various economic and political structures.

As valuable as these thousands of documents from the sands of Egypt have been, however, in so far as understanding the language and world of the New Testament, some scholars have persisted in raising questions regarding how representative and useful these texts are for studying the linguistic complexities of the Graeco-Roman world.[5] For example, some have maintained that the Greek of Egypt as represented in the papyri came under Semitic, perhaps even Hebrew, influence because of the large Jewish population in the region. According to this view, the papyri thus already had a Semitic

---

4.   See A. Deissmann, *Bibelstudien* (Marburg: Elwert, 1895) and *Neue Bibelstudien* (Marburg: Elwert, 1897), translated as *Bible Studies* (trans. A. Grieve; Edinburgh: T. & T. Clark, 1901 [2nd edn, 1909]), and *Licht vom Osten* (Tübingen: Mohr, 1908 [4th edn, 1923]), translated as *Light from the Ancient East* (trans. L.R.M. Strachen; London: Hodder & Stoughton, 1910 [4th edn, 1927]) (see p. 346 n. 4); J.H. Moulton, *Prolegomena*, vol. 1 of *A Grammar of New Testament Greek* (Edinburgh: T. & T. Clark, 1906 [3rd edn, 1908]), and with G. Milligan, *The Vocabulary of the Greek Testament Illustrated from the Papyri and Other Non-Literary Sources* (London: Hodder & Stoughton, 1914–29). Van Minnen ('Century of Papyrology', p. 17) issues a challenge to papyrologists to make methodological advances, such as the application of modern linguistic categories to analysis of the papyri. See Bagnall, *Reading Papyri*, pp. 1-8, who challenges papyrologists to move beyond simply editing texts to questions of method.

5.   For a discussion of the major issues, and a collection of important essays on this topic, see S.E. Porter (ed.), *The Language of the New Testament: Classic Essays* (JSNTSup, 60; Sheffield: JSOT Press, 1991).

cast.[6] Others have argued that the Greek of Egypt was influenced by Coptic, which is, according to this view, similar syntactically to the Semitic languages. This would result in apparent linguistic similarities between New Testament Greek, influenced by Aramaisms, and the documentary papyri, influenced by Coptic.[7] There are at least three important and telling responses to be made to these hypotheses. The first is that, as Teodorsson has indicated, no other kind of Greek has ever been found in Egypt.[8] One is left with the rather implausible assertion that the supposed Semitic influence was so pervasive that it coloured all of the Greek in use throughout Egypt, since the papyrus finds have covered a range of over 300 miles along the Nile. At many of these sites, however, no evidence of Jewish habitation has been found.[9] The second response is that the examples from Coptic used for comparison date to the third century CE at the earliest, although Greek papyrus finds date from as early as the fourth century BCE.[10] The logical implication instead is that Coptic may well have been influenced by Greek rather than the reverse. The third response (the one being pursued in this paper) is that discussion has been too confined to the finds from Egypt, without fully appreciating a number of important documentary papyri archives from outside of Egypt that, to my mind, confirm the hypothesis that the Greek of the papyri, both

6. See, for example, G. Dalman, *The Words of Jesus: Considered in the Light of Post-Biblical Jewish Writings and the Aramaic Language* (trans. D.M. Kay; Edinburgh: T. & T. Clark, 1902), p. 17; R.R. Ottley, *A Handbook to the Septuagint* (London: Methuen, 1920), p. 165; and J. Courtenay James, *The Language of Palestine and Adjacent Regions* (Edinburgh: T. & T. Clark, 1920), pp. 57-75.

7. See, for example, L.-T. Lefort, 'Pour une grammaire des LXX', *Muséon* 41 (1928), pp. 152-60; J. Vergote, 'Grec Biblique', in *DBSup3* (ed. L. Pirot; Paris: Letouzey et Ane, 1938), cols. 1353-60; F. Gignac, *A Grammar of the Greek Papyri of the Roman and Byzantine Periods* (2 vols.; Milan: Istituto Editoriale Cisalpino, 1976, 1981), I, pp. 46-48; *idem*, 'The Language of the Non-Literary Greek Papyri', in D.H. Samuel (ed.), *Proceedings of the Twelfth International Congress of Papyrology* (Toronto: Hakkert, 1970), pp. 159-72; *idem*, 'The Papyri and the Greek Language', *Yale Classical Studies* 28 (1985), pp. 157-58.

8. S.-T. Teodorsson, *The Phonology of Ptolemaic Koine* (Gothenburg: Acta Universitatis Gothoburgensis, 1977), pp. 25-35.

9. Cf. the indications of places of major papyrus finds and Jewish communities in Egypt in Turner, *Greek Papyri*, map at the back, and W. Horbury and D. Noy, *Jewish Inscriptions of Graeco-Roman Egypt* (Cambridge: Cambridge University Press, 1992) plate 1.

10. Gignac (*Grammar*, I, p. 50) has pointed this out.

Egyptian and otherwise, is in fact our best guide to the Greek of the Graeco-Roman world and hence to that of the New Testament.

The finds of papyri outside of Egypt—especially in the Roman near east—that should be considered in discussion of the Greek of the Graeco-Roman world are far more abundant than is generally realized.[11] Besides the finds at Herculaneum, which are philosophical texts,[12] and those of Vindolanda from the time of Hadrian in Britain, of the slightly more than 600 documentary papyri originating in the Roman near east, roughly 400 of them are in Greek. These numbers do not include literary texts (of which religious and sectarian texts such as those from Qumran are a subset),[13] but do include a significant number of texts from the Roman province of Arabia (many in the Babatha archive, to be discussed further below), even if they were written before provincial status was conferred in 106 CE. One of the major features of these documents is the fact that, although Greek is clearly the predominant language, with Latin the second most prominent (especially in texts concerning military matters), there are also texts in Hebrew and a variety of Aramaic dialects (Palestinian Aramaic, Nabataean, Palmyrene, and Syriac), plus a few other languages. In this respect, these documents are clearly in harmony with the multilingual character of the Graeco-Roman world,[14] in which Greek was the *lingua franca*, used widely for trade, commerce, administration and government by all strata of society, while other languages may also have been used for a variety of other purposes. This would have included indigenous languages such as Aramaic in the Roman near east, and possibly Hebrew, as a politically induced religious language during the time of Bar Kokhba, since Hebrew suddenly

11. The most complete listing to date is H.M. Cotton *et al.*, 'The Papyrology of the Roman Near East: A Survey', *JRS* 85 (1995), pp. 214-35. Cf. also F. Millar, *The Roman Near East 31 BC–AD 337* (Cambridge, MA: Harvard University Press, 1993), pp. 545-52. Van Minnen's article, as Cotton *et al.* note (p. 214 n. 1), does not mention papyri outside of Egypt.

12. See Turner, *Greek Papyri*, pp. 17-18 and 171.

13. Besides Cotton *et al.*, 'Papyrology of the Roman Near East', pp. 216-17, see, for example, Turner, *Greek Papyri*, pp. 38-39; Bagnall, *Reading Papyri*, p. 10 with notes; and A. Calderini, *Papyri: Guida allo studio della papirologia antica Greca e Romana* (Milan: Ceschina, 1962), pp. 23-31.

14. See G. Cavallo, 'Le tipologie della cultura nel riflesso delle testimonianze scritte', in *Settimane di studio del Centro italiano di studi sull'alto medioevo* (vol. 34; Spoleto: Panetto & Petrelli, 1988), p. 467.

seems to appear on non-literary papyri during this time in the Judaean finds.[15] The Babatha archive, for example, has texts in Nabataean, Palestinian Aramaic, and Greek, and the Bar Kokhba documents have Hebrew, Aramaic and especially Greek. Furthermore, a noteworthy feature is not merely the presence of this variety of languages in documentary texts, but the use of two or more of these languages, even on the same document, such as the body of the text being written in one language and the signatures of witnesses in others. As a result of these factors, there are numerous loan words in these documents, especially Latin words found in Greek, but also Greek and Latin words found in the Semitic languages.[16] This multilingualism is consonant with what we know from the Egyptian papyri. One of the most impressive recent publications in this regard is a quadrilingual— Greek, Latin, Demotic, and a fourth, unknown language—fragment of accounts from the time of Augustus, possibly originating in Alexandria, though probably found at Oxyrhynchus.[17]

Among the discoveries in the Roman near east of this period, there are at least five major finds, three of which are especially worth commenting upon in this paper. The major finds include those from Dura Europos in Syria (on the Euphrates);[18] the Bar Kokhba archive from the so-called Cave of Letters in Wadi Habra/Nahal Hever (designated P.Yadin*);[19] the Babatha archive from the so-called Cave of Letters in Wadi Habra/Nahal Hever (designated alternatively as P.Yadin,[20] or P.Babatha, to the frustration of papyrologists), to which further similar texts are still being added in recent publications (many of them to be designated P.Se'elim although they probably also originated in the Wadi Hebra/Nahal Hever); those from Wadi Murabba'at (designated either P.Mur., or DJD, 2);[21] and those from Palestine late

15. See Cotton *et al.*, 'Papyrology of the Roman Near East', p. 214.

16. Cotton *et al.*, 'Papyrology of the Roman Near East', p. 215.

17. See R. Coles, 'A Quadrilingual Curiosity in the Bodleian Library in Oxford', in *Proceedings of the XVI International Congress of Papyrology* (Chico, CA: Scholars Press, 1981), pp. 193-97 with plate.

18. See G.D. Kilpatrick, 'Dura-Europos: The Parchments and the Papyri', *GRBS* 5 (1964), pp. 215-25.

19. The asterisk is meant to indicate that these texts are unpublished, what it really seems to mean is that they are either unpublished or not published in an 'authorized' collection by Yadin.

20. Note that there is no asterisk with this designation.

21. There are also a few other Greek fragments from Cave 7 at Qumran,

in the Roman Empire (fifth and sixth century), P.Nessana from the Negev and P.Petra from Petra.[22] All of these archives are significant in various ways. The Dura Europos collection illustrates the multilingualism of a second- and third-century Roman settlement on the outermost frontiers of the empire, including the multilingualism of its synagogue. The finds in the Negev and Petra are useful in establishing a trajectory for later development. However, these fall outside the purview of this paper.

The archives of greatest importance for understanding the world of the Roman east, and hence of the New Testament, especially its language, are those found near the Dead Sea. Among the fifteen letters found in the Bar Kokhba archive in the Cave of Letters, eight letters or more are in Aramaic and between three and five are in Hebrew (differentiating between Aramaic and Hebrew is not always possible), with two letters in Greek. Arguably the most interesting of all of these documents is P.Yadin *52 (also known as 5/6Hev 52 and SB VIII 9843),[23] the letter from a certain Soumaios to Jonathe and Masabala. Whereas most documentary papyri are lucky to have a single edition, this text has been repeatedly edited and discussed. It was first cited as letter 3 by Yadin in his report of his excavations in 1960 in the *Israel Exploration Journal*,[24] along with a second Greek letter, letter 6

published in DJD, 3, with their hand being reassessed later by Professor Peter Parsons in DJD, 8 (pp. 19-26). Included in these fragments is 7Q5, which J. O'Callaghan has argued is a fragment of Mark 6.52-53 ('Papiros neotestamentarios en la cueva 7 de Qumrân?', *Bib* 53 [1972], pp. 91-100), supported by C.P. Thiede, *The Earliest Gospel Manuscript? The Qumran Papyrus 7Q5 and its Significance for New Testament Studies* (Exeter: Paternoster Press, 1992), esp. pp. 23-41. These claims have generally been dismissed by both papyrologists and New Testament scholars. See G. Stanton, *Gospel Truth? New Light on Jesus and the Gospels* (London: HarperCollins, 1995), pp. 20-32.

22. The documents from Masada should be mentioned, but the remains in Greek are highly fragmentary (for example Doc.Masada 743, 745, 746, 791, 792, 793, 794) or simply lists of names (for example Doc.Masada 744, 748, 749, 784–90). There are also five Greek papyri from Cave Abi'or near Jericho awaiting publication. See Cotton *et al.*, 'Papyrology of the Roman Near East', p. 215, for these descriptions.

23. This text is also cited as no. 19 in Millar, *Roman Near East*, p. 551.

24. Y. Yadin, 'Expedition D', *IEJ* 11 (1961), pp. 36-52, esp. pp. 42-43 for letter 3, and p. 44 for letter 6. For a fascinating first hand account of the discoveries, see Y. Yadin, *Bar-Kokhba: The Rediscovery of the Legendary Hero of the Last Jewish*

(P.Yadin *59 = 5/6Hev 59 = SB VIII 9844),[25] with the promise of an edition by Lifshitz. The edition of Lifshitz published the entire text, with critical notes and commentary, along with an edition of the second Greek text.[26] Yadin included further discussion of the papyrus in his book on Bar Kokhba, although the beautiful full page photograph that he includes has been badly misaligned, so that the left hand fragment is one line (or slightly more) too low.[27] This papyrus was introduced to biblical scholars in a widely accessible form by Fitzmyer, who published it in his presidential address to the Catholic Biblical Association, subsequently revised.[28] The edition of Lifshitz was then 'corrected' at its most vulnerable point by Howard and Shelton, and further by Rosén.[29] The papyrus has been edited twice more since then, by the papyrologist Obbink and by Lapin.[30]

Editing of the text certainly has benefited from such effort. Nevertheless there are still several larger and smaller issues that remain open for discussion.[31] One of the first issues is regarding the

Revolt against Imperial Rome (London: Weidenfeld and Nicolson, 1971), esp. pp. 124-39.

25. Cited as no. 21 by Millar, *Roman Near East*, p. 551.

26. B. Lifshitz, 'Papyrus grecs du désert de Juda', *Aeg* 42 (1962), pp. 240-56, with plates.

27. Yadin, *Bar-Kokhba*, p. 131.

28. J.A. Fitzmyer, 'The Languages of Palestine in the first Century AD', *CBQ* 32 (1970), pp. 501-31; repr. with corrections in *idem*, *A Wandering Aramean: Collected Aramaic Essays* (Chico, CA: Scholars Press, 1979), pp. 29-56; and repr. with corrections in Porter (ed.), *Language of the New Testament*, pp. 126-62 (cited below).

29. G. Howard and J.C. Shelton, 'The Bar-Kokhba Letters and Palestinian Greek', *IEJ* 23 (1973), pp. 101-102; H.B. Rosén, 'Die Sprachsituation im römischen Palästina', in *Die Sprachen im römischen Reich der Kaiserzeit* (Beihefte der Bonner Jahrbücher, 40; Cologne: Rheinland, 1980), pp. 215-39, here p. 224 and n. 19, with reference to Lk. 6.7.

30. D. Obbink, 'Bilingual Literacy and Syrian Greek', *BASP* 28 (1991), pp. 51-57; H. Lapin, 'Palm Fronds and Citrons: Notes on Two Letters from Bar Kosiba's Administration', *HUCA* 64 (1993), pp. 111-35. There are a number of unfortunate oversights in Lapin's edition, although he usefully provides a complete critical apparatus of variant readings.

31. It must be noted that all of my observations are based on examination of the photograph in Yadin's *Bar-Kokhba*, p. 131. I am always suspicious of readings arrived at without first-hand examination of the papyrus, my own readings included. Nevertheless, examination of the editions, including Obbink's, in relation to the

author of the letter. The Greek name in the opening and closing is coυμαîoc (ll. 1 [reconstructed], 20). Lifshiftz argued that this was a hypocoristicon or pet name of Simon ben Kosibah, the leader of the second Jewish revolt (132–35 CE).[32] Scholars have divided on this point. On the one hand, Gichon seems to accept Lifshitz's estimation, speaking of the letters as part of Bar Kokhba's military correspondence.[33] Fitzmyer tends to accept the attribution, although acknowledging that, if the letter was not from Bar Kokhba himself, it was from 'someone very closely associated with him, who writes to the same two lieutenants to whom Bar Cochba wrote in other letters—and, indeed, about the same matter'.[34] In fact, all but one of the so-called Bar Kokhba letters found together in this bundle in the Cave of Letters are addressed to one or both of these same men. Sevenster, on the other hand, is more skeptical. Whereas he concedes that the writer of the letter was close to Bar Kokhba, he doubts the association, agreeing with Yadin that it requires further comment. One of the questions Sevenster legitimately raises is what this might imply regarding Bar Kokhba: 'How is it possible that, in a purely Jewish milieu during a ruthless war against the Romans, the man who called himself prince of Israel used alternatively three different languages, one being Greek, in communicating with Jewish leaders in a truly Jewish area?'[35] The answer he suggests is the use of scribes.

In defending the position that the letter was sent by Simon ben Kosibah, Lifshitz argues that transcriptions from Hebrew to Greek vary, and that Soumaios could be a possible transcription of Simon ben Kosibah. This may well be true, but none of the examples he cites can produce Soumaios from Simon ben Kosibah. In fact, the second

plates, indicates that there are still problems with the editions, not least whether certain readings really can be seen on the papyrus, and the degree of certainty indicated in a number of instances. My own diplomatic text is provided at the end for comparison, along with a tentative translation.

32. Lifshitz, 'Papyrus grecs', pp. 243-44. On Simon Bar Kokhba, see J.A. Fitzmyer, 'The Bar Cochba Period', in his *Essays on the Semitic Background of the New Testament* (SBLSBS, 5; Missoula, MT: Scholars Press, 1974), pp. 305-54, esp. pp. 312-16.

33. M. Gichon, 'New Insight into the Bar Kokhba War and a Reappraisal of Dio Cassius 69.12-13', *JQR* 77 (1986), pp. 15-43, esp. p. 40.

34. Fitzmyer, 'Languages of Palestine', p. 142.

35. J. Sevenster, *Do You Know Greek? How Much Greek Could the First Jewish Christians Have Known?* (NovTSup, 19; Leiden: Brill, 1968), p. 170.

Greek letter (P.Yadin *59) actually has cίμων χωcιβᾶ (l. 2), the Greek transcription one would expect. The second letter is addressed to one of the same two people that the first is, Jonathe. The subject matter is also similar. Although it is possible to believe that Bar Kokhba could refer to himself with a pet name, while others did not, the nature of a pet name seems to require that others know and use it as well. Such evidence is lacking here. Instead, it is to be noted that Soumaios is a name found twice in lists of witnesses in the Babatha archive (P.Yadin 12.16 and 19.34), in the midst of Aramaic or otherwise clearly Semitic names.[36] This indicates that the author of this letter was probably not Bar Kokhba himself, even though he may well have been one of the Jewish revolutionaries from Nabataea, with a name apparently fairly common to men in Nabataea (Arabia) at the time.[37]

A second factor to consider in evaluating this letter is the reconstruction of l. 13, which seems to indicate the reason for the letter having been written in Greek. Lifshitz proposed that the line read τ[ὸ ὁρ]μᾶν, 'desire'. Thus, in the context of ll. 11-15, the sense would be that 'it [the letter] was written in Greek because *the desire* was not found to write in Hebrew'.[38] This is a difficult reading for three reasons. The first is paleographical. The papyrus is broken along a line that runs from l. 1 to the bottom, thus affecting the ability to read the second or third letter of virtually every line. The second is the grammatical one that the spelling in this rendering is the Doric form of the accusative singular of the feminine noun, which in Hellenistic Greek should be spelled ὁρμήν.[39] The third reason is the sense. It seems odd to explain the uncustomary use of Greek over 'Hebrew' (or Aramaic) for so trivial a reason as not feeling like it, when the majority of the letters are written in Aramaic.

The paleography poses by far the greatest difficulty, since the hand of the writer was irregular. The second, regarding the spelling, is not as serious as might at first be imagined. For one thing, there are many misspelled words in the papyrus, as Lifshitz, Fitzmyer, Obbink and

36. Contra Lapin, 'Palm Fronds and Citrons', p. 116, who thinks that Soumaios may have been a Gentile.

37. Obbink, 'Bilingual Literacy', p. 57.

38. Lifshitz, 'Papyrus grecs', p. 247, claiming that the passive verb εὑρηθῆναι with the reconstructed noun is a Hebraism.

39. Howard and Shelton, 'Bar-Kokhba Letters', p. 102, followed by Fitzmyer, 'Languages of Palestine', p. 143.

Lapin have noted.[40] Although the change from *eta* to *alpha* would be unusual,[41] there are other, somewhat similar vowel changes (for example ε > αι in ll. 8, 11). Therefore, it is not inconceivable, even if unlikely, that this is another phonetic misspelling. The third difficulty, regarding intention, is not particularly compelling, except as it comes into contact with various paleographical and linguistic factors. In the light of these difficulties, several proposals have been made. Howard and Shelton, recognizing the grammatical difficulty, restore l. 13 with τ[ὸ Ἑρ]μαν, giving a hypocoristic name to the missing scribe *exempli gratis* for any name that fits the space and traces.[42] Their translation is: 'the letter was written in Greek because [Her]mas could not be found to write in Hebrew'.[43] Whereas Fitzmyer accepts the difficulty of the originally proposed reading, τὸ ὁρμᾶν, he does not accept the name Ἑρμαν (or any other), especially because Howard and Shelton do not explain how to understand the resulting Greek, that is, the man's name preceded by the neuter article.[44] Obbink raises the objection that this would seem to imply that Hermas was the only one capable of writing in Hebrew—something that Howard and Shelton suggest[45]—yet how does this correlate with the number of other letters in Hebrew or Aramaic? Obbink also has questions about the resulting syntax, especially how to construe the name with the infinitive γράψασθαι ('write') in l. 15.[46] Similarly, Yadin's 1971

40. See Lifshitz, 'Papyrus grecs', pp. 241-42; Fitzmyer, 'Languages of Palestine', p. 143; Obbink, 'Bilingual Literacy', p. 54; Lapin, 'Palm Fronds and Citrons', p. 114.

41. See L.R. Palmer, *The Greek Language* (London: Duckworth and Bristol Classical Press, 1980), p. 177; and Teodorsson, *Phonology of Ptolemaic Koine*, *passim*, who cites no example.

42. See BDF §125 on hypocoristic names, especially in ας.

43. Howard and Shelton, 'Bar-Kokhba Letters', pp. 101 and 102.

44. Fitzmyer, 'Languages of Palestine', pp. 142-43 n. 1.

45. Howard and Shelton, 'Bar-Kokhba Letters', p. 102. They find that the explanation that he did not feel like writing Hebrew 'is hardly satisfactory'. They continue: 'If the average soldier had had this skill [to write Hebrew or Aramaic], there would have been no need to single out one individual by name or to write Greek because that man was absent'.

46. Obbink, 'Bilingual Literacy', p. 52, although I question this reading of the line. Lapin ('Palm Fronds and Citrons', p. 122) reads ἐ[γγρά]ψασθαι. While I agree that *epsilon* begins the line, I do not think there is enough space for his reading, and simply cannot see the *psi*.

translation, 'the letter is written in Greek as we have no one who knows Hebrew [or Aramaic]',[47] Fitzmyer rightly criticizes, since it is even more difficult to correlate this with the Greek text—both ὁρμάν and Ἕρμαν have disappeared, with 'no one' appearing instead. Nevertheless, Gichon accepts Hermas as the scribe, and builds a theory as to the use of Greek upon it. He notes that there were non-Jews participating in the second Jewish revolution (for example Tyrsis and Aelianus, according to Yadin), and since this foreign element was so pronounced, 'part of [Bar Kokhba's] military correspondence was conducted in Greek'. He states further that 'In one letter it is explicitly mentioned that Greek was being used..."since Hermas is unable to (read and) write Hebrew". Hermas is *clearly* a pagan name, not used by Jews.'[48] The problem is, of course, that this is based upon a highly disputed textual reconstruction (never meant to propose a specific name) and thus is anything but clear, besides the fact that nothing is said about not being able to read Hebrew. Gichon seems to want to make an unwarranted, if not that untypical, distinction, similar to that posed by Sevenster, noted above, that Jews of the time writing to each other, especially those at the forefront of a Jewish revolution, would not, or even could not, use Greek.

Obbink, rejecting the original and the second reading, argues that a better restoration is τὸ [ἀφο]ρμάς, 'opportunity'. He argues this on two grounds. The first is paleographical, contending that the traces on the papyrus reveal a final *sigma* rather than a *nu*.[49] My examination of the photograph shows that l. 13 is much more difficult to read than most others of the papyrus. To be fair, Obbink does diplomatically transcribe the crucial letters as τ [...] μας.[50] Although the line is intact, the space for the first two or three letters after the joining of the two fragments is seriously abraded. The *sigma* that Obbink suggests is far from a certainty, with only enough of the letter present to make it a *possible* restoration. A further difficulty is the amount of space to be left between the left fragment and the major piece—

47. Yadin, *Bar-Kokhba*, pp. 130, 131.
48. Gichon, 'Bar Kokhba War', p. 40 (emphasis added).
49. Obbink, 'Bilingual Literacy', p. 52 with n. 9.
50. Nevertheless, this diplomatic transcription could easily be overlooked, and his restoration given more credence than is perhaps warranted. See Lapin, 'Palm Fronds and Citrons', p. 122 n. 31, who notes that Obbink offered his restoration to conform with Lifshitz's edition.

Obbink's diplomatic transcription appears to have too many spaces (four) for his own reconstruction (with three letters). In fact, the shape of the two fragments indicates that there is probably no actual space betwen the two, and hence square brackets are probably inappropriate, certainly for four spaces. I am not convinced that there is enough room for the letters he suggests. As for the rest of the word, I can see nothing of the omicron apart from some ink marks that may be any number of letters,[51] then there is an abraded portion of probably three letters, then faint outlines that I take as *mu* and *alpha*, with some question of the *mu*, and then the marks that may be a *sigma*. At best, I would transcribe this line as follows: τ...μας—a better though far from certain, match with Lifshitz's original reading.

Obbink's second reason for his solution is that this reading is suggested by the Greek idiom 'to have an opportunity' + the infinitive of what is to be done. The idiom is common in Hellenistic prose, and is found twice with εὑρεῖν ('find'), both in papyri. One is BGU II 615.6 (second century CE) 'finding opportunity I wrote to you, etc', and the other is BGU III 923.22 (first or second century CE) 'if you might find opportunity replying, etc'.[52] As a result of Obbink's analysis, not only is there a more plausible (though far from certain) idiomatic solution provided, but what Lifshiftz thought was a Hebraism has been eliminated. The phrasing is seen to be thoroughly Greek.[53] Nevertheless, the text is not clear, so perhaps the reason that Greek was used cannot be finally determined, apart from recognizing that it was indeed used.[54]

51. See Lapin, 'Palm Fronds and Citrons', p. 122 n. 31, who believes that he can see the outline of the omicron.

52. Obbink, 'Bilingual Literacy', pp. 52-53.

53. The only study I know that is devoted to assessing Semitisms and other linguistic influences on Greek texts of these Judaean archives is N. Lewis, *The Documents from the Bar Kokhba Period in the Cave of Letters: Greek Papyri* (Jerusalem: Israel Exploration Society, Hebrew University of Jerusalem, Shrine of the Book, 1989), pp. 13-19. This not the place to assess Lewis's work on this issue, but a preliminary examination indicates that some of the evidence marshalled requires re-thinking. For example, Lewis cites the use of a curse introduced by λέγων as indicating 'one of the most familiar Hebraisms of the Greek Old and New Testaments' (p. 14). However, this idiom is found in a range of non-translation and non-biblical Greek authors. See S.E. Porter, *Verbal Aspect in the Greek of the New Testament with Reference to Tense and Mood* (New York: Lang, 1989), pp. 138-39.

54. Rosén ('Die Sprachsituation', p. 224) proposes τ[ὸ μη]δ[έν](α), which is

A third and final issue to mention is the use of the closing ἔρρωσο ('farewell').[55] In his first mention of the letter, Yadin noted that the letter ended in ἔρρωσο, 'which is equivalent to the conclusion of הוה שלום in the Hebrew and Aramaic letters'.[56] However, although this Greek closing may perform the same function as the Hebrew and Aramaic conclusion, there is no further relationship to be noted, since this is a standard Greek epistolary closing.[57]

What conclusions can be drawn from this discussion? The first is with regard to epistolary form and use of epistolary conventions. This letter is clearly written in the form of a standard Greek letter, with a number of the usual epistolary formulas. For example, the letter follows the standard three-part structure of opening, body and closing. In the opening, the pattern of 'A [in the nominative case] to B [in this case B and C, in the dative case], χαίρειν ['greeting']' (ll. 1-3) is followed exactly. The body of the letter is introduced by ἐπειδή[58] ('since'), a frequent convention for establishing the circumstances or background of a request or instruction.[59] Here Soumaios says that 'since I sent to you Agrippa', Jonathe and Masabala are to send things in return. The body of the letter includes a request that cτελεούc (beams)[60] or, better according to my reading of the papyrus, θύρcουc (branches or palm fronds)[61] and citrons be sent for the κιτρειαβολήν of the Jews,[62] or the Feast of Tabernacles. Several times forms of the

paleographically difficult on several accounts, including the ink on the papyrus and the author's scribal tendencies.

55. Lapin ('Palm Fronds and Citrons', p. 114) reads ἔρρωσω, but this must be a mistake.

56. Yadin, 'Expedition D', p. 42.

57. See J.L. White, *Light from Ancient Letters* (Philadelphia: Fortress Press, 1986), p. 200: 'almost all papyrus letters have "A to B greeting" as their initial formula and ἔρρωσο as the word of farewell'.

58. Lapin ('Palm Fronds and Citrons', p. 114) reads ἐπ]ηδή, but this appears to be a mistake, since the letter uses *iota* adscript (l. 1), and I can see none here.

59. White, *Light*, p. 208.

60. See Fitzmyer, 'Languages of Palestine', p. 143, following Lifshitz, 'Papyrus grecs', p. 241, although with questions and discussion.

61. Lapin, 'Palm Fronds and Citrons', pp. 116-18, who reconstructs this line much differently from previous editors.

62. See Lifshitz, 'Papyrus grecs', pp. 241, 245-46; Sevenster, *Do You Know Greek?*, p. 172 n. 1, who note that the word κιτρειαβολήν, if it is correct, is a neologism, perhaps a Hebraism coined by Greek-speaking Jews. The reference to the feast as 'of the Jews' does not mean that the writers are not Jews. As Obbink notes,

verb ποιέω ('do'), often used to make requests and give instructions in letters,[63] are used (ll. 11, 15-16). The letter closes with a signature by Soumaios and the farewell. As White says, 'The typical word of farewell in letters which begin with this initial phrase [as cited above] is ἔρρωσο'.[64] The elegance of the closing signature may well be taken to indicate that the author was competent in Greek, even though someone else wrote the letter. The writer of the letter was almost assuredly not a professional or trained scribe, since the hand is sloppy and many of the letters are ill-formed. Thus those involved in the revolt used the letter, the standard form of written communication in the Graeco-Roman world for which we have thousands of equivalent examples from Egypt and elsewhere.

Secondly, this letter reveals, even among the reactionary Bar Kokhba revolutionaries, a multilingual milieu. Since the text fails us at the very point where we would hope to find out the reason for writing in Greek, we cannot rely on various proposed suppositions to reveal the reason. Nevertheless, Greek is the language used for two of the letters in this small archive. This is clearly consonant with a vast number of other texts found throughout the Roman east during this period, as well as what we know of the linguistic milieu of the larger Graeco-Roman world, and thus does not distinguish this letter, or, by inference, those involved in the Bar Kokhba revolt, from other ethnic groups distributed throughout the Roman Empire. Depending upon where they lived, many in Palestine and elsewhere in the Roman east may well have used a native local language, but it appears that a significant number of them also knew and used Greek. This Greek was sufficient to carry on necessary business transactions and personal communication, even under the pressure of an emergency such as a national revolution. This scenario is reinforced here by virtue of the simple fact that, not only did the writer use Greek, but he used it with the expectation that the readers, Jonathe and Masabala, would be able to read the letter themselves or have others around them who could read it for them. As Obbink emphasizes, this letter reflects what, on the basis of the textual evidence, must have been frequent in this part

even in New Testament books written by Jews there is this kind of identification ('Bilingual Literacy', p. 56). Lapin ('Palm Fronds and Citrons', p. 121) argues for παρεμβολήν, 'camp', but this does not seem to fit the markings of the papyrus.

63. White, *Light*, p. 208.
64. White, *Light*, p. 198.

of the world during this time, even though direct references to it are infrequent—widespread bilingual competence, including the possibility of those who could serve for others as interpreters.[65] In this instance, however, it is most likely that Jonathe and Masabala knew Greek, Hebrew and Aramaic, since they have letters in each of the three languages addressed to them in the corpus (besides P.Yadin *52 in Greek being addressed to both men, and P.Yadin *59 in Greek being addressed only to Jonathe, P.Yadin *50, *54, *55, *56 and *58 in Aramaic are to both, and P.Yadin *53 and *60 in Aramaic are to Jonathe alone, and P.Yadin *49 in Hebrew is to both).[66]

Thirdly, there is no need to posit what might be called an iconicity between language, ethnicity and region. In other words, rather than positing, as Gichon does, that Greek would have only been used to speak with foreigners, or, as Sevenster rhetorically suggests, that it is difficult to imagine the leader of the Jewish revolution using Greek—it seems perfectly plausible that, for a variety of purposes, including various administrative tasks, Greek was used throughout the region by all sorts of people, including Jewish revolutionaries. This seems to offer further support for the proposal regarding Acts 6.1 of Moule, endorsed by Fitzmyer, that there were Jews in Palestine who habitually spoke Greek, whether or not they spoke a Semitic language.[67] The speaking of Greek, as the vast array of papyri indicates, was something that not only Egyptians or Diaspora Jews could have done, but those in the Roman east as well. This conclusion has been reinforced by recent publications of Jewish inscriptions from this area.[68] In the case of Soumaios, Jonathe and Masabala, in the light of the letter being

65. Obbink, 'Bilingual Literacy', p. 55, with n. 16 for bibliography.

66. See Sevenster, *Do You Know Greek?*, p. 171.

67. See C.F.D. Moule, 'Once More, Who Were the Hellenists', *ExpTim* 70 (1958–59), pp. 100-102; J.A. Fitzmyer, 'Jewish Christianity in Acts in Light of the Qumran Scrolls', in L.E. Keck and J.L. Martyn (eds.), *Studies in Luke–Acts* (Philadelphia: Fortress, 1980 [1966]), pp. 233-57, repr. in his *Essays in Semitic Background*, pp. 271-303; referred to in Fitzmyer, 'Languages of Palestine', p. 144. See now also Lapin, 'Palm Fronds and Citrons', p. 116; H.A. Brehm, 'The Meaning of Ἑλληνιστής in Acts in Light of a Diachronic Analysis of ἑλληνίζειν', in S.E. Porter and D.A. Carson (eds.), *Discourse Analysis and Other Topics in Biblical Greek* (JSNTSup, 113; Sheffield: JSOT Press, 1995), pp. 180-99.

68. See S.E. Porter, 'Jesus and the Use of Greek in Galilee', in B. Chilton and C.A. Evans (eds.), *Studying the Historical Jesus: Evaluations of the State of Current Research* (NTTS, 19; Leiden: Brill, 1994), pp. 129-47.

written in Greek and signed in Greek, along with the other evidence in the Babatha archives, Soumaios was probably a Nabataean Jew who 'customarily read and wrote Greek but not Hebrew or Aramaic',[69] and Jonathe and Masabala were probably Judaean Jews who knew Aramaic and Hebrew, as well as Greek.

The fact that these letters were found in the cave along with the Babatha archive raises the question of why they would have been preserved. In the light of all but one of the letters being addressed to Jonathe, and sometimes Masabala, it is most plausible that these letters were saved by one of these two men, probably Jonathe, and taken to the Cave of Letters. Was this in anticipation of victory, or with the realization of defeat? With victory in hand, would they emerge to resume their positions, probably as leaders for Bar Kokhba in Engedi, or were they simply taking last remembrances of an abortive effort?

Thus, let me provide the following translation of the crucial letter: '(1) Soumaios to Jonathe (2) son of Baianos and Ma(3)sabala, greeting. (4) Since I sent to (5) you Agrippa, ende(6)avour to send to me (7) branches and citrons. (8) But them you will return (9) for [the] Feast of Tabernacles of (10) [the] Jews and not otherwise (11) will you do. It (the letter) is written (12) however in Greek because (13) the desire *or* opportunity [?] was not to be (14) found in Hebrew (15) to write. Him [Agrippa] (16) release immediately (17) on account of the feast (18) and not otherwise will you (19) do. (20) Soumaios. (21) Farewell.'

One must be cautious in using a single letter to make too sweeping generalizations about the ancient world. Nevertheless, this linguistic scenario is confirmed in several ways by the Murabba'at and the Babatha archives. I will discuss them briefly in regard to their pertinence for the issues raised above. In several respects, the Murabba'at archive is consistent with what has been said above.[70] The first is that the collection of documents is multilingual, including Greek, Aramaic, Latin, and Hebrew, in order of predominance. This reflects the kind of distribution of languages found in other archives in the Roman east. It is difficult to date many of these texts, and there is not any necessary unity to the documents regarding senders and receivers. An early

69. Obbink, 'Bilingual Literacy', p. 57.
70. See P. Benoit, J.T. Milik and R. de Vaux (eds.), *Les grottes de Murabba'ât* (DJD, 2; 2 vols.; Oxford: Clarendon Press, 1961), I, pp. 3-13 on the discovery.

second-century date of writing is indicated by the fact that several of the Aramaic letters appear to have been sent by Bar Kokhba (P.Mur. 43 and probably 44; cf. 42, from an administrator of Beth-Masiko to the same person as in the previous two). Some of the documents may be dated slightly later. The Aramaic documents include a number of different types (mostly financial, with a few letters and lists of names, often fragmentary), some of them specifically datable to the time of the second Jewish revolution (for example P.Mur. 22, 23, 25, 30), although the vast majority are probably earlier (for example P.Mur. 19, 20, 26, 27, 28, 31, 32, 33, 34, 35, 37, 38–40, 41). The same is true of the few Hebrew documents, with some datable to the time of the revolt (P.Mur. 24, 29), but a few earlier (for example P.Mur. 7).[71]

The largest number of these texts, however, is in Greek. The majority of them cannot be dated with any certainty, nor can their place of writing be established. All that can be determined is that the vast majority are financial documents of some sort found in caves in the Wadi Murabba'at (P.Mur. 89, 90, 91, 92, 93, 94, 95, 96, 97, 98–102, 103–107, 118, 119, 120, 121, 122, 123, 124, 125, 126–55). Nevertheless, among these Greek texts, several merit brief attention. One is a double deed[72] contract for remarriage between two Jews, Elaios and Salome, who had been divorced and then reconciled, along with payment of a dowry (P.Mur. 115 = SB X 10305).[73] The text, originating at Bethbassi near Hebron, is dated to 124 CE (by regnal, civil and calendrical dates, as are most of the datable texts).[74] One of the features noted by the original editors is that this rare practice of remarriage is paralleled by a few other papyri from Egypt (for example BGU IV 1101 [13 BCE]), and seems to reflect (much more

71. Note that for P.Mur. 49–52 and 53–70 it cannot be determined whether they are Hebrew or Aramaic.

72. On the double deed (a contract written twice, with one copy sealed as a permanent record, and the other for reference), see Lewis, *Documents*, pp. 6-10, correcting Yadin, *Bar-Kokhba*, pp. 229-31.

73. See also C. Spicq, *Theological Lexicon of the New Testament* (3 vols.; trans. J.D. Ernest; Peabody, MA: Hendrickson, 1994 [1978, 1982]), II, p. 264, who cites P.Oxy. 1473 (third century CE) also; S.E. Porter, Καταλλάσσω *in Ancient Greek Literature, with Reference to the Pauline Writings* (Estudios de Filología Neotestamentaria, 5: Córdoba: Ediciones El Almendro, 1994), pp. 67-68 (correct the lines to 5-6).

74. On dating these and related documents, see Lewis, *Documents*, pp. 27-28.

than has often been realized) typically Graeco-Roman practices even by Jews, so much so that the editors refer here to syncretism.[75] One must be careful in defining syncretism, since what appears to be the case here is simply Jews living by the legal conventions of the Graeco-Roman world. Similar is a recently published fragmentary canceled marriage double deed contract between two Jews, Aqaba and Selampious (?), dated to 130 CE (XHev/Se Gr. 2, probably to be traced to the Nahal Hever Cave of Letters). This text also probably originated near Hebron.[76] Another marriage contract also involves a woman named Salome, this time marrying a man named Aurelius (P.Mur. 116). The text is fragmentary, missing most of the first three lines, and hence cannot be dated precisely. Paleographically it probably dates to the first half of the second century CE. There are many similarities with P.Mur. 115. A last example to note is an example of legal proceedings between two Jewish women, Mariam and Salome, and a Roman soldier (P.Mur. 113). The fragmentary nature of the text makes it uncertain regarding the nature of the litigation involved. Paleographically, the text has been dated to the second half of the second century. Although it is highly unlikely that Salome in each of these documents is the same woman, since the name was frequent, that these letters have been found together in the same archive suggests that they may be linked in some way that is not altogether clear.

There are at least four significant results of this evidence from the Muraba'at archive that merit mention. First, there is a trajectory that seems to begin before and continue after the second Jewish revolution. Even though Jews are involved, Roman law and institutions, although perhaps adapted to the particular context, are firmly in place, especially as represented by marriage contracts. Secondly, there appear to be many similarities between these texts and those found in Egypt, thus indicating a common legal, cultural, and even linguistic grounding of the Roman east and Egypt. Thirdly, one must keep in mind that these texts indicate that a high degree of Romanization has penetrated deeply into eastern Palestine, even among a population apparently fairly far removed from the major population centres. Fourthly, in a multilingual milieu, with several indigenous languages and/or dialects,

75. Benoit, Milik and de Vaux (eds.), *Les grottes de Murabba'ât*, p. 248.

76. See H.M. Cotton, 'A Cancelled Marriage Contract from the Judaean Desert (XHev/Se Gr. 2)', *JRS* 84 (1994), pp. 64-86.

Greek and Latin are also found in the archive, with Greek predominant in the extant texts.

The Babatha archive is arguably the most important single archive for this discussion.[77] A second, somewhat similar, archive has recently been identified and published from the Cave of Letters, but it contains only six documents.[78] The Babatha archive also comes from the Cave of Letters, and consists of 36 (or 37) items, 26 of which are Greek documents (9 of these with subscriptions and signatures in Aramaic and/or Nabataean), the rest being in Nabataean and Aramaic. The story of Babatha cannot be repeated in detail here, but a summary is perhaps warranted.[79] Babatha was a woman of some financial status, although not from the upper or noble class of Jewish residents in the Province of Arabia (founded in 106 CE, so, actually, Babatha had lived in Nabataea when it was a semi-autonomous kingdom).[80] She was apparently married twice. Her first husband, Joshua, died, leaving her with an orphaned son placed in the care of guardians. She married a second time, to a man named Judah, who was already married to a woman named Miriam.[81] When he died two years later, Babatha

77. See Lewis, *Documents*, *passim* for publication. See also the article by A. Wasserstein, 'A Marriage Contract from the Province of Arabia Nova: Notes on Papyrus Yadin 18', *JQR* 80 (1989), pp. 93-130; and responded to by Lewis in 'The World of P.Yadin', *BASP* 28 (1991), pp. 35-41. An account of finding the letters is in Y. Yadin, 'Expedition D—The Cave of the Letters', *IEJ* 12 (1962), pp. 231, 247-48. Additional texts of direct relevance from the so-called P.Se'elim collection are H.M. Cotton, 'Fragments of a Declaration of Landed Property from the Province of Arabia', *ZPE* 85 (1991), pp. 263-67; *idem*, 'Another Fragment of the Declaration of Landed Property from the Province of Arabia', *ZPE* 99 (1993), pp. 115-21; *idem*, 'Rent or Tax Receipt from Maoza', *ZPE* 100 (1994), pp. 547-57; with the documents dated to around 125 CE. See also the list in J.C. Greenfield, 'The Texts from Nahal Se'elim (Wadi Seiyal)', in J.T. Barrera and L.V. Montaner (eds.), *The Madrid Qumran Congress* (Leiden: Brill; Madrid: Editorial Complutense, 1992), II, p. 665.

78. See H.M. Cotton, 'The Archive of Salome Komaise Daughter of Levi: Another Archive from the "Cave of Letters"', *ZPE* 105 (1995), pp. 171-208. The documents are all financial, including a marriage agreement published in the Babatha archive (P.Yadin 37).

79. See Lewis, *Documents*, pp. 3-5; Yadin, *Bar-Kokhba*, pp. 222-53. See also H.M. Cotton and J.C. Greenfield, 'Babatha's Property and the Law of Succession in the Babatha Archive', *ZPE* 104 (1994), pp. 211-24.

80. See T. Mommsen, *The Provinces of the Roman Empire from Caesar to Diocletian* (2 vols.; trans. W.P. Dickson; London: Macmillan, 1909), II, pp. 116-59.

81. Polygamy was apparently more widespread among Jews during this time

became embroiled in a number of legal battles, since her husband's second wife and family failed to provide her with the dowry to which she was legally entitled, including providing an adequate means of support for her son. As a result, she was sued and counter-sued, through a 'guardian' or 'lord', as per Roman law. Her archive spans the years of 94 to 132 CE, many of the documents precisely dated by regnal, provincial and calendrical dates, some of the documents apparently even overlapping with the start of the second Jewish revolt. Her residence was in Arabia, in the village of Maoza on the south-eastern side of the Dead Sea.[82] It appears that, when the revolution broke out, she, along with other villagers, may have gone to En-gedi, which was a stronghold of the revolutionaries, probably fleeing to the caves when events turned against them. She apparently took her most important legal documents, spanning almost forty years of litigation and establishing her legal claim to a variety of properties, etc., along with a number of valuable artifacts,[83] for a time when she might need them to establish her claims. Whether she died in the Cave of Letters is not known. What is known is that the documents were never used for that purpose.

Included in the archive are the following Greek documents, many of them double documents: a series of texts regarding her orphaned son and his guardians (P.Yadin 27–30), including extracts of council minutes on the appointments of the guardians (P.Yadin 12), a petition to the Roman governor regarding the care of the son (P.Yadin 13), a summons of the guardians (P. Yadin 14), and a deposition (P.Yadin 15);[84] several financial documents, including a census report that establishes her wealth (P.Yadin 16); two documents regarding her first husband's daughter (P.Yadin 18, 19), perhaps implying that the daughter was also in the cave; and a series of litigation-related

than many have recognized. See Lewis, *Documents*, pp. 22-24.

82. See H.M. Cotton, 'Babatha's *Patria*: Mahoza, Mahoz 'Eglatain and Zo'ar', *ZPE* 107 (1995), pp. 126-34.

83. The artifacts are some of the best specimens of their kind. They are described in Yadin, *Bar-Kokhba*, *passim*. Two other sets of finds are worth noting. The first is Roman bronze objects with pagan figures defaced, and the second is Roman glass. As Yadin says, finding these objects, including specimens of beautiful Roman glass bowls in England and the Judaean desert, should not surprise us, since 'at that time, after all, the whole area was one Roman common market!' (p. 205).

84. See H.M. Cotton, 'The Guardianship of Jesus Son of Babatha: Roman and Local Law in the Province of Arabia', *JRS* 83 (1993), pp. 94-108.

documents concerning Babatha's inheritance when her second husband died (P.Yadin 20–26). A number of fragmentary texts also appear to be financial or administrative documents (P.Yadin 31–35). There was also a marriage contract for Salome Komaise (P.Yadin 37), a woman from the same village, whose own archive has been found. Since Babatha apparently did not survive the revolution, it is impossible to continue the trajectory plotted above. Nevertheless, the pattern is well enough established to be able to point to several facts consistent with those noted above.

The first is that Babatha was a woman who was fully conversant with and involved in the established Roman legal system of the time, even if she herself did not speak or write Greek (this cannot be determined). This social-political system apparently allowed for—or, more probably, encouraged—the suitable documents to be recorded, filed and preserved in Greek (no matter what other languages may also have been used). Since Arabia had only been a province since 106 CE, it might come as a surprise to find that the span of Babatha's documents precedes that time. In other words, by the time of direct Roman rule over the area there was already a distinct and clear understanding and use of the Roman legal system, established under Nabataean local rule in the first century, beginning with Augustus, although also probably reflecting earlier Greek laws or customs.[85] The second feature to note is the use of Greek as the clearly predominant language of these administrative, financial and legal documents. Whereas it is clear that indigenous Semitic languages continued to be maintained, and were probably still widely used for personal contact, the language of commerce, trade, and governmental administration, including the courts, was Greek. The multilingual character of many of the documents, and certainly of the archive itself, illustrates that there were numerous bilinguals, and that many needed to know Greek in order to perform their regular duties. As Cotton states,

> Most of the people involved in this [the Babatha] archive are Jews; but, as there is nothing specifically Jewish about the Greek part of the archive, we are perfectly justified in regarding the Jews as representative of the provincials in general. Moreover, they represent that part of the provincial

---

85. See Wasserstein, 'Marriage Contract', esp. pp. 117-26, who notes the level of assimilation of the Jews, as reflected by reference to ἑλληνικὸς νόμος (P.Yadin 18.51; cf. P.Yadin 37.9-10).

population which was less tainted by the 'epigraphic habit' of the Graeco-Roman world, i.e. they come from the less Hellenized section of the provincial population. Precisely because of this we can be sure that their dealings with the Roman authorities constitute a faithful picture of the realities of life in the province.[86]

So what can be concluded regarding the evidence presented here in relation to the world of the Roman east, and, by implication, of the New Testament? The first is that traditional boundaries between Jew and non-Jew in the world of the first few centuries CE, even in the Roman east of which Judaea was a part, need to be further re-evaluated, especially in terms of language.[87] The pervasiveness of Graeco-Roman culture is illustrated by the fact that, by the time of the late first century, it was a dominant influence on daily life of even those who lived at the furthest reaches of the empire. The local inhabitants, even though they may not have spoken Greek as their native tongue, had sufficient recourse to those who did, so much so that they became actively involved in the governmental, financial and legal workings of the time. In some instances this may have been an elective involvement, but for others it was probably forced upon them when they needed to protect their rights and property. These papyri give an insightful view into life in eastern Judaea and western Arabia during the late first century and into the middle part of the second century. Secondly, within this cultural milieu, there is much to be learned about the use of the Greek language of the time. Although there has been much attention devoted to the Ptolemaic papyri of Egypt, and recently more attention to the Roman papyri there, more work still needs to be done on the Greek of the Roman east. Most work done to this point has concentrated on unhelpful contrasts being drawn between this Greek and the Greek of the New Testament, often in terms of its supposed Semitisms. What is necessary is a thorough study of the various archives in terms of the dialects of Greek to be found.

---

86. Cotton, 'Guardianship of Jesus', p. 107.

87. M. Hengel has done significant work in this area in his *Judaism and Hellenism: Studies in their Encounter during the Early Hellenistic Period* (Philadelphia: Fortress Press, 1994); *The 'Hellenization' of Judaea in the First Century after Christ* (London: SCM Press, 1989); and *Jews, Greeks and Barbarians* (London: SCM Press, 1980), among other works. The latest evidence allows the breaking down of these imaginary barriers to continue in more outlying areas of the empire. See Millar, *Roman Near East*, pp. 337-436, for an excellent survey.

Nevertheless, what also emerges from this brief study is that the work done on the language of the Egyptian papyri must form the basis of this further study. Thirdly, and finally, consistent patterns of similarity with Egypt begin to emerge as well. This apparent and evident overlap should provide a basis for more informed analysis of the Roman east. As Cotton rightly says,

> The greatest surprise caused by the final publication of the Greek part of the Babatha Archive has been the striking similarity between the documents from the province of Arabia and those from Egypt, notwithstanding the fact that the people who wrote these documents or are attested in them were mostly Jews. Their 'Jewishness' is expressed in nothing except their names... Babatha and her litigants show no awareness of an existing normative rabbinic law, but are strongly influenced by Roman law, while their diplomatics resemble those of Egyptian papyri. The degree of assimilation of non-Hellenized Jews—most of them do not know Greek—into their environment seems to upset some deeply entrenched views about the contrast between Jews and non-Jews in the Greco-Roman world.[88]

It seems to me that the evidence is now at hand to be able to redress these wrong-headed views and to grasp a more realistic picture of the Roman east, including the world of Judaea and of the New Testament.

*Diplomatic Text and Translation of P.Yadin *52*[89]

1 cου[.]αιρ[..]ωναθηι
   .[..]ανουκαιμα
   .]αβαλα χαιρειν
   .]ηδηεπεμcαπρος
5 .]μαcα[.]ριππανcπ[.]υ
   δ[...]τεπεμcεμοι
   θ[.]ρ.ο..καικιτρια
   α[...]δαγαcθηcεται
   ι.[..]τρε..βοληνιου

88. Cotton, 'Marriage Contract', pp. 64-65. See also Lewis, 'World of P.Yadin', pp. 40-41.

89. The tentative translation attempts to capture the sense of the diplomatic text. I wish to thank the members of the Biblical Studies Research Cluster of the Centre for Advanced Theological Research, Roehampton Institute London, for their suggestions regarding this paper, especially with regard to the diplomatic text and translation.

10 δ[..]ωνκαιμηαλως
    π[..]ηϲηταιεγραφη
    δ[.]ελην ϲτιδια
    τ...μα.μηευρη
    θ[.].αι εβραεϲτι
15 ε[..].. αϲθαιαυτον
    απ[.].υϲαιταχιον
    δ.[..]..γεορτην
    κ[...].αλλωϲποιη
    ϲ.[..].

20 ϲουμαιοϲ
    ερρ[.]ϲο

1   Sou[m]aio[s to J]onathe
    son of Bai]anos and Ma-
    s]abala, greeting.
    Si]nce I sent to
5   y]ou A[g]rippa, en[d]e-
    a[vou]r to send to me
    b[r]a[n]ch[es] and citrons.
    But t[hem] you will return
    for Feast of Tabernacles of Je-
10 w]s and not otherwise
    will you do. It is written
    how[ever] in Greek because
    th[e de]sir[e *or* th[e oppo]rtuni[ty (?) was not to be
    f[ou]nd in Hebrew
15 to w[rit]e. Him
    rel[ea]se immediately
    o[n account of th]e feast
    a[nd not] otherwise will you
    d[o].

20 Soumaios
    Fare[w]ell

Part IV

THE SCROLLS AND EXTRA-BIBLICAL TEXTS

'WRESTLING AGAINST WICKEDNESS IN HIGH PLACES': MAGIC IN THE WORLDVIEW OF THE QUMRAN COMMUNITY

Philip S. Alexander

> For we wrestle not against flesh and
> blood, but against principalities, against
> powers, against the rulers of the darkness
> of this world, against spiritual wickedness
> in high places (Eph. 6.12, AV)

To judge by the contents of their library it is probable that the Dead Sea community practised certain forms of magic,[1] despite the biblical injunctions to the contrary (Deut. 18.9-14), which are quoted almost

---

1. In the present paper I work with a pragmatic, commonsense definition of magic which, since I am dealing with Jewish tradition, takes as its starting-point Deut. 18.9-14. Deut. 18.9-14, like most ancient law codes, gives a rather clear indicative definition of magic. The forbidden activities listed there would be readily categorized by English speakers as 'magic'. More importantly they were recognized as forming a category within the Jewish tradition: see, for example, the profound discussion of the definition of magic (*kishuf, keshafim*) in *b. Sanh.* 65a-68a. The Qumran texts discussed in this paper deal with incantation and with divination—two activities which fall within the category: hence my title, '*magic* in the worldview of the Qumran community'. The problem is not so much that the category itself is unclear, but that the Qumran group, who apparently accepted the authority of Deuteronomy, engaged in such 'forbidden' activities. I offer no solution to this problem here, but simply note that it is not solved by dropping the category 'magic'. The category is, of course, 'fuzzy', as are most cultural and religious categories, and what unifies the category is not obvious (other than that the acts listed, like many other acts, are forbidden). It is tempting for academics to try and sharpen up the definition, but little is achieved by this if it produces a private definition divorced from common usage. 'Magic' is an important category within religions and historians of religion should continue to use it, however difficult it may be. In this paper I do not use 'magic' in any pejorative sense, and do not imply a contrast between 'magic' and 'religion', or 'magic' and 'science'. The pejorative overtones of 'magic' are much stronger in rarefied academic discourse than in common speech.

verbatim in the Temple Scroll (11QTemple col. lx, ll. 16-21). That fact in itself is hardly surprising, since most Jews in the late Second Temple period believed to some extent in the power of magic.[2] However, I would suggest that magic played an unusually prominent role in the worldview of the Qumran sect, and that they had a deeply magical outlook on life. The magical texts from Qumran fall into two broad groups: first, texts concerned with defence against demons and evil spirits, and, secondly, texts concerned with divination, augury and prediction of the future. In this paper I shall survey the main texts in both these groups and then offer some concluding observations on the place of magic in the life and theology of the Dead Sea sect.

Defence against Demons

4Q510 (4QSongs of the Maskil[a]) and 4Q511 (4QSongs of the Maskil[b])
4Q510 and 511 are the remains of two very fragmentary Hebrew scrolls which appear to have contained a series of 'songs' (*shirim*) of a strongly incantatory character.[3] Both are in Herodian hands and palaeographically date to the late first century BCE or the beginning of the first century CE. Similarities in content and language suggest that they are two copies of the same composition. Two rubrics of the songs are partially preserved which indicate that they were of the form: למשכיל שׁיר[ראשׁו]ן (4Q511 frag. 2, col. i, l. 1) and למשכיל שׁ[יר שׁני (4Q511 frag. 8, l. 4). The songs, therefore, appear to have been numbered and designated as למשכיל. Baillet and others have taken למשכיל as meaning 'composed by the Maskil', the *lamed* being *lamed auctoris*, as, traditionally, in מזמור לדוד.[4] In context, however, this may not be correct. למשכיל here may be analogous to למשכיל in 1QS col. iii, l. 13 and have the sense, 'a song for the Maskil to sing'. The 'voice' of the songs is clear at 4Q510 frag. 1, l. 4 and it is that of the Maskil.

The songs contained various literary elements which Bilhah Nitzan in her penetrating analysis has designated as praise, incantation and

---

2.   See P.S. Alexander, 'Incantations and Books of Magic', in E. Schürer, *The History of the Jewish People in the Age of Jesus Christ*, III.1 (rev. G. Vermes, F.G.B. Millar and M.D. Goodman; Edinburgh: T. & T. Clark, 1986), pp. 342-80.

3.   M. Baillet, 'Cantiques du Sage', in *Qumrân Grotte 4, III (4Q482–4Q520)* (DJD, 7; Oxford: Clarendon Press, 1982), pp. 219-86.

4.   Baillet, *Qumrân Grotte 4*, p. 215.

thanksgiving,[5] but they are thematically strongly unified and the pivot of each composition is the incantation. The purpose of the incantation emerges at 4Q510 frag. 1, ll. 4-8:

> 'And I, a Maskil, proclaim the majesty of his beauty
> to frighten and ter[rify] all the spirits of the angels of destruction and the
> spirits of the bastards, demons, Lilith, 'howlers and [yelpers' (Isa. 13.21)
> ...]—
> those who strike suddenly to lead astray the spirit of understanding and to
> appall their hearts and their so[uls]
> during the period of the domini[on] of wickedness and the times
> appointed for the humiliation of the Sons of Lig[ht] on account of (their)
> guilt in the times they are afflict[ed] by iniquities—
> not for eternal destruction [but on]ly for the period of (their) sinful
> humiliation'.

(4) ואני משכיל משמיע הוד תפארתו לפחד ולב[ה]ל (5) כול רוחי מלאכי
חבל ורוחות
ממזרים שד אים לילית אחים ו[ציי]ם...(6) והפוגעים פתע פתאום לתעות
רוח בינה
ולהשם לבבם ונ[פשו]תם בקץ ממשל[ת] (7) רשעה ותעודות תעניות בני או[ר]
באמת
קצי נגוע[י] עוונות ולוא לכלת עולם (8) [כי א]ם לקץ תעניות פשע[6]

In other words, the proclamation of God's majesty which the Maskil has just made in the section of praise which precedes this quotation is for the purposes of frightening the demons. Articulated here is a theory of prayer as a defence against demonic attack. The element of thanksgiving in the songs also alludes to this apotropaic function of prayer. Thus at 4Q511 frags. 8-9, ll. 4-10 the Maskil thanks God for

5.   B. Nitzan, *Qumran Prayer and Religious Poetry* (STDJ, 12; Leiden: Brill, 1994), pp. 236-72. See further B. Nitzan, 'Hymns from Qumran לפחד לבהל Evil Ghosts (4Q510-4Q511)', *Tarbiz* 55 (1986), pp. 19-46, with the responses to this article by J.M. Baumgarten and I. Ta-Shma on pp. 440-45 and with Nitzan's reply on pp. 603-605 [Hebrew].

6.   The text is a conflate of 4Q510 frag. 1, ll. 4-8 and 511 frag. 10, ll. 1-6. Note: (1) משכיל, though anarthrous, is probably used as a title. (2) The conjunction in והפוגעים is epexegetical, that is, הפוגעים does not denote a further category of malevolent spirit, but rather defines the harm inflicted by all the spirits previously listed. (3) The suffixes on לבבם ונ[פשו]תם refer forward to בני או[ר], or to 'the men of the Community', understood from the context. (4) ולוא לכלת עולם וגו' probably implies that the punishment which the Maskil metes out to the evil spirits is a partial punishment which endures only for this age. In the age to come, however, God will bring upon them utter annihilation.

his protection, implicitly against demonic attack, using words that echo that well-known psalm of protection, Psalm 91 (on which more anon),[7] and at 4Q511 frags. 48-49+51, col. ii, ll. 1-6 he thanks God for revealing to him how to defend himself against evil spirits.

The Songs of the Maskil are probably a sectarian composition. At a general level they are redolent of the siege mentality of sectarianism, but more particularly they reflect some of the distinctive language of the Qumran group, terms like 'Sons of Light' (4Q510 frag. 1, l. 7) and 'Men of the Covenant' (4Q511 frags. 63-64, col. ii, l. 5), as well as the designation of the spiritual leader of the sect as 'Maskil'. It is unclear whether the Maskil recited these songs as a private office or as a public liturgy. That the latter was the case is suggested by 4Q511 frag. 63, col. iv, ll. 1-3, which preserves the concluding benediction of the work:

> May they bless all Your works continually,
> and blessed be Your name for ever and ever.
> Amen, amen.

'Amen' in early Jewish prayer often involves a communal response, or the response of another, on hearing someone else recite a prayer. If this is the case here, then a vivid picture emerges of the Maskil standing as the agent and spiritual champion of the congregation and reciting these songs to defend it against demonic attack, with the congregation supporting his efforts by affirming 'Amen, amen!' The scenario envisaged is not an exorcism, at least if we take exorcism in its precise sense of expelling a demon from the body of an individual. Rather the Maskil is, through prayer, erecting or maintaining a spiritual cordon round the Community, *pre-emptively* to keep at bay the encircling forces of darkness.

A formidable array of spiritual forces is ranged against the Community: the demonology is complex. In 4Q510 frag. 1, quoted earlier, we have: the spirits of the angels of destruction (*ruhei mal'akhei hevel*); spirits of the bastards (*ruhot mamzerim*); demons (*shedim*); Lilith; and 'howlers and yelpers' (*'ohim ve-ṣiyyim*—an allusion to Isa. 13.21). 'Spirits of the bastards' is attested again at 4Q511 frag. 35, l. 7 and at 4Q511 frags. 48-49+51, col. ii, ll. 2-3, and 'congregation of the bastards' (*'adat mamzerim*) at 4Q511 frag. 2, col. ii, l. 3. At 4Q511 frag. 1, l. 6 we have the generic terms 'destroyer' (*mashhit*) and 'evil spirits'

---

7. Cf. frag. 8, l. 6 שדי בסתר with Ps. 91.1, יושב בסתר עליון בצל שדי יתלונן.

(*ruhei resha'*). The background to the demonology of the Songs of the Maskil lies in the Enochic literature and in the book of *Jubilees*, which, though not sectarian in origin, were closely studied at Qumran and deeply affected the sect's worldview.

1 Enoch 7, 10 and 15 offer a remarkable aetiology of demons, according to which demons arose from the bodies of the Giants after they had been killed as a punishment for their arrogant rebellion against God and the divine order of society. The Giants were the monstrous offspring of fallen angels, the Watchers, and human women. They represent mythologically the forces of chaos, and their 'spirits', which survived them, continue their evil work. Implicit in this account seems to be a generic distinction between 'angels' and 'demons'. 'Demons' are not just fallen angels, but a different order of beings that is part angelic and part human. The evil spirits, says *1 Enoch*, have been given authority to attack and to destroy the sons of men until the day of judgment, when they shall be finally dealt with (*1 En.* 16.2). *Jubilees* 10 takes up and expands these ideas. The evil spirits fathered by the Watchers were beginning to lead astray the sons of Noah after the Flood and to make them err in order to destroy them. Noah prayed to God for relief from their oppressions and God sent his angels to bind the demons. However, Mastema (or Satan, as he is also called), the chief of the evil spirits, interceded with God and argued that if all his spirits are bound he would not be able to perform his function of punishing human wickedness. He was left a tenth of his spirits so that he could fulfil his role until the day of judgment, but an angel taught Noah how to deal with these remaining demons, explaining to him 'all the medicines of their diseases, together with their seductions, how he might heal them with the herbs of the earth'. Noah wrote this information down in a book which he passed on to Shem.

The influence of these ideas on the Songs of the Maskil is clear. The 'spirits of the bastards', which they mention several times, are the spirits of the Giants, who were born of the illicit union of angels and women. That the demons are allowed to afflict humankind on account of their sin only till the day of judgment and the final reckoning is implied in the rather obscure language of 4Q510 frag. 1, ll. 7-8, quoted earlier: 'not for eternal destruction but only for the period of [their, that is, the Community's] sinful humiliation'. The Maskil is seen in a Noahic role, interceding for his Community and defending them against spiritual evil. The Qumran literature shows a marked interest in the biblical story of the Flood, possibly because the Community believed that the evil conditions which provoked the Flood were being replicated in their days. They too were living at the end of history, just prior to a cataclysmic divine judgment of God on the wickedness of their generation. Like righteous Enoch and Noah they had to stand out against the prevailing evil and warn their contemporaries of the impending doom. It is vital for a correct understanding of the Songs of the Maskil and of the level of their magic to appreciate their strong conceptual framework. Behind them is a powerful and coherent mythological worldview, which runs through all the major sectarian texts. They are integral to that worldview. We have already noted the allusion at 4Q510 frag. 1, ll. 7-8 to the eschatological defeat of evil. This idea was understood in cosmological terms by some in Second Temple Judaism, and there may be a reference to this cosmological interpretation of the final defeat of evil in the very broken passage at 4Q511 frag. 30, ll. 1-3, which mentions God's sealing of the abysses. The implication probably is that evil spirits represent the irruption into this world of the forces of chaos and disorder which God overcame and sealed at the time of creation. Fittingly at the end of history these forces will be once again consigned to their proper place in the abyss and creation fully restored.

The Maskil's magical defence of his Community is conspicuous for the absence of *materia magica*, of technical magical rituals and formulae and of divine names. The Maskil simply reminds the demons of the majesty and power of God, and of his impending judgment on them. He may also have invoked the protection of the good angels. There are allusions to good angels at 4Q511 frag. 2, col. i, ll. 7-8, where it may be implied that each of the tribes of Israel has its tutelary angel. 4Q511 frag. 20, col. i, l. 2 refers to the 'angel of his glory' (*mal'akh kevodo*), and if the striking phrase *rosh memshalot*, 'chief of dominions', at 4Q511 frag. 2, col. i, l. 3 denotes, as Baillet conjectured,[8] an archangel, we may have here an early allusion to the ranking of the angels into hierarchies such as 'thrones, dominions, principalities and powers'.[9] Basically the Maskil warns the demons not to meddle with him and his Community, because they have got 'protection'. By

8. *Qumrân Grotte 4*, p. 222. However, I am not sure that the reference here is to 'un archangel *déchu*'.

9. Cf. Col. 1.16, εἴτε θρόνοι εἴτε κυριότητες εἴτε ἀρχαὶ εἴτε ἐξουσίαι.

reciting the power of God and his angels he confuses and terrifies them and prevents them from striking. In a word he engages in psychological warfare against the demons.

To anyone who knows the later Jewish magical texts the absence of *nomina barbara* in the Songs of the Maskil is striking. The Qumran Community was clearly very reluctant to pronounce the divine name,[10] and this may have inhibited their development of *nomina barbara*, but the means employed in the Songs of the Maskil are particularly appropriate to the end which they envisage. According to the Songs of the Maskil the specific damage which the demons do is to 'appall' the hearts and souls of the Sons of Light and to lead them into error. In other words they attack their minds and intellects, leading them to doubt the truth. The use of a psychological counter-attack is, therefore, appropriate. The Maskil in his turn 'confuses' and 'terrifies' the demons, who, because they are partially human, are equally susceptible to psychological warfare. Behind all this may be a shrewd perception that what the members of the Community need to sustain their identity and loyalty is to be constantly reminded of their privileged relation to God. The Songs of the Maskil would appear to work because through them the Community would be assured of divine protection against the demons of doubt. *Jubilees* also sees one of the primary activities of the demons as being 'to lead astray the children of the sons of Noah and to make them err' (*Jub.* 10.1), but it also holds them responsible for physical illnesses which can only be cured by *materia medica*. That the Essenes engaged in herbalism and physical healing is asserted by Josephus,[11] but there is little evidence of this activity, perhaps by chance, among the Scrolls. The Songs of the Maskil seem primarily to be concerned with protection against affliction of the soul and not of the body. [12]

---

10. See 1QS col. vi, l. 27–col. vii, l. 2; CD col. xv, ll. 1-2, and note the use of *yod* for the Tetragram at 4Q511, frag. 10, l. 12, on which see G.W. Nebe, 'Der Buchstabenname *Yod* als Ersatz des Tetragrams in 4Q511, Fragm. 10, Zeile 12?', *RevQ* 12 (1986), pp. 283-84.

11. *War* 2.136, σπουδάζουσι δ' ἐκτόπως περὶ τὰ τῶν παλαιῶν συντάγματα, μάλιστα τὰ πρὸς ὠφέλειαν ψυχῆς καὶ σώματος ἐκλέγοντες· ἔνθεν αὐτοῖς πρὸς θεραπείαν παθῶν ῥίζαι τε ἀλεξητήριοι καὶ λίθων ἰδιότητες ἀνερευνῶνται. See further G. Vermes, *Post-Biblical Jewish Studies* (SJLA, 8; Leiden: Brill, 1975), pp. 8-29.

12. On the unremitting psychological warfare of Belial and his demonic cohorts against the Sons of Light, see also 1QS, col. iii, ll. 20-24, 'The Angel of Darkness

11Q11 (11QApocryphal Psalms[a])

Many of the themes and motifs of the Songs of the Maskil are repeated in 11Q11.[13] This badly damaged scroll, in a Herodian hand of the early first century CE, contained at least four psalms which were recited as incantations against demons. The final preserved text is a version of Psalm 91, 'He that dwells in the secret place of the most high shall abide under the shadow of the almighty', a psalm frequently quoted in Jewish amulets and incantations right down to the present day and invoked as a sovereign remedy against demons in Talmudic literature.[14] The two preceding texts are otherwise unattested psalms attributed to David. Their opening rubrics were probably the same: לדויד על דברי לחש בשם יהוה. Here לדויד, unlike למשכיל in the Songs of the Maskil, is probably intended to indicate authorship. The technical description of the text which follows as 'words of incantation' (*divrei laḥash*) is noteworthy. Even more noteworthy—not to say surprising—is the fact that the Tetragram is written out in full, a point to

---

leads all the children of righteousness astray, and until his end, all their sin, iniquities, wickedness, and all their unlawful deeds are caused by his dominion in accordance with the mysteries of God. Every one of their chastisements, and every one of the seasons of their distress shall be brought about by the rule of his persecution; for all his allotted spirits seek the overthrow (להכשיל) of the sons of light' (trans. Vermes). 4Q174 [4QFlorilegium] frags. 1-3, col. i, ll. 7-9, 'And as for what he said to David, "I shall obtain for you rest from all your enemies" (2 Sam. 7.11), it means that he shall obtain for them rest from all the Sons of Belial, who cause them to stumble (המכשילים), to destroy them [on account of] their [   ], when they come in accordance with Belial's design to cause the Sons of Light to stumble (להכשיל), and to plot against them evil designs, so as to ha[nd th]em over to Belial through their wicked error'.

13. For text, translation and commentary, see J.P.M. van der Ploeg, 'Le Psaume xci dans une recension de Qumran', *RB* 72 (1965), pp. 210-17 (+ Pls. VIII-IX); *idem*, 'Un petit rouleau de psaumes apocryphes (11QPsAp[a])', in G. Jeremias, H.W. Kuhn and H. Stegemann (eds.), *Tradition und Glaube: Festgabe für K.G. Kuhn* (Göttingen: Vandenhoeck & Ruprecht, 1971), pp. 128-39 (+ Pls. II-VII); E. Puech, '11QPsAp[a]: Un rituel d'exorcismes. Essai de reconstruction', *RevQ* 14 (1990), pp. 377-408; *idem*, 'Les deux derniers psaumes davidiques du rituel d'exorcisme 11QPsAp[a] IV,4–V,14', in D. Dimant and U. Rappaport (eds.), *The Dead Sea Scrolls: Forty Years of Research* (Leiden: Brill, 1992), pp. 64-89. Further Nitzan, *Qumran Prayer and Religious Poetry*, pp. 232-36; M. Delcor, 'L'utilisation des psaumes contre les mauvais esprits à Qumran', in P. Grelot (ed.), *La vie de la parole: De l'Ancien au Nouveau Testament* (Paris: Desclée, 1987), pp. 61-70.

14. *y. 'Erub.* 10.11 [26c]; *b. Shebu.* 15b.

which we shall return later. These compositions have been plausibly linked with the four 'songs for singing over the afflicted' mentioned in the list of David's writings in 11QPsalms[a] col. xxvii, ll. 9-10.

Despite their similarities the scenario envisaged in 11Q11 is, I think, rather different from that of the Songs of the Maskil. The Songs of the Maskil are apotropaic and preventative. In 11Q11, however, a demon has breached the defences and successfully attacked a member of the Community, causing illness. 11Q11 contains texts to be recited over him to expel the demon. In other words here we *are* dealing with exorcism in the strict sense of the term. The songs address the afflicted one in the second person singular. This is the case not only in Psalm 91 (note, for example, כי הואה יצילך מפח יקוש in v. 3), but also with the apocryphal psalms: note, for example, קרא בכו[ל עת אל השמ]ים אשר]יבוא אליך בלי[על וא]מרתה אליו, 'Call to the heavens whenever Belial comes to you, and say to him...' (in col. iv, ll. 4-5). I see no reason to suppose that a congregation is being addressed here. Rather an individual is in view, and the situation is one of specific crisis. Consequently the responsum 'Amen, Amen, Selah' should be taken as the reply of the individual. I would, therefore, restore at col. v, l. 14, ויע[נה אמן אמן] סלה, 'And *he* shall answer, "Amen, Amen, Selah"', not ויע[נו אמן אמן] סלה, 'And they shall answer, "Amen, Amen, Selah"'. The formula, 'Amen, Amen Selah', is not found in the Bible, but it is very common in Jewish amulets. That sickness is envisaged is suggested by Psalm 91, with its references to plague and pestilence, and by the allusions to healing in the broken contexts of col. i, l. 8 and col. iv, l. 3. The songs are recited over the sick one, who may be too weak to recite them himself, but who assents to them with the response, 'Amen, Amen, Selah'.

The two surviving apocryphal psalms are strongly hortatory in tone. The victim is exhorted to exert himself and to confront the demon. An element of self-healing is, therefore, involved, and the absence of technical magical praxis is once again striking. The warfare is psychological. The afflicted one is invited to abuse the devil to his face at col. iv, ll. 4-8:

> [When]ever Beli[al] comes to you, you [shall s]ay to him:
> 'Who are you? [You should be afraid of] man and of the seed of the sa[in]ts.
> Your face is a face of [fu]tility and your horns are the horns of a dr[ea]m.
> You are darkness and not light, [perver]sity and not righteousness'.

(4) בכו[ל עת]. . . (5) [.]אשר [יבוא אליך בלי[על ואל[מרתה אליו (6) מי

אתה [תירא מ]אדם ומזרע הקד[ושי]ם פניך פני

(7) [ש]ו וקרניך קרני חל[ו]ם חושך אתה ולוא

(8) אור [עו]ל ולוא צדקה[15

Most take the reference here to 'horns' as figurative, but I think it may be intended literally. This may be the earliest mention of the physiognomy of the devil as a horned being.

The afflicted one is further exhorted to remind the devil of the divine protection which he enjoys. He invokes God's creative power, mythologized as a defeat of the forces of chaos and as a sealing of the abyss (11Q11 col. i, ll. 10-13; col. ii, ll. 1-3). He invokes angelic protectors, warrior angels such as Raphael and possibly Michael under the title 'Prince of the Host' (col. iv, l. 8), who can incarcerate Belial in the abyss, the dark horrors of which are described with a positively Miltonic exuberance (col. iii, ll. 7-11; col. iv, ll. 8-10). As in the Songs of the Maskil, the idea is implied that evil represents the eruption into the ordered world of the forces of chaos which God subdued at the creation and sealed into the abyss. These dark forces, which re-emerged through the breach of human sin and the fall of the Watchers, will once again be subdued at the end of days and confined to their proper realm in the deeps. Belial is reminded not only of the eschatological judgment which he will undergo, but of the earnest of that judgment in the punishment of the Watchers (11Q11 col. ii, ll. 7-8). Column iv, ll. 11-12 perhaps alludes to the idea that each righteous individual has his own specific guardian angel, who can defend him when Satan attacks.

There are hints in the text of a complex demonology. 4Q510 frag. 1, l. 4 may have listed spirits, devils, Lilith, and 'howlers and yelpers'. But the villain of this piece is unquestionably Belial himself, referred to as 'Satan' (11Q11 col. iv, l. 12), as the 'prince of enmity' and 'ruler of the abyss of darkness' (col. i, ll. 5-6), and as 'ruler of the earth' (col. iii, l. 9). The ontological status of Belial at Qumran is somewhat unclear. Cosmologically he is obviously a very powerful figure, the chief opponent of Michael and the good angels. He cannot be a demon. Demons are the foot-soldiers of the forces of darkness. He must, therefore, belong to the category of angel, but where did he come from? Is he one of the fallen Watchers? If he is an angel, then

15. After Puech in Dimant and Rappaport, *The Dead Sea Scrolls*, p. 68.

he cannot be the direct cause of the illnesses envisaged in 11Q11, since an angel cannot penetrate the body of a human. That is possible only for a demon or an evil spirit.

Is 11Q11 a sectarian text? It contains no distinctively sectarian terminology such as we find in the Songs of the Maskil. Its leading ideas, though closely parallel to those of the Songs of the Maskil, are not distinctively Qumranic, but were probably widely shared by other groups in late Second Temple Judaism. However, there is equally little to suggest that the text is pre- or non-Qumranic. The fact that the Tetragram is written out normally is no evidence of a pre-Qumranic or non-Qumranic origin. There are other probably sectarian scrolls in which the Tetragram is written fully and without substitutes.[16] Here this practice may have a precise function since the text specifically invokes the protection of the Name of God, though it does not take this idea to the lengths of later Jewish magical texts, which develop elaborate magical variations of the Tetragram. Moreover, we should bear in mind that the text palaeographically dates from the early first century CE. If it is much older and has been handed down and copied at Qumran, why did the Qumran scribes not use a substitute? On balance I think that 11Q11 was probably composed at Qumran, though it may reflect more widely held ideas. The parallelism with the Songs of the Maskil suggests that these were psalms recited by the Maskil. Defence of the Community against spiritual attack and exorcism belonged naturally to the province of the spiritual mentor of the Sect.

11Q11 may be compared with descriptions of healings in a number of literary texts preserved among the Scrolls. The most complex example of these is in the book of Tobit, a novelistic work of non-sectarian origin, but popular, it seems, at Qumran. In Tobit, Tobias expels the demon Asmodaeus from his bridal chamber through a combination of prayer and magical praxis (he burns the heart and liver of a certain type of fish on the ashes of incense).[17] The warrior angel Raphael is also involved in the action, both in advising Tobias and in pursuing and binding Asmodaeus (Tob. 6.16-17; 8.3; cf. 4Q196 [4QTobit[a]] and 4Q197 [4QTobit[b]]). A second example is 1QGenesis Apocryphon col. xx, ll. 16-22, where Abram prays and lays his hands

16. See Puech's discussion of the problem in Dimant and Rappaport, *The Dead Sea Scrolls*, p. 80.

17. Tob. 8.1-9.

on Pharaoh's head to expel an evil spirit which has afflicted him
because he took Sarai into his house (cf. Gen. 12.10-20 and 20.1-18).
The third example is in the Prayer of Nabonidus (4Q242): Nabonidus
is cured of an 'evil ulcer' through praying to God most high and
through the attentions of a Jewish 'exorcist' (*gazer*), who 'forgave'
him his sin. The account of the healing, however, is extremely com-
pressed and unclear, and it has been suggested that we should read גֵּיר,
'resident alien' and not גָזֵר, 'exorcist'. If this is correct then the link
between sickness and demons would be weakened, if not completely
broken.[18]

4Q560 (4QAgainst Demons)

The magical character of the very fragmentary Aramaic scroll 4Q560
has now, I believe, been demonstrated beyond reasonable doubt.[19] It
contains an adjuration against demons which attack pregnant women,
cause various illnesses and disturb sleep. A complex demonology is
clearly implied, though the categories of some of the demons are hard
to identify. Beelzebub, the prince of the demons, may be mentioned at
col. i, l. 1. This text probably comes from a spell-book which would
have contained a collection of such adjurations. A healer or exorcist
would have copied from the book onto skin, papyrus or a thin sheet of
metal an appropriate spell and personalized it for a client by inserting
his name. This text, encased in a small container, would then have
been worn as an amulet or buried at a suitable position in the house
(for example, at the threshold). Such amulets may be compared with
Tefillin and *Mezuzot*, examples of which have been found at
Qumran.[20] We do not know whether the Community saw the latter as

18. See A. Lange and M. Sieker, 'Gattung und Quellenwert des Gebets des
Nabonid', in H.J. Fabry, A. Lange and H. Lichtenberger (eds.), *Qumranstudien*
(Schriften des Institutum Judaicum Delitzchianum, 4; Göttingen: Vandenhoeck &
Ruprecht, 1996), pp. 3-34. It should also be noted that the common translation of גָזֵר
in the Prayer of Nabonidus as 'exorcist' (so, for example, García Martínez) is questionable. A גָזֵר is, strictly speaking, a 'diviner' or 'soothsayer' (Dan. 2.27; 4.5; 5.7;
5.11), not an 'exorcist'.

19. D.L. Penney and M.O. Wise, 'By the Power of Beelzebub: An Aramaic
Incantation Formula from Qumran (4Q560)', *JBL* 113 (1994), pp. 627-50. See also
R.H. Eisenman and M.O. Wise, *The Dead Sea Scrolls Uncovered* (Shaftesbury,
Dorset: Element Press, 1992), pp. 265-67.

20. *Tefillin*: 1Q13 (DJD, 1, pp. 72-76); 4Q128–48 (DJD, 6, pp. 48-79);
unknown provenance: Y. Yadin, *Tefillin from Qumran (X Q Phyl 1-4)* (Jerusalem:

a protection against demons or simply as a literal fulfilment of the injunctions of Deut. 6.8-9. However, the common Greek term for *Tefillin*, φυλακτήρια, suggests that they were widely regarded as charms of some sort. 4Q560 is almost certainly not itself the amulet, since the skin on which it is written shows no signs of rolling or folding. The spell which it contains is a general apotropaic. It does not imply that the wearer is actually afflicted with the illnesses mentioned (he or she would be in a sorry state if they were). Rather it would be worn to prevent such illnesses striking. It is probable that the spell simply adjured the demons in the name of YHWH not to strike. There is absolutely nothing in this text which is distinctively Qumranic. Its type of magic was commonplace throughout the ancient Near East. However, the fact remains that it was discovered among the Dead Sea Scrolls and it fits in well with the ethos of 4Q510–11 and 11Q11. I would suggest that such a recipe-book may have been the property of the Maskil and that the writing of protective amulets may also have been seen as belonging peculiarly to his province.

Augury and Divination

I turn now to the other great area of magic at Qumran, namely, augury and divination. Here I shall be more brief since I have already published on this subject.

4Q186 (4QAstrological Physiognomy) and 4Q561 (4QPhysiognomy)
Though the two physiognomic texts, 4Q186 and 4Q561,[21] are similar

Israel Exploration Society/The Shrine of the Book, 1969); *Mezuzot*: 4Q149–55 (DJD, 6, pp. 80-85).

21. Edition of 4Q186: J.M. Allegro, 'An Astrological Cryptic Document from Qumran', *JSS* 9 (1964), pp. 291-94; Allegro, DJD, 5, pp. 88-91, pl. XXXI, with J. Strugnell, 'Notes en marge du volume V des "Discoveries in the Judaean Desert of Jordan"', *RevQ* 7 (1969–71), pp. 274-76. Interpretation of 4Q186: M. Delcor, 'Recherches sur un horoscope en langue hébraïque provenant de Qumran', in M. Delcor (ed.), *Religion d'Israel et proche orient ancien* (Leiden: Brill, 1976), pp. 306-307; P.S. Alexander, 'Physiognomy, Initiation and Rank in the Qumran Community', in H. Cancik, H. Lichtenberger and P. Schäfer (eds.), *Geschichte–Tradition–Reflexion: Festschrift für Martin Hengel zum 70. Geburtstag*, I (Tübingen: Mohr [Paul Siebeck], 1996), pp. 385-94; F. Schmidt, 'Astrologie juive ancienne: Essai d'interpretation de 4QCryptique (4Q186)', *Orion International Symposium, Jerusalem 12–14 May, 1996* [unpublished]. Edition of 4Q561: Eisenman and Wise,

in content it is unlikely, as Florentino García Martínez suggests,[22] that one is a copy or translation of the other. The texts differ from each other in significant ways: 4Q186 is in Hebrew, 4Q561 in Aramaic; 4Q186 is in code, 4Q561 is not; above all, 4Q186 links physiognomy with astrology, though it is misleading to call it a horoscope, whereas 4Q561, at least in its preserved portions, does not.

4Q186, which dates palaeographically to the early or middle Herodian period, attempts to determine the nature of a man's 'spirit' by observing the form of certain parts of his body. Significantly these bodily parts are all visible (teeth, toes, fingers, thighs, eyes, beard) and can be inspected without involving intimacy: the person can be shrewdly appraised without them realising that this is happening. Certain physiognomic methods (for example palmistry and metoposcopy) involve close inspection of the body and require the subject's co-operation. 4Q186's criteria do not belong to this class. On the basis of this inspection it can be determined how many parts a man's spirit has in the 'house of light' (*bet ha-'or*) and how many in the 'pit of darkness' (*bor ha-ḥoshekh*). A nine-point scale is used. Whatever the origins of this may be, it clearly implies that any individual must be predominantly good or predominantly bad. No-one can be evenly balanced and, in the rabbinic sense, morally 'intermediate' (*beinoni*). Every person can, therefore, be assigned to one of two 'lists' or 'columns'—righteous or wicked, 'son of light' or 'son of darkness'.

A good case can be made out for 4Q186 as a sectarian composition, though physiognomy, of course, was by no means confined to Qumran. Its language strongly echoes the Sermon on the Two Spirits in 1QS col. iii, l. 13–col. iv, l. 26, and like that text it is deterministic. This determinism is expressed in two ways. First, through the idea of the two 'columns'. I have proposed elsewhere that this refers to the idea of the heavenly books. Normally these are thought of as books on which the deeds of men are recorded and which are consulted on the Day of Judgment to determine whether a man goes to heaven or hell. But sometimes the heavenly scroll is conceived of as a sort of foreordained script according to which future events will be played out. History is then pictured as the unrolling of this scroll. A similar idea is expressed in later Heikhalot literature through the concept of the

The Dead Sea Scrolls Uncovered, pp. 263-65.

22. F. García Martínez, *The Dead Sea Scrolls Translated* (Leiden: Brill, 2nd edn, 1996), p. 513.

heavenly curtain (the *Pargod*) on which are embroidered all the generations of mankind, from Adam till the end of history. Every man is inscribed in one of the two columns from birth, indeed from before birth. Physiognomy is a way of discovering in which column he is inscribed.[23]

The second way in which the determinism is expressed is through the astrology. There is no necessary connection between physiognomy and astrology: it is absent, as we noted in 4Q561. By making the link 4Q186 is introducing very explicitly the notion of fatalism. The sign under which one is born determines the nature of one's spirit, and this in turn registers on one's physiognomy. What the text is interested in knowing is the nature of a man's spirit. Theoretically this could have been deduced either from the astrology or from the physiognomy. The physiognomy was obviously easier, since few commoners in antiquity probably knew with any precision the time of their birth, and so casting a nativity was problematic. The astrology also gives the text a certain cachet, since astrology was widely regarded in antiquity as the queen of the sciences, and it chimes in with the sect's well-documented interest in astronomical and calendric lore.

I have suggested elsewhere that the Qumran sect, like the Pythagoreans and the later Heikhalot mystics, may have attempted secretly to apply physiognomic criteria to determine who was fit to join the Community.[24] The wording of the Sermon on the Two Spirits is suggestive: the purpose of the Sermon is 'to instruct all the sons of light and teach them the nature of all the children of men according to the kind of spirit which they possess, the signs identifying their works during their lifetime, their visitation for chastisement, and the time of their reward' (1QS col. iii, ll. 13-15). The 'signs' apparently envisaged by the Sermon are moral 'fruits of the spirit', but someone may have tried to give this a harder, more technical edge, in the form of physiognomic criteria. We know from palaeography that the Sermon on the Two Spirits was already extant in the early first century BCE (the palaeographic date of 1QS). Palaeographically 4Q186 is early Herodian at the earliest, so it may represent a secondary exegesis of the 'signs' in the Sermon of the Two Spirits. As with the other texts, I would suggest that physiognomy was distinctively Maskilic lore at Qumran. The fact that one of the two physiognomic texts is in code is

23. Alexander, 'Physiognomy, Initiation and Rank', pp. 388-89.
24. Alexander, 'Physiognomy, Initiation and Rank', pp. 391-93.

suggestive. A plausible case can be made out for all the coded texts as representing secret doctrine to be kept within the circle of the Maskil.

Two narrative texts from Qumran confirm the sect's interest in physiognomy. The first, 4Q534 (4QElect of God), describes the birth of a wonder-child whose special qualities are marked by certain phsyiognomic features. The references to 'lentils' (= freckles) and 'moles' as significant can be paralleled in the mediaeval Jewish physiognomies.[25] There has been a great deal of speculation as to who this wonder-child might be. Some have suggested an eschatological, messianic figure; others Noah. The two proposals are not as exclusive as might at first appear, since it is a commonplace of folklore that *any* child born to affect history in any dramatic way will bear in his body the marks of his singular destiny. The other narrative where physiognomy fleetingly makes an appearance is the description of Sarai's beauty in 1QGenesis Apocryphon col. xx, ll. 2-8. There long, supple fingers are seen as a positive feature, in contrast to the negative characterization of short, fat fingers in 4Q186.

4Q318 (4QBrontologion)

The Aramaic scroll 4Q318[26] is basically a brontologion, a well-known type of divinatory text found also in Akkadian, Greek and mediaeval Hebrew.[27] A brontologion interprets thunder as an omen portending important events. The Qumran example is complex, as Michael Wise has shown.[28] It opened with a selindromium which assigned the moon to one of the twelve signs of the zodiac for each day of the month throughout the whole year. This selindromium was then used in the second half of the work to explain the significance of the thunder: for

25. Alexander, 'Incantations and Books of Magic', p. 365.

26. Edition: Eisenman and Wise, *The Dead Sea Scrolls Uncovered*, pp. 258-63. Interpretation: Alexander, 'Incantations and Books of Magic', pp. 365-66; J.C. Greenfield and M. Sokoloff, 'Astrological and Related Omen Texts in Jewish Palestinian Aramaic', *JNES* 48 (1989), pp. 201-14; M.O. Wise, 'Thunder in Gemini: An Aramaic Brontologion (4Q318) from Qumran', in *idem, Thunder in Gemini and Other Essays on the History, Language and Literature of Second Temple Palestine* (Sheffield: JSOT Press, 1994), pp. 13-50; J.C. Greenfield and M. Sokoloff (with Appendices by D. Pingree and A. Yardeni), 'An Astrological Text from Qumran (4Q318) and Reflections on Some Zodiacal Names', *RevQ* 16 (1995), pp. 507-25.

27. A late Hebrew example in the John Rylands University Library Manchester (Rylands Gaster H1840) shows some interesting verbal similarities to 4Q318.

28. Wise, 'Thunder in Gemini'.

example, frag. 2, col. ii, l. 9: 'If thunder occurs (when the moon is) in Gemini, (it portends) fear and distress caused by foreigners…' (אם בתאומיא ירעם דחלה ומרע מנכריא).

There is nothing distinctively sectarian about this text, but it does fit in comfortably with the Qumranic worldview. Once again we find an interest in astrology. Brontology does not necessarily involve astrology. The astrological element in 4Q318 is, therefore, significant, as is its use specifically of the moon to link the thunder to the zodiac. Moreover, the interest in prodigies is understandable in a Community that believed it was living at the end of history. It is a commonplace of apocalyptic that signs and wonders in the heavens will foretell the end. Josephus (*War* 6.291) states that prodigies and portents were eagerly studied in first-century Palestine and that the interpretation of omens required great skill. It may have been seen specifically as a priestly prerogative. There may also be a stronger theological message to this dry and formal text than at first meets the eye. Wise notes that a reconstruction of the selindromium, possible because the text was so regular and formulaic, shows that for its author the first sign of the zodiac was Taurus. This is curious, for when he was writing the first sign of the zodiac would have been Aries, because the sun in his day would have risen in Aries at the vernal equinox. The sun would have risen in Taurus only much earlier in history, due to the phenomenon of the precession of the equinoxes. Wise cleverly suggests that the selindromium is based on the configuration of the heavens at the time of creation. If this is so, then the thunder which occurs now invokes, so to speak, an order inscribed on nature at the time of creation. Have we once again a reference to determinism? Here the idea may be that events are predetermined since the creation of the world. There may be more. The author of the selindromium may have held that the vernal point was at the beginning of Taurus when the world was created. This would mean that he would have dated creation to around 4400 BCE. From ca. 4400 to ca. 2200 BCE the vernal point would have precessed across Taurus till around 2200 BCE it moved into Aries. The author of the selindromium may have been aware that it was now on the edge of Aries and about to move into Pisces. Perhaps he saw this as heralding the end of the world and the dawning of a new age. (Modern astrologers, of course, note that the vernal point is moving into Aquarius, and hail this as the dawn of new age—'the Age of Aquarius'.)

All this is very speculative, but there can be no doubt that 4Q318 is an exceedingly learned text, one which could only have been fully understood by someone well-versed in contemporary astrology. Its doctrine is certainly attested outside Qumran, but as with the other texts the fact remains that it was found at Qumran. I would suggest, once again, that we have distinctively Maskilic lore. The interpretation of prodigies and calculations of the end may also have been his province. The fact that part of the text is a selindromium may be significant in this regard. Lunar lore was sensitive at Qumran, because of possible conflicts it might have engendered with the solar calendar, which was the basis of the sect's worship. Some texts about the moon are in code. It is possible that lunar doctrine at Qumran would have been confined to the circle of the Maskil.

Magic in the Worldview of Qumran

I shall conclude by drawing together the separate threads of the foregoing analysis in some general observations, and by briefly setting the ideas found in the texts which we have examined in the wider context of the history of religions.

First, it is clear that magic is integral to the worldview of Qumran. Behind the magic lies the basic dualism of the sect as articulated in the Sermon on the Two Spirits. The present age is a battlefield between the forces of light and the forces of darkness. This battle, like a game of three-dimensional chess, is being waged on a multiplicity of levels—terrestrial and celestial, spiritual and physical. On the one side are ranged Satan/Belial/Melchiresha and his minions—the demons and the 'sons of darkness', the wicked human opponents of the sect. Ranged on the other side are Michael/Melchizedek, the good angels and the 'sons of light', the members of the sect. The liturgies of the sect are weapons in this cosmic battle, aimed at defending the sons of light against spiritual attack. The concept of liturgy as spiritual warfare seems to have been pervasive at Qumran. It explains the numerous texts of cursing in which Belial and his minions (demonic and human) are ritually damned, and the equally numerous texts of blessing in which benedictions are heaped on the heads of the members of the Community. Even the physiognomies fit into this pattern, since they too echo the dualism of the Two Spirits, and may have been employed in the spiritual defence of the sect, to prevent 'sons of darkness' from being admitted into the Community of the 'sons of light'.

Secondly, the magic at Qumran is a learned magic. It is sometimes rather thoughtlessly assumed that magic is almost by definition a socially low-level activity.[29] This is quite wrong. Magic spans the whole social spectrum. The magic at Qumran is not the magic of the ignorant, uneducated magician plying his trade in the market or on the street corner. It is a high-level, learned magic, comparable in sophistication to the magic found later in the Great Magical Papyrus of Paris (*PGM* IV), or in the Hebrew Book of Secrets (*Sefer ha-Razim*). As in these texts, the magic is set in a strong conceptual framework of mythology, theology and cosmology. And in the Qumran texts the magical praxis is markedly restrained. As I have argued consistently this magical lore at Qumran was probably seen as belonging especially to the province of the Maskil. As the spiritual mentor of the Community, it was his duty to learn, apply and transmit this magical doctrine.[30]

Finally, Qumran provides us with a striking example of prayer viewed as spiritual warfare. The history of religions abounds with groups which held similar views. There may be antecedents in the Bible. It is surely arguable that Psalm 91 was actually being used by the Qumranians in a way consistent with the intention of its original author. Prayer as spiritual warfare is equally well attested in later Judaism in the Qabbalah and in the mysticism of the Hasidei Ashkenaz. Early Christian literature contains similar ideas. Note for example the famous passage on the whole armour of God in the deutero-Pauline letter to the Ephesians, which forms the motto of the present paper (Eph. 6.10-18). Any Qumranite could have said a hearty amen to the words, 'Our wrestling is not against flesh and blood, but against the principalities, against the powers, against the world-rulers of this darkness, against the spiritual hosts of wickedness in the heavenly places'. Having described the various parts of the armour of God, the writer concludes with the crucial exhortation to engage in 'all prayer

29. So, for example, J.M. Hull, *Hellenistic Magic and the Synoptic Tradition* (London: SCM Press, 1974), pp. 9 and 44.

30. For some perceptive remarks on the Maskil's role at Qumran, see C.A. Newsom, 'The Sage in Qumran Literature: The Function of the Maskil', in J.G. Gammie and L.G. Perdue (eds.), *The Sage in Israel and the Ancient Near East* (Winona Lake, IN: Eisenbrauns, 1990), pp. 373-82.

and supplication, praying at all seasons in the Spirit, and watching thereunto in all perseverance and supplication for all the saints'. Later Celtic Christianity was to exploit this idea to a conspicuous degree: prayers like St Patrick's Breastplate are as much magical incantations for protection against demons as prayers in the normally accepted sense of the term. The parallels are rich and thought-provoking, but to pursue them in any depth would require another essay.

Is 4Q525 a Qumran Sectarian Document?

Jacqueline C.R. de Roo

Introduction

The document 4Q525, also known as 4QBeat, has evoked the interest of several scholars. This is mainly due to the collection of beatitudes in frag. 2 which immediately call to mind the series of makarisms found in the Gospels (Mt. 5.3-12; Lk. 6.20-23). Most studies on 4Q525 have only focused on its beatitudes and compared them to the Matthean makarisms. This article will look at 4Q525 as a whole and try to place it in its proper context, discussing the similarities and differences between 4Q525 and traditional wisdom literature. Moreover, I will attempt to answer an important question which has not yet been addressed by scholars: Is 4Q525 a Qumran sectarian document? In other words, was 4Q525 composed by a member of the Qumran community?[1]

The Similarity of 4Q525 to Traditional Jewish Wisdom Literature

When we read the opening section of 4Q525 we immediately notice a striking resemblance to Jewish wisdom literature. In frag. 1 someone is said to have spoken 'in the wisdom God gave him'. The words which follow, 'to know wisdom and discipline, to understand...',

---

1. Recently some scholars have challenged the concept of a 'Qumran community'. They have suggested that the ideas prevalent in Qumran literature may well have been widespread within Judaism of the time and were in all likelihood not only characteristic of a small esoteric group living at Khirbet Qumran in isolation from their fellow-Jews. In this article the expression 'Qumran community' refers not only to people living at Khirbet Qumran, but also to those who lived elsewhere and abided by the Qumranites' teachings and lifestyle.

recall the beginning of Proverbs 1.[2] In Prov. 1.7 'the fear of the Lord' is said to be 'the beginning of wisdom' (see also Prov. 9.10). It is possible that this thematic statement was also a part of the beginning of 4Q525. We do not know this for sure, because 4Q525 is somewhat fragmentary. However, it is quite likely for two reasons. First, as Puech observed, the beginning of 4Q525 strongly recalls the beginning of Proverbs. Secondly, frag. 4 of 4Q525 speaks of the fear of the Lord while connecting it to wisdom. '[Those] who fear God keep its ways...' (l. 8), that is, wisdom's ways. The Hebrew literally says '*her* ways' (דרכ'ה). This means that only a singular feminine noun can be its antecedent: it must refer back to 'wisdom' (חוכמה) in l. 7. So, as in Proverbs, keeping wisdom's ways is seen as the result of fearing God. Another wisdom book which makes the same connection between wisdom and fearing God is Ben Sira. According to Ben Sira 'the root (or beginning) of wisdom is the fear of the Lord' (1.14, 20).[3]

Both the style and the content of 4Q525 remind us of Proverbs and even more of Ben Sira. Its phrases, expressions, and ideas bring to mind these two wisdom books. Numerous parallels in addition to the similarities described above could be mentioned. I will limit discussion to the most important ones.

(1) As in Proverbs and Ben Sira 'the pursuit of wisdom (חוכמה)' is a main emphasis in 4Q525. 'Blessed is the man who attains wisdom' (frag. 2, col. ii, l. 2, compare in particular with Prov. 3.13 and Sir. 14.20, but also with Prov. 4.5, 7; 8.11; 15.33; Sir. 1.14; 25.10; 45.26). The third singular feminine suffix which is present throughout the list of beatitudes undoubtedly stands for the feminine singular noun 'wisdom' (חוכמה) mentioned in l. 3. However, it could refer to 'the law of the Most High (תורת עליון)' in l. 4 as well, because תורה is also

---

2. É. Puech, '4Q525 et les péricopes des béatitudes en Ben Sira et Matthieu', *RB* 98 (1991), p. 83.

3. Ben Sira dates from ca. 180 BCE. See C.A. Evans, *Noncanonical Writings and New Testament Interpretation* (Peabody, MA: Hendrickson, 1992), p. 13. On the basis of archaeological, palaeographic, and literary evidence most scholars have come to the conclusion that the Qumran sect was formed during approximately this time period, probably mid second century BCE. See L.H. Schiffman, *Reclaiming the Dead Sea Scrolls* (Garden City, NY: Doubleday, 2nd edn, 1995 [1994]), pp. 90-91. Similarities with Proverbs are found in almost every part of Ben Sira. Since Ben Sira is later, these similarities strongly suggest a dependence on Proverbs. See A.A. Di Lella, *The Wisdom of Ben Sira* (AB, 39; Garden City, NY: Doubleday, 1987), p. 43.

a feminine singular noun.[4] This ambiguity and the juxtaposition of 'attaining wisdom' and 'walking in the law of the Most High' as two identical things suggest that the identity of wisdom and the law is presupposed. This identification is already present in a subtle way in Prov. 7.1-4. However, it is more apparent in Sir. 24.22-23.[5] It is also striking that the Greek equivalent of the Hebrew expression תורת עליון (frag. 2, col. ii, l. 4), that is, νόμος ὕψιστος, occurs seven times in Ben Sira,[6] whereas we do not find it anywhere else in the Apocrypha, nor in the Old Testament. Parts of the Hebrew text of Ben Sira have been found in the Cairo Geniza. The Hebrew phrase תורת עליון is fully present in 49.4 and has been partially preserved in 41.8.[7] Moreover, like 4Q525, Ben Sira has a whole list of beatitudes which speaks of the pursuit of wisdom (14.20-27).[8]

(2) The pre-eminence of wisdom over gold, silver, and precious jewels is stressed both in 4Q525 and in Proverbs. In Prov. 3.13-15 the man who finds wisdom is called happy, because its gain is better than silver, gold, or jewels. Nothing a person can desire compares with wisdom. The expression שוה ב 'to compare with' in Prov. 3.15 is also found in 4Q525 frag. 2, col. iii, l. 1. This line is very fragmentary, but context (frag. 2, col. iii, ll. 1-7) suggests that it too may have been a reference to the incomparable nature of wisdom. In 4Q525 the pre-eminence of wisdom over silver, gold, and jewels is stressed in a slightly different way than in Proverbs: it is impossible to obtain wisdom with these precious objects.

(3) The contrast between sincerity and deceitfulness occurs in 4Q525, as well as in Proverbs and Ben Sira. Prov. 12.5-6, 17, 19-20 and 14.8 speak of the deceit (מרמה) which resides in the heart of wicked men and compare it to the sincerity of the righteous. Likewise, 4Q525 frag. 2, col. ii, l. 3 refers to deceit (מרמה) found in the heart and contrasts it with seeking wisdom with pure hands, that is, in all

4.   J.A. Fitzmyer, 'A Palestinian Collection of Beatitudes', in F. Van Segbroeck *et al.* (eds.), *The Four Gospels* (Festschrift Frans Neirynck; 4 vols.; Leuven: Peeters/Leuven University Press, 1992), II, p. 513.

5.   B.T. Viviano, 'Eight Beatitudes at Qumran and in Matthew?', *SEA* 58 (1993), p. 77.

6.   See Sir. 9.15; 19.17; 23.23; 24.23; 39.1; 42.2; 44.20.

7.   I. Lévi, *The Hebrew Text of the Book of Ecclesiasticus* (Semitic Studies Series, 3; Leiden: Brill, 1904), pp. 51, 69.

8.   See also discussion above.

sincerity. Both in Sir. 1.28-29 and in 4Q525 frag. 2, col. ii, l. 3 there is a warning against hypocrisy. Ben Sira tells his readers not to approach God with a divided heart and not to be a hypocrite in men's sight. The author of 4Q525 warns against searching wisdom with a deceitful heart.

(4) Both in Proverbs and 4Q525 folly is contrasted to wisdom and prudence. In Prov. 14.18 the wisdom (חכמה) of the prudent (ערום) is described as the opposite of the folly (אולת) of fools. Likewise, in 4Q525 those who burst out on the paths of folly (אולת) are contrasted with those rejoicing in wisdom (חכמה, frag. 2, col. ii, ll. 2-3) and the prudent (ערומים) who recognize wisdom's (חכמה) ways (frag. 4, l. 11).

(5) The idea of a wholesome tongue versus a perverse tongue is found in Proverbs and Ben Sira, as well as in 4Q525. Wise, wholesome words will result in good things. According to Prov. 21.23 he who guards his tongue keeps himself out of trouble. Ben Sira tells us that kind words multiply friends (6.5). The author of 4Q525 calls the person who speaks with a clean heart blessed (frag. 2, col. ii, l. 1). Foolish, perverse words, on the other hand, will cause trouble. It results in calamity (Prov. 17.20), shame, condemnation (Sir. 5.14), destruction (22.27), or ensnarement (Sir. 28.26; 4Q525 frag. 14, col. ii, l. 27). Ben Sira stresses the tendency of humans to sin with their tongue. In 19.16 he wonders: 'Who has never sinned with his tongue?' It is so easy to make a slip of the tongue without intending it. There are even more who have fallen by misuse of the tongue than by the edge of the sword (28.18). This proneness in humans to use their tongue unwisely is also implied in 4Q525. In frag. 14, col. ii, ll. 18-28 the speaker finds it necessary to warn even a discerning person (l. 18) against sinning in speech (compare also 4Q525 frag. 2, col. ii, l. 1; frag. 14, col. ii, ll. 18-28 with Prov. 10.20, 31-32; 12.18-19; 15.2, 4; 18.21; 31.26; Sir. 5.13; 19.6; 20.18; 51.2-6).

(6) Humility is viewed as a quality which goes hand in hand with fearing God in Proverbs, Ben Sira and 4Q525. In Prov. 22.4 riches, honor, and life are the result of both humility and fearing God. According to Ben Sira those who fear the Lord will humble themselves before him (2.17). Likewise, in 4Q525 loving God means showing humility (frag. 4, l. 12; see also frag. 2, col. ii, l. 6).

Besides the parallels described above there are larger conceptual similarities between Proverbs, Ben Sira, and 4Q525. Each of these wisdom documents explains not only how, but also why one should lead a wise life. All three refer to the consequences of one's behavior both in the present and in the end-time. 4Q525 emphasizes the latter in particular. This eschatological orientation is already present in the beatitudes to which I turn now.

In frag. 2, col. ii of 4Q525 we find five beatitudes.[9] This collection of beatitudes has an important function within the document. Spicq makes the interesting comment that 'the originality of the Old Testament is to frame exhortations to virtue in makarisms'.[10] Likewise, the Qumran beatitudes should be read as exhortations. They all exhort the reader to live a wise life, that is, a life in accordance with the commandments of the Lord. It is important to realize that these exhortations also imply a warning. Each beatitude begins by declaring a person blessed because that person does good. It continues by calling this same person blessed because of not doing evil. An example of this is 'Blessed are those who *hold fast to* its (that is, wisdom's or the law's) statutes and *do not hold fast to* the ways of injustice' (frag. 2, col. ii, ll. 1-2). So there is an exhortation to do good, but there is also a warning not to do evil.

What are the consequences of living wisely or foolishly according to the author of 4Q525? Do they take place in the present as the logical result of one's actions or in the end time as a reward or punishment from God? Does the answer in 4Q525 to this question differ from the one found in traditional Jewish wisdom literature?

4Q525 contains practical advice on how to do well in life. Fragment 14, col. ii, ll. 18-28 is somewhat fragmentary; nevertheless, it is fairly clear that the speaker in this section refers to the unpleasant moments in life which a word spoken in haste may cause. An example of this is: 'Be very careful of causing offense with your tongue [...] lest you be entrapped by your own lips' (ll. 26-27).

9.   Part of the first beatitude has been reconstructed by Puech, '4Q525', as follows: '[Blessed is the one who speaks the truth] with a pure heart and does not slander with his tongue'. His reconstruction seems a quite plausible one to me. First, the remaining words strongly recall Ps. 15.2-3. Secondly, his reconstruction matches the antithetical parallel which follows (pp. 88-89). Whenever there is a reference in the rest of this article to the first beatitude of 4Q525, it will be to the one reconstructed by Puech.

10.   C. Spicq, 'Μακάριος', *Theological Lexicon of the New Testament* (3 vols.; trans. and ed. J.D. Ernest; Peabody, MA: Hendrickson, 1994 [1978]), II, p. 435. Spicq is referring to the LXX. Therefore, he uses the term 'makarisms'.

4Q525 resembles traditional wisdom literature in this regard. Wisdom books like Proverbs and Ben Sira contain many practical instructions for successful living. They deal 'in generalities: (...) well-doing does generally tend toward well-being'.[11] Often the author simply points to the logical result of one's actions as these examples illustrate:

> Without counsel plans go wrong, but with many advisers they succeed (Prov. 15.22).
> If you have found honey, eat only enough for you, lest you be sated with it and vomit it (Prov. 25.16).
> Bring not everyone into your house, because many are the wounds inflicted by the slanderer (Sir. 11.29).

However, 4Q525 also speaks of the final outcome of one's actions. At first sight the Qumran beatitudes only seem to speak of the blessings which rest upon those who lead a wise life. However, by implication their antithetical parallels also speak of the curses which are upon those who lead a foolish life. The implicit warning in the Qumran beatitudes not to lead an unwise and wicked life is made explicit in context. For here a vivid description of the day of judgment is presented to the reader. This section is very fragmentary, but there are enough clues given to suggest this. Fragment 15 talks about 'darkness (אופל)', 'eternal curses (אררות נצח)', 'flame[s of] death (מות [י] רשפ)' which fly about, 'flaming brimstone (להבי גופ[ר]ית)' and 'perdition (שחת)'. Fragment 22 speaks of 'the depths of the pit (ירכתי בור)' and 'the fiery furnace (כור חרון)'. There are references in frag. 21 to 'those cursed of God con[tinually...] (זעומי אלוהים תמ[יד)', 'dark places (מן]חשכים)' and the gathering of wrath (ת]קבץ חרון). Whose wrath is spoken of here? In the Qumran sectarian documents the word חרון sometimes refers to God's wrath (for example CD 10.9).[12] The phrase 'on the day designated (וביום נחרצה)' in frag. 22 strongly suggests that the author of 4Q525 is speaking of the day of God's wrath. This section of 4Q525 has many affinities with the book of Joel which is highly eschatological in nature. Like 4Q525 it speaks of the day on which God is going to pour out his wrath and bring judgment. It will be 'a

---

11. D. Kidner, *The Wisdom of Proverbs, Job, and Ecclesiastes* (Downers Grove: Inter-Varsity Press, 1985), p. 119. Kidner only refers to Proverbs, not to Ben Sira.

12. If 4Q525 is Qumran sectarian, which I believe it is (see discussion below), this would lend support to the idea that חרון could refer to God's wrath in 4Q525 as well.

day (יום) of darkness (חשך)' (Joel 2.2; compare 4Q525 frag. 15, l. 6; frag. 21, l. 1; frag. 22, l. 2 where יום and חשך also occur, though not combined). Like 4Q525, Joel contains numerous expressions of fire-imagery to depict this awesome day (compare Joel 1.19; 2.3, 5 with 4Q525 frag. 15, ll. 3, 5-6; frag. 22, l. 4).

Are there references in traditional Jewish wisdom literature to the eschatological destiny of the wise and foolish? Yes, there are. Wisdom books like Proverbs and Ben Sira deal not only 'in generalities', but also 'in ultimates'.[13] Both books contain references to the final out-come of one's behavior in the end-time. Even the author of Proverbs speaks of the day of judgment, though in the only reference he does not depict it graphically like 4Q525. 'Riches do not profit in *the day of wrath*, but righteousness delivers from death' (Prov. 11.4).[14] Ben Sira's description of the day of judgment resembles somewhat more the one found in 4Q525. As in 4Q525 vivid fire-imagery is used. It is very likely that the author of 4Q525 wanted to convey a similar mes-sage to his readers as Ben Sira in 5.7-8:

> Delay not your conversion to the Lord; put it not off from day to day—
> For suddenly *His wrath flames forth*; at *the time of vengeance you will be destroyed*. Rely not upon deceitful wealth; it will be no help *on the day of wrath*.[15]

Ben Sira 7.16-17, 16.18, 21.9-10, and 36.7-8 might contain an implicit reference to the day of God's wrath, though this is not always clear from context. There is only one more explicit reference to the day of judgment in Ben Sira, that is, in 18.24. Here also a reminder of the approach of this day is given in order to motivate obedience to God's commandments.[16] However, its description is not graphic. The only *graphic* depiction of the day of judgment in Ben Sira is found in 5.7-8 and it is not very elaborate like in 4Q525. If we consider how very small 4Q525 is in comparison to Ben Sira, we realize that its concentration of eschatological vocabulary and descriptions is much higher.

---

13. Kidner, *Wisdom of Proverbs*, pp. 118-19. Again, Kidner does not speak about Ben Sira in particular.

14. J.G. Gammie, 'Spacial and Ethical Dualism in Jewish Wisdom and Apocalyptic Literature', *JBL* 93 (1974), p. 378.

15. See also Sir. 18.24.

16. Occasionally Ben Sira reminds his readers of death in order to motivate them to live in accordance with God's commandments (8.7; 14.12-17; 28.6).

There is a striking resemblance between 4Q525 and traditional Jewish wisdom books such as Proverbs and Ben Sira. As in these wisdom books the concept of wisdom, in particular the close connection between being wise and fearing God, is central in 4Q525. Also, humility is seen as an important virtue in honoring and loving God. The contrasts between wisdom and folly, sincerity and deceitfulness, and a wholesome tongue and a perverse tongue occur in all three documents. Moreover, all three point to the consequences of one's behavior both in the present and in the end-time. In some respects 4Q525 resembles more Ben Sira than Proverbs. The expression 'the law of the Most High' occurs both in 4Q525 and in Ben Sira, whereas we do not find it anywhere else in the Apocrypha, nor in the Old Testament. Moreover, like 4Q525 Ben Sira contains a graphic depiction of the end-time which is lacking in Proverbs. However, the concentration of eschatological vocabulary and descriptions is much higher in 4Q525 than in Ben Sira. Nevertheless, 4Q525 contains enough elements similar to those found in traditional wisdom literature to be called a wisdom document.

The Distinctive Qumran Sectarian Elements of 4Q525

I have looked at the many similarities in style and content between 4Q525 and traditional Jewish wisdom books such as Proverbs and Ben Sira. However, it has been shown that 4Q525 also differed from these books: its high concentration of eschatological elements is not typical of traditional Jewish wisdom literature. As will be shown, 4Q525 deviates from traditional Jewish wisdom literature in more ways. This could be a hint that it is sectarian. In order to be able to interpret the content of 4Q525 properly it is necessary to determine whether this document is distinctively Qumranian. Was it composed by members of the sect themselves or was it written elsewhere and brought to Qumran? The orthography of 4Q525 is similar to the one used in other Qumran sectarian documents. Moreover, some important verbal and conceptual elements in 4Q525 suggest that it is Qumranian. These will be discussed below when I will place 4Q525 in the thought-world of Qumran.

a. *The orthography of 4Q525*
In his article on the orthography and language of the Dead Sea Scrolls, E. Tov divides the Scrolls into two major groups. The spelling convention of one group very closely resembles that of the Masoretic text

and it consists primarily of biblical scrolls. It is relatively defective, that is, the shorter spelling for a particular word will be used. For example, the negative particle is spelled לא instead of לוא.

The other group is characterized by 'a special system of orthography and by peculiar grammatical forms'. These scrolls' orthography is relatively full. This means that many words are lengthened by the addition of an א, ה, or ו. For example, the second masculine singular suffix is written כה- instead of ך-. Tov argues that they were all either copied or written at Qumran.[17] Their spelling convention and language are typically Qumranian.[18]

It is clear that 4Q525 belongs to this latter group. For instance, the negative particle לא, the masculine singular noun כל, and the second masculine plural suffix כם- are always written full in 4Q525 (לוא instead of לא, כול instead of כל, כמה- instead of כם-). The longer form of the second masculine singular suffix, that is, כה-, occurs thirty one times in 4Q525. The shorter form ך-, on the other hand, occurs only three times (frag. 14, col. ii, ll. 4, 7, 13). Many other words are written full in 4Q525. These include: אלוהים instead of אלהים (for example frag. 1, l. 1; frag. 4, l. 8), מואדה instead of מאד (frag. 14, col. ii, ll. 24, 26), אורחות instead of ארחות (frag. 15, l. 8). The only word which is always written defectively in 4Q525, even though the full form is much more often used in Qumran sectarian documents, is the particle כי. However, Tov warns us that 'in only a few cases do all the features appear together in one scroll, such as 4Q174'. We should not forget that the Scrolls were not all written or copied by the same scribe. Although the Qumran scribes were 'working within a specific tradition', they 'also retained a certain individuality'. Therefore, we cannot expect all Qumran documents to have exactly the same features.[19]

As demonstrated above, 4Q525 is written in the so-called 'Qumran orthography'.[20] However, this does not prove that 4Q525 was composed by a person belonging to the Qumran community. The so-called

17. E. Tov, 'The Orthography and Language of the Hebrew Scrolls Found at Qumran and the Origin of these Scrolls', *Textus* 13 (1986), pp. 31-57.

18. Even though he sees this system as typically Qumranian, Tov ('The Orthography') does not suggest that it is unique to Qumran. It is only for convenience that he describes it as such. For besides the Qumran scrolls no other manuscripts have been found which employ the same system. See p. 38.

19. Tov, 'The Orthography', p. 36.

20. For the use of this expression, see Tov, 'The Orthography', p. 38.

'Qumran orthography' is characteristic of the Qumran documents, but it may not be unique to Qumran. It is true that no documents of the same time period have been found which contain the same spelling convention. However, this does not prove that it was not employed by other groups as well. It is difficult to know, because not many documents of this time period have been discovered.[21] The document 4Q525 could simply have been copied by a scribe at Qumran like some of the biblical and apocryphal material, which has also been written in the 'Qumran orthography'. It may be concluded that the orthography of 4Q525 leaves the possibility open that it is a Qumran sectarian document, that is, composed by a person of the Qumran community, though on its own the orthography is not enough evidence to prove this.

b. *The Use of Vocabulary in 4Q525*

The use of vocabulary in 4Q525 strongly suggests that it is a Qumran sectarian document. Several words are employed in this work which have a Qumranian flavor to them. They are not necessarily unique to Qumran, but they occur with lesser frequency in the Old Testament. Moreover, several of them are key words in Qumran theology.[22]

---

21. Tov, 'The Orthography', p. 38.

22. The ideal would be to compare 4Q525 to Hebrew wisdom literature of the same time period, both Qumranian and non-Qumranian. However, this is impossible. The only contemporary Hebrew wisdom literature was found at Qumran. Most of this material has been published relatively lately. Not much of it has been labelled as distinctively Qumranian. One of the reasons is that few scholars have worked on it. Lacking the ideal material for comparison, I have decided to compare the vocabulary of 4Q525 to that of the five largest and virtually undisputed Qumran sectarian documents (the Community Rule, the Damascus Document, the Thanksgiving Hymns, the War Scroll, the Pesher Habakkuk) and to the Old Testament. It is important to keep in mind that the Old Testament is at least six times, if not seven times, larger than these five Qumran sectarian documents together. Of course, 4Q525 is quite small and fragmentary. In order to maintain a 'safe' method of comparison, I have only selected those words as typically Qumranian which occur more often in this small body of Qumranian manuscripts than in the Old Testament. In other words, my method of comparison does not entirely depend on the *percentage* of frequency. Moreover, unlike the Old Testament, the Qumran material used for comparison does not contain any documents belonging to wisdom literature. Therefore, any remarkable similarity in vocabulary between 4Q525 and the five selected Qumran documents is not simply due to a similarity in genre of literature.

(1) The word עולה (frag. 2, col. ii, ll. 2, 7; frag. 4, l. 10; frag. 10, l. 4)[23] meaning 'injustice, unrighteousness, wrong' is much more often used in Qumran sectarian documents than in the Old Testament.[24] Moreover, the particular expression דרכי עולה 'the ways of injustice' (frag. 2, col. ii, l. 2) never occurs in the Old Testament. However, we do encounter a very similar expression in the Thanksgiving Hymns: דרך עולה 'the way of injustice' (6.26). עולה is an important word at Qumran. The spirit belonging to the lot of Belial is characterized as a רוח עולה 'spirit of injustice' (1QS 4.9, 20). The use of the word עולה is often set in opposition to words for truth and righteousness (1QS 4.17, 19, 20, 24; 10.20; 1QH 19.26). God hates עולה forever (1QH 6.25). Therefore, at the appointed time he will extinguish it (1QS 4.20-23).

(2) The word ענוה meaning 'humility' is used four times in 4Q525 (frag. 2, col. ii, l. 6; frags. 8–9, l. 4; frag. 14, col. ii, l. 20; frag. 26, l. 2).[25] It occurs only seven times in the whole Old Testament. In the Community Rule alone ענוה is used eight times.[26] Moreover, the particular idiom בענות נפשו 'in the humility of his soul' which we find in 4Q525 (frag. 2, col. ii, l. 6) also occurs in 1QS 3.8, whereas it is not found in the Old Testament.

In the Qumran sectarian documents 'humility' functions as an important theological concept. In 1QS 4.3 humility is the first quality mentioned of the spirit of light. Since the Qumranites saw themselves as representing the lot of the spirit of light, they considered humility to be one of the essential characteristics of the *Yaḥad*, that is, the Qumran community (1QS 2.24). Moreover, the Qumranites stressed the importance of humility in their doctrine of salvation. Only the sins of those who show humility will be covered (1QS 3.8).[27]

23. Two of the four references are reconstructed.

24. The word עולה occurs only 29 times in the Old Testament. In the Thanksgiving Hymns and the Community Rule together it is used more often (21 times in 1QH and 10 times in 1QS), despite their much smaller size.

25. The last reference is a reconstruction.

26. ענוה does not occur as often in the other main Qumran documents. We encounter it only once in the Thanksgiving Hymns and in the Damascus Document. The War Scroll and the Pesher Habakkuk do not mention the word ענוה. However, if we consider how large the size of the Old Testament is in comparison to 1QS, 1QH, 1QM, CD, and 1QpHab together, we realize that the occurrence of ענוה is relatively more frequent in the Qumran documents.

27. I do not believe that בענות נפשו means 'in the distress of his soul', although this would make a nice parallel to the other references to trial and distress in the same

(3) Besides the word ענוה the Qumranites used other expressions in their documents to convey the notion of humility. The verb צנע is an example which is normally translated as 'to be modest, to be humble'.[28] It is encountered in 4Q525 frag. 4, l. 12 as well as three times in the Manual of Discipline (4.5; 5.4; 8.2). In the Old Testament צנע occurs only once (Mic. 6.8).

(4) The document 4Q525 contains the expression הלך תמים 'to walk in perfection, to walk blamelessly' (frag. 4, l. 10), which is more often used in the Qumran sectarian documents than in the Old Testament. In the whole Old Testament it occurs only four times, whereas in a relatively small document like the Community Rule alone we encounter it nine times. There are important theological connotations attached to the phrase הלך תמים. 'The men of God's lot' are characterized as those 'who walk perfectly in all his ways' (1QS 2.2). However, the Qumranites realized fully that even in their holy community a perfect walk of life was an ideal to strive for, rather than a reality. They were very aware of the sinful nature of *every* human being, including those belonging to God's lot. Therefore, 'the *Yahad* of holiness, those who walked perfectly (הלך תמים) as he commanded', at times still needed to take disciplinary actions against those members within their own community who did not live up to this ideal (1QS 8.20ff.). Sometimes the transgressor was 'expelled from the Council of the *Yahad*' forever (1QS 8.22, 23). Nevertheless, the Qumranites realized that even a genuine member of their community could fall into sin. In such a case he was not allowed to 'touch the pure meal of the men of holiness or know anything of their counsel until his deeds (were) purified from all injustice and he (walked) perfectly (תמים הלך) again'. Afterwards he was readmitted (1QS 8.17-19).

(5) The word תוכחה 'chastisement' which is found in 4Q525 (frag. 4, l. 9) occurs at least nine times in the principal Qumran sectarian

---

sentence (frag. 2, col. ii, l. 5). First, the word ענות never occurs in 4Q525 whereas ענוה at least two other times. Moreover, 4Q525 also contains another word related to humility, צנע 'to be humble' (frag. 4, l. 12). Humility is an important theme in this document. Secondly, the expression 'in the distress of his soul' is not found in Qumran literature, nor in the Old Testament. In contrast, the idiom 'in the humility of his soul' occurs in 1QS 3.8. Thirdly, in 1QH 4.22 a close connection between distress and humility is made. Distress is viewed as a chastisement from God to make a person humble. The same is done in the fifth Qumran beatitude.

28. BDB, p. 857.

documents (6 times in the Thanksgiving Hymns; 3 times in the Pesher Habakkuk). In the Old Testament it is used only four times. The speaker of the Thanksgiving Hymns often uses תוכחה to refer to divine chastisement. According to Qumran theology God's chastisements were sanctifying. It is 'in the mystery of his wisdom' that God chastises (יכה) his people for their own good, because in the end his chastisement (תוכחה) will bring 'joy and gladness' (1QH 17.24). Moreover, it is an expression of his righteousness (1QH 17.33).[29]

(6) The phrase חמת תנינים 'poison of snakes' occurs in 4Q525 (frag. 15, l. 4). This expression is found only one time in the Old Testament (Deut. 32.33) whereas it is used at least four times in the Qumran sectarian documents.[30]

(7) The expression אבני חפץ 'stones of desire, precious stones' is found in 4Q525 (frag. 2, col. iii, l. 3). It is used only once in the Old Testament (Isa. 54.12) whereas it occurs four times in the War Scroll alone.[31]

To conclude, the terms עולה 'injustice', ענוה 'humility', צנע 'to be humble', הלך תמים 'to walk perfectly', תוכחה 'chastisement', חמת תנינים 'poison of snakes', and אבני חפץ 'stones of desire' which are found in 4Q525 all occur with more frequency in the Qumran sectarian documents than in the Old Testament. Also, the particular phrase דרכ(י) עולה 'the way(s) of injustice' and the idiomatic expression בענות נפשו 'in the humility of his soul' are not used in the Old Testament at all, but they do occur in 4Q525, as well as in the Qumran sectarian documents. Moreover, many of these words and phrases represent important concepts in Qumran thought. This strongly suggests that 4Q525 is a Qumran sectarian document.

c. *The Teachings Found in 4Q525*

In the previous section I have classified 4Q525 as a Qumran sectarian document on the basis of typical Qumranian words and expressions it contains.[32] The next question which comes to mind is: How does 4Q525 fit into the thought-world of Qumran? In this section I will

---

29. See also discussion below.

30. 1QH 13.10, 27; CD 8.9; 19.22. To be sure, the last two references are quotations of Deut. 32.33.

31. The Community Rule, the Thanksgiving Hymns, the Damascus Document, and the Pesher Habakkuk do not contain the phrase אבני חפץ.

32. I do not mean to suggest that they are unique to Qumran.

show how the teachings found in 4Q525 are compatible with the Qumran doctrines on major issues like human nature, election and responsibility, and the end-time.

1. *To whom is the warning in 4Q525 addressed?* The warning in 4Q525 against leading a sinful life is not directed in particular to the foolish or wicked. In frag. 14 the speaker tells 'the discerning one' to listen (1. 18) and warns him not to use his tongue unwisely by complaining too soon (1. 23) or by offending someone (1. 26).[33] Related to this is the interesting paradox found in frag. 16: not those who lack understanding, but 'the discerning ones' are led astray (1. 3). In traditional Jewish wisdom literature, on the other hand, it is always the naive, the foolish, who are misguided by the wicked. They are among the ones who are told to listen and who receive a warning as these few examples illustrate:

> I saw among *the naive* (...) a young man *lacking sense* (...) and, behold, a woman comes to meet him, dressed as a harlot (...) with her flattering lips *she seduces him*. Suddenly he follows her... (Prov. 7.7-22).
> The idols of the heathen have become (...) *a snare* to the feet of *the foolish* (Wis. 14.11).
> O *naive ones*, discern prudence; And, O *fools*, discern wisdom, *listen*, for I shall speak noble things (Prov. 8.5, 6).

On this point 4Q525 surely deviates from traditional Jewish wisdom literature, but not from Qumran sectarian literature, as these quotations demonstrate:

> And now, *listen, all you who know righteousness*, and understand the works of God (CD 1.1).
> *Listen, O wise men* (חכמים), meditate upon knowledge (...) Be of steadfast mind [...] Increase prudence (...) O *righteous men* (צדיקים), put away iniquity! Hold fast [to the Covenant], *all you perfect of way* (וכול תמימי דרך), 1QH 9.35-36).

Notice the paradox in the last quotation. Why would righteous men need to put away iniquity? This is not merely sarcasm, though it is difficult to miss the irony. In order to be able to answer the question

---

33. In a later section of my paper I try to show that the second person singular in frag. 14 is used generically as it is in the rest of the document. In other words, a group of people is addressed instead of a specific individual.

we need to determine who the wise, the righteous, and the perfect of way are. I believe that these three expressions all refer to the same group of people, that is, to the men of God's lot, the Qumran community. First, CD 6.2-5 speaks of 'the discerning ones (נבונים) from Aaron' and 'the wise (חכמים) from Israel' who 'dug the well'. The well symbolizes the Law[34] and the diggers are 'the converts of Israel who went out of the land of Judah to sojourn in the land of Damascus'. In the Damascus Documents the name 'Damascus' is used as a symbol for Qumran.[35] So 'the wise' and 'the discerning ones' represent the Qumran community. Secondly, in 1QS 2.2 it is 'the men of the lot of God' who are characterized as those 'who walk perfectly in all his ways (ההולכים תמים בכול דרכיו)'.[36] Thirdly, those who belong to the lot of God are described as 'the sons of righteousness (בני צדק)' (1QS 3.20-22).[37] 'All the sons of righteousness' are led astray by 'the Angel of Darkness' (1QS 3.22). This explains why 'the righteous men' in 1QH 9.36 are told to 'put away iniquity'. It also clarifies why 'the discerning men' in 4Q525 frag. 16, l. 3 are led astray.

Interestingly, another wisdom fragment found at Qumran, 4Q184, also known as 'The Wiles of the Wicked Woman', speaks of a harlot who attempts to lead astray 'upright men' (l. 14). It is 'the meek' whom she tries to make rebel against God (l. 16). Her goal is to keep 'the righteous chosen ones' from obeying God's commandments (ll. 14, 15). Harrington has argued that there is nothing 'distinctively Qumranian' about 4Q184. According to him it could have been composed somewhere else.[38] Harrington has overlooked an important

---

34. It is interesting that 'the wise (חכמים)' are digging the well which represents 'the Law (תורה)', because in 4Q525 there is also a close connection between wisdom and the law (see discussion above).

35. Schiffman (*Reclaiming the Dead Sea Scrolls*, pp. 93-94) has convincingly argued for this.

36. Notice the resemblance in wording between 'all you perfect of way' and 'who walk perfectly in all his ways'.

37. Notice the resemblance in wording between 'the righteous ones' and 'the sons of righteousness'.

38. D.J. Harrington, 'Wisdom at Qumran', in E. Ulrich and J.C. VanderKam (eds.), *The Community of the Renewed Covenant: The Notre Dame Symposium on the Dead Sea Scrolls* (Notre Dame: University of Notre Dame Press, 1994), p. 138. In a later work Harrington seems to connect 4Q184 more closely to the Qumran community when he states: 'If this text is not clearly sectarian, at least its content and terminology would have appealed to and have been readily appropriated by the

element in this document. The ones who are seduced by the harlot are 'the righteous chosen ones' (l. 14), those already walking in 'the ways of righteousness' (l. 16).[39] It is typical for Qumran only to instruct, warn and reprove those who belong to the righteous ones, that is, the people of their community. This Qumranian peculiarity can be found in 4Q525, 4Q184, as well as in the undisputed Qumran sectarian documents. The Master (משכיל), one of the leaders at Qumran, is not supposed to 'rebuke the men of the Pit (אנשי השחת) nor dispute with them' (1QS 9.16). The Qumranites did rebuke their own people, as passages like 1QS 5.24–6.1, 6.24–7.25, and 4Q477 make evident.[40] The Master is commanded to 'conceal the teaching of the Law from men of injustice'. He should only instruct 'those who have chosen the Way' (1QS 9.17-18). The Qumranites did not feel responsible for the souls of people outside their community. It is possible that in the beginning stage of the sect the Qumranites were still concerned about outsiders and tried to have them join their group.[41] However, when we read the Qumran sectarian documents we do not receive the impression that the Qumranites saw it as their duty to be an 'outreach' to those who did not belong to their sect. Lacking this sense of obligation, they withdrew themselves from society and lived in the wilderness.

Likewise, the addressees in frags. 8–9, l. 3 'Pay attention to me, all

Qumran sectarians'; see D.J. Harrington, *Wisdom Texts from Qumran* (London: Routledge, 1996), p. 34.

39. This interesting feature has already been observed by Moore who likewise believes that 4Q184 is Qumran sectarian. Moore also makes the important connection between 4Q184 and 1QS 3.24. See R.D. Moore, 'Personification of the Seduction of Evil: "The Wiles of the Wicked Woman"', *RevQ* 10 (1981), p. 518.

40. These passages are discussed in more depth below.

41. The typical sectarian document 4QMMT is directed to outsiders who are asked in a gentle manner to turn from their wrong path and adhere to the law of God as interpreted by the Qumran community. However, this letter was very likely written in the beginning stage of the sect when the Qumranites had not yet developed a 'hatred for outsiders'. Over time they developed 'the sectarian mentality of the despised, the rejected, the abandoned; so they began to look upon themselves as the true Israel and despise all others'. Moreover, the outsiders addressed in the letter might have belonged, at one time, to their own group. This would explain the Qumranites' sense of responsibility for them. For an overview on this theory, see L.H. Schiffman, 'The Sadducean Origins of the Dead Sea Scrolls Sect', in H. Shanks (ed.), *Understanding the Dead Sea Scrolls* (New York: Random House, 1992), pp. 35-49. See also L.H. Schiffman, 'The New Halakhic Letter and the Origins of the Dead Sea Sect', *BA* 53 (1990), pp. 64-73.

you sons of…' (…שיבו לי כול בני[ק[ה])[42] must be the Qumranites. The most common address in Proverbs and Ben Sira is 'son' or 'sons'.[43] Generally speaking it is the young man without much life-experience who is addressed. He is not necessarily a fool, but neither has he yet proven to be wise. He is still at a stage where he needs to make a choice between leading a wise or foolish life. His lack of experience and youthful lusts could lead to foolishness.[44] In 4Q525 the word 'sons' must have been modified by a noun.[45] Unfortunately the text is so fragmentary that we do not know which noun, but it may have said 'all you sons of righteousness' (cf. 1QS 3.20, 22) or 'all you sons of light' (cf. 1QS 1.9) or 'all you sons of truth' (cf. 1QS 4.5). Unlike the young man in Proverbs and Ben Sira, these 'sons' belonging to the lot of God have already made a choice in life. They chose to separate themselves from the other Israelites in order to join the Qumran community.

2. *A warning to live as God's chosen ones: Be who you are!* In frag. 4 of 4Q525 a key warning is given under which all other warnings found in the document[46] could be categorized: '[…Do not] forsake (עזב) […] your [inheritan]ce (נחלה) or your lot (גורל) to foreigners' (l. 7). This command reminds us of a similar one given in the Old Testament. In Numbers 36 the tribes of Israel are commanded to each hold to its own inheritance. They are not supposed to transfer lots, that is, pieces of land, to other tribes (see in particular vv. 7, 9, 12). Is this also the meaning of the statement in our text? This is doubtful. A specific commandment like not selling a piece of land to an outsider would be somewhat out of place in context. Though frag. 4 is quite fragmentary, it is obvious that the author is speaking in more general terms about obeying God's commandments, without discussing concrete

42. The Hebrew literally says 'all the sons of…'

43. See Prov. 1.8, 10, 15; 2.1; 3.1, 11, 21; 4.1, 10, 20; 5.1, 7, 20; 6.1, 3, 20; 7.1, 24; 8.32; 19.27; 23.15, 19, 26; 24.13, 21; 27.11; 31.2; Sir. 2.1; 3.17; 4.1; 6.18, 23, 32; 7.3; 10.28; 11.10; 14.11; 16.24; 18.15; 21.1; 31.22; 37.27; 38.9, 16; 39.13; 40.28.

44. See in particular Prov. 7; 23.19-21; Sir. 6.18-20.

45. The Hebrew word בני must be a construct form of בנים, because כול indicates that it is a plural noun as opposed to a singular noun with a first singular pronominal suffix attached to it. So its meaning is 'sons of…' not 'my son'.

46. Some of these warnings are given in a more subtle way than others.

examples of specific situations in life. The warning not to forsake one's inheritance or lot is followed by a description of the wise or the righteous:

> [Those] who fear God keep its (that is, wisdom's) ways... (1. 8) ... and do not reject its chastisements (1. 9). Those who walk perfectly turn aside injustice and do not reject its punishments... (1. 10). The shrewd recognize its way and its depth... (1. 11). Those who love God demonstrate a humble walk in it... (1. 12).

The above quotation is more than merely a description of how the wise or the righteous *are* and *behave*. It is meant to be a description of how those who belong to the group of the righteous *ought to be* and *ought to behave*. It illustrates what it means not to forsake one's lot to foreigners.

I believe that the word גורל 'lot' in frag. 4, 1. 7 is a reference to the lot of God (cf. 1QS 2.2; 1 QM 13.5; 17.7), also called the lot of light (CD 13.12) or the lot of the holy ones (1QS 11.7, 8). The Qumran sect believed that there were two lots. God had set two spirits over humankind: the spirit of truth and the spirit of iniquity. The former is associated with light, truth and righteousness, the latter with darkness, falsehood and unrighteousness (1QS 3.17-26). Each of these spirits has a group of followers, both angels and humans, called the 'lot'. One lot belongs to Belial, the other to God (1QS 2.2-5). The Qumranites viewed themselves as the sons of God's lot. All those who did not belong to their community were seen as part of the lot of darkness.

The lot of the sons of light was viewed as an inheritance received from God by all chosen ones. 'And he has caused them [namely, his chosen ones][47] to inherit the lot of the holy ones' (וינחילם בגורל קדושים, 1QS 11.7-8). This explains why the author of 4Q525 speaks in frag. 4 of forsaking one's lot (גורל) as forsaking one's inheritance (נחלה).[48]

The author of 4Q525 warns his readers not to forsake God's lot to which they belong by joining those outside the sect, that is, 'the foreigners' (בני נכר). This should not be taken as merely a warning against physical separation. A person could forsake the lot of God while still being a member of the Covenant by 'walking among the idols of his heart' (1QS 2.11-14), that is, by 'doing his own thing' and

---

47. The antecedent of 'them' is 'his chosen ones' in l. 7a.
48. I must mention that the word נחלה 'inheritance' in 4Q525 frag. 4, 1. 7 is a reconstruction.

ignoring God's precepts as interpreted by the Community.

'Do not forsake your lot (that is, God's lot) to foreigners (that is, Belial's lot)' is a key warning in 4Q525. It is the sum of all other warnings in 4Q525 against sin, because for the Qumranites all sin was associated with the lot of Belial which stood in opposition to God's lot (1QM 1.1-5).

The Qumran sect's emphasis on God's predestination of all humans before they ever existed, either for good or evil (1QS 3.13-25), did not make them deny human responsibility.[49] On the contrary, belonging to the assembly of the elect brought with it a great responsibility. One had to act in accordance with divine election. In frag. 4 of 4Q525 the author gives a serious warning to his readers:

> God in his mercy gave you a place among the sons of light. Now live as God's chosen ones. You belong to those who fear God. Therefore, keep wisdom's ways! (cf. l. 8). You belong to those who walk perfectly.[50] Therefore, turn aside injustice![51] (cf. l. 10). You belong to those who love God. Therefore, walk humbly in wisdom's ways! (cf. l. 12).

The exhortation can be summarized as follows: Be who you are![52]

3. *A warning to fight against one's sinful tendencies.* In the previous section I have mentioned the purpose of the antithetical parallels to the beatitudes. They function as warnings. I have come to the conclusion that in each beatitude there is an exhortation to do good, but there is also a warning not to do evil. This indicates that the author of 4Q525 takes the human tendency to sin very seriously. He was much aware of

49. M.G. May refers to the emphasis on predestination in the Qumran sectarian documents and to the tension between God's sovereignty and humanity's responsibility. He rightly states that 'the Qumranites were not theologians seeking a system of belief neatly and consistently set forth in theological terms; they did not permit their "system" to deny the responsibility of man'. See M.G. May, 'Cosmological Reference in the Qumran Doctrine of the Two Spirits and in the Old Testament Imagery', *JBL* 82 (1963), p. 5.

50. Cf. 1QS 2.2.

51. The spirit belonging to the lot of Belial is characterized as a עולה רוח 'spirit of injustice' (1QS 4.9, 20). Not forsaking God's lot means not letting oneself be influenced by the spirit of Belial's lot.

52. What Moore, 'Personification', has said about 4Q184 could also be said about 4Q525: 'Indeed it might just be that the desire to maintain the significance of human responsibility in the midst of a predestinarian outlook was the real motivation behind this Qumranian work' (p. 516).

the sinful nature of *every* human being, including those belonging to God's lot.

The Qumranites realized fully that in their holy community a perfect walk of life was an ideal to strive for, rather than a reality.[53] Even though the Qumran sect thought that the sons of light were elected by God from the very beginning to do good (1QS 3.13-17), they nevertheless believed that the evil spirits of Belial's lot would try to cause the sons of light to stumble (cf. 1QS 3.24). According to Qumran theology, 'the Angel of Darkness leads *all* the sons of righteousness astray', not one is excluded. Even the speaker in the Community Rule describes himself as belonging 'to wicked mankind'. He speaks of his sinful tendencies, which belong 'to those who walk in darkness' (1QS 11.9-10).

Although the Qumranites strove for perfection, they did not believe that they could reach perfection as long as the Angel of Darkness was still active (1QS 3.21-23). In the hearts of all human beings, including those of the sons of righteousness, two spirits struggle: the spirit of truth and the spirit of injustice. As a result, 'they walk in both wisdom (חכמה) and folly (אולת)' (1QS 4.23-24). Therefore, the author of 4Q525 exhorts the people of his community to 'attain wisdom (חכמה)' and warns them not to 'burst forth on paths of folly (אולת)' (frag. 2, col. ii, l. 2). The Qumranites did not view the domains of light versus darkness as entirely separated. As Wernberg-Møller has so aptly written:

> The difference between light and darkness, righteousness and sin was, of course, felt to be radical; but the two domains of these opposites were not kept strictly apart. Perversion and darkness made inroads upon the realms of truth and light, because the sons of righteousness, in spite of their name and election, like the rest of mankind, had two 'spirits', two opposing inclinations, constantly at war with one another...[54]

4. *A warning to persevere in times of chastisement and trial.* In 4Q525 God's blessing rests upon those who hold on to wisdom (frag. 2, col. ii). The author of 4Q525 calls in particular that person blessed who

> does not forsake it (wisdom or the law) in the face of [his] trials (מצר), and at the time of distress (צוקה) does not abandon it, and does not forget

---

53. P. Wernberg-Møller, 'A Reconsideration of the Two Spirits in the Rule of the Community (1 Q Serek 3.13–4.26)', *RevQ* 3 (1962), p. 427.

54. Wernberg-Møller, 'Reconsideration', p. 427.

> it [in the day of] terror (פחד), and in the humility (ענוה) of his soul does
> not abhor it. But he meditates on it continually, and in his trial (צרה) he
> reflects on the law... (frag. 2, col. ii, ll. 5-6).

It seems that the author wants to emphasize this point, because the phrases 'in the face of his trials', 'at the time of distress', 'in the day of terror', and 'in his trial' are all referring to the same difficult time period. Context makes clear which tough circumstances the author speaks of. In the immediately preceding line the person called blessed is the one who 'restrains himself by its (wisdom's/the law's) disciplines (יסור), and is continually satisfied with its scourges (נגע)' (l. 4). It is very likely that ll. 3b-7 form one single beatitude,[55] because all clauses within these lines are dependent on אשרי 'blessed' whereas the beatitudes in the preceding section are all separately introduced by אשרי.[56] So the trial (צרה, מצר), distress (צוקה), and terror (פחד) should be interpreted as the direct cause of wisdom's disciplines (יסור) and scourges (נגע).

The word יסור also occurs in frag. 4, l. 10, where 'those who walk in perfection' are characterized as not rejecting wisdom's disciplines (יסור). Moreover, in ll. 8-9 of frag. 4 'those who fear God' are described as not rejecting wisdom's chastisements (תוכחה).

I believe that the words נגע, יסור, and תוכחה are close to synonymous, if not entirely synonymous in 4Q525. They all three refer to divine chastisements.[57] Moreover, the four terms פחד, צוקה, מצר, and צרה all refer to or are very closely associated with the stressful situation caused by divine chastisement. This interpretation is supported by the way these expressions function in various Qumran sectarian documents. They often occur in combination in a context which speaks of divine chastisement, both in the Thanksgiving Hymns and in the Community Rule.

A very clear example is found in 1QH 17. In this section four of the seven above mentioned words occurring in 4Q525 are used. The speaker in the Thanksgiving Hymns talks about his scourges (נגע) in

55. After l. 7 the text is so fragmentary that we do not know whether the following lines are also dependent on אשרי.

56. The situation in this text is different from the one encountered in Sir. 14.20-27. Ben Sira 14 contains eight separate beatitudes, all dependent on the word אשרי which is mentioned only once.

57. Even though I believe that 'chastisement' would be the best English equivalent for all three words, I have avoided identical renderings in order to avoid confusion.

which he delights (l. 10). He is able to delight in them, because he knows that it was God who rebuked (יכח)[58] him in the mystery of his wisdom (l. 23). God's chastisement (תוכחה) is an expression of his righteousness (l. 33). Yet God in his mercy also comforted the speaker in his distress (צוקה, l. 13). Moreover, he 'will bring healing to [his] wound' (...) 'and everlasting space to the distress (צרה) of [his] soul' (ll. 27-28). The speaker realizes that God's chastisements (תוכחה) and scourges (נגע) are for his own good. God's chastisement (תוכחה) will become his 'joy and gladness' (l. 24). His scourges (נגע) 'will turn to [eternal] healing and everlasting [peace]' (l. 25). The speaker attaches eternal value to the divine chastisement he receives. This coincides with the words found in 4Q525 frag. 2, col. ii, l. 4: 'Blessed is the man...who restrains himself by [wisdom's/the law's] disciplines (יסור) and is continually satisfied with its scourges (נג)'. It strongly suggests that the blessings pronounced in 4Q525 pertain to eternity as well.

The speaker in the Thanksgiving Hymns also uses the word יסור to refer to divine chastisement. He understands that God keeps his chosen one from sinning against him by 'restoring to him his humility (ענוה) through [his] corrections (יסור)' (1QH 4.22). It is interesting to observe that in 1QH 4.22 humility is seen as the desired result of divine chastisement. In 4Q525 humility is a virtue which a person shows in not abhorring wisdom (or the law) when God chastises him (frag. 2, col. ii, l. 6). The difference is merely a matter of emphasis. In the *Hodayot* the stress is on God's gracious work in a sinner's heart through chastisement. In 4Q525, on the other hand, the human's responsibility to show humility when being chastised is emphasized.

Wisdom's chastisements in 4Q525 may be equated with God's chastisements in other Qumran sectarian manuscripts for several reasons. First, in 4Q525 there is a very close connection between wisdom and God. Wisdom is given by God (frag. 1, l. 1). Fearing God means keeping wisdom's ways (frag. 4, ll. 8-9). Secondly, the use of vocabulary in 4Q525 to refer to chastisement and the distress which accompanies it is very similar to the one found in the other Qumran sectarian documents.[59] Thirdly, in the *Hodayot* God chastises the speaker 'in the mystery of his wisdom (חכמה)' (1QH 17.24). Wisdom's

58. The word תוכחה (4Q525 frag. 4, l. 9) comes from the same root as the verb יכח (see BDB, p. 407).

59. See discussion above.

chastisements in 4Q525 are the chastisements of *God's* wisdom. Hence, they are God's chastisements.

In Qumran theology God chastises his people in several ways. He often does it by making use of others, both members of the lot of God and members of the lot of Belial. In 1QS 5.24–6.1 the members of the Community are told to 'rebuke (יכח) one another in truth, humility, and charity'. A man should rebuke his companion on the same day he commits a transgression, lest he continues in sin. The Qumranites were not only taught responsibility for their own actions, but also for those of their fellow members. In 4Q477 'A Record of Disciplinary Action' the actual names of some members of the Qumran community who transgressed their precepts are mentioned. They were chastised. The word יכח 'to chastise, to reprove', representing the same root as the noun תוכחה[60] (cf. 4Q525 frag. 4, l. 9), occurs several times in this document (for example, frag. 1, col. i, l. 3; col. ii, ll. 5, 7). They chastised (יכח) a certain Johanan, because he was quick-tempered (frag. 1, col. ii, l. 4). The Hebrew says: הואה קצר אפים. These words are almost identical to the ones occurring in 1QS 6.26, 'Whoever has answered his companion with obstinacy, or has addressed him in impatient anger (קוצר אפים)…shall do penance for one year…' This is one of the prescribed chastisements we find in the Community Rule. 1QS 6.24–7.25 contains a whole list of rules by which a transgressor within the Community is to be judged. Depending on how severe his transgression is, he has to do penance for ten days (for example, 7.9-10), one month (for example, 7.13-14), two months (for example, 7.8), three months (for example, 7.9), six months (for example, 7.5), one year (for example, 7.4), or two years (for example, 7.18-19). Only in exceptional cases, for example, when someone has slandered the Congregation, 'he shall be expelled from among them and shall return no more' (7.17). Most of the time the sinner receives a chance to repent from his sin. Again, this shows how the chastisements of God's wisdom were meant for a person's own good to bring him to repentance and thus to a state of blessedness (cf. 4Q525 frag. 2).

Not only members of God's lot, but also members of Belial's lot are used by God to chastise his people. In 1QH 17.21-28 the speaker says that it was God himself who strengthened his enemies against him (l. 21) in order to reprove him 'in the mystery of [his] wisdom'

---

60. See above.

(l. 23). The *Hodayot*-speaker knows that God in a mysterious way uses evil for good. 'You have caused light from darkness to shine for me' (ll. 26-27). God allows the Angel of Darkness to scourge (נגע) and bring distress (צרה) to the sons of righteousness. Even their succumbing to temptation is all 'in accordance with the mysteries of God'. The tension between the two opposing spirits which reside in each person's heart is at its strongest in times of distress when the spirits of Belial try to cause the sons of light to stumble (1QS 3.22-24). The Qumranites are urged not to 'abandon God during the dominion of Satan because of fear (פחד) or terror or affliction' (1QS 1.17-18). God will only bless them when they persevere in times of trial by holding on to his wisdom and his Law (cf. 4Q525 frag. 2, col. ii, ll. 3b-7).

5. The consequences of heeding versus ignoring the warning. I have already mentioned that the Qumran beatitudes should be read as both exhortations and warnings. The first part of each beatitude exhorts the reader to lead a wise life in accordance with God's commandments. The second part warns him not to lead a foolish, sinful life.

A curse is implied in the antithetical parallel to each beatitude. At first sight the Qumran beatitudes only seem to speak of those who are blessed. However, by implication they also talk about those who are not blessed because of the 'eternal curses (אררות נצח)' which await them (see frag. 15, l. 4; frag. 21, l. 2). Already in the beginning section of 4Q525 the author wants to draw a contrast between the righteous and the wicked. That this is indeed his intention is evident from the section which follows the beatitudes. Fragment 4 describes the righteous and wise. In frags. 7, 10, and 13 descriptions of the wicked and unwise are given. Moreover, the author shows the consequences of righteous versus wicked behavior. Fragments 12 and 14 specify what it means to be blessed. Fragments 15, 21 and 22 point out what it means to be cursed.

The author of 4Q525 encourages those who persevere in holding on to wisdom or the law, despite the difficulties it entails. He calls them blessed (frag. 2, col. ii), because of the future honor and peace which await them. Fragments 12 and 14 describe this future state of blessing.

In frag. 14 someone is addressed directly. The second person masculine singular suffix is used quite frequently in this fragment, that is, 33 times, whereas it occurs only 3 times in the rest of document. This

observation raises several important questions. How does frag. 14
relate to the rest of 4Q525? Who is the addressee in this fragment? It
is significant that neither the first, nor the second person singular
occurs only in frag. 14. The former is also found in frags. 8–9, 13,
21–23. The latter also occurs in frags. 8–10, 38. So besides frag. 14,
frags. 8–9 is the only other place[61] in 4Q525 where the first and
second person singular occur together. Both in frag. 14 and frags. 8–9
the speaker tells his addressee to listen to him. 'And now, O discerning one, listen to me' (ועתה מבין שמעה לי, frag. 14, col. ii, line 18).
'Pay attention to me, all you sons of...' (...הן[ק]שיבו לי כול בני, frags.
8–9, l. 3). We can only guess how the last sentence would have ended.
It may have said 'all you sons of righteousness' (cf. 1QS 3.20, 22) or
'all you sons of light' (cf. 1QS 1.9) or 'all you sons of truth' (cf. 1QS
4.5). In frags. 8–9, l. 6 the speaker continues by giving a promise: 'If
you do good, He (that is, God) will do good to you... (א[ם]
תטיב ייטיב לכה)'. The second person in this sentence is not plural, but
singular. Nevertheless, it is clear from context that a group is
addressed, not just one individual (cf. l. 3, 'all you sons of...').
Likewise, 'you' in frag. 14 is probably generic, referring to a body of
people. As we have already seen above, we have good reason to think
that the sons of God's lot, that is, the members of the Qumran community, are addressed. In frag. 14 the speaker gives a more detailed
depiction of the goodness from God's hand which he promised in
frags. 8–9. Notice the recurrence of the root טוב in frag. 14. 'He (that
is, God) will fill your days with good (טוב)' (col. ii, l. 13). In frag. 14
the requirement on the basis of which God's goodness may be
obtained is no more mentioned, at least not in the incomplete material
which we possess. However, the condition 'if you do well' (cf. frags.
8–9) is surely the backdrop against which the description of God's
blessing in frag. 14 should be read.

In frag. 14 the speaker tells his audience: 'You shall be blessed
(תתברך)' (col. ii, l. 7). The Hebrew word for 'blessed' here is not
אשרי (cf. frag. 2), but a form of the verb ברך. However, even though
their semantic ranges are not identical, the two words are often interchangeable. Both denote a happiness due to God's good favor toward

---

61. According to Wacholder and Abegg's reconstruction frags. 8–9 form one
piece. See B.Z. Wacholder and M.G. Abegg, Jr, *A Preliminary Edition of the
Unpublished Dead Sea Scrolls: The Hebrew and Aramaic Texts from Cave Four.
Fascicle Two* (Washington: Biblical Archaeology Society, 1992), pp. 185-203.

the person involved. The blessing implies 'abundance of peace (רוב שלום)' (frag. 14, col. ii, l. 13; see also frag. 12, l. 1), 'honor (כבוד)' (frag. 14, col. ii, l. 14), 'goodness (טוב)' (frag. 14, col. ii, l. 13), and deliverance 'from every evil (מכול רע)' (frag. 14, col. ii, l. 12).

From the Community Rule it is known that the priests have to bless (ברך) 'all the men of God who walk perfectly in all his ways' (2.1-2). Their pronouncement of blessing contains vocabulary which is similar or identical to some of the terms found in the description of blessing in 4Q525, in particular frag. 14.[62]

> May he bless you (ברך, cf. frag. 12, l. 1; frag. 14, col. ii, l. 7) with all good (טוב, cf. frag. 14, col. ii, l. 13) and preserve you from all evil (מכול רע, cf. frags. 8–9, l. 6; frag. 14, col. ii, l. 12). May he lighten your heart with life-giving wisdom and grant you eternal knowledge. May he raise his merciful face toward you for everlasting peace (שלום, cf. frag. 12, l. 1; frag. 14, col. ii, l. 13).

The author of 4Q525 warns those who lead foolish and wicked lives. I have argued that he refers to the day of judgment when the wicked will be punished. Several words and phrases suggest this. Fragment 15 talks about 'darkness (אופל)', 'eternal curses (אררות נצח)', 'flame[s of] death (רשפן[י] מות)' which fly about, 'flaming brimstone (להבי גו[פ]רית)' and 'perdition (שחת)'. Fragment 22 speaks of 'the depths of the pit (ירכתי בור)' and 'the fiery furnace (כור חרון)'. There are references in frag. 21 to 'those cursed of God con[tinually...] (זעומי אלוהים תמ[יד])', 'dark places (מ]חשכים])' and the gathering of wrath (ת]קבוץ חרון]). As I have shown above, the phrase 'on the day designated' in frag. 22 strongly suggests that this is a reference to the day of God's wrath. Like Ben Sira and Joel, the author of 4Q525 wants to warn his readers against the coming day of judgment when God will punish all those who led foolish lives. Blessed are those 'who do not hold fast to the ways of injustice'...'who do not burst forth on the paths of folly'...'who do not search for [wisdom] with a deceitful heart'...who do not abandon, forget, or abhor wisdom in times of trial and chastisement (cf. frag. 2), because they will not go into 'the fiery furnace' (frag. 22, l. 4)...'on the day designated' (frag. 22, l. 2). By leading a wise life in accordance with the law of the Lord they have not provoked God's wrath as the unwise have.

In the Community Rule the priests are told to bless the men of God's

---

62. The similarities have been marked between brackets.

lot (1QS 2.1-4).[63] The Levites are supposed to curse the men of Belial's lot (1QS 2.5-11). However, in this same passage it is also made clear that being a member of the Qumran community does not guarantee God's favor. The priests and the Levites will curse 'the man who enters this covenant while walking among the idols of his heart, who sets up before himself a stumbling-block of sin so that he may backslide' (1QS 2.11-12). It is significant that the pronouncement of the curse upon the men of Belial's lot was done by the Levites alone. The pronouncement of the curse upon those leading a sinful life *within* the Community is done by both the priests and the Levites. This suggests that the curse upon wicked people within the Community is heavier than the curse upon outsiders. When a Covenant member persists in acting wickedly 'all the curses of the Covenant shall cling to him and God will set him apart for evil' (1QS 2.15-16). Even though he belonged at one time to the Qumran community, 'he will be cut off from the midst of all the sons of light... His lot will be among those who are cursed forever' (1QS 2.16-17). So ultimately he will become part of Belial's lot, because he forsook God's lot. It is in this light that we should read the warning given in 4Q525 frag. 4, l. 7: 'Do not forsake your lot!' If you do, God will treat you as one belonging to Belial's lot and you will not escape his severe punishment.

In the Community Rule and in 4Q525 the description of God's judgment upon the wicked is very similar.[64] In 1QS 2.5, 7, 11, 17 those who act wickedly are called cursed (ארר). This is reminiscent of 'the eternal curses (אררה)' mentioned in 4Q525 frag. 15, l. 4. In 1QS 2.7-8 the men of Belial's lot are called damned (זעם). The author of 4Q525 warns his readers that they will also be among those who are damned (זעם) by God continually, if they choose depravity (frag. 21, ll. 2-4). In both documents imagery of darkness and fire is used to depict the fierceness of God's wrath and punishment. In the Community Rule the wicked are 'damned in the *darkness* of everlasting *fire*' (2.8). There will be made an end to them 'in the *fire* of the *dark* places (מחשכים)' (4.13). The author of 4Q525 also speaks of '*darkness*' (frag. 15, ll. 1, 6) and '*dark* places (מחשכים)' (frag. 21, l. 1). Fire-imagery is used as well: there are references to '*flaming* brimstone' (frag. 15, l. 6) and 'the *fiery* furnace' (frag. 22, l. 4).

63. See also above.
64. Similarities are mentioned in italics. Verbal parallels in Hebrew are put between brackets.

6. *Who gives the warning?* Who is the speaker in 4Q525? It is difficult to answer this question. We can only speculate about his identity. The recurrence of the first person singular in 4Q525 is quite striking,[65] because its use is relatively infrequent in the Qumran sectarian documents. It only occurs in the latter part of the Community Rule (chs. 10–11), in the Thanksgiving Hymns, and in the opening section of the Damascus Document (chs. 1–2).[66] Of course, this does not mean that the speaker in 4Q525 needs to be the same as in one of the above mentioned Qumran sectarian texts, though the possibility is certainly not excluded.

The first person singular in the Thanksgiving Hymns has often been identified as the Teacher of Righteousness. However, G. Jeremias and H.W. Kuhn have argued that the Teacher is only the speaker in certain portions of the *Hodayot*. In all other cases the first person singular is the voice of other Hymn-writers belonging to the Qumran community who wanted to imitate his style.[67] Could the speaker in 4Q525 be the Teacher of Righteousness? This is a possibility. It is interesting how the Scrolls emphasize the importance of listening to the Teacher of Righteousness (CD 20.32; 1QpHab 2.2). Likewise, the speaker in 4Q525 repeatedly urges his readers to listen to him: 'And now, o discerning one, listen to me (ועתה מבין שמעה לי)' (frag. 14, col. ii, l. 18, see also frag. 2, col. ii, l. 12 and frag. 13, l. 6);[68] 'Hearken to me (האזינו לי)' (frag. 23, col. ii, l. 2).

The first address is almost identical to the one we find in CD 2.2,

65. See, for example, frags. 8–9, l. 3; frag. 13, l. 6; frag. 14, col. ii, ll. 18, 28; frag. 22, l. 2; frag. 23, col. ii, l. 2.

66. The first person singular also occurs in later sections of the Damascus Document, but only in biblical quotations with God as speaker (for example 7.16; 8.3; 9.19).

67. Jeremias believes that the first person singular is the Teacher of Righteousness in the following portions of the Thanksgiving Hymns: 2.1-19; 2.31-39; 3.1-18; 4.5–5.4; 5.5-19; 5.20–7.5; 7.6-25; 8.4-40 (all references are according to Sukenik's numbering system). See G. Jeremias, *Der Lehrer der Gerechtigkeit* (Göttingen: Vandenhoeck & Ruprecht, 1963). Likewise, Kuhn has separated the 'true Teacher's hymns' from the hymns composed by his followers. He argues that the Teacher of Righteousness is speaking in the following sections of the *Hodayot*: 2.1-19; 4.5-29; 5.5-19; 5.20–6.36; 7.3-25; 8.4-40 (again, Sukenik's numbering system is used). See H.W. Kuhn, *Enderwartung und gegenwärtiges Heil* (Göttingen: Vandenhoeck & Ruprecht, 1966).

68. The last two references are partially reconstructed.

14, except that the imperative of שמע is plural instead of singular (ועתה שמעו אלי). However, it is unlikely that the speaker in the Damascus Document is the Teacher of Righteousness, because he refers to him (see CD 1.1). The same address also occurs in Prov. 5.7, 7.24, 8.32. In Prov. 8.32 wisdom is the speaker. In Prov. 5.7 and 7.24 it is not clear who the speaker is. It does not seem that the expression 'and now, listen to me' is only used by one particular person. It could be employed by anyone who would want to give weight to his words. The only thing which is close to certain about the speaker in 4Q525 is that he was someone who had a position of authority within the Community.

Not only the vocabulary, but also the content of 4Q525 suggests that it is a Qumran sectarian document. The paradoxical reference to discerning men who are led astray (frag. 16, l. 3) is typical for Qumran sectarian literature. It is not found in traditional Jewish wisdom books. 4Q525 is clearly addressed to the members of the Qumran sect. The addressees in frags. 8–9 'all you sons of...' are in all likelihood 'the sons of light, truth, and righteousness' (cf. 1QS 1.9; 3.20, 22; 4.5), that is, the Qumran community. The speaker, who is probably a leader within the community, gives an important warning against sin in general in frag. 4, l. 7. Here he tells the Qumranites not to forsake their lot, that is, the lot of God, in order to join foreigners, namely, those outside the community, in their sinful practices. The author of 4Q525 was much aware of the sinful nature of *every* human being, including of those belonging to God's lot. According to Qumran theology 'the Angel of Darkness leads *all* the sons of righteousness astray' (cf. 1QS 3.24), not one is excluded. Therefore, the author of 4Q525 urges the Qumranites to live as God's chosen ones by fearing him while humbly walking in wisdom's ways (frags. 2; 4). If they heed his warning, they will be blessed (frags. 12; 14). If they ignore it, they will be cursed (frags. 15; 21–22).

Conclusion

There are many similarities in style and content between 4Q525 and wisdom books such as Proverbs and Ben Sira. 4Q525 is clearly a wisdom document. However, 4Q525 also deviates from traditional Jewish wisdom literature, because it is a typical Qumran sectarian document. The most striking Qumranian element of 4Q525 is found in frag. 16, l. 3 which speaks of discerning people who are led astray. This interesting type of paradox does not occur in traditional Jewish wisdom literature, but it does show up in Qumranian manuscripts. Moreover, the high concentration of eschatological elements in 4Q525 is not found in traditional wisdom books like Proverbs and Ben Sira. The vocabulary of 4Q525 also strongly suggests that it is a Qumran sectarian document. The terms עולה 'injustice', ענוה 'humility', צנע 'to be humble', הלך תמים 'to walk perfectly', תוכחה 'chastisement', חמת תנינים 'poison of snakes', and אבני חפץ 'stones of desire', which we find in 4Q525, all occur with more frequency in the Qumran sectarian literature than in the Old Testament. Also, the particular phrase עולה דרכ(י) 'the way(s) of injustice' and the idiomatic expression בענות נפשו 'in the humility of his soul' are not used in the Old Testament at all, but they do occur in 4Q525 as well as in the Qumran sectarian documents. Moreover, the teachings of 4Q525 are entirely compatible with the Qumran doctrines on major issues like human nature, election and responsibility, and the endtime.

GEOGRAPHIC ASPECTS OF NOACHIC MATERIALS
IN THE SCROLLS AT QUMRAN

James M. Scott

Introduction

The Qumran scrolls contain a surprising amount of Noachic material, and scholars have recently shown a great deal of interest in it. While some of this material is rather loosely tied to Genesis,[1] most of it simply follows the narrative sequence of the Hebrew Bible, whether by summarizing, paraphrasing, or even more radically, rewriting the biblical text.[2] The purpose of this paper is not to survey all of this Noachic material, but rather to examine part of the alleged evidence for the lost 'Book of Noah' and role of the Qumran scrolls in reconstructing it.

The Lost 'Book of Noah'

While some scholars question whether the 'Book of Noah' ever even existed, others believe that the lost book can be reconstructed on the basis of fragments which remain of it in later works, such as the books of Enoch and *Jubilees* and some Qumran manuscripts. Florentino García Martínez is perhaps the main proponent of this latter view. Based on his reconstruction from various ancient sources, he summarizes the contents of the lost 'Book of Noah' as follows.[3]

---

1.   For example, 4QExhortation based on the Flood (4Q370) and the incidental citation of Gen. 7.9 in the Damascus Document (CD 5.1).

2.   For example, the Genesis Apocryphon (1QapGen), 4QCommGen[a] (4Q252), the Genesis section of 4Q422, the extra-canonical Daniel tradition in 4Q243–245, 551 and a passage in the Damascus Document (CD 3.1).

3.   F. García Martínez, '4QMess Ar and the Book of Noah', in his *Qumran and Apocalyptic: Studies on the Aramaic Texts from Qumran* (STDJ, 9; Leiden: Brill, 2nd edn, 1994), pp. 1-44 (here pp. 43-44).

(1) The 'Book of Noah' began with a description of the fall of the Watchers and its disastrous consequences for humanity (cf. *Jub.* 7.21-24; 5.6-11; 1Q19 1.2; 1Q20; and *1 En.* 60.7-10, 24).

(2) The 'Book of Noah' continued with a description of Noah's marvellous birth, the doubts to which it gave rise, and the resolution of those doubts thanks to the appeal to Enoch, who foretold Noah's future and his salvation from universal punishment (cf. *1 En.* 106–107; 1QapGen 1–4; 6Q8 1; and 1Q19 3–11).

(3) The 'Book of Noah' then gave an autobiographical account of Noah's life before the Deluge, which included the angels' prediction of the Flood (cf. 1QapGen 6 and *1 En.* 10.1-3).

(4) The book continued with the Flood narrative and Noah's salvation (cf. *Jub.* 5.24-28 and 1QapGen 7–9).

(5) The book then included Noah's sacrifice after the Flood, his covenant with God, prescriptions concerning blood deriving from this covenant, and Noah's instructions to his sons (cf. *Jub.* 6.2-4; 6.10-14; 7.23-37; 1QapGen 10–15; and a manuscript of the *Testament of Levi* from Mount Athos).

(6) The book concluded with the partition of the earth among the sons of Noah (cf. *Jub.* 8.9–9.15; 1QapGen 16–17; and an excerpt from Abydenos in the *Chronography* of Syncellus [47.11-13]).[4]

In this way, García Martínez pieces together the broad outline of the lost 'Book of Noah' from the extant sources which allegedly preserve it. My purpose here is not to examine his whole reconstruction but to consider merely the final section—the division of the earth among the sons of Noah. Let us begin by looking at each of the three sources upon which the reconstruction is based.

First, García Martínez finds a fragment of the supposed last section of the lost 'Book of Noah' in *Jub.* 8.9–9.15. Indeed, *Jub.* 8.11 makes explicit reference to a 'book' of Noah, which García Martínez curiously fails to mention. The text states: 'When he [namely, Noah] summoned his children, they came to him—they and their children. He divided the earth into the lots which his three sons would occupy. They reached out their hands and took the book from the bosom of

---

4.   According to García Martínez ('4QMess Ar and the Book of Noah', p. 44), the 'Book of Noah' possibly also included a reference to another Noachic writing, a medical treatise on the healing properties of some herbs (cf. *Jub.* 10.12-14).

their father Noah.'⁵ Without this explicit mention of the 'book' of Noah, García Martínez has difficulty in attributing *Jub.* 8.9–9.15 to the lost work, but he nevertheless does so because 'the reference of Syncellus which makes the partition of the earth an important part of the Noachic work, and the remains of col. XVI and XVII of *1QapGn*, which have preserved part of the same partition, lead us to attribute these chapters of *Jubilees* to the influence of the *Book of Noah*'.⁶

The circularity of García Martínez's argument is apparent. Moreover, since *Jub.* 10.14 refers to 'all the books that he [namely, Noah] had written', we may doubt whether the quest for a single, all-inclusive 'Book of Noah' is advisable at all.⁷ More probably, we should see the division of the earth among the sons of Noah as constituting an independent 'Book of Noah' which is separate from books of Noah on other subjects (cf., for example, *Jub.* 10.12-14). This is confirmed, at least for a later period, by the fact that *Jubilees* 8–9 circulated independently in the Διαμερισμὸς Γῆς ('Division of the Earth') tradition, which is found, for example, in Hippolytus's *Chronicon* and the Alexandrian World-Chronicles.⁸ However, before we can assume that such a 'Book of Noah' existed already in the second century BCE, when *Jubilees* is usually dated, additional evidence is needed, for *Jubilees* 8–9 is available only in the much later Ethiopic version, which is based on a Greek translation of the original Hebrew text of *Jubilees*.⁹ Of the 14 or 15 *Jubilees* fragments found at Qumran,¹⁰ none retains any part of *Jubilees* 8–10, the section in

5.   García Martínez refers merely to *Jub.* 10.13 and 21.10 ('4QMess Ar and the Book of Noah', p. 24).

6.   García Martínez, '4QMess Ar and the Book of Noah', p. 39.

7.   Cf. García Martínez, '4QMess Ar and the Book of Noah', p. 24, who argues that the existence of the 'Book of Noah' is 'attested by two explicit allusions in *Jubilees*' (that is, *Jub.* 10.13; 21.10).

8.   Cf. P.M. Fraser, *Cities of Alexander the Great* (Oxford: Clarendon Press, 1996), pp. 11-12; J.M. Scott, 'The Division of the Earth in *Jubilees* 8.11–9.15 and Early Christian Chronography', in M. Albani *et al.* (eds.), *Studies in the Book of Jubilees* (TSAJ; Tübingen: Mohr [Paul Siebeck], forthcoming); R.W. Cowley, *Ethiopian Biblical Interpretation: A Study in Exegetical Tradition and Hermeneutics* (Cambridge: Cambridge University Press, 1988), pp. 31-33.

9.   Cf. J.C. VanderKam, *The Book of Jubilees* (2 vols.; CSCO, 510–11; Scriptores Aethiopici, 87-88; Leuven: Peeters, 1989), I, pp. vi-xxxi.

10.   That is, 1Q17–18; 2Q19–20; 3Q5; 4Q176 frags. 21–23 (two copies?); 4Q216; 4Q218–23/24; 11Q12. See J.C. VanderKam, 'The *Jubilees* Fragments from

which the book reworks the material in Genesis 10.[11]

García Martínez not only finds a fragment of the last section of the lost 'Book of Noah' in *Jubilees* 8–9, but, secondly, he finds one in the Genesis Apocryphon cols. xvi–xvii. Whereas most other scholars consider the Genesis Apocryphon to be dependent on *Jubilees*,[12] García Martínez regards it is an independent and more faithful witness to the lost 'Book of Noah'.[13] Although here as elsewhere the Genesis Apocryphon is highly fragmentary, cols. xvi–xvii obviously cover much of the same material as the division of the earth among Noah's sons and grandsons described in *Jubilees* 8–9.[14] Hence, we may assume that there is a literary relationship of some kind between the two documents, and we may be assured as well of the antiquity of the material in *Jubilees* 8–9.

Since the publication of García Martínez's article, new information has come to light about the Genesis Apocryphon, which bears on the issues that he raises. It has been announced, for example, that, using special imaging techniques, the words 'Book of the Words of Noah' (כתב מלי נוח) can be read on a blackened fragment of the Genesis Apocryphon.[15] According to Elisha Qimron, this fragment originally

Qumran Cave 4', in J. Trebolle Barrera and L. Vegas Montaner (eds.), *The Madrid Congress: Proceedings of the International Congress on the Dead Sea Scrolls, Madrid 18–21 March 1991* (2 vols.; Leiden: Brill, 1992), II, pp. 535-648; J.C. VanderKam and J.T. Milik, '*Jubilees*', in *Qumran Cave 4. VIII. Parabiblical Texts, Part 1* (DJD, 13; Oxford: Clarendon Press, 1994), pp. 1-185.

11. For this section the surviving witnesses are: (a) the Ethiopic version (complete text of *Jubilees*); (b) citations from the chapters in an anonymous Syriac Chronicle (for *Jub*. 8.2-4, 11-12, 22-27, 29-30; 10.29) and (c) citations from the chapters in the writings of several Greek authors, including the *Chronography* of Syncellus (for *Jub*. 10.1, 3, 7-9). All of the versional evidence for *Jubilees* is collected in VanderKam, *The Book of Jubilees*, II, pp. 328-68 (pp. 334-35 for the Syriac Chronicle).

12. Cf., for example, J.A. Fitzmyer, *The Genesis Apocryphon* (BiOr, 18; Rome: Pontifical Biblical Institute, 2nd edn, 1971), pp. 16-19.

13. Cf. García Martínez, '4QMess Ar and the Book of Noah', p. 40.

14. Cf. J.M. Scott, *Paul and the Nations: The Old Testament and Jewish Background of Paul's Mission to the Nations with Special Reference to the Destination of Galatians* (WUNT, 84; Tübingen: Mohr [Paul Siebeck], 1995), pp. 30-33.

15. R.C. Steiner, 'The Heading of the *Book of the Words of Noah* on a Fragment of the Genesis Apocryphon: New Light on a "Lost Work"', *DSD* 2 (1995), pp. 66-71.

comes from col. v, near the beginning of l. 29, that is, right at the beginning of a new section. In that case, the words 'Book of the Words of Noah' stand as the heading of what follows in the Genesis Apocryphon: a first-person account of Noah about his family. Unlike García Martínez's reconstruction, therefore, this 'Book of Noah' does not include an account of Noah's miraculous birth.

Furthermore, new portions of 1QapGen 12 have recently been published which, among other things, introduce genealogical material about Noah's children drawn from Genesis 10 (cf. 1QapGen 12.10-12).[16] This material is pertinent to our discussion, because it shows the influence of Genesis 10 not only in cols. xvi–xvii but also earlier in the Genesis Apocryphon. Moreover, this new genealogical material actually contradicts the book of *Jubilees* in a significant way. For whereas the Genesis Apocryphon makes it clear that the five sons of Shem avoided intermarriage with the families of Ham and Japheth by marrying the five daughters of Shem after the flood, *Jubilees* unpolemically presupposes that intermarriage between the families of Shem and Japheth occurred already in the first post-diluvian generation.[17] If there is such sharp disagreement between the Genesis Apocryphon and *Jubilees* on such a fundamental point based on Genesis 10, what does that say about the relationship between these two documents vis-à-vis the alleged last section of the 'Book of Noah'? Do both versions go back to one original, as García Martínez supposed, or does the Genesis Apocryphon represent a reaction against the *Jubilees* account? Perhaps the full publication of the Genesis Apocryphon will provide some answers to these questions. For the present, however, the Genesis Apocryphon cannot be shown to be independent of *Jubilees* at this point.

Besides finding a fragment of the last section of the 'Book of Noah' in *Jubilees* 8–9 and in the Genesis Apocryphon cols. xvi–xvii, García Martínez finds a fragment, thirdly, in an extract from Abydenos cited in the *Chronography* of Syncellus. Reporting on the division of the earth among the sons of Noah, the text states: 'Upon making these partitions and his will once engraved, as they say, he handed his sealed

---

16. Cf. J.C. Greenfield and E. Qimron, 'The Genesis Apocryphon Col. XII', *Abr-Nahrain Supplement* 3 (1992), pp. 70-77.

17. Cf. J.C. VanderKam, 'The Granddaughters and Grandsons of Noah', *RevQ* 16 (1994), pp. 457-61.

testament to them'.[18] Unfortunately, the use of this extract as evidence for the 'Book of Noah' is more problematic than García Martínez seems to realize. Syncellus is citing a passage on the Tower of Babel from the second-century historian Abydenos, which itself is apparently an embellishment of Eusebius's citation of Alexander Polyhistor (first century BCE),[19] who in turn relies on the *Babyloniaca* of Berossus, reportedly written in the time of Antiochus I (c. 324–261 BCE). Furthermore, although Polyhistor includes this legend of the Tower of Babel among his excepts from Berossus,[20] he does not attribute it to Berossus. Instead, he identifies the 'Sibyl' as its source.[21] A comparison of Polyhistor's quotation with the extant fragments from the *Sibylline Oracles* reveals that Polyhistor was quoting from material now found in the third book of the Sibyllines, that is, the so-called 'Jewish Sibyl', particularly *Sib. Or.* 3.97-161.[22] The mention of the war between Titan and Kronos in the extract makes this virtually certain. It is difficult to know, however, whether Polyhistor himself added this Sibylline material to Berossus's work,[23] or whether he found it already interpolated in the *Babyloniaca*.[24] In any case, it is

18. A.A. Mosshammer (ed.), *Georgii Syncelli Ecloga Chronographica* (Leipzig: Teubner, 1984), 47.11-13.

19. Syncellus undoubtedly quotes the Abydenos extract from Eusebius, who also does not include the material which García Martínez cites. Cf. J. Karst (ed.), *Eusebius Werke*. V. *Die Chronik aus dem Armenischen übersetzt* (GSC, 20; Leipzig: Hinrichs, 1911), 17.11-23. The Polyhistor fragment which Abydenos cites is also included separately in Eusebius's *Chronicon* (cf. 12.1-9).

20. Eusebius, *Chron.* 4–34 (ed. Karst). For a convenient display of the Polyhistor fragments, see Felix Jacoby, *FGrHist* IIIA, frags. 79–81.

21. Eusebius, *Chron.* 12.10 (ed. Karst).

22. Polyhistor himself, in another work, entitled Περὶ Ἰουδαίων, cites a very similar version of this story from an anonymous (Samaritan?) author whom he incorrectly identifies as Eupolemus, a Jewish historian of the second century BCE. See further below.

23. For example, A. Kuhrt, 'Berossus' *Babyloniaka* and Seleucid Rule in Babylonia', in A. Kuhrt and S. Sherwin-White (eds.), *Hellenism in the East: The Interaction of Greek and non-Greek Civilizations from Syria to Central Asia after Alexander* (London: Gerald Duckworth, 1987), pp. 32-56 (here p. 34).

24. Cf. W. Adler, *Time Immemorial: Archaic History and its Sources in Christian Chronography from Julius Africanus to George Syncellus* (Dumbarton Oaks Studies, 26; Washington, DC: Dumbarton Oaks Research Library and Collection, 1989), pp. 35-38.

not sufficient to cite Abydenus as evidence for the lost 'Book of Noah' without considering his sources.

As I have mentioned, García Martínez's citation of Abydenos in Syncellus embellishes the Polyhistor extract. Writing in the eighth century CE, Syncellus stands at the end of a long stream of tradition which has undergone a tremendous transformation in the process, including interpolations, revisions, and omissions. We know that Syncellus himself often used *Jubilees* as a source, probably an abridgment of some kind, which he could freely rework and mix with other sources he was citing, often without express attribution.[25] In fact, García Martínez's citation of Abydenos in Syncellus (*Chron.* 47.11-13) strongly reminds us of *Jub.* 8.11, for it is the only other text which speaks of Noah's giving his sons a title deed to the territories which they had received on earth. If we are correct that this citation is ultimately dependent on *Jub.* 8.11, which Syncellus has added to the Abydenos extract,[26] then Syncellus and Abydenos cannot be used as separate evidence that *Jubilees* 8–9 stems from the 'Book of Noah'.[27]

To summarize our results to this point, we have seen that García Martínez's reconstruction of the supposed final section of the 'Book of Noah' presents several difficulties, not least that the sources which he

25. Cf. Adler, *Time Immemorial*, pp. 10, 182-88. See esp. pp. 182-83: 'Of all the extra-biblical Jewish sources that Syncellus and the other Byzantine chronographers consulted in their treatment of primordial history, *Jubilees* is the most extensively used, and at the same time subject to some of the most thoroughgoing reworking. When he first appeals to *Jubilees*, Syncellus... acknowledges dependence on intermediaries, whom he identifies as "some historians". Like other Byzantine chronographers, he appeals repeatedly to *Jubilees*, even though he initially warns his readers that the work does not appear to be authoritative. While typically referring to *Jubilees* by the name by which it was best known among the chronographers—ἡ λεπτὴ Γένεσις or some variant of it—, he is aware that the work also circulated under the name *Apocalypse of Moses*, and occasionally identifies it in this way. In many other cases, excerpts are cited from that work without express attribution.' Alder, *Time Immemorial*, p. 183: 'As in the case of other Byzantine chronographers who cite from *Jubilees*, Syncellus never quotes verbatim from it. Unlike his fairly faithful citations from *1 Enoch*, Syncellus' citations from *Jubilees* and the allied *Life of Adam* are, as he himself knows, epitomized forms of these works.'

26. The skeptical ὡς φασιν in Syncellus's *Chron.* 47.12 is probably an addition of Syncellus to the reworked *Jubilees* text. On Syncellus's scepticism about the authority of *Jubilees*, see the previous note.

27. *Pace* García Martínez, '4QMess Ar and the Book of Noah', p. 39.

uses in this reconstruction cannot be shown to be independent of *Jubilees* 8–9. Moreover, the whole attempt to reconstruct a single, all-inclusive 'Book of Noah' becomes questionable in view of the reference in *Jubilees* to a plurality of 'books' written by Noah (cf. *Jub.* 10.14). Hence, the way forward seems to lie in another direction. If we take seriously *Jub.* 8.11-12, then *Jubilees* 8–9 gives the contents of a more narrowly focused 'Book of Noah', which concentrated on the division of the earth among Noah's sons, albeit, as we shall see, with an apocalyptic agenda. This smaller 'book' later circulated independently in the Διαμερισμὸς Γῆς ('Division of the Earth') tradition, which is found, for example, in Hippolytus's *Chronicon* and the Alexandrian World-Chronicles. However, evidence of the *Jubilees* tradition is also found already both in the Third Sibyl and in the War Scroll, to which we now turn.

Jubilees *8–9 and the Third Sibyl*

Following the lead of Syncellus, I begin by comparing *Jubilees* 8–9 and the Third Sibyl, both of which stem from the second century BCE. *Jubilees* 8–9 contains two corresponding accounts of the division of the earth. First, in *Jub.* 8.10-30, Noah divides the earth by lot among his three sons, following the order given in Gen. 10.1: Shem receives the temperate 'middle of the earth' (*Jub.* 8.12-21), with Mt Zion 'in the middle of the navel of the earth' (v. 19); Ham receives the hot southern portion (vv. 22-24); and Japheth receives the cold portion (vv. 25-30). The geographical extent of these portions and the physical boundaries between them are described in great detail, following a more or less circular path in each case. Each description ends with a formula indicating that the portion allotted to that son became a possession to him and his descendants 'forever' (vv. 17, 24, 29).

Secondly, in *Jub.* 9.1-15, the sons of Noah, still in the presence of their father (v. 14), divide the portions given to them among their own sons. The text reverses the order of presentation in the first account, so that the sons are now listed from south to north: the sons of Ham (v. 1), the sons of Shem (vv. 2-6), and the sons of Japheth (vv. 7-13). After the distribution of the land, Noah compels his sons and grandsons to swear an oath to curse anyone who desires to seize a portion that does not belong to his lot (vv. 14-15):

In this way Noah's sons divided (the earth) for their sons in front of their father Noah. He made (them) swear by oath to curse each and every one who wanted to occupy the share which did not emerge by his lot. All of them said: 'So be it!' So be it for them and their children until eternity during their generations until the day of judgment on which the Lord will punish them with the sword and fire because of all the evil impurity of their errors by which they have filled the earth with wickedness, impurity, fornication, and sin.[28]

Here there seems to be a connection between violation of territorial boundaries and the future divine judgment.[29]

How does *Jubilees* 8–9 compare with the Third Sibyl? The latter recounts the biblical story of Noah and his three sons in much the same way as *Jubilees* does, albeit with a thick overlay of Greek mythology. The Sibyl, herself a daughter (or daughter-in-law) of Noah (cf. *Sib. Or.* Prol. 33; 1.288-90; 3.827), explains that after the Flood, the earth was divided by lot (κατὰ κλῆρον) into three territories according to the three sons of Gaia and Ouranos: Kronos, Titan, and Iapetos (*Sib. Or.* 3.110-14). The Iapetos of Hesiod (*Theog.* 18, 134, 507, 746), who is equivalent to the biblical Japheth,[30] facilitates

28. See also *Jub.* 10.22: 'Come, let us go down and confuse their tongues so that they do not understand one another and are dispersed into cities and nations and one plan no longer remains with them until the day of judgment'.

29. Cf. J.C. VanderKam, 'Putting Them in Their Place: Geography as an Evaluative Tool', in J.C. Reeves and J. Kampen (eds.), *Pursuing the Text: Studies in Honor of Ben Zion Wacholder on the Occasion of his Seventieth Birthday* (JSOTSup, 184; Sheffield: JSOT Press, 1994), pp. 46-69, who considers the under-lying purpose of *Jubilees* 8–10 to be an explanation of the presence of non-Shemite peoples in Shemite territory. Cf. D. Mendels, 'The Concept of Territory: Borders and Boundaries (200–63 BCE)', in his *The Rise and Fall of Jewish Nationalism* (Garden City, NY: Doubleday, 1992), pp. 81-105 (here pp. 94-95). Note that an Ethiopic text includes the division of the earth among the sons of Noah between a comment on the destruction and rebuilding of Jericho (Josh. 6.26) and the story of Achan (Joshua 7), perhaps because 'it may be considered to be related to the themes of Israelite resettlement in Canaan, and the fact and the morality of the dispossession of other peoples...' (Cowley, *Ethiopian Biblical Interpretation*, p. 31).

30. On the identification of Iapetos and Japheth, see C. Westermann, *Genesis* (3 vols.; BKAT, 1; Neukirchen-Vluyn: Neukirchener Verlag, 3rd edn, 1983), I, p. 674; D. Neiman, 'The Two Genealogies of Japheth', in H.A. Hoffner (ed.), *Orient and Occident: Essays Presented to Cyrus H. Gordon on the Occasion of his Sixty-Fifth Birthday* (AOAT, 22; Kevelaer: Butzon & Becker; Neukirchen-Vluyn: Neukirchener Verlag, 1973), pp. 119-126 (here pp. 123-26); M.L. West, *Hesiod: Theogony,*

the connection between the Greek myth and the Table-of-Nations tradition in Genesis 10.[31] Each son reigned over his own territory and was bound by oath not to violate the other's portions (vv. 115-16). But after Ouranos died, the sons began to transgress their oaths by stirring up strife against each other 'as to who should have royal honor and reign over all men' (vv. 110-20). At first, diplomacy was able to bring about an uneasy truce that allowed the eldest son, Kronos, to rule over all on a provisional and temporary basis (vv. 121-31). However, when Titan discovered that Kronos had deceived him, a war broke out between the families (vv. 147-53), a war which is described as 'the beginning of war for mortals' (vv. 154-55). The subsequent list of nations shows that the struggle for world empire continued even after all the descendants of Titan and Kronos had died (vv. 156-58). As the text states, 'But then as time pursued its cyclic course, the kingdom of Egypt arose, then that of the Persians, Medes, and Ethiopians, and Assyrian Babylon, then that of the Macedonians, of Egypt again, then of Rome' (vv. 158-61). The point of the Third Sibyl is that the oath imposed by the father was broken, that a struggle for world domination began among the three sons, and that before setting up his own kingdom, implicitly with Israel,[32] God will judge all nations by sword and fire (cf. vv. 2, 492-519), including Magog (cf. vv. 319, 512-13, both passages with Gog [Ezek. 38.1]). The parallel to *Jubilees* 8–9 is obvious, for there too three sons after the Flood are assigned portions by lot (cf. *Jub.* 8.11), and the territories are held inviolable by an oath imposed by their father, which, if broken, would bring a curse upon the offender and ultimately divine judgment by sword and fire (cf. *Jub.* 9.14-15).[33] Apparently, therefore, the 'Book of Noah' preserved in *Jubilees* 8–9 also circulated in

Edited with Prolegomena and Commentary (Oxford: Oxford University Press, 1966), pp. 202-203.

31. According to Pseudo-Eupolemos (in Eusebius, *Praep. Evang.* 9.17.9, citing Alexander Polyhistor's 'On the Jews'), the Babylonians held that Kronos was the father of Canaan, the father of the Phoenicians, who was the father of Chus (= Ethiopia) and Mitzraim (= Egypt). Thus, Kronos occupies a genealogical position analogous to that of Ham, who was the father of Cush, Mitzraim, Put, and Canaan (cf. Gen. 10.6). On J. Freudenthal's widely followed emendation of Χανααν to Χαμ, see, however, R. Doron, 'Pseudo-Eupolemus', *OTP*, II, p. 881 n. *u*.

32. Cf. Scott, *Paul and the Nations*, pp. 37-40.

33. For other similarities between the Third Sibyl and *Jubilees* 8–9, see Scott, *Paul and the Nations*, pp. 36-40.

Alexandria, Egypt, the place where the Third Sibyl originated and later the Alexandrian World-Chronicles as well. Since *Jubilees* and the Third Sibyl both stem from the second century BCE, we may surmise that the apocalyptically oriented 'Book of Noah' which is reflected in both writings existed before the second century.

Jubilees 8–9 *and the War Scroll*

Another text to which to compare *Jubilees* 8–9 is the War Scroll (1QM). The first two columns detail the sequence of events during the (forty-year) war of the Sons of Light against all the nations of the world, led by the Kittim, that is, the Romans (cf. Dan. 11.30).[34] This war is proleptically summarized in 1QM col. i, ll. 1-7, culminating in ll. 6-7: '…and the supremacy of the Kittim shall cease, that wickedness be overcome without a remnant. There shall be no survivors of [all Sons of] Darkness'. Clearly alluding to Dan. 12.1, this war is further described as the last and greatest tribulation: 'It is a time of distress fo[r al]l the people who are redeemed by God. In all their afflictions none exists that is like it, hastening to its completion as an eternal redemption. On the day of their battle against the Kittim, they shall g[o forth for] carnage in battle' (col. i, ll. 11-13). According to Dan. 12.1 (NRSV), 'There shall be a time of anguish, such as has never occurred since nations first came into existence. But at that time your people shall be delivered, everyone who is found written in the book'.[35] This can be compared to 1QM col. x, ll. 14-15, which, alluding to Genesis 10–11, refers to the 'confusion of language (בלת

34. Cf. H. Lichtenberger, 'Das Rombild in den Texten von Qumran', in H.-J. Fabry *et al.* (eds.), *Qumranstudien: Vorträge und Beiträge der Teilnehmer des Qumranseminars auf dem internationalen Treffen der Society of Biblical Literature, Münster, 25.-26. Juli 1993* (Schriften des Institutum Judaicum Delitzschianum, 4; Göttingen: Vandenhoeck & Ruprecht, 1996), pp. 221-31. On 4Q285, see J.J. Collins, *The Scepter and the Star: The Messiahs of the Dead Sea Scrolls and Other Ancient Literature* (ABRL; Garden City, NY: Doubleday, 1995), p. 59. Gog does not figure prominently in the War Scroll (cf. merely 1QM col. xi, l. 16) and Magog not at all. 4QpIsa^a frag. 7, col. iii, l. 11 refers to the battle of the Kittim, and there are several other mentions of the Kittim in the context of battle; 4QpIsa^a frags. 7-10, col. iii, l. 25 mentions Magog.

35. Alternatively, Dan. 12.1 may be referring to the time of trouble 'such as has not occurred since they [namely, the people of Israel] became a nation (גוי) until that time'.

(לשון)³⁶ and the separation of peoples (עמים ומפרד),³⁷ the dwelling-place of clans (מושב משפחות)³⁸ (15) and the distribution of lands (ונחלת ארצות)'.³⁹ After thus alluding to the Table of Nations and the Tower of Babel, cols. xi–xii go on to list the nations by name that will be defeated in battle.⁴⁰ Hence, like Dan. 12.1, the War Scroll

36. This expression has no apparent Qumran parallel. Cf. E. Qimron, *The Hebrew of the Dead Sea Scrolls* (HSS, 29; Atlanta: Scholars Press, 1986), p. 99, who lists בְּלָה 'confusing' under 'Words Mainly Attested in the DSS and in the Tannaitic and Amoraitic [MH²] Literature'. Note, however, that the verb בלל 'confuse' is used in Gen. 11.7, 9 of the confusion of language at the Tower of Babel.

37. This expression has no apparent Qumran parallel, but Gen. 10.5, 32 uses the *niphal* of פרד of peoples separating or dividing from parent stock: 'From these [namely, the sons of Javan] the coastland peoples separated... (32) These are the families of Noah's sons, according to their genealogies, in their nations; and from these the nations separated on the earth after the flood.'

38. The term משפחה 'clan' in the wider sense of people or nation occurs in Gen. 10.5, 18, 20, 31, 32; 12.3; 28.14. Gen. 10.30 refers to the territorial 'dwelling-place' (מושב) of the descendants of Joktan, which extended from Mesha in the direction of Sephar, the hill country of the east. CD 3.1 refers to 'the sons of Noah and their clans' (בני נח ומשפחותיהם). Note especially 1QM col. ii, ll. 13-14: 'During the following ten years, the war shall be divided against all the sons of Ham (14) according to [their clans in] their [set]tlements (למ]שפחותם במו[שבותם). During the remaining ten years, the war shall be divided against all [the sons of Japh]eth in their settlements'. See also 4Q287 (4QBlessingsᵇ) frag. 5, l. 13: 'the families of the earth' (משפחות האדמה).

39. This phrase does not occur in the Hebrew Bible, but see Deut. 19.14: 'You must not move your neighbor's boundary marker, set up by former generations, on the property that will be allotted to you in the land that the LORD your God is giving you to possess'. This seems to correspond to the view of *Jubilees*: just as Israel was not to move the inner-tribal boundaries in the Land, so also the nations were not to remove the international boundaries on the earth. *Jubilees* also has the concept of the division of the earth among the sons and grandsons of Noah into territorial 'lots' (cf. *Jub.* 8.11) or '(hereditary) shares' (*Jub.* 8.17, 21, 22, 24, 25, 29; 9.2, 3, 4, 6, 8, 9, 10, 11, 12, 13, 14). The whole issue is 'inheritance' (cf. *Jub.* 9.13).

40. That is, 'the seven nations of vanity' (col. xi, ll. 8-9; cf. col. iv, l. 12; col. vi, l. 6; col. ix, l. 9), the 'Kittim' (col. xi, l. 11; cf. col. xv, l. 2; col. xvi, ll. 6, 8; col. xvii, ll. 12, 14, 15; col. xviii, ll. 2, 4; col. xix, ll. 10, 13), 'Asshur' (col. xi, l. 11; cf. col. xviii, l. 2; col. xix, l. 10), 'all lands' (col. xi, l. 13), the 'peoples' (col. xi, l. 13), 'all the sons of man' (col. xi, l. 14), 'the nations' (col. xi, l. 15; col. xii, ll. 11, 14), 'Gog' (col. xi, l. 16), the 'nations' (col. xii, l. 11), the 'ki]n[gdoms' (col. xii, l. 15). Also in much of the rest of the War Scroll there is a heavy emphasis on the war against '(all) the (wicked) nations' (cf. col. xiv, ll. 5, 7; col. xv, ll. 1, 2, 13; col. xvi, l. 1; col. xix, ll. 6, 10).

juxtaposes the *Urzeit* and the *Endzeit*, the beginning of the nations and their cataclysmic end.

The forty-year war is to be conducted in two phases interrupted by sabbatical years at the appropriate times. In the first phase, the entire holy congregation is to participate in a six-year war against Israel's neighbors and traditional enemies (Edom, Moab, Ammon, etc.), the Kittim, and the offenders against the covenant. After the conclusion of the first phase and a sabbatical year, selected units from the tribes of Israel are to continue the fight for twenty-nine years, with four intervening sabbatical years (totalling thirty-three years), against the remaining nations. 1QM col. ii, ll. 10-14 outlines the plan of attack during this twenty-nine-year period, listing the nations to be fought according to the order given in Gen. 10.1. Thus, the first nine years of this last major offensive is to be fought against the sons of Shem (1QM col. ii, ll. 10-13); the next ten years of the war are to be fought against 'all the sons of Ham according to their clans in their dwelling-places' (col. ii, ll. 13-14), where the phrase 'according to their clans' (למשפחתם) comes from Gen. 10.20; and the final ten years of the war is to be fought against 'all the sons of Japheth in their dwelling-places' (col. ii, l. 14).[41] The War Scroll expects that the nations will fall under divine judgment, and that universal sovereignty will pass from the Kittim to Israel. Indeed, 1QM col. xvii, ll. 7-8 refers to 'the dominion of Israel over all flesh' (cf. also col. xix, l. 8). Hence, like *Jubilees* 8–9 and the Third Sibyl, the War Scroll uses the division of the earth among Noah's sons to express an expectation of eschatological divine judgment by fire and sword.

Conclusion

The attempt to reconstruct from disparate sources a single 'Book of Noah' that includes everything from the fall of the Watchers to the division of the earth among Noah's sons not only seems arbitrary, lacking the necessary controls for ascertaining what was included in the original work, but it also fails adequately to reckon with the fact that, according to *Jubilees*, many books of Noah were in circulation on various subjects. It seems safer and more fruitful, therefore, to begin

---

41. On the war against Japheth, see also 1QM col. xviii, l. 2 'and the shout of the holy ones when they pursue Asshur; the sons of Japheth will fall, never to rise again; the Kittim will be crushed without...'.

with a document, such as *Jubilees* 8–9, which explicitly claims to constitute a 'Book of Noah' and which has a demonstrably independent *Nachleben*.

THE SHEKINAH IN THE COPPER SCROLL:
A NEW READING OF 3Q15 12.10

Al Wolters

The Copper Scroll (3Q15) is subdivided into a large number of small sections (most scholars count 64), each describing a hiding place and a treasure hidden there. The hiding place is usually a place in or near Jerusalem, and the treasure most often consists of a quantity of silver and gold. As I have argued elsewhere, the way in which the different sections are structured and phrased shows a high degree of parallelism between them, such that the overall literary pattern can serve as a useful heuristic guide for interpreting obscure words or phrases.[1]

However, the last section of the Copper Scroll (usually numbered 64) is to some degree an exception to this widespread parallelism. Although it is true that the literary structure and stereotypical phraseology of this section conform to the overall pattern of the scroll as a whole, the description of both the hiding place and the material hidden there is different from that found in the preceding 63 sections. In my own recently published edition and translation of the Copper Scroll, this last section reads as follows:

> In the cavern of the Presence on the north of Koḥlit—its opening is north and tombs are at its mouth: a duplicate of this document, and the interpretation, and 'their oils', and the *protokollon* of the one and the other.[2]

---

1. See A. Wolters, 'Literary Analysis and the Copper Scroll', in S.J. Kapera (ed.), *Intertestamental Essays in Honour of Józef Tadeusz Milik* (Cracow: Enigma Press, 1992), pp. 239-52, and *idem*, 'Paleography and Literary Structure as Guides to Reading the Copper Scroll', in G.J. Brooke (ed.), *Copper Scroll Studies: Papers Presented at the International Symposium on the Copper Scroll, Manchester, September 1996* (Sheffield: Sheffield Academic Press, forthcoming).

2. A. Wolters, *The Copper Scroll: Overview, Text and Translation* (Sheffield: Sheffield Academic Press, 1996), p. 55.

It will be noted that the 'treasure' in this case does not consist of silver and gold, or of other standard valuables, but of a mysterious 'duplicate' (משנא) of the Copper Scroll itself, along with three equally mysterious additional hidden items: 'the interpretation', 'their oils', and 'the *protokollon* of the one and other'. Especially the last three items have been the subject of considerable scholarly disagreement, and my own interpretation of them has been disputed.[3] What is clear, however, is that the 'treasure' component of section 64 constitutes something of a special case in the Copper Scroll as a whole. What I will be arguing in what follows is that the hiding place in this section is also something of a special case. I will be defending the thesis that the hiding place in question is indeed 'the cavern of the Presence', and that it contains what is probably the earliest documented case of the Hebrew word שכינה in the sense of 'Shekinah' or divine presence.

What we are dealing with is essentially the reading and interpretation of the first dozen or so characters in l. 10 of col. xii—letters which constitute the beginning of the last section of the scroll. In addition to my own interpretation, the following readings and translations have been proposed:

(1) Milik 1956:   בשית שכנה בצפון
                         'In the pit nearby, towards the north'[4]
(2) Allegro 1960:   בשית שכינה בצפון
                         'In the Pit adjoining on the north'[5]
(3) Milik 1962:   בשית שבצח בצפון, 'Dans la galerie du Rocher Lisse
                         au nord'[6]

3. See P. Mandel, 'On the "Duplicate Copy" of the *Copper Scroll (3Q15)*', *RevQ* 16 (1993), pp. 69-76, in which my interpretation of each of the three additional items is challenged.

4. J.T. Milik, 'The Copper Document from Cave III, Qumran', *BA* 19 (1956), pp. 60-64 (63). Milik gives the Hebrew text on which his translation is based in his article 'L'édition des manuscrits du désert de Juda', *Volume du Congrès, Strasbourg 1956* (VTSup, 4; Leiden: Brill, 1957), p. 22. Milik's initial interpretation is also reflected in the press release of 1 June 1956; see H.W. Baker, 'Notes on the Opening of the "Bronze" Scrolls from Qumran', *BJRL* 39 (1956–57), pp. 45-56 (56). I understand that Émile Puech, in his recent French translation of the Copper Scroll (which I have not seen), also accepts the reading שכנה.

5. J.M. Allegro, *The Treasure of the Copper Scroll* (London: Routledge & Kegan Paul, 1960), p. 55. Allegro is followed by B.-Z. Luria, *The Copper Scroll from the Desert of Judah* (Jerusalem: Kiryath Sepher, 1963), p. 126 [in Hebrew].

6. J.T. Milik, 'Le rouleau de cuivre provenant de la grotte 3Q (3Q15)', in *Les 'petites Grottes' de Qumrân* (DJD, 3; Oxford: Clarendon Press, 1962), pp. 200-302

(4) Pixner 1983: בשית בצדהב צפון

'In the underground passage that is in Ṣehab north'[7]

(5) Lefkovits 1993: בשית שבינח בצפון

'In the deep-pit which is in Janoah in the north'[8]

(6) Wilmot/Wise 1996: בשית >שבצדא< בצפון

'In the dry well that is at the north'[9]

It is clear that all scholars are agreed that the relevant sequence of characters begins with בשית and ends with צפון. Although there is some uncertainty about the meaning and vocalization of שית, this is not a matter which need detain us in the present context. I will assume that the noun means 'cavern' and was vocalized *šêt*, although the meaning

(298). Milik's revised interpretation is already reflected in his English translation of the Copper Scroll; see J.T. Milik, 'The Copper Document from Cave III of Qumran: Translation and Commentary', *Annual of the Department of Antiquities of Jordan* 4/5 (1960), pp. 137-55 (142). His new interpretation is adopted by M.A. Rodrigues, 'Aspectos linguísticos do documento de cobre de Qumran (3Q15)', *Biblos, Revista de Faculdade de Letras, Universidade de Coimbra* 39 (1963), pp. 329-423 (348); L. Moraldi, *I manoscritti di Qumrān* (Turin: Unione tipografico-editrice torinese, 1971), p. 722; and G. Vermes, *The Dead Sea Scrolls in English* (Harmondsworth: Penguin Books, 4th edn, 1995), p. 378.

7. B. Pixner, 'Unravelling the Copper Scroll Code: A Study of the Topography of 3Q15', *RevQ* 11 (1983), pp. 323-61 (358). Pixner is followed by García Martínez, although the latter appears to read the toponym as צחב, with a *het* rather than a *he* as middle consonant. See F. García Martínez, *Textos de Qumrân* (Madrid: Editorial Trotta, 2nd edn, 1993), p. 480 ('En el túnel que hay en Sejab, al Norte'), and *idem*, *The Dead Sea Scrolls Translated: The Qumran Texts in English* (trans. G.E. Watson; Leiden: Brill, 1994), p. 463 ('In the tunnel which is in Sechab, to the North').

8. J.K. Lefkovits, 'The Copper Scroll—3Q15, a New Reading, Translation and Commentary' (unpublished PhD dissertation, New York University, 1993), pp. 927-31. The same reading is adopted, apparently independently of Lefkovits, in K. Beyer, *Die aramäischen Texte vom Toten Meer. Ergänzungsband* (Göttingen: Vandenhoeck & Ruprecht, 1994), pp. 232-33.

9. For the Hebrew text, see the conclusion of M.O. Wise, 'David J. Wilmot and the Copper Scroll', in Brooke (ed.), *Copper Scroll Studies*; for the translation, see M.O. Wise in M.O. Wise, M.G. Abegg, Jr, and E.M. Cook, *The Dead Sea Scrolls: A New Translation* (New York: HarperCollins, 1996), p. 198. Wise's translation is based, not only on Wilmot's reading, but also on the latter's understanding of שית as 'dry well' (private communication).

'pit' and the pronunciation *šît* are also defensible.[10] The crucial point of difference between the rival interpretations is the way in which the characters immediately following שׁית are read.

The problem here is in the first place a paleographical one. The script of the Copper Scroll makes no distinction between *beth* and *kaph,* and often no distinction between *he* and *ḥet* either.[11] Consequently, the shape of the letters does not tell us whether we should read the letter after the *shin* as a *kaph* (as Milik did in 1956), or as a *beth* (as Milik did in 1962). Furthermore, we cannot be sure that the letter preceding בצפון is a *he* (so Milik in 1956) or a *ḥet* (so Milik in 1962). In such cases, the choice between competing readings will have to be decided by non-paleographical considerations, such as context and lexicography.

It *is* possible, however, to use paleographical criteria to decide on another disputed reading, namely the letter or letters which precede the *he/ḥet*. The correct reading is *nun* according to some (Milik in 1956), *yod-nun* according to others (Allegro and Lefkovits), and *sade* according to still others (Milik in 1962 and Pixner). It can be shown that the third reading is almost certainly wrong, since it assumes an unprecedented form of the *sade*. As a chart of the various forms of this letter in the Copper Scroll makes clear (see Figure 1), the 'branch' at the upper right of the *sade* regularly consists either of two roughly equal strokes, one vertical and one horizontal, or of a curved diagonal line. But the putative *sade* here (if we follow the facsimile published by Milik[12]) has neither of these features: there is only a short vertical line very close and parallel to the main downstroke, with only the hint of a horizontal line connecting the two verticals. In fact, Milik's own facsimile seems to suggest the letters *yod-nun*, and not the letter *sade*. The problem with the reading of a *sade* here is compounded by the fact that those who adopt it are forced to postulate

10. The vocalization *šêt* is the one given in G.H. Dalman, *Aramäisch-neu-hebräisches Wörterbuch zu Targum, Talmud und Midrasch* (Göttingen: Pfeiffer, 1938; repr. Hildesheim: Georg Olms, 1967 [1901]), s.v.; M. Jastrow, *A Dictionary of the Targumim, the Talmud Babli and Yerushalmi, and the Midrashic Literature* (New York: G.P. Putnam's Sons, 1886–93; repr. New York: Judaica Press, 1971), gives the vocalization *šît* and the meaning 'pit'. See also Milik, 'Le rouleau de cuivre', p. 241 (sub C 38).

11. For a discussion of lookalike letters in the Copper Scroll, see Wolters, 'Paleography and Literary Structure'.

12. See DJD, 3, *Planches* (pl. LXX).

an otherwise unattested word: the noun צה in the case of Milik,[13] and the toponym צהב in the case of Pixner.[14] Consequently, even if we base our conclusions on Milik's own facsimile, it is possible to show on paleographical grounds that his reading of a *ṣade* here should be disallowed.

This conclusion is clinched by direct examination of the relevant segment of the Copper Scroll in Amman. On the basis of my own inspection of the original in Amman in July 1991, I can state that the short vertical of Milik's facsimile looks like an accidental scratch or discoloration (it is not punched into the metal like the strokes of the surrounding letters), and that there is no horizontal line connecting the two verticals. In other words, the correct reading is neither *ṣade* nor *yod-nun*, but simply a single *nun*.

If the text does not contain a *ṣade*, we can also safely dismiss Wilmot's hypothesis of a scribal error, which seems to have been based on the assumption that שבצה was a false start for שבצפון. And if the text does not contain a *yod-nun* either, there is no longer any reason to postulate a *ḥet* after this disputed character, as Milik and Lefkovits have done. (In any case, Milik's צה, as we have seen, is unattested as a noun elsewhere, and Lefkovits's ינה is an ambiguous biblical toponym which is elsewhere spelled ינוה.)[15] What is decisive is that שכנה spells a well-attested Hebrew common noun, while the remaining possible permutations do not (שכנח, שבנה, or שבנה).[16] Consequently, we can be fairly certain that שכנה is in fact the correct reading. Ironically, Milik's original reading of 1956 appears to have been right all along.

---

13. Milik, 'Le rouleau de cuivre', pp. 240 (sub C 22) and 298.

14. See Pixner, 'Unravelling the Copper Scroll Code', p. 358 n. 52.

15. Two places called ינוה (written *plene*) are mentioned in the Bible: one in the territory of Ephraim (Josh. 16.6) and one in Galilee (2 Kgs 15.29). See Lefkovits, *The Copper Scroll*, pp. 929-31. An argument in favour of this reading was the fact that the second component of the stereotypical pattern of the Copper Scroll ('Specification') often begins with שב-, 'which is in' (see Lefkovits, p. 928). However, without a *yod*, the following noun here would be נה or נה, neither of which offers a plausible sense.

16. It is true that שבנה is a biblically attested proper noun, so that the translation 'In the cavern of Shebna' is also possible. However, this possibly non-Jewish name appears to have been unique to a single individual in eighth-century Judah (see *HALAT* and the biblical dictionaries).

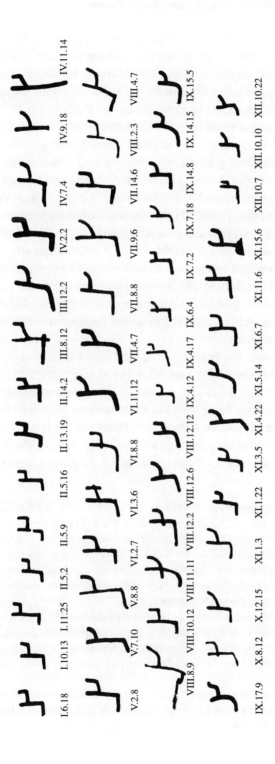

Figure 1

Unfortunately, the Hebrew word which now emerges in the text is still ambiguous on the lexical level. It could spell either *šᵉkēnâ*, the feminine word for 'neighbour', or *šᵉkīnâ*, 'divine Presence'. It is the former possibility which was chosen by Milik in 1956, as well as Allegro (although he took the word to be spelt *plene*, as שכינה).[17] However, this seems a most unlikely interpretation. For one thing, if *šᵉkēnâ* is taken as an adjective meaning 'neighbouring', we would expect it to be preceded by an article, since the first components of the sections of the Copper Scroll are regularly definite. For another, according to the comprehensive Hebrew dictionaries of Ben Yehuda and Even-Shoshan, the word שכן (*šākēn*), and its feminine counterpart שכנה (*šᵉkēnâ*), are always used as nouns (meaning 'neighbour') and never as adjectives (meaning 'neighbouring').[18] Consequently, if this is the word that we find in the last section of the Copper Scroll, then the description of the hiding place should be translated, not as 'in a neighbouring cavern', but as 'in a cavern of a neighbour lady'. Not surprisingly, no one has suggested this as the appropriate meaning for the phrase in this context.

On the other hand, the reading שית שכנה (*šêt šᵉkīnâ*) does yield a plausible sense. It finds a close parallel in the phrase בית שכינה, 'house of the Presence', which is found in the *Targum Neophiti* of Exod. 15.17 as a designation of the Temple.[19] Similarly, in rabbinic literature we frequently find the expression מחנה שכינה, 'camp of the Presence', as a designation of the area surrounding the inner sanctuary of the Temple in Jerusalem.[20] The absence of the article is not surprising, since שכינה

17. See Milik, 'L'édition des manuscrits', p. 22 ('avoisinante'), and Allegro, *Treasure of the Copper Scroll*, p. 55 ('adjoining') and p. 170 n. 314 ('neighbouring').

18. See E. Ben Yehuda, *Thesaurus Totius Hebraitatis et Veteris et Recentioris* (Jerusalem: Ben-Yehuda, 1951–52), s.v. (14.7108), and A. Even-Shoshan, *Millon Ha'ivri Hamerukkaz* (Jerusalem: Kiryath Sepher, 1982), s.v. Some dictionaries of Modern Hebrew do recognize an adjectival use of the word, but this appears to be an innovation with respect to pre-modern usage.

19. See A. Díez Macho, *Neophyti 1. Targum Palestinense MS de la Biblioteca Vaticana. Tomo II: Éxodo* (Madrid/Barcelona: Consejo Superior de Investigaciones Científicas, 1970), p. 101. Cf. M. Sokoloff, *A Dictionary of Jewish Palestinian Aramaic of the Byzantine Period* (Ramat Gan: Bar-Ilan University Press, 1990), s.v. בית (p. 95b).

20. See A.M. Goldberg, *Untersuchungen über die Vorstellung von der Schekhinah in der frühen rabbinischen Literatur—Talmud und Midrasch* (SJ, 5; Berlin: de Gruyter, 1969), pp. 103-108.

in mishnaic Hebrew is often used as the equivalent of a proper name, without article.[21] As so often, the Copper Scroll uses vocabulary which is characteristic of mishnaic Hebrew.[22] In fact, the nominal pattern $q^e t\bar{\imath}l\hat{a}$, which is virtually absent from biblical Hebrew, but very frequent in Mishnaic Hebrew, is found in several other places in the Copper Scroll (notably $y^e r\bar{\imath}d\hat{a}$ in col. i, l. 13, where the form is spelt defectively, as here).[23] From a philological point of view, there is nothing odd or surprising about the reading $\check{s}^e k\bar{\imath}n\hat{a}$ in the present context.

It may be objected that it is implausible to find a reference to the Shekinah in a document usually dated to shortly before the fall of Jerusalem in 70 CE, since it has been claimed that the term 'Shekinah' was not commonly used until well into the second century.[24] However, Arnold M. Goldberg, the author of the most comprehensive study to date of the concept of the Shekinah in rabbinic Judaism, adduces grounds for suggesting an earlier date. Specifically, he suggests that the well-known expression שכינה מחנה, 'the camp of the Shekinah', may have originated before 70 CE.[25] Ephraim E. Urbach, in his magisterial study entitled *The Sages*, states quite definitely that it is inconceivable that the concept of Shekinah should have been unknown before the destruction of the Temple.[26] Similarly, Bruce D. Chilton has argued in a more recent study that the earliest 'framework' of the Isaiah Targum, which frequently associates the Shekinah with the Temple,

21. See Goldberg, *Untersuchungen*, p. 443: 'Die Verwendung des Artikels scheint indifferent zu sein. Eher auffällig ist das häufige Fortlassen des Artikels, wo man einen solchen erwarten würde...'

22. See A. Wolters, 'The *Copper Scroll* and the Vocabulary of Mishnaic Hebrew', *RevQ* 14 (1990), pp. 483-95.

23. See Milik, 'Le rouleau de cuivre', p. 234 (sub B 19b), and E. Qimron, *The Hebrew of the Dead Sea Scrolls* (HSS, 29; Atlanta: Scholars Press, 1986), p. 65 (§330.1b). On the reading $y^e r\bar{\imath}d\hat{a}$ in l. 13 see A. Wolters, 'The Fifth Cache of the Copper Scroll: "The Plastered Cistern of Manos"', *RevQ* 13 (1988), pp. 167-76 (175-76).

24. See C.R. Koester, *The Dwelling of God: The Tabernacle in the Old Testament, Intertestamental Jewish Literature, and the Old Testament* (Washington: Catholic Biblical Association, 1989), p. 72.

25. Goldberg, *Untersuchungen*, p. 443.

26. E.E. Urbach, *The Sages: The World and Wisdom of the Rabbis of the Talmud* (Cambridge, MA: Harvard University Press, 1987), p. 44. (The Hebrew original of this work was published in 1971.)

'was developed in the difficult period from shortly before 70 until the revolt of Bar Kokhba'.[27] Strikingly, this is precisely the range of dates which has been suggested for the Copper Scroll. Consequently, there is nothing anachronistic about the reading *šᵉkînâ* in the present context.

Our conclusion is therefore that the last hiding place of the Copper Scroll is as unique as its last 'treasure'. The place where the duplicate of the scroll was hidden (together with the three enigmatic items associated with it) was in all likelihood 'the cavern of the Shekinah'. If the Copper Scroll is to be dated to around 68 CE, as it commonly is, then this is probably also the earliest attested occurrence of the central Jewish theologoumenon שכינה.

The implications of this conclusion are potentially quite significant. If Goldberg and Chilton are right, the earliest stage of the evolution of the concept of Shekinah connected it exclusively with the Temple in Jerusalem. It was there that the Shekinah dwelt, and it was only in connection with the prospect, and later the reality, of the Temple's destruction that the notion was entertained that the Shekinah could be separated from the Temple. In Chilton's analysis, the earliest framework of the Isaiah Targum, dated to about the same time as the Copper Scroll, comprised two strata: 'one of which assumes that the cult continues to function and that the Shekinah is present in the Temple, while the other presupposes the temporary removal of the divine presence'.[28] It is possible that the Copper Scroll represents a point in time when the perspective of the second stratum of the Isaiah Targum is beginning to emerge: the Shekinah is still closely tied to the Temple and its cult, but has been temporarily removed to an alternative sanctuary which was given the designation, not בית שכינה, 'the house of the Shekinah', but שית שכינה, 'the cavern of the Shekinah'. This would fit well with the view of the majority of students of the Copper Scroll today, namely that the treasure of the Copper Scroll represents part of the wealth of the Second Temple, hidden in anticipation of the Temple's destruction in 70 CE. Since this treasure also included a very significant proportion of Temple-related cultic items,

27. B.D. Chilton, *The Glory of Israel: The Theology and Provenience of the Isaiah Targum* (JSOTSup, 23; Sheffield: JSOT Press, 1983), pp. 69-75.

28. Chilton, *The Glory of Israel*, p. 75.

as I have argued elsewhere,[29] it may be that the Copper Scroll is part of a major undertaking to provide for a temporary alternative to the Jerusalem Temple, where the cult could be continued and the Shekinah have its dwelling. Such a hypothesis is of course based on a number of disputed assumptions, and can only be called speculative. It is, however, consistent with the description of the last hiding place of the Copper Scroll as 'the cavern of the Shekinah', which we have argued is the most plausible reading in 12.10.

29. A. Wolters, 'The Cultic Terminology of the Copper Scroll', in Z.J. Kapera (ed.), *Intertestamental Essays in Honour of Józef Tadeusz Milik*, II (Cracow: Enigma Press, forthcoming).

INDEXES

INDEX OF REFERENCES

OLD TESTAMENT

NEW TESTAMENT

PSEUDEPIGRAPHA

DATE DUE